The Foreign Policies
of Arab States

Also of Interest

†*A Concise History of the Middle East,* Second Edition, Revised and Updated, Arthur Goldschmidt, Jr.

†*Rich and Poor States in the Middle East: Egypt and the New Arab Order,* edited by Malcolm H. Kerr and El Sayed Yassin

†Available in both hardcover and paperback.

About the Book and Authors

The Foreign Policies of Arab States

Bahgat Korany and Ali E. Hillal Dessouki

with contributions by Ahmad Yousef Ahmad, Raymond A. Hinnebusch, A. G. Kluge, Paul C. Noble, Mohamed E. Selim, and I. William Zartman

Designed specifically to fill the existing gap in materials for courses dealing with foreign policy in the Arab world, the Middle East, or the Third World in general, this textbook investigates the foreign policies of six influential Arab states—Algeria, Egypt, Iraq, Libya, Saudi Arabia, and Syria—and the Palestine Liberation Organization within the framework of their domestic, regional, and global environments. Approaching foreign policy as a role played by the state on the international scene, the authors make a crucial distinction between a state's role conception (that is, its general foreign policy objectives, world view, or orientation) and its role enactment (that is, its actual international behavior).

Organized around a coherent conceptual framework and written in a straightforward style that avoids jargon, this text combines clarity of presentation with rigorous critical analysis of existing literature and original sources. It will be a valuable resource for researchers, as well as a welcome addition to teaching materials on the Arab world and the Middle East.

Bahgat Korany is professor of political science and director of the Arab studies program at the University of Montreal. As a visiting professor, he has taught at Laval University in Quebec (1976), the Patterson School of International Affairs at Carleton University (1977, 1978), and the University of Dakar in Senegal (1977, 1978), and he has been a Fellow of the Center for International Affairs, Harvard University (1979-1980). His book *Social Change, Charisma and International Behavior* (1976) was awarded the Hauchman Prize for the Study of International Relations in Switzerland.

Ali E. Hillal Dessouki is professor in the Faculty of Economics and Political Science at Cairo University. Professor Dessouki has also been an advisor to the Minister of Information, Egypt (1975-1976) and a Fellow of the Center of International Studies, Princeton University (1980-1981). His book *Politics and Government in Egypt* (in Arabic, 1978) was awarded Egypt's State Prize for Best Book in Political Analysis.

The Foreign Policies of Arab States

Bahgat Korany and
Ali E. Hillal Dessouki

---

with contributions by
Ahmad Yousef Ahmad
Raymond A. Hinnebusch
A. G. Kluge
Paul C. Noble
Mohamed E. Selim
I. William Zartman

Westview Press • Boulder and London

The American University in Cairo Press • Egypt

Copyright © 1984 by Westview Press, Inc.

Published in 1984 in the United States of America by Westview Press, Inc., 5500 Central Avenue, Boulder, Colorado 80301; Frederick A. Praeger, Publisher

Published in 1984 in Egypt by The American University in Cairo Press, 113 Sharia Qasr El Aini, Cairo

Library of Congress Catalog Card Number: 83-51344
ISBN (Westview) 0-86531-697-X
ISBN (Westview) 0-86531-698-8 (pb)
ISBN (AUC) 977-424-023-5 (pb)

Printed and bound in the United States of America

10   9   8   7   6   5   4   3

Contents

Illustrations

Figures

Preface

This book is intended to fill a gap in the literature on Arab foreign policies. Its objective is to underline the basic features of the foreign policy of a number of influential Arab states. Though the book is written primarily to serve as a textbook or general introduction to the subject, we have kept in mind its conceptual relevance to students of the foreign policy of Third World countries.

The book has been written, to the best of our ability, in lucid and clear language, avoiding unwarranted jargon. However, it is not an exercise in "contemporary political history." We aspire to combine clarity of presentation with rigorous analysis. The framework of analysis used in all chapters conceptualizes foreign policy as a role on the international scene. Each chapter deals with foreign policy orientation, the decision-making process, and foreign policy behavior. The book will, we hope, prove useful not only to those interested in knowing more about Arab and Middle Eastern international politics, but also to those interested in generating hypotheses and accumulating knowledge for theory building. We also hope that our quest for relevance will make the book useful to practitioners—to functionaries of foreign ministers, journalists, and international civil servants.

Our thanks go first and foremost to our distinguished colleagues who kindly responded to our invitation to contribute to the book and whose chapters explore certain unstudied areas of Arab countries. Lynne Rienner of Westview Press has been a patient but persistent publisher. Jean-Benoit Gauthier of the Department of Political Science at the University of Montreal and Gamal Zahran of Cairo University were very efficient research assistants. We would also like to thank Mrs. Johan Sarrazin and Mr. Arthur St.-Germain for their editorial work. Holly Arrow of Westview Press worked hard on the manuscript to make it read like a book.

The final manuscript was typed at the University of Montreal by Nicole Laberge and Renée Nadeau of the Department of Political Science and by Christiane Aubin of the Arab Studies program. It was Christiane who slaved over the tables and kept track of all the parts of the manuscript. During the last hectic days, Iglal Dessouki and Margaret Korany were involved in everything from typing to editing. Without their involvement, we might not have been able to submit the manuscript in time for publication.

It may be of interest to our English-speaking readers to know that no similar book exists in Arabic and that an Arabic edition will appear soon. We collaborated in writing Chapters 1, 2, and 11, discussing each one at length and agreeing on its content. The order of our names on the chapters, however, indicates which one of us took final responsibility for the actual writing. We hope that this book offers a modest contribution to the scientific study of Arab foreign policies and that it will be a source of encouragement to others to further explore this field of study.

Bahgat Korany and Ali E. Hillal Dessouki

The Foreign Policies
of Arab States

The Arab World

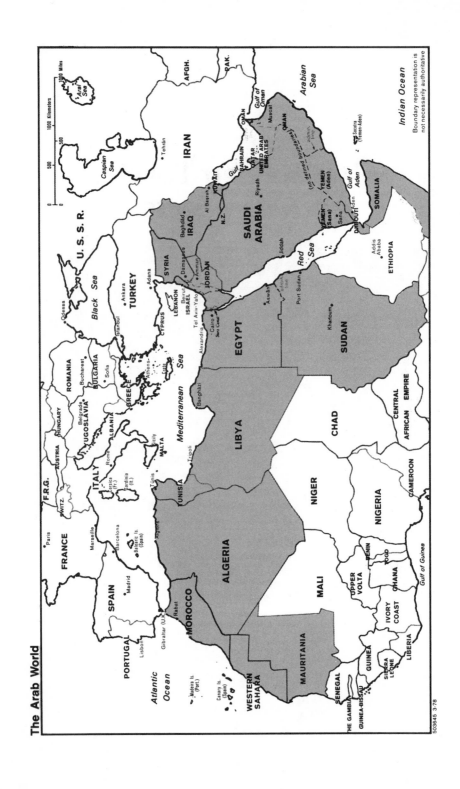

503645 3-78

Introduction

Arab states have been studied from many angles. We have books on Arab governments and politics, history and political evolution, ideologies and intellectual trends, inter-Arab relations and the great powers' policies in the region, but very little on Arab states' foreign policies or on how these countries view the world and their role in it.

This statement is confirmed by the results of our survey of the literature on Arab foreign policies, written in eight languages. The results, reported in Chapter 1, reveal for instance that in 1983, there was only one book in English dealing with Egyptian foreign policy, and it deals only with Egypt's Arab policy during the Nasser era (1952–1970). Similarly, no book exists on Syrian foreign policy, with the exception of one on Syria's intervention in Lebanon.[1] We could not even find a systematic essay on Lebanon's foreign policy. Books devoted to one Arab country usually have sections on external relations or foreign affairs, such as those by Majid Khadduri and by the Penroses on Iraq.[2] But this is not always the case; the two major books on Egypt published in the 1970s[3] have no such chapters. Finally, although scores of books on the domestic politics of Arab countries exist, there is but a single book on foreign policy–making in the Middle East, dealing with Israel and three Arab countries.[4]

With a few exceptions, the existing literature suffers from a number of limitations. It is of a descriptive or prescriptive genre, rarely linked to recent conceptualization in foreign policy analysis. Most of it belongs to the tradition of diplomatic political history or commentary on current affairs.[5] Finally, other than statements about the role of leaders and personalities, there is almost no treatment in existing books of how foreign policy is actually made and implemented.

Four factors may account for this poverty in the literature. First is the underdeveloped state of the discipline of foreign policy analysis in Third World countries (which we examine more closely in Chapter 1). Between 1950 and 1965, Western scholars viewed these newly independent countries as having no purposeful foreign policies of their own. Their external behavior was analyzed as a reaction to the great powers' policies toward them, and hence emphasis was placed on the international relations of the country rather than on its foreign policy proper. Moreover, theories of foreign policy analysis at that time dealt primarily with developed countries and were not applicable to developing ones. A second factor is the limited data available in a rapidly changing environment, in which foreign policy affairs are shrouded in secrecy and widely perceived as a matter of utmost national security. Third, students of Arab politics have focused more attention on regional dynamics than on single-actor behavior. There is no lack of analyses dealing, for instance, with inter-Arab relations or the Arab-Israeli conflict. The fourth factor concerns the present state of Arab (and Middle Eastern) scholarship in Europe and the United States.

An evaluation of this literature is not our objective here. We want only to emphasize the weakness in methodology and lack of analytical rigor; literature on the Arab countries has not as yet contributed to the body of social science as has, for instance, the literature on Latin America. Our field has been plagued by inadequate conceptualization, overemphasis on historicism and the uniqueness of the Islamic-Arab situation, and neglect of a truly comparative outlook.

Why should we study the foreign policies of Arab states? By Arab states, we mean those twenty-two states that belong to the League of Arab States, founded in 1945.[6] They are primarily distinguished by cultural-linguistic homogeneity. These countries occupy a strategic part of the world; their lands stretch from the Atlantic Ocean in the west to the Indian Ocean in the east, and from the Horn of Africa in the south to the "northern tier" in the north. They control a number of important waterways: the Suez Canal, Bab Al-Mandeb, the Gulf of Aqaba, the Gulf, and the Straits of Hormuz. They perform crucial roles in Islamic, African, and nonaligned councils. Finally, oil wealth has enabled some of them to accumulate enormous financial resources that may be placed at the service of their foreign policies.

We started our research with four main propositions on Arab foreign policies in mind:

1. Arab states share a number of norms and pan-Arab core concerns such as Arabism, the Palestine problem, and nonalignment. All Arab states—particularly those desiring to perform an influential regional role—address themselves to these core concerns. In addition to being part of the Arab collective political culture, these concerns have been used by Arab regimes as a legitimizing device and as a weapon to discredit opponents.
2. Arab foreign policies are primarily regional in orientation. This regional emphasis is the result of three factors. First, small or medium powers are usually regionally oriented. Second, the Arab-Israeli conflict is perceived as a general Arab problem. Third, the belief system of Islam or Arab nationalism encourages regional trans-state interactions.
3. There is an intimate relationship between domestic and external policies in most Arab countries. In Syria and Jordan, for instance,

the Palestine issue has direct implications for internal stability. For Saudi Arabia, the future of Jerusalem is a question intimately related to the regime's legitimacy. Among influential Arab states, Egypt provides an exceptional example of dissociation between domestic and regional foreign policies that allows the Egyptian leadership a noticeable degree of external maneuverability. The more a regime or leadership derives its legitimacy from a certain policy behavior, the less freedom of action it enjoys.

4. There is latent tension in the orientation of Arab foreign policies between the norm of pan-Arabism and the interests of each state, between role conception and role performance. There is growing discrepancy between the pan-Arab belief system and state behavior based on raison d'état. Thus one notices a difference between the sources of a particular policy, which are in many cases specific state interests, and the justification of that policy—usually articulated in pan-Arab rhetoric.

Beneath this rhetoric, what are the differences among the foreign polices of Arab states? Arab foreign policies can be classified according to a number of criteria. One is *orientation in the global system* (e.g., pro-U.S. or pro–Soviet Union). Although all Arab states are technically nonaligned, in most cases they tilt toward one or the other of the superpowers. A second criterion is *degree of involvement* in Arab politics (quietism versus activism). A closely related criterion is *distribution of resources and influence*, for in most cases activism is a function of a strong or rich country. A fourth criterion is *type of actor*. The Arab world has included a number of nonstate actors, such as the League of Arab States, the Provisional Government of the Republic of Algeria (GPRA), and the Palestine Liberation Organization (PLO). Another interesting example is Lebanon, a state that, for the last few years, not only has had no independent foreign policy, but whose territory has become an arena for the foreign policy of other regional actors.

On what grounds were certain countries chosen over others for this study? Our choice of seven actors (Algeria, Egypt, Iraq, Libya, the PLO, Saudi Arabia, and Syria) was influenced by four criteria: orientation, degree of involvement, distribution of resources and influence, and type of actor. The bias was toward influential Arab actors whose foreign policies make a difference for the Arabs and the world. We made sure to represent countries from the Arab East (the Mashreq) and the Arab West (the Maghreb), rich and poor states, and a nonstate actor (the PLO).

The structure of the book reflects our concerns. The first chapter is conceptual and deals with three issues: various approaches to the study of the foreign policy of developing countries, a survey of the literature on Arab foreign policies, and the framework of analysis to be applied in the seven case studies. Thanks to the authors of the different chapters, the framework was followed closely. Depending on the availability of data or the importance of a particular variable to the analysis of an actor's foreign policy, the authors differed in their emphasis. Some put two variables together under one title. In certain cases, the impact of history was so important that the author felt obliged to discuss historical legacy. Notwithstanding these variations, all the case studies address the same major questions.

Chapter 2 analyzes the global system and Chapter 3 the regional system as they relate to Arab foreign policies. The objective of these two chapters is to outline how the external environment presents constraints or opportunities for different Arab actors. The seven case study chapters take up the seven Arab actors in alphabetical order. The last chapter deals briefly with some other Arab states, underlines patterns of Arab foreign policy for 1970–1980, and suggests some theoretical conclusions that may be of relevance to developing countries in general.

NOTES

1. Adeed I. Dawisha, *Syria and the Lebanese Crisis* (New York: St. Martin's Press, 1980).

2. Majid Khadduri, *Socialist Iraq* (Washington, D.C.: Middle East Institute, 1978); and Edith Penrose and E. F. Penrose, *Iraq: International Relations and National Development* (Boulder, Colo.: Westview Press, 1978).

3. Richard H. Dekmejian, *Egypt under Nasser* (Albany: University of New York Press, 1971); Raymond W. Baker, *Egypt's Uncertain Revolution Under Nasser and Sadat* (Cambridge, Mass.: Harvard University Press, 1978). Recent books on Egypt's political economy establish more linkage with the country's international relations, but still without analyzing its foreign policy. See Mark Cooper, *The Transformation of Egypt* (Baltimore: Johns Hopkins University Press, 1982); and John Waterbury, *The Egypt of Nasser and Sadat: The Political Economy of Two Regimes* (Princeton, N.J.: Princeton University Press, 1983).

4. R. D. McLaurin, Mohammed Mughisuddin, and Abraham Wagner, *Foreign Policy Making in the Middle East* (New York: Praeger Publishers, 1977).

5. For instance, see the only book on Jordan, by Mohamed I. Faddah, *The Middle East in Transition: A Study of Jordan's Foreign Policy* (London: Asia Publishing House, 1974).

6. The twenty-two members are: Algeria, Bahrain, Egypt, Iraq, Djibouti, Jordan, Kuwait, Lebanon, Libya, Mauritania, Morocco, North Yemen, Oman, Palestine, Qatar, Saudi Arabia, Somalia, South Yemen, Sudan, Syria, Tunisia, and the United Arab Emirates. Egypt's membership was suspended in 1979. *Arab Report*, published by the Arab League, 1984.

A Literature Survey and a Framework for Analysis

Ali E. Hillal Dessouki
Bahgat Korany

This book deals with the foreign policies of a number of developing or Third World actors. The study of developing countries' foreign policies has often been described as "underdeveloped" or "undeveloped." We have no intention of adding to the confusion of theories, models, and analytical frameworks already existing in the field. The objectives of this introductory chapter are rather: (1) to summarize the main trends and approaches in the study of developing countries' foreign policies, (2) to survey the literature on Arab foreign policies, and (3) to suggest a framework for analysis that takes into account the major conceptual contributions in foreign policy theory in the last two decades.

THE FOREIGN POLICY OF DEVELOPMENT:
APPROACHES TO THE STUDY OF
DEVELOPING COUNTRIES' FOREIGN POLICIES

For a long time the analysis of developing countries' foreign policies was dominated by three approaches:[1]

1. The psychologistic approach views foreign policy as a function of the impulses and idiosyncrasies of a single leader. According to this view, kings and presidents are the source of foreign policy; war and peace become a matter of personal taste and individual choice. Foreign policy is perceived not as an activity designed to achieve national or societal goals but, as E. Shills wrote in 1962, as "a policy of public relations"[2] whose objectives are to improve the image of the state, enhance the popularity of the leader, and divert attention from domestic troubles to illusory external victories.

There are at least three criticisms of this view. First, it makes foreign policy appear to be an erratic, irrational activity not subject to systematic analysis. Second, it ignores the context (domestic, regional, and global) within which foreign policy is formulated and implemented. There are certain systemic constraints that most leaders will not or cannot usually challenge. Third, it ignores the fact that because of their interest in political survival, most leaders downplay eccentricities that run counter to dominant attitudes, public mood, and political realities. For instance, in 1970–1973 President Anwar Al-Sadat of Egypt concealed his dislike of the Soviets in his public pronouncements. He even accused Egyptian critics of the Soviet Union of being traitors to the cause of the homeland. Under different circumstances (discussed in Chapter 5), Egyptian policies became increasingly influenced by Sadat's personal feelings. It has been argued that only those idiosyncrasies that neither challenge prevailing values nor threaten a regime's stability are likely to be expressed in foreign policy.

We cannot rule out idiosyncratic variables in many developing countries, but what is more important is to analyze how the context of policy-making encourages certain leadership types and not others; how it allows certain idiosyncrasies but not others; and how a leader's idiosyncrasies may alter the context, affecting the foreign policy orientation of other leaders.[3]

2. The great powers approach, dominant among traditionalists such as Hans Morgenthau,[4] views foreign policy as a function of East-West conflict. Briefly stated, the foreign policies of developing countries are seen as lacking autonomy; affected by external stimuli, they react to initiatives and situations created by external forces. The main weakness of this approach is its neglect of domestic sources of foreign policy. Moreover, it implies that developing countries lack purposeful foreign policies of their own.

3. The reductionist or model-builders approach[5] views the foreign policies of the developing countries as determined by the same processes and decisional calculi that shape the foreign policies of developed countries. The basic difference is quantitative; the former have fewer resources and capabilities and therefore conduct foreign policy on a smaller scale. This view is predicated on the assumption that the behavior of all states (big and small, rich and poor, developed and developing) follows a rational actor model of decision-making; that all states seek to enhance their power, and that all are motivated by security factors. The conclusion is that the foreign policies of developing countries are exactly like those of the developed ones, but at a lower level of material resources. This approach does not account for specific features of the developing countries such as modernization, the low level of political institutionalization at home, and dependency status in the global stratification system abroad.

Since the 1970s, students of Third World countries' foreign policies have looked beyond the idiosyncrasy variable to consider the structural factors of these societies. They have sought to identify the specific features of these societies that distinguish them from developed societies and to apply more rigorous analytical frameworks. These efforts have resulted in more interaction between students of comparative politics and foreign policy analysis—enriching both subdisciplines—and more interaction between theorists and those engaged in field research.[6] The net outcome has been the emergence of a new body of literature on what can be called "the foreign policy of development."

One common element of the new literature is the emphasis on domestic sources of foreign policy and on how the processes of modernization and social change affect the external behavior of developing countries. East and Hagen, for example, underline the resource factors, distinguishing between size factors (absolute amount of available resources) and modernization factors (the ability to mobilize, control, and use these resources). Modernization is perceived as the process by which states increase their capability to control and use their resources. The more modernized states thus have a greater capacity to act.[7] A second example is Weinstein's pioneering work on Indonesia, in which he defines three foreign policy objectives: defense of the nation's independence against perceived threats, mobilization of external resources for the country's development, and the achievement of objectives related to domestic politics (e.g., isolating one's political opponents from their foreign supporters, lending legitimacy to domestic political demands, and creating symbols of nationalism and national unity).[8]

An equally important element in the new literature is the emphasis on the political economy of an actor's position in the global stratification system. In this context, inequality becomes a core focus, for developing countries exist in a world social order characterized by inequality between states at the levels of socioeconomic development, military capability, political stability, and prestige. This results in the penetration of developing countries' decision-making processes from the outside, with external actors participating authoritatively in the allocation of resources and the determination of national goals.[9] Much has been written on the role of the International Monetary Fund (IMF), international private banks, multinational corporations, and the big powers' foreign aid in this regard.[10] The situation in most developing countries is characterized by domination and unequal exchange. It is a dependency situation involving highly asymmetrical patterns of transactions between states.

A proper analysis of the foreign policies of Third World countries should accept that foreign policy is part and parcel of the general situation of the Third World and reflects the evolution of this situation. In this sense, the foreign policy process cannot be separated from the domestic social structure or domestic political process. To understand a country's foreign policy, we have to open the "black box" of Third World society. The countries of the Third World are part and parcel of a world system; they are greatly affected by international stratification and inequality. Formal state sovereignty notwithstanding, a Third World society can be permeated, penetrated, and even dominated. It is thus important to see how external constraints and global structures (e.g., relations with big powers or multinational companies) affect its foreign policy–making process as well as its international behavior.

From reviewing the literature, it seems that developing countries are faced by three major issues in the conduct of their foreign policies. The first is *the aid/independence dilemma*, i.e., the trade-off between the need for foreign aid and the maintenance of national independence. Some leaders, such as Nasser, Nkrumah, and Sukarno, have been more concerned with independence; others, such as Sadat or Suharto, have attached more importance to foreign aid. The difference in emphasis cannot be understood only in terms of social background and political values; other structural factors, such as the characteristics of the global system, perceived security threats, and economic problems, are of equal importance.

The second issue is *the resources/objectives dilemma*, which is more pressing in developing than in developed countries. It refers to the ability of foreign policy–makers to pursue objectives within the realm of their country's capabilities. This seems a commonsense proposition; but examples abound of countries pursuing unfeasible objectives. In the 1940s, King Abdallah of tiny Transjordan followed an activist policy for unity with Syria; in the 1950s, Iraq, despite an obvious imbalance of resources, projected itself as an alternative to Egyptian regional leadership; and in the 1960s Egyptian resources were drained by the protracted war in Yemen against Saudi Arabia.

Third is *the security/development dilemma*, a modern version of the age-old guns-or-butter debate. Some scholars perceive foreign policy primarily as a process or an activity whose main objective is the mobilization of external resources for the sake of societal development. Students of Egypt's foreign policy, for instance, cannot escape this conclusion. Sadat's rapprochement with the United States and peace with Israel were motivated by economic troubles at home and the desire to attract foreign investment, as demonstrated in Chapter 5. For other states, such as Syria, threat perceptions and security considerations remain the paramount factors in their foreign policy, as shown in Chapter 10.

Although security threats of a military nature cannot be overlooked, particularly in regions—such as the Middle East and southern Africa—experiencing endemic long-standing conflicts, for most developing countries the real security threat is hunger and malnutrition. In its third annual report on world development in 1980, the World Bank stated that 78 million people are living in absolute poverty. The number is likely to increase in the 1980s because of the worsening economic outlook for developing nations and because of population growth. The earth's present population of 4.3 billion is expected to reach 6 billion by the end of the century. One of the most explosive forces in many developing countries is the frustrated desire of poor people to attain a decent standard of living. Poverty, population explosion, failure of developmental efforts, and food insecurity lie at the heart of the national security issue for these countries. Consequently, the concept of national security must be redefined and broadened to include nonmilitary as well as military threats.

THE STUDY OF ARAB
FOREIGN POLICIES, 1965–1981

The "underdeveloped study of underdeveloped countries" is nowhere more clearly demonstrated than in the analysis of Arab foreign policy, as conclusions reached in the late 1970s by nine specialists dealing with the Third World indicate.[11] As stated in 1977 by one of the present coauthors, "the systematic analysis of foreign policy in the Middle East is an underdeveloped area of study. Only in the last few years have academics undertaken foreign policy studies of Middle Eastern states."[12]

To go beyond general impressions and get a data-based view of the state of the art for foreign policy studies of the Arab countries, we conducted a survey of the literature for the seventeen-year period from 1965 to 1981. Books published on Arab foreign policies can be counted on one's fingers. Consequently, we inventoried articles from various periodicals as well as some unpublished Ph.D. dissertations.

Four initial criteria served as guidelines in selecting items for inclusion.

1. The item should go beyond pure information to shed light on the conceptual and empirical issues in the field of foreign policy analysis.
2. The item should be a scholarly work rather than one adopting a "propagandistic" or "current affairs" approach.
3. Consequently, the search for survey items should be restricted to the pages of well-established specialized journals.
4. Selection would be limited to those items published in English or French.

The strict application of these criteria—laudable as they were—resulted in a harvest of items too scanty to be informative or useful. Indeed, the scarcity of scholarly and systematic works on Arab foreign policy during a seventeen-year period is in itself a telling condemnation of the state of this subfield. We subsequently amended our criteria, making some realistic modifications. Rather than limiting ourselves to purely scholarly publications, we added periodicals dealing with current affairs but still possessing a recognized status among students of international relations. These additions range from *Foreign Policy* to *World Today*. We included articles in Arabic, German, Hebrew, Japanese, and Spanish. We also added some of the standard specialized magazines whose coverage of the area has been credible and of use to scholars in the field. (Examples

TABLE 1.1
Articles on Sixteen Arab Countries and Palestine, by Language of Publication, 1965-1981

| Country | Language of Publication | | | | |
	Arabic	English	French	Others[a]	Total
Algeria	--	15	15	--	30
Egypt	2	40	8	2	52
Iraq	--	8	2	--	10
Jordan	--	1	--	--	1
Libya	--	14	7	--	21
Kuwait	--	2	--	--	2
Mauritania	--	--	1	--	1
Morocco	--	1	2	--	3
Oman	1	--	--	--	1
Palestine	--	2	--	--	2
Saudi Arabia	3	22	3	4	32
Sudan	--	5	1	--	6
Syria	--	3	--	--	3
Tunisia	--	2	3	--	5
United Arab Emirates	--	2	--	--	2
North Yemen	--	1	1	--	2
South Yemen	--	1	--	--	1
TOTAL	6	119	43	6	174

[a]German, Hebrew, Japanese, and Spanish.

are the bimonthly *Jeune Afrique*—Paris, the monthly *Middle East*—London, and the monthly *New Outlook*—Tel Aviv.

The result was a total of 297 items. Because of our relaxed criteria, however, the articles did not fall into a neat classification between, for instance, internal, regional, and international politics on the one hand and foreign policy proper on the other. This again reflects the underdevelopment of the foreign policy subfield. We distinguished instead between two categories of articles: those dealing *primarily with an Arab country's foreign policy*, and those dealing with what we dubbed *system dynamics*, i.e., inter-Arab politics, great power influences on one or two Arab states, or regional politics as such.

This categorization gave us 124 articles for system dynamics, leaving 174 articles that deal with the foreign policies of Arab countries (see Table 1.1). From the classification of articles in Table 1.1, several conclusions are apparent: the dominant language for foreign policy studies is still English (articles in Arabic are much more numerous in the category of system dynamics); articles in French are concentrated—for obvious historical reasons—on the Maghreb, including Libya; and the distribution of the 174 articles among countries is very uneven.

Egypt and, increasingly, Saudi Arabia are relatively overpublished. The six publications in languages other than Arabic, English, and French focus on these two countries. Many other countries—even crucial ones such as Kuwait, Syria, or the Sudan, are underpublished. Particularly striking is the complete absence in our survey of any publications on Lebanon's foreign policy.

By the end of the decade 1965–1975, not a single book in Arabic, English, or French had been published on the foreign policy of Egypt— an overpublished country according to our inventory. The number of articles on Egypt for the same decade amounted to 23, totaling 369 pages—an average of about 37 pages a year.

From a *qualitative* point of view, the situation is even worse. Among the 23 authors of the articles on Egypt whose professional affiliations could be ascertained (12 in all), 10 had an academic background. The majority of articles were written under the pressure of events or for a specific occasion, without the benefit of in-depth research. As a result, these works neither reflect the recent advances in comparative foreign policy conceptualization nor attempt to link data and theory.

Our review of the literature published between 1965 and 1975 revealed three important theoretical problems. First, the works of this decade did not provide an operational definition of the "what" of foreign policy: the output itself. Authors tended to deal with goals, objectives, strategies, general declarations, and official statements, actions, and transactions— accepting all of these as foreign policy. No distinction was made between general orientation or world view and specific behavior or action. Second, with the exception of reporting gossip or practicing a modern version of the "great man" theory of history, the dynamics and intricacies of the foreign policy–making process were largely neglected. The "black box" remained closed. Third, although most authors attempted to interpret and analyze the sources or determinants of foreign policy, their efforts suffered from conceptual fuzziness and a lack of explicitness.

The year 1975 was a watershed for the study of Arab foreign policy. The breakthrough came with a new generation of researchers who were graduate students at the time and who combined both the knowledge of the area specialist and the methodology of social science in their Ph.D. dissertations. Examples include Adeed Dawisha's Ph.D. dissertation at London University on Egypt; Nicole Grimaud's, Marlène Nasr's, and Ghassan Salama's dissertations at the University of Paris on Algeria, Egypt, and Saudi Arabia respectively; Mohamed Selim's work at Carleton University on Nasser's operational code; Walid Mubarak's study at Indiana University on Kuwait; and Ahmad Yousef's and Mustafa Elwi's dissertations at Cairo University on Egypt's foreign policy decisions in 1962 and 1967.[13]

Some of these dissertations were published, initiating a debate on the present state of theory in foreign policy analysis for developing countries and on the problems of relevant hypotheses and data collection in a context of agonizing social change and underdevelopment.

THE FRAMEWORK FOR ANALYSIS

To ensure coherence and continuity between the chapters of the book, the analysis of each actor's foreign policy has been based on the same fundamental concepts and categories. An important task is the precise description of foreign policy output. Does "foreign policy" mean general objectives, specific acts, critical choices and decisions, or all of these combined? In his oft-cited 1966 article, Rosenau deals extensively with foreign policy determinants (the independent variables) and their comparative influence, but neglects to define what he means by foreign policy as an output.[14] The 1968 article by the *International Encyclopedia of the Social Sciences* follows Rosenau's example and offers no definition. Even textbooks neglect this conceptual task.

Our solution is to conceptualize foreign policy output as a *role*. The role concept is very handy for our purposes, as it allows the disaggregation of foreign policy output into its relevant components: the actor's general objectives, orientation, or strategy (role conception) and the specific foreign policy behavior (role performance or role enactment). This breakdown of foreign policy output into general objectives and concrete behavior attracts attention to an important question in both foreign policy empirical analysis and theory building: How does the foreign policy role conception (general strategy and declaratory objectives) conform to or depart from the role performance (actual behavior)? What is the disparity ratio between "say" and "do," between conception and behavior? What determines the variations in disparity ratio between different regimes and countries? Is it a question of *intra-elite* conflict, with political elites agreeing on a consensual foreign policy orientation but disagreeing on the manner of implementation? Is it a question of *inter-role* conflict, with objectives and actions at the regional level conflicting with those at the global level? Or is it only a question of *role strain*, when the realization of foreign policy objectives is beyond the capabilities of the Third World actor or beyond the capabilities of a regime lacking the legitimacy to mobilize needed resources?

The introduction of role theory to foreign policy analysis inspires numerous theoretical leads that might help the field to sharpen and operationalize its conceptual distinctions, and thus proceed more quickly in overcoming its handicaps and limitations.

The contribution of role theory is not limited to its conceptual capital; it is also of empirical relevance. For instance, the election of former actor Ronald Reagan to the highest political office in the United States, and the crucial political roles played by Mao's wife, Jiang Qing, and Evita Peron, who both worked as actresses, establish a link between role theory and political analysis more direct than most leaders would like to consider. The empirical relevance of the role concept to foreign policy analysis can be quite explicit. Witness the assertion made by a prominent Third World leader—Gamal Abdel Nasser of Egypt—at the beginning of his career: "I always imagine that in this region there is a role wandering aimlessly about in search of a hero to play it. . . . It is we, and we alone in virtue of our position, who can play the part."[15] Nasser relates role to position or status. In retrospect, this quotation reminds us that if objectives are not tailored to capabilities, the result is foreign policy *crises or failures* (e.g., Egypt's 1967 war with Israel, initiated when the better part of the Egyptian army was in Yemen). Foreign policy crises can lead to foreign policy *change* (e.g., Sadat's replacing the USSR with the United States as Egypt's dominant role partner and his signing of a formal peace treaty with Israel with all its bilateral and regional repercussions). In other words—as Linton reminded us forty-five years ago and as Nasser confirmed almost thirty years ago—opportunities and constraints, rights and duties, are inseparable properties of the actor's position and status.

The proposed framework of analysis consists of the following fourfold scheme: domestic environment, foreign policy orientation, decision-making process, and foreign policy behavior.

Domestic Environment

Each of the following factors is analyzed as either enhancing or con-straining the foreign policy options of a country.

Geography. A state's geographic position has long been considered an important determinant of its foreign policy. The impact of geography, however, is not static. We know that states change their foreign policy and that the significance of geographic position varies over time. In the twentieth century, geographic considerations have been tempered by modern military weaponry and advanced communications technology.

This is not to suggest that geography has lost all significance. In many cases, certain national interests and objectives are obviously dictated by geographic considerations. The location of a country among its immediate neighbors contributes to the development of national identity. A state's potential development is also influenced by its geography: material endowments (size, topography, climate, and natural resources) play a vital role in determining whether a country will develop industry or agriculture or both; whether it can support a large population; and whether it has elements of power such as a strong economic base or easily defendable borders. A nation's access to natural resources within its boundaries affects its ability to enforce its own foreign policy demands and to resist pressures by other states. Finally, geographic factors influence the actions of a ruling elite. The significance of this influence depends upon the perception and interpretation of geographic factors by policy-makers.[16]

In the case of developing countries, two issues are of particular importance. The first is the issue of artificial boundaries: a number of African boundaries, for instance, were drawn along latitudes and lon-gitudes in the colonial offices of London, Paris, and other European capitals. These political divisions ignore geographic, ethnic, and economic considerations. The second issue concerns the proliferation of ministates that lack the ingredients of independent existence. This situation results in continuous dependence on larger countries for economic aid, political support, and military assistance.

Population and Social Structure. The size, composition, and geographic distribution of a country's population are factors in the calculus of national power. Although a large population does not guarantee international influence, states with small populations are usually at a disadvantage. The size of population is not in itself a sufficient index of power. It is the composition of the population—its social cohesiveness, education, and distribution of skills—that really makes a difference. Like geographic factors, population is not a static element; it must be viewed in relation to the sociopolitical context. It may surprise many to know that in the wars of 1948, 1956, and 1967, little Israel mobilized combat forces that were larger in number than the combined forces of its Arab adversaries, whose total population was fifteen to twenty times greater than Israel's. The issue of social or national integration is particularly important in developing countries; most have ethnic, religious, and racial problems. The existence of minority groups in frontier areas further complicates matters for developing countries, especially when they seek help from a neighboring country.

Economic Capability. This factor refers to the natural resources of a country (availability) and to its ability to mobilize them at the service of its foreign policy (control). Economic capability affects both a state's objectives and its means of implementing them. Poor states, for instance, are likely to have a low level of diplomatic representation. In the case of developing countries, two questions are investigated: to what extent is the economic infrastructure (agriculture, industry, and services) capable of satisfying the economic needs of the population, thus reducing the need for foreign aid; and does economic development tend to enhance or decrease dependence on foreign sources?

Military Capability. This capability is both quantitative (number of troops and weapons) and qualitative (level of weapons systems and training, past experiences, and cohesiveness). Almost all developing countries depend for their armaments on a limited number of sources in the developed world. Arms sales have indeed been a major avenue for influence and penetration. Most developing countries, however, aspire to establish large, strong armies. The army is viewed as a symbol of national independence and as an embodiment of the nation's dignity. The literature underlines three areas where armaments and foreign policy interact: first, countries that follow activist or change-oriented foreign policies usually embark on a policy of arms acquisition; second, the existence of large armies may entice decision-makers to use the military instrument in their foreign policy; and third, the army acts as a constraint, influencing the choice between foreign policy options.

Political Structure. Here we discuss to what extent the political structure provides opportunities or imposes constraints on decision-makers. A political structure may constitute a resource, depending on its stability, legitimacy, degree of institutionalization, and level of public support. Conversely, political factionalization and domestic instability may constrain the conduct of a purposeful foreign policy.

The low level of political institutionalization and the high level of political instability in most developing countries have several results. One is the primacy of the executive, particularly in the development of a presidential center that dominates the policy-making process. The presidential center usually enjoys relative freedom of action due to the absence of a free press or a strong opposition. In these countries the link between domestic and foreign policy is more direct than in the developed countries: foreign policy is employed for the achievement of domestic objectives. This point will be further developed in our discussion of the decision-making process.

Foreign Policy Orientation

The concept of orientation refers to one component of foreign policy output; the other components are decisions and actions. Orientation is the way a state's foreign policy elite perceives the world and its country's role in it. Kal Holsti defines orientation as a state's "general attitudes and commitments toward the external environment, its fundamental strategy for accomplishing its domestic and external objectives and aspirations and for coping with persisting threats."[17] Taking the degree of involvement in international politics as a criterion, he identifies three basic types of global orientation: isolation, nonalignment, and coalition building or alliance construction. Orientations are necessarily stable, though by no means rigid or unchanging. They may change due to a radical alteration in the domestic political structure, the regional balance of power, or the global system.

The analysis of a country's orientation may address questions such as: What are the country's general objectives and strategy at the global and regional levels? How do we explain their adoption by the ruling elite? How do orientations change over time and what are the sources of change?

The Decision-Making Process

There has been an overemphasis in the literature on the personalized character of the decision-making process and on the lack of political institutionalization in developing countries. Although this emphasis is essentially valid, it gives a simplistic and reductionist image of the decision-making process. An individual leader may have the ultimate say in the choice between alternatives, but he or she must take into consideration a great number of variables and must weigh the responses of various influential domestic groups. Moreover, in many instances the primary unit of decision-making is not the president as an individual but the presidency as an institution. Individual politicians in developing countries are directly involved in foreign policy–making, but this process takes place in a specific social and institutional context. Even in the most authoritarian regimes, institutional arrangements constitute an intermediary variable between individual decision-makers and their environment.

In developing countries, the number and the relative influence of participants in the decision-making process vary according to type of political regime and issue area (for example, "high" versus "low" politics). These differences, however, do not affect the general decision-making pattern, which is dominated by the executive power around or through *el señor presidente* or *la monarchie présidentielle*. Robert L. Rothstein argues that the pattern of this political process is a function of two characteristics: conflict and poverty. Conflict is caused by the fractionalization of the polity into primordial or economic divisions that may be tribal, ethnic, religious, regional, or class-oriented. The frequency and the intensity of conflict are heightened by ever-increasing poverty caused by rising demands and insufficient resources. This situation leads to constant struggle between the various groups for control of the state.[18]

If foreign policy as an area of choice is a field of opportunities and constraints, the developing country enters this arena with the double burden of an "international system of increasing complexity" and a "domestic base that is less secure and less manageable."[19] The impact of underdevelopment on policy-making is heightened by the fact that "new and inexperienced elites [are] forced to decide critical strategic issues without much knowledge or expertise, without many useful precedents, and in the face of sharp economic cleavages and serious foreign pressures."[20]

The conceptualization of the decision-making process in developing countries as a "resource gap problem" involving group conflicts is a big step toward removing the blinders of psychological reductionism. It opens the door to further investigation of how and when an alliance between domestic and external groups can influence the resource gap and determine the decisions to be taken. It also explains the infiltration by outside groups into a developing country's decision-making process.

Foreign Policy Behavior

This includes the concrete actions, positions, and decisions that the state takes or adopts in the conduct of its foreign policy. Foreign policy behavior is the concrete expression of orientation in specific acts, and it is analyzed in this book in relation to the superpowers as well as to other regional actors.

The behavior of developing countries has been generally characterized by support for the United Nations and other international organizations, advocacy of change in the global system, promotion of the idea of a new international economic order (NIEO), and emphasis on regional issues.

In brief, we think that this framework for analysis has certain merits. It reflects conceptual advances in foreign policy analysis. It is interdisciplinary, relevant to the specific situation of developing countries, and applicable to the Arab countries with which this book is concerned.

NOTES

1. Bahgat Korany, "Foreign Policy Models and Their Empirical Relevance to Third World Actors: A Critique and an Alternative," *International Social Science Journal* 26 (1974), pp. 70–94.

2. Quoted in Franklin Weinstein, *Indonesian Foreign Policy and the Dilemma of Dependence* (Ithaca, N.Y.: Cornell University Press, 1976), p. 21.

3. *Ibid.*, p. 26.

4. See for instance his analysis of Afro-Asian neutralism. Hans Morgenthau, "Neutrality and Neutralism," *The Year Book of World Affairs* (London) 11 (1957), pp. 47–75.

5. James Rosenau, Michael Brecher, and Margaret Hermann all follow this approach.

6. For an overview of the field see Bahgat Korany, "The Take-off of Third World Studies? The Case of Foreign Policy," *World Politics* 35, 3 (1983), pp. 465–487. See also John Stremlau (ed.), *The Foreign Policy Priorities of Third World States* (Boulder, Colo.: Westview Press, 1982).

7. Maurice A. East and Joe I. Hagen, "Approaches to Small States' Foreign Policy: An Analysis of the Literature and Some Empirical Observations," Paper presented to the International Studies Association meeting, Toronto, Canada, February 25–29, 1976.

8. Franklin Weinstein, "The Use of Foreign Policy in Indonesia: An Approach to the Analysis of Foreign Policy in Less Developed Countries," *World Politics* 24 (1972), pp. 356–382.

9. Bahgat Korany, *Social Change, Charisma and International Behavior* (Leiden, Netherlands: Sijthoff, 1976), pp. 140–159.

10. In general see Thomas Biersteker, *Distortion or Development? Contending Perspectives on the Multinational Corporation* (Cambridge, Mass.: MIT Press, 1978), pp. 1–26. For an analysis of Egypt's situation, see Ali E. Hillal Dessouki, "Policy-Making in Egypt: A Case Study of the Open Door Economic Policy," *Social Problems* 28, 4 (1981), pp. 410–416.

11. Korany, "The Take-off," pp. 465–466.

12. Adeed Dawisha, "The Middle East," in Christopher Clapham (ed.), *Foreign Policy-Making in Developing States: A Comparative Approach* (London: Saxon House, 1977), p. 70.

13. Adeed Dawisha, *Egypt in the Arab World: The Elements of Foreign Policy* (London: Macmillan, 1976); Nicole Grimaud, "La politique étrangère de l'Algérie," Ph.D. diss., University of Paris, 1982, forthcoming as a book in 1984; Marlène Nasr, "L'idéologie nationale arabe dans les discours de Gamal Abdel Nasser: 1952–1979," Ph.D. diss., University of Paris–Sorbonne IV, 1979 (Arabic edition published by the Center for Arab Unity Studies, Beirut, 1981); Ghassan Salama, "La politique étrangère de l'Arabie Saoudite," Ph.D. diss., University of Paris, 1979 (Arabic edition published by the Institute for Arab Development, Beirut,

1980); Mohamed Selim, "The Operational Code Belief System and Foreign Policy Decision-Making: The Case of Gamal Abdel-Nasser," Ph.D. diss., Carleton University, Ottawa, 1979 (Arabic edition published by the Center for Arab Unity Studies, Beirut, 1983); Walid Mubarak, "Kuwait's Quest for Security, 1961–1973," Ph.D. diss., Indiana University, 1979; Ahmad Yousef Ahmad, "Egypt's Role in Yemen 1962–1967," Ph.D. diss., Cairo University, 1978 (in Arabic); and Mustafa Elwi, "Egypt's International Behavior During the Crisis of May–June 1967," Ph.D. diss., Cairo University, 1981 (in Arabic).

14. James Rosenau, "Pre-theories and Theories of Foreign Policy," in Barry Farrell (ed.), *Approaches to Comparative and International Politics* (Evanston, Ill.: Northwestern University Press, 1966), pp. 27–93.

15. Quoted in Peter Willetts, *The Nonaligned Movement: The Origins of a Third World Alliance* (New York: Nichols Publishing Co., 1978), p. 9.

16. Norman Hill, *International Politics* (New York: Harper & Row, 1963), p. 226; and Harold Sprout and Margaret Sprout, *Foundations of International Politics* (New York: D. Van Nostrand Co., 1962), p. 288ff.

17. K. J. Holsti, *International Politics* (Englewood Cliffs, N.J.: Prentice-Hall, 1977), p. 109.

18. Robert L. Rothstein, *The Weak in the World of the Strong: The Developing Countries in the International System* (New York: Columbia University Press, 1977), pp. 181–182.

19. *Ibid.*, p. 62.

20. *Ibid.*, p. 90.

2

The Global System
and Arab Foreign Policies:
The Primacy of Constraints

Bahgat Korany
Ali E. Hillal Dessouki

INTRODUCTION

In both academic and political parlance, the expression "the dependent status of Third World countries" is widely accepted. Indeed, the label "Third World" is a translation of the French term *tiers monde*, which was inspired by the subordinate position of the *tiers état* in France's political system just prior to the 1789 French Revolution. But instead of addressing the major impact of external factors on Third World political behavior that the label expresses, foreign policy model-builders—influenced by the context of developed countries—have emphasized domestic factors.[1] On the rare occasions when the relationship of global system and foreign policy is addressed, the resulting statements are either confused or too general.

This chapter starts by defining the global system and summarizing the different approaches to its analysis. The "dependency perspective" is singled out as the most relevant in confronting the problematique that interests us here: international stratification and inequality and their effects on developing countries. However, this perspective is found wanting for two reasons: it addresses the linkage of global system and foreign policy in terms that are too general, and it lumps together the different parts of the Third World as if specific variations among different regions did not exist. After reviewing the literature on the global system/ foreign policy linkage, the chapter concentrates on the specific features of the Arab world, demonstrating the primacy of constraints in the formation of foreign policy.

DEFINING THE GLOBAL SYSTEM

By global system we mean the pattern of interactions among international actors, which take place according to an identifiable set of rules. This simple definition contains three basic elements:

First, international actors include both states and nonstate actors: international organizations such as the Organization of Petroleum Exporting Countries (OPEC) and the Arab League, multinational companies (the Seven Sisters, Aramco), and national liberation movements (the PLO; Algeria's Provisional Government, 1958–1962). These actors differ in capabilities, characteristic structure, and objectives.

Second, relations among actors follow regular patterns of international conflict and cooperation. These patterns constitute a whole; the system is more than the mere sum of relations among its members. Moreover, relations embrace different issue areas: diplomatic, economic, cultural, and military.

Third, these relations are governed by a set of rules that are usually incorporated into international law, the deliberations of international organizations, and the practice of states. These rules can be well-established, explicit, and written; or evolving, implicit, and more or less consensual. International law includes treaties as well as international practice and custom. Implicit rules should not be understood, however, as being less important, for they can be crucial in the functioning of the system, as is the case in the field of nuclear deterrence.

Although the literature basically agrees on the definition of the global system, no consensus exists on what is the best means of analyzing it. Approaches and schools of thought conflict on this issue.

APPROACHES TO THE ANALYSIS OF THE GLOBAL SYSTEM

Differences over how to study the global system are part of a larger debate in the sociology of international relations. Basically, the debate has turned on two major issues: the methodological-conceptual one (traditionalism versus behavioralism) and the ideological-substantive one (liberal versus Marxist, developed country versus dependency approaches).[2]

The Traditionalism-Versus-Behavioralism Debate

Students of political analysis believe that the study of the global system passed through a methodological-conceptual revolution in the 1950s under the impact of the behavioral movement in political science.[3] This behavioral movement was a reaction to *traditional approaches* to the study of politics, which were based on the following common assumptions:

- Both empirical (factual) and normative (value-judgment) questions are proper subjects of enquiry.

- Formal institutions, legal systems, and historical description of political events are the proper focus of research.
- Quantitative methods should be used sparingly, if at all.
- Conclusions are drawn on the basis of informed judgment and careful study or observation, not from statistical probabilities based on many observed cases.
- It is doubtful whether scientific methods, in any sense other than careful and systematic inquiry, can be successfully transferred to the study of human behavior.

The new *behavioralist* wave, on the contrary, focused on individuals and their behavior rather than on formal/legal structures. The behavioralists' greatest emphasis was on rigor and precision in research. Their objective was the elaboration of law-like generalizations, a theoretical base for the "science of politics."[4] To attain this objective, they followed four steps: (1) the formulation, at the outset of the research project, of explicit hypotheses defining the relationship between dependent and independent variables (the phenomenon to be explained and its possible determinants); (2) the measurement of quantitative indicators of variables that test the relationship; (3) the use of mathematical-statistical techniques whenever possible to achieve maximum precision in testing the different hypotheses; and (4) the carrying out of necessary cross-national research and the collection of comparative data to make generalizations reliable.

Some welcome concerns of the behavioralists were the importance of rigor in social research, the relevance of concepts borrowed from other social sciences to promote interdisciplinary analysis, and the utility of discovering patterns of political behavior rather than being limited to individual cases. However, the behavioralists overdid their case to the extent that some founders of the movement became skeptical and raised the possibility of a "postbehavioral era." This self-scrutiny and skepticism were inspired by the excesses of the behavioralist school: a preoccupation with method to the exclusion of substantive issues, a focus on the most readily quantifiable hypotheses rather than on the relevant and meaningful ones, the promotion of expensive research tools such as computers and databanks and jargon incomprehensible to the policy-maker, and the relative neglect of some major ethical questions in a world of poverty, hunger, violence, and a nuclear balance of terror.[5]

Western Approaches, Marxism, and Dependencia

By the 1960s, a Third World perspective was coalescing around the dependency perspective to counterbalance established approaches. At first, this dependency perspective was associated with classical Marxism, and thus suffered from the poisoned atmosphere of the Cold War, but with the increasing excesses and failures of behavioralism in the late 1960s, young political scientists and politicians turned more and more

TABLE 2.1
Different Analytical Approaches to the Global System

	◄——— The Ideological Debate ———►	
	Traditionalism	Marxism-Leninism
↑ The Methodological Debate ↓	The historian's analysis of the nineteenth-century balance-of-power system; the works of Hans Morgenthau	The analysis of the European capitalist system; Marx and Engels
	Behavioralism	Dependencia
	Systems analysis inspired by social and natural sciences; the works of M. Kaplan and D. Easton	Adoption of a political economy approach that emphasizes the characteristics and role of the periphery; the contributions of S. Amin and F. Cordoso

toward the dependency perspective. By the early 1970s, the field of global system analysis included the schools listed in Table 2.1.

The traditional approach to the analysis of the global system concentrated only on inter-European politics, treating all events in the Third World purely as extensions of this major conflict. Indeed, traditionalists treated all international relations as inter-state phenomena, emphasizing the separation between domestic and external policies. They followed the so-called billiard-ball model of the state, which envisions borders as impenetrable barriers. Behavioralism attacked traditionalism for its methodological sloppiness and stressed the role of nonstate actors[6] as well as the linkage[7] between domestic and foreign policies. Methodological refinement notwithstanding, behavioralism was still as Eurocentric as traditionalism. Most importantly, however, behavioralists overemphasized academic neutrality, mistrusted "ideological issues," and hence made many of the substantive sociopolitical problems of the world taboo.

The drawbacks of behavioralism account for the general seductiveness of Marxism and the popularity of Lenin's theory of imperialism. Marxism focused on the impact of nonstate actors and linkages in an interdisciplinary way, emphasizing the "real life issues" of exploitation, inequality, and the hierarchy among major political actors. But even this approach was elaborated in terms of Europe, the system's center. Marxism also seemed to neglect the role of the superstructure in an age of populism and the interventionist corporatist state.[8] Marxism's frowning upon nationalism and its de-emphasis of the role of peasants (a massive proletariat is still absent in the predominantly agrarian Third World societies) were additional drawbacks.

Though sharing Marxism's emphasis on the importance of real life issues and on the system's structural properties, dependencia tried to cope with deficiencies and anachronisms by bringing the "periphery" in. Building on previous advances in social analysis (e.g., rigor, inter-disciplinarity, and the dialectical approach), the dependency perspective concentrates on the relationship between the global system and Third World societies, and hence comes nearest to our chosen problematique.

As useful surveys of the perspective are now available,[9] we will limit ourselves to analyzing its basic propositions[10] (six in all) to see how they help in dealing with the global system and its influence on foreign policy–making.

THE DEPENDENCY PERSPECTIVE: ITS BASIC PROPOSITIONS

1. Present problems of Third World underdevelopment and development cannot be studied in isolation from their historical and global context. In a nutshell, Third World underdevelopment and development are part of a global dynamic: the process of change in the worldwide capitalist system.

2. Although internal structure and processes do play a role in Third World societies, most important changes in these societies are ultimately determined by external forces. This reveals the inability of Third World societies to exert much control over their own destinies, let alone over the larger world system. The use of the term "dependent" to describe this situation is amply justified both in practice and in theory.

3. Rather than being an isolated, mechanistic process, economic change is part of the general societal process and reflects the roles of different groups at the national and international levels. Two consequences follow: (1) the real object of our study is neither economics nor politics, but political economy, which is the interaction between the two; and (2) the state's sovereignty and frontiers are analytical concepts rather than barriers: in short, separation between the domestic and foreign policies of the penetrable Third World society is either a fiction or an aberration. Consequently, all social institutions—from the family and culture to religion and the media—are linked to the world political economy and the world domination patterns that underlie it.

4. The influence of the worldwide (capitalist) system is no longer exerted through an impersonal market, but through an important nonstate actor: the multinational company (MNC). Though the MNCs behave with visible and deliberate purpose, they do not necessarily have the interests of the Third World at heart. For example, the industrialization that the MNCs sponsor is based on sophisticated technology (which has to be imported) and thus requires lots of foreign currency (which is scarce) but little local labor (which is plentiful).[11] The list of ensuing

harmful effects can be extensive. Multinational companies drive out locally owned businesses; export scarce capital through profit remittances, transfer payments, and patent royalties; create unnecessary and alien consumption patterns; corrupt local politicians; and contaminate social values.

5. An examination of the pattern of international stratification—essential for an understanding of Third World foreign policies—shows that many local groups are consciously or unconsciously dependent on the existing system and hence unlikely to challenge it. These groups include landowners, the growing state bureaucracies, and the entrepreneurial bourgeoisie.

6. The road to change is therefore a difficult one. Some degree of dissociation of the dependent periphery from the system's core may be necessary as the only way to recreate another, more just structure.

The dependency perspective has three advantages as far as Third World foreign policy analysis is concerned. First, it emphasizes the role of structural factors that could account for foreign policy better than traditional approaches. For example, patterns of social organization and institutions could be emphasized instead of psychological or idiosyncratic factors. Second, it is a dynamic perspective that emphasizes both the role of social change in a global context and the linkage between the different levels of analysis—from the global to the subnational—through the hierarchical network of different social groups. The state is no longer seen as the compact and impermeable billiard ball traditionalists assumed it to be. And third, the advocates of dependency theory pushed aside rigid discipline boundaries to emphasize the close relationship between political, economic, historical, and sociological phenomena.

However, the perspective has two main drawbacks for an analysis of the linkage between the global system and foreign policy. For one, it is much more concerned with general patterns of national underdevelopment and development than with the systematic analysis of a dependent country's foreign policy. For instance, according to proposition 6 above, a country's policy-makers are advised to reverse dependency through dissociation from the system, but many questions remain unanswered. For instance, what form will the dissociation take? What groups can lead the effort? What specific policies should they adopt? This high level of generality is related to the second drawback: the perspective's homogenizing tendency to lump together all Third World societies. A common Third World position in the global system notwithstanding, there are variations among Third World regions. These variations[12] involve patterns of precolonial evolution and types of colonial relationship, social organization, and phases of development (e.g., Black Africa versus Latin America; India versus Honduras). In short, we need to sort out the common features of the Third World as a whole from the specific characteristics of its regions. Distinguishing general and specific traits will help make the analysis of the relationship between global system and foreign policy much more concrete. We shall deal with problems presented by each of these drawbacks in order to attune the dependency perspective to the analysis of Arab and Third World foreign policies.

How Does the Global System Influence Foreign Policy?

Four features characterize what little literature[13] we have on this linkage. First of all, there is unanimous affirmation of the influence of global systemic factors on foreign policy. Almost all authors agree that the behavior and interaction of nations are more influenced by the system than vice versa.

Second, authors do not go beyond stating the existence of this linkage; they fail to specify its degree. In the literature, we find propositions such as: (1) there is a relationship between a nation's regional position (a systemic factor) and its support for, or voting record in, the UN (a foreign policy behavior); (2) there is a relationship between a nation's status in the international system and its diplomatic interactions with other nations; and (3) the Cold War determines the linkage between states.

A third aspect of the literature is that authors confuse purely external factors (e.g., geographical distance from the USSR or the United States, number of formal allies or enemies) and proper systemic factors (e.g., bipolar or multipolar structure, overall level of interaction patterns, "rules of the game," or the system's political culture and values). Disregarding this difference between external and systemic factors, McGowan and Shapiro use the two categories interchangeably. Many of their propositions on "systemic" factors actually cover external ones, as these examples show: (1) the less geographical and socioeconomic distance between nations, the greater the interaction between them; (2) the less distance between nations in terms of governmental attributes, the greater the interaction between them; (3) the policies of international organizations constrain the foreign policy activities of nations; and (4) the activities of the great powers limit the attempts of smaller states to maintain neutrality and independence.

Finally, if little is available on the actual linkage between the global system and foreign policy, even less exists on how the dominant system does in fact influence the foreign policy of the dependent or developing country. If there is a dependent foreign policy, what does it look like?[14]

Some proponents of the empirical approach have tried to deal with this question. For instance, Richardson[15] asks whether and how the economic dependence of Third World countries is reflected in their foreign policy behavior. He decides to equate "dependent" with "compliant" or "deferential" behavior. Compliance in this respect means that the behavior's "wellsprings are external rather than internal to the nation," i.e., "the foreign policy behavior of a dependent country will be more or less in accord with the preferences of the country that dominates its economic life." He then tests the relationship between dependency on the United States and the degree of compliance in the foreign policy behavior of 23 Third World countries (19 from Latin America, and 4 from Africa and Asia). He measures foreign policy behavior by one indicator: roll-call UN votes. The results of this test indicate that no relationship exists between dependency and foreign policy behavior, at least at this level.

Despite rigor in data collection and analysis, two difficulties arise as a result of this empiricist school of thought. If measurement is the only way to test the relationship of global system and foreign policy, we should wonder whether the diversity of a country's foreign policy can be reduced to the single indicator of UN votes and also whether dependency as a global pattern is properly expressed as unequal relations between a Third World country and the United States alone. As the propositions of the dependency perspective show, dependency is not limited to unequal bilateral relations as such; rather, this inequality is seen as a reflection of a historically determined macrostructure characterized by specific stratification patterns and modes of production. If this historical-structural conceptualization of the world system is what distinguishes dependency from other macroapproaches (Kaplan or Aron), it is not enough to test the relations between dependent countries and the United States. Any dependent country may switch from one patron to another—say from the United States to Great Britain, or France, or Japan—but this does not change a country's dependent status, only its dominant partner.

In short, very few of the hypotheses of the scanty literature on the relationship between the global system and foreign policy have been tested, probably because many of these hypotheses have been formulated in very general terms, without taking into account the specificities of different Third World regions. This brings us to our second criticism of the dependency perspective: its homogenizing treatment of Third World regions.

What Elements Are Specific to the Arab World?

Despite common socioeconomic features and interests, the Third World is not a uniform group. Third World members vary in level of development (Brazil versus Upper Volta), GNP per capita (Argentina's $2,390 versus Bangladesh's $130), political orientation (Cuba versus Malawi), and historical experience (Senegal versus "noncolonized" Ethiopia). The Arab world, however, possesses several common elements that predominate over inter-Arab variations and make this group a distinct entity within the larger group of developing or dependent countries. These shared features include cultural homogeneity, concentration of relevant resources, and the constant plague of a protracted social conflict (the Palestine-Zionist issue).

Cultural Homogeneity. As a people, Arabs enjoy a high degree of linguistic and cultural homogeneity. Notwithstanding subnational variations due to the local history of each community, the Arabs belong to the same religion, the same cultural tradition; they share a common history and converse in the same language. One of the dominant intellectual and political trends in the Arab world in the twentieth century has been Arab nationalism and the call for Arab unity. The pan-Arab trend was manifested in scores of cultural and literary clubs at the turn of the century, in political movements with branches in a number of Arab countries—the Ba'th party and the Arab nationalist movement are two, and in Egypt's policies of the 1950s and 1960s.

According to this pan-Arab ideology, the Arab world is one nation, and its division into separate states is an aberration resulting from "foreign designs." The daily circulation of Egyptian or Lebanese newspapers in different Arab countries, the use of common films and television programs, the presence of Arab students of all nationalities in the universities of Cairo, Baghdad, or Kuwait, and more recently the increasing labor migration: all indicate a level of exchange in the Arab world unparalleled in other Third World regions.

The high level of Arab interaction belies some established theories of the global system, e.g., Galtung's notion of a feudal pattern of international interaction.[16] According to this pattern, interaction is intense among top dogs (developed countries), quite high between developing and developed countries, and very limited among underdeveloped or dependent countries (the underdogs). Moreover, interaction among underdeveloped countries usually takes place through developed countries, according to Galtung.

Not only does Arab cultural homogeneity make Galtung's theory of the global system inapplicable to the Arab world, but it has also had political consequences at the regional Arab level. Arabs see themselves as having played a distinct and glorious part in the world civilization. They believe that they have a special role within Islam and the Moslem world. Islam was revealed to an Arab; its sacred shrines are in an Arab country; and its book, the Qur'an, can only be recited in Arabic. Because of their relatively early independence (mostly in the 1940s in the Arab East and the 1950s and 1960s in the Arab West), certain Arab countries (particularly Egypt) also played a significant role in the anticolonial movement in Africa and in the development of the nonaligned movement. In the 1970s, other Arab countries (Libya, Saudi Arabia, Algeria, and Morocco) played roles far beyond their immediate borders, as described in Chapters 4, 7, and 9.

A basic component of Arab political culture is the belief that Arab nationhood will be translated into Arab statehood, and that the present division of the Arab nation into several states is both artificial and temporary. This explains the enthusiasm with which the Arab masses accepted the union of Egypt and Syria as the United Arab Republic (1958–1961). This last case, in fact, confirms another important characteristic of Arab politics: intense involvement by the masses. It is almost as if inter-Arab relations are not really foreign relations but part of the politics of the extended family instead. Thus, Arab leaders tend to talk directly to the citizens of other Arab states. Moreover, pan-Arab issues (e.g., the Palestine problem) become a component of political legitimacy for many Arab regimes. The condemnation of Sadat's 1977 Jerusalem visit and the 1978 Camp David agreements was less an expression of opposition to peace with Israel than a protest against Sadat's go-it-alone diplomacy on a pan-Arab issue.

Arab cultural homogeneity has also led to occasional confrontation with the big powers. These powers are concerned over the potential emergence of a unified Arab state that could constitute an effective barrier to their influence in the region and their desire to control Arab resources. Both the West and the USSR clashed with Nasser on the occasion of the constitution of the United Arab Republic.[17]

The Protracted Palestinian-Zionist Conflict.[18] All Arab countries—secular and religious, radical and conservative—view the dispersion of the Palestinians as a blatant case of injustice against all Arabs. Already in 1960, the cofounder of the Ba'th Pan-Arab party and the former prime minister of Syria, Salah Eddin Al-Bitar, emphasized the "Western betrayal" and linked it to the foreign policy that the "Arab nation" should follow: "Western imperialism divided the Arab homeland, maintained it in a divided condition, took away Palestine, drove out its people, made it Jewish. . . . Thus the Arab position must reflect an attitude toward the West which is in harmony with the lack of Western justice."[19]

This perception of the Palestinian problem and of Western policy toward the Arabs is the major reason that Arab nationalists in the mid-1950s refused participation in Western alliances and adopted a policy of nonalignment.

Oil. If the popular image of the Arab as a bedouin has been replaced, it is by the image of the rich oil sheikh. The Algerians may be right when they say that oil is only another primary product, and hence that oil producers are like any other raw-material producers in the Third World. However, the realities of the 1970s indicated that oil has a very special impact on the global system. The shock of the 1973 oil embargo, associated in developed countries with long lines at petrol stations and talk of hard winters with minimum heating oil, showed that oil was special.

The embargo by Arab oil producers could carry such clout for two reasons: they possessed a substantial percentage of world oil exports (see Table 2.2) and they acted in concert in the context of an energy-hungry world. The results of their action were a global systemic crisis and increased bargaining power for Arab oil producers. Saudi Arabia saw its international status change almost overnight from that of a purely Islamic leader to that of an oil power. The fact that Saudi Arabia was invited to sit on the IMF board of directors shows that Arab oil producers could, if they chose, influence many aspects of the global economy.

TABLE 2.2
Arab Oil Power in 1971 and 1980

Country	1971		1980	
	Oil Production (bpd)[a]	Oil Revenue (millions US$)	Oil Production (bpd)	Oil Revenue (millions US$)
Saudi Arabia	4.545	2,160	9.990	104,200
Kuwait	2.975	1,395	1.425	18,300
Iraq	1.700	840	2.645	26,500
United Arab Emirates	1.060	421	1.005	19,200
Qatar	0.430	198	0.470	5,200
Libya	2.765	1,766	1.790	23,200
Algeria	0.780	320	1.040	11,700
TOTAL	14.255	7,100	18.365	208,300

Source: Adapted from Michael Field, "Oil in the Middle East and North Africa," in *The Middle East and North Africa 1982-1983* (London: Europa Publications, 1982), pp. 98-134.

[a]Barrels per day.

Oil wealth also gave impetus to the idea of a new grouping in the global system: the African-Arab-European dialogue. The rationale for this triangle of cooperation was to capitalize on the assets of the three groups: Africa with its enormous potential in agricultural and mineral sectors, but lack of technology, capital, and trained manpower; the Gulf Arabs with their oil and cash surplus; and the OECD (Organization for Economic Cooperation and Development) countries with their technology, skilled labor, and banking facilities for recycling petrofunds.

This example of cooperation is significant because it confirms how oil, one element of the specific Arab condition, has intensified the mingling of regional and global politics. From 1956 to 1973, there have been eleven interventions by the big powers in the Arab East alone.[20] This high level of big power attention may reflect several factors: the strategic position of the Arab world; Soviet interest in the warm waters of the Mediterranean; Western dependence on oil and fear of a Soviet threat; the influence of various transnational actors such as multinational oil companies and the Zionist movement; and the growing Arab market for arms and other goods. Whatever the reasons, the high level of big-power involvement in the region's affairs has blurred the distinction between purely regional and global issues. This brings us to the last point of this chapter: the impact of the global system on Arab foreign policies.

THE PRIMACY OF GLOBAL CONSTRAINTS

To the majority of international actors, the global system presents an arena of both constraints and opportunities. In the case of Arab countries—

TABLE 2.3
Major Arms Deals of Ten Arab Countries
from July 1980 to June 1981 (in millions US$)[a]

Country	Amount
Algeria	1,500
Egypt	1,200
Iraq	8,300
Jordan	575
Morocco	950
Qatar	40
Saudi Arabia	3,000
Syria	3,300
Tunisia	80
United Arab Emirates	370
TOTAL	19,315

Source: Adapted from Hans Maull, "The Arms Trade with the
Middle East," in *The Middle East and North Africa 1982-1983*
(London: Europa Publications, 1982), pp. 135-144.

[a]The dominance of the West in Arab arms deals is unquestionable.
Some of these figures include deals with the Soviet Union
(Algeria, Syria, and Iraq), but the list does not include Saudi
Arabia's $9-billion AWACS deal with the United States.

as with the rest of the developing or dependent countries—the constraints outnumber the opportunities. We will show the primacy of constraints in examining three main issues: the imposition of an arms control regime, the limits of oil as resource power, and Israel's extraterritoriality and Jewishness.

The Arms Control Regime

Arab-Israeli relations in the last thirty-five years have cost the Arab East six major wars, including the 1948 war at the creation of Israel, the 1982 Lebanese invasion, and the 1969–1970 War of Attrition between Egypt and Israel. It is no wonder, then, that Israel and the countries of the Arab East have been the largest arms purchasers in the world during the 1970s (Table 2.3). On both ethical and social grounds, any attempts are welcome that eliminate or at least limit wars that kill, maim, and waste needed development energies and funds.[21] But arms control regimes (a set of rules imposed by the great powers) have used the political context provided by the escalating Arab-Israeli conflict to buy influence and promote their own political objectives rather than to pursue political solutions.

A good example of the use of an arms supply and control regime as a means of domination over the recipients' policies is the May 1950 Tripartite Declaration on the Middle East by the three major Western powers of the period: the United States, Great Britain, and France. The statement recognized the need of the Arab states and Israel "to maintain a certain level of armed forces for . . . their internal security and legitimate self-defence to permit them to play their part in the defence of the area as a whole."[22] Thus arms were to be supplied according to the "good conduct" of each nation as judged by Washington, London, or Paris; no alternative arms supplier, of course, could ever be used. In this way, the declaration attained two objectives: it maintained a Western monopoly over the region, and it maintained the territorial status quo.

Israel welcomed the declaration. None of the Arab countries were consulted. In a joint statement, the Arabs reaffirmed their "pacific intentions," but stressed the "sovereign right of each State to evaluate its arms needs." However, when pan-Arabists like Nasser asserted this sovereign right (by negotiating the 1955 Soviet arms deal following the West's refusal to supply such arms), immediate coercive measures were applied. These ranged from economic pressure and the withdrawal of aid to blatant military intervention (the 1956 Suez invasion). An immediate objective was to defeat this revolt against the system, or at least to impose a high price for disobedience and thus discourage its repetition elsewhere.[23]

The 1955 Soviet arms deal also demonstrates the opportunities that could be exploited by a dependent country; for Egypt's attempts to loosen the system's straitjacket control would not have been successful without an alternative power both available and ready to counterbalance the domination of the "capitalist core." In 1955, the Cold War context accelerated Soviet readiness to be involved, thereby helping Nasser to break free from the West.

This last point shows that a dependent or dominated state can still maneuver to maximize opportunities resulting from the system's structure and the global context; however, it is impossible to eliminate the constraints.[24] For example, by the early 1970s Egypt had changed its dominant international partner by establishing close military and economic cooperation with the Soviets. Yet Egypt was still very constrained in the type of weapons it could receive and by limits on their use. Thus in Sadat's mind the departure of Soviet experts in 1972 was a necessary prerequisite for launching the October War of 1973. Following the war, Sadat's Egypt changed dominant partners again and was reintegrated into the Western core, but constraints remained. We have only to think of Egypt's dependence on U.S. food shipments, the $1.3 billion in annual U.S. aid, and the borrowing facilities on the international market that Egypt would not have access to without the help of the United States.

To conclude, the present structure of the global system and the proliferation of "limited wars" have given the central powers huge leverage over their Third World subordinates. Though arms transfers and arms control measures have often been couched in moralistic and altruistic terms, historical evidence indicates that control of the arms traffic has been used as a privileged instrument of the central powers to exploit a favorable regional context. Their major aims were to promote their own political objectives and gain unilateral benefits against their global opponents—at the expense of local powers if necessary.

The Limitation of Resource Power

If any primary product could have an effect on the global system in the 1970s, it was certainly oil. In less than a decade, the price of a barrel of oil rose from $2 in 1972 to $42 at the end of 1981. From 1974 to 1976, OPEC countries increased their investments in U.S. commercial banks and in treasury and portfolio securities from $5.5 to $8.9 billion.[25] As a result, fragile and even vulnerable countries have come to occupy the center of world politics, as data on the increase of diplomatic representation and visits to Saudi Arabia show. Stereotyped notions of "oil power" and "the Arabs are coming" aside, does the possession of oil by a few Arab countries open a range of opportunities for some developing states?

The 1973 oil embargo had a great impact because of its surprise effect; the oil-hungry system was quite unprepared for the sudden cutoff of supplies. But global demand can decline almost as quickly as it can rise, and this could shatter the oil-based economies of these countries. The impact of fluctuations shows how dependent the so-called oil powers are on the economies of the developed countries and on global economic policies as a whole.

For instance, between 1979 and 1982, oil demand in the noncommunist world dropped from 52.4 million barrels per day (bpd) to only 45.5 million.[26] Perhaps half of this decline was due to the worldwide recession—U.S. factories, for example, were operating at only 60% of capacity, but the developed countries' policy of conservation has turned out to be an even more important factor in the market place. Between 1973 and 1980, economic output in the major industrial countries increased by 19%, while total energy consumption grew by only 4%, and petroleum use actually declined. The problem for OAPEC (Organization of Arab Petroleum-Exporting Countries) is that the market loss due to conservation is irreversible. Even lower oil prices will not induce homeowners to rip the insulation out of their attics, or persuade automakers to build gas-guzzling cars.[27]

Developed countries have also demonstrated the fragility of oil power by entering the market as new producers with oil and gas fields of their own—in Alaska and the North Sea, for example. Because of this increased competition and sagging oil demand, OPEC's sales started to slide in 1982 for the first time in nearly two decades. By February 1983, OPEC's share of the noncommunist world's total oil supply stood at 46%, down from 68% in 1976.[28] Between 1979 and 1982, world demand dropped by 9.5 million bpd, and OPEC's production fell by more than 12 million bpd, to 17.75 million bpd. Yet according to one estimate, OPEC members need to produce about 21 million bpd to meet the needs of their own economies.[29] Even if the Arab oil producers are not yet in the same economic plight as Nigeria, which had to evict hundreds of thousands of foreign workers almost overnight, the writing is on the wall. Although they appear powerful, oil producers are in fact hostages to the global system and the short-term fluctuations of developed economies.

Even before the 1982–1983 world oil glut, oil power could not guarantee the success of the 1975 Paris conference on North-South relations, nor achieve the global change insisted on by Algeria, nor establish the New International Economic Order (NIEO) that the Third World demanded. In this respect, Saudi minister of finance Abu Al-Khail's statement in 1975 is very relevant: "Saudi Arabia has surplus cash." But it is wealth rather than cash—as Adam Smith showed two centuries ago—that adds to a country's economic-military capabilities, and allows it to increase the ratio of global opportunities to global constraints. One may even argue that because of the present structure of the global system, even oil cash is recycled to Western countries, as data on Saudi arms purchases and imports show. In this sense, the system's core enjoys both the oil and its revenue.

The 1973 oil embargo also failed at the regional level to attain some of its most explicit objectives: the settlement of the Palestinian issue and the evacuation of Arab lands occupied by Israel in the 1967 war. It should be remembered that when OAPEC decided on the embargo, the resolution stated explicitly that this embargo and curb on production would not be lifted before Arab territories (Syria's Golan Heights, Egypt's Sinai, and Jordan's West Bank) were evacuated. A few months later, however, Secretary of State Kissinger managed to restore the status quo ante: normal oil flow without the return of Arab lands. This brings us to the Israeli issue as it relates to the primacy of global constraints.

Israel as an Extraterritorial Actor

It has been argued that the presence of Israel in the area encourages unity among Arab countries. This argument is predicated on the assumption that Arabs are united less by positive or constructive ideology than by their hostility toward Israel.

Leaving aside political rhetoric, this proposition can still be substantiated by the theory of conflict. According to this theory, when a group—a nation, a party, or a family—faces a serious external danger, it tends to downplay or forget internal conflicts in order to close ranks in the face of the outside threat. This model does indeed apply in both Arab and Israeli societies; the governments of both have occasionally used the conflict to cement national unity. Though important, this factor can be misleading if no account is taken of the other aspects of Arab-Israeli relations.[30] One such aspect is the specific character of Israel as an extraterritorial state.

Based on historical and sociological considerations, Israeli leaders insist on the conception of Israel as the embodiment of the Jewish dream of statehood. As a result a very complicated set of delicate and original problems, as Nahum Goldman, ex-head of the World Zionist Organization and World Jewish Congress, put it, faces Israel in its relations with the Diaspora.[31] In his three-volume classic on Israel's foreign policy, Michael Brecher dealt with this issue in relation to foreign policy analysis:

> The presence of externally based foreign policy interest groups is widespread in an age of "penetrated political systems": no state is totally immune from group pressures stemming from beyond its territorial boundaries. None is comparable to Israel in this respect, however. Israel is a self-conscious *Jewish* state; indeed that is its *raison d'être*; and Israel is the only Jewish state, indissolubly linked to world Jewry in the minds of her leaders and of most Jews—and of most non-Jews in the Euro-American world as well.[32]

Among these Diaspora Jews, the 6 million of North America stand out. Not only are they double the Jewish population of the state of Israel, but they have also provided Israel's basic means of political, financial, and economic support.[33] Without them,[34] Israel would not have achieved international recognition so quickly[35] and surmounted its political, economic, and military challenges so successfully.[36]

The result is that the influence of the central powers has been continuously felt in the daily evolution of the Arab system. From the very beginning, the creation of Israel and the subsequent conflict between Arabs and Israelis was determined by external events[37] such as the 1917 Balfour declaration giving Britain's promise of a Jewish national home, the Hitler Holocaust and the subsequent Western desire to compensate the Jews by helping them to settle in Palestine, and then the decision to partition Palestine.

Even at the level of policy-making and implementation, European and American Jews participated directly in deciding the evolution of the Middle East. In the early years following the establishment of the state of Israel, the World Zionist Organization attempted to secure for its president, Nahum Goldman, an invitation to attend Israeli cabinet meetings.[38] Israel's prime minister at the time, Ben Gurion, refused. Goldman returned to this subject in his writings,[39] reviewing the proposals for a joint decision-making organ between Israel and the Jewish Diaspora (e.g., the establishment of a senate, in addition to the Israeli Parliament, where the elected representatives of the Diaspora would sit; the creation of a permanent assembly where equal numbers of Israelis and representatives of world Jewry would sit). In the absence of any common decision-making institution, Goldman found the existing practice unsatisfactory: periodic visits to Israel by leaders of Jewish organizations to discuss with the members of the Israeli government the current state of affairs. Israel's extraterritoriality has brought the global system even more concretely into the region's affairs. Possible lines of demarcation between regional interactions and global politics have become even more blurred.

CONCLUSION

Does the primacy of constraints indicate that dependent actors are helpless in the face of "systemic tyranny," as stated by Kaplan, or "world hegemony," as dependencia maintains? The adoption of such a deterministic view would imply that nothing other than the system counts in the making of a country's foreign policy. Global constraints notwithstanding, other factors continue to play an important part in the country's foreign policy orientation and behavior: national leadership patterns, economic and military capabilities, the size and composition of the population, and the style of mobilizing and managing resources. Even for a dependent country, the constraint/opportunity ratio could change as a result of the country's possession of the "right" resources and its leadership's will to use them. If maintained for some time, a foreign policy based on the use of these resources could eventually modify aspects of the systemic structure. It is thus the interaction between national capabilities and dispositions, on the one hand, and existing systemic structures, on the other, that determines a country's foreign policy and its degree of success.

NOTES

1. James N. Rosenau, *The Scientific Study of Foreign Policy* (New York: Free Press, 1971); Michael Brecher, Blema Steinberg, and Janice Stein, "A Framework for Research on Foreign Policy Behavior," *Journal of Conflict Resolution* 13 (1969), pp. 75–102.

2. This debate, which has been raging for some time, has shaped the thought of professors, international civil servants, journalists, and students, affecting what and how many of us write.

3. The assumptions and propositions of the different approaches are scattered here and there in the basic books and articles of social science methodology and international relations theory. The best introduction to the international relations debate is still Klaus Knorr and James N. Rosenau (eds.), *Contending Approaches to International Politics* (Princeton, N.J.: Princeton University Press, 1969). Hans Morgenthau is most representative of the "traditional approach"; see his *Politics Among Nations*, 5th ed., rev. (New York: Alfred A. Knopf, 1978).

4. Good representatives of this school in international relations are Karl Deutsch, Bruce Russett, and J. David Singer. For a representative collection of papers, see J. David Singer (ed.), *Quantitative International Politics* (New York: Free Press, 1968); see also a collection of biographical and autobiographical studies of the main behavioralists, of their disciples, and of their main research projects in James N. Rosenau (ed.), *In Search of Global Patterns* (New York: Free Press, 1976).

5. Charles W. Kegley, Jr., and Eugene Wittskopf, *World Politics: Trend and Transformation* (New York: St. Martin's Press, 1981). Two points must, however, be emphasized here. First, the traditionalism/behavioralism dichotomy is not as neat or well-demarcated as our synopsis might suggest. Many social scientists cannot be classified as belonging to either school, having accepted some views of each. Second, the traditionalism/behavioralism debate has been concentrated in the West, especially in North America. Social scientists in the rest of the world have remained onlookers, uninformed or even unconcerned.

6. Robert O. Keohane and Joseph S. Nye, Jr. (eds.), *Transnational Relations and World Politics* (Cambridge, Mass.: Harvard University Press, 1972); Richard Mansbach et al., *The Web of World Politics: Non State Actors in the Global System* (Englewood Cliffs, N.J.: Prentice-Hall, 1976).

7. This concept has been popularized and systemized by Rosenau, *Scientific Study*.

8. Corporatism in its pure form entails the presence in society of various interest associations, yet these formal institutions are in fact controlled by the state or its representatives. Voluminous literature exists on the corporate form of state in the Third World. For a recent discussion of this issue in an Arab context, see John Waterbury, *The Egypt of Nasser and Sadat: The Political Economy of Two Regimes* (Princeton, N.J.: Princeton University Press, 1983), especially pp. 3–40, 307–388; a more general treatment in the context of developed (capitalist and socialist) countries is Gerhard Lembruch and Jack Hayward (eds.), *Interest Intermediation: Toward New Corporatism(s)*, a special issue of the *International Political Science Review*, vol. 4 (Beverly Hills, Calif.: Sage Publications, 1983).

9. The most useful answers and evaluations are to be found in A. Foster-Carter, "From Rostow to Gunder Frank: Conflicting Paradigms in the Analysis of Underdevelopment," *World Development* 4 (1976), pp. 167–180; Richard Bath and Dilmus James, "Dependency Analysis of Latin America," *Latin American Research Review* 11 (1976), pp. 3–55; Antonio C. Peixoto, "La théorie de la dépendance: Un bilan critique," *Revue Française de Science Politique* 27 (1977), pp. 601–629; Gabriel Palma, "Dependency: A Formal Theory of Underdevelopment or a Methodology for the Analysis of Underdevelopment?" *World Development* 6 (1978), pp. 881–924; and J. Samuel Valenzuela and Arturo Valenzuela, "Modernization and Dependency: Alternative Perspectives in the Study of Latin American Underdevelopment," *Comparative Politics* 10 (1978), pp. 535–557.

10. John S. Gitlitz and Henry A. Landsberger, "The Inter-American Political Economy: How Dependable Is Dependency Theory?" in John D. Martz and Lars Schoultz (eds.), *Latin America, the United States and the Inter-American System* (Boulder, Colo.: Westview Press, 1980), pp. 45–70.

11. With the sudden influx of oil cash, this situation has been reversed in Saudi Arabia and other Gulf countries, which now import several million migrant workers. Scarce foreign currency and abundant labor is still the norm in the Third World, however.

12. A good illustration of these variations is Edward Williams's "Comparative Political Development: Latin America and Afro-Asia," *Comparative Studies in Society and History* 11 (1969), pp. 342–354.

13. A good introduction to this literature is Patrick McGowan and Howard Shapiro, *The Comparative Study of Foreign Policy: A Survey* (Beverly Hills, Calif.: Sage Publications, 1973).

14. For some good attempts to examine this external influence on foreign policy, see Leon Gordenker, *International Aid and National Decisions: Development Programs in Malawi, Tanzania and Zambia* (Princeton, N.J.: Princeton University Press, 1976); R. Peter Dewitt, Jr., *The Inter-American Development Bank and Political Influence* (New York: Praeger Publishers, 1977); Teresa Hayter, *Aid as Imperialism* (New York: Penguin Books, 1971). For the specific Arab context, see Bahgat Korany, "Hypothèse marxiste et méthodologie behavioraliste: Une analyse empirique," *Etudes Internationales* 7 (1976), pp. 51–66; "Underdevelopment and Foreign Policy Change: Sadat's Egypt in Comparative Perspective," Paper submitted to the Canadian Political Science Association, Halifax, Nova Scotia, May 1981; and "Egypt's Policy Shift 1971–1981," Paper submitted to the meeting on "The Impact of Money: Dynamics of Power and Dependency in the Arab World," Boston, June 1982. The papers of this meeting are to be published soon. For an analysis of the effects of the global system on the structure of the Arab region, see Bahgat Korany, "Allah's Wish: Premises and Promises of Contemporary Arab Economy," Paper submitted at the conference on "South-South Relations" organized by the Chinese Academy of the Social Sciences and the Third World Foundation, Beijing, April 1983.

15. Neil R. Richardson, *Foreign Policy and Economic Dependence* (Austin and London: University of Texas Press, 1978), especially pp. 69–70, 136, 143, 147, 152.

16. Johan Galtung, "A Structural Theory of Imperialism," *Journal of Peace Research* 8 (1971), pp. 81–117.

17. For a solid and insightful tracing of how the different great powers of different historical periods have resisted moves toward Arab unity, see Galal Amin, *The Arab East and the West* (Beirut: Center for Arab Unity Studies, 1980) (in Arabic).

18. A protracted conflict involves economic, social, religious, political, and psychological dimensions at the level of the individual, the different social groups, the society itself, and even the global system. As Azar, Jureidini, and McLaurin have said, these conflicts are "hostile interactions which extend over long periods of time with sporadic outbreaks of open warfare fluctuating in frequency and intensity. These are conflict situations in which the stakes are very high—the conflicts involve whole societies and act as agents for defining the scope of national identity and social solidarity. While they may exhibit some breakpoints during which there is a cessation of overt violence, they linger on in time and have no distinguishable point of termination. It is only in the long run that they will 'end' by cooling off, transforming or withering away; one cannot expect these conflicts to be terminated by explicit decision. Protracted conflicts, that is to say, are not specific events or even clusters of events at a point in time; they are processes." Edward Azar, Paul Jureidini, and Ronald McLaurin, "Protracted Social Conflict: Theory and Practice in the Middle East," *Journal of Palestine Studies* (1978), pp. 41–61.

19. Salah Eddin Al-Bitar, *Arab Policy* (Beirut: 1960), pp. 23–27 (in Arabic).

20. Yair Evron, "Great Powers' Military Intervention in the Middle East," in Milton Leitenberg and Gabriel Steffer (eds.), *Great Power Intervention in the Middle East* (New York and Toronto: Pergamon Press, 1979), pp. 17–45.

21. Ali E. Hillal Dessouki, "The Effects of Arms Race and Defence Expenditures on Development: A Case Study of Egypt," Research paper, Cairo University, Cairo, 1980.

22. Paul Jabber, *Not by War Alone: Security and Arms Control in the Middle East* (Los Angeles and London: University of California Press, 1981), and "The

Tripartite Declaration," in Yaacov Shimoni et al. (eds.), *Political Dictionary of the Middle East in the 20th Century* (New York: Quadrangle, 1974), p. 388.

23. The 1957 Eisenhower Doctrine continued the same line of thinking. In 1967, "the renewal of U.S. interest in limiting the transfer of weaponry to the Middle East . . . came at a time when Israel had just achieved a position of clear regional military supremacy . . . [In] his address of June 19, 1967, President Johnson's call for limits on the 'wasteful and destructive arms race' was made while the Syrian, Egyptian, and Jordanian military machines lay practically in ruins," Jabber, *op. cit.,* pp. 181–182.

24. In the 1970s, arms purchases from the Soviet Union were not as taboo as they had been in the mid-1950s, but petrol sales were. Only the form of the constraint had changed.

25. Michael Field, "Oil in the Middle East and North Africa," in *The Middle East and North Africa 1982–1983* (London: Europa Publications, 1982), pp. 93–134.

26. *Time,* February 7, 1983, pp. 34–38.

27. *Newsweek,* February 7, 1983, pp. 50–54.

28. *Time,* February 7, 1983, pp. 34–38.

29. *Newsweek,* February 7, 1983, pp. 50–54.

30. For a further discussion of Israel's impact on the region, including Israeli influence upon Arab unity and disunity, see Bahgat Korany, "Structure et processus du système international arabe 1961–1983," in *Le Moyen-Orient: Enjeux et perspective* (Quebec: Presses de l'Université Laval, Collection Choix, 1983).

31. Nahum Goldman, *Où va Israël?* (Paris: Calmann Levy, 1975), p. 119.

32. Michael Brecher, *The Foreign Policy System of Israel* (London and New York: Oxford University Press, 1972), p. 137.

33. I. L. Kenen, *Israel's Defense Line: Her Friends and Foes in Washington* (Buffalo, N.Y.: Prometheus Books, 1981). Mr. Kenen has worked for U.S. support for Israel for more than forty years. At the time of publishing his book, he was honorary chairman of the American Israel Public Affairs Committee, which he helped establish in 1951, and editor emeritus of the *New East Report,* which he founded in 1957. His book has been described by Henry Kissinger as "fascinating and informative."

34. Nancy Jo Nelson, "The Zionist Organizational Structure," *Journal of Palestine Studies* 10 (1980), pp. 80–93; Walter Lehn, "The Jewish National Fund," *Journal of Palestine Studies* 4 (1974), pp. 73–96. See especially pp. 95–96 for the impressive data on the acquisition of territory in Palestine by the fund between 1905 and 1950.

35. Two notable analyses in this respect are Richard Stevens, *American Zionism and U.S. Foreign Policy 1942–1947* (New York: Pageant Press, 1962); and Evan Wilson, *Decision on Palestine: How the U.S. Came to Recognize Israel* (Stanford, Calif.: Hoover Institution Press, 1979). Wilson was a foreign service officer on the Palestine desk, watched U.S. policy in the making, and took part in its implementation. Drawing on heretofore unpublished documents, he describes how the White House, Congress, and the State Department were buried under an avalanche of paper from different Zionist groups engaged in a world-wide campaign of pressure politics. This pressure politics worked. In explaining his decision to recognize Israel, Truman said frankly to a group of State Department officials: "I am sorry, gentlemen, but I have to answer to hundreds of thousands who are anxious for the success of Zionism: I do not have hundreds of thousands of Arabs among my constituents." Wilson, *op. cit.*

36. Ghassan Bishara, "Israel's Power in the U.S. Senate," *Journal of Palestine Studies* 10 (1980), pp. 58–79. Mr. Bishara is the Washington correspondent of *Al-Fajr* (Jerusalem). See also Marvin Feuerwerger, *Congress and Israel: Foreign Aid Decision-Making in the House of Representatives* (London: Greenwood Press, 1979). Dr. Feuerwerger has several years' experience in Washington politics, having served as a legislative aide for the American Israel Public Affairs Committee, and as the principal deputy to President Carter's "advisor on Jewish Affairs." Feuerwerger demonstrates how Congress approves aid to Israel, often adding to administration requests. From 1970 to 1977, Congress increased economic aid to Israel by 30% over administration requests, at a time when Congress was cutting foreign and worldwide aid by almost 25%. Congress also eased Israel's burden by offering loans on easy terms and waiving repayment of major debts during this period. Congress earmarked foreign aid funds for Israel, a practice generally discouraged by the White House because it limits administration flexibility. See also the excellent review by John Richardson in *Journal of Palestine Studies* 10 (1980), pp. 80–85.

37. Historically, "Zionism was very much the child of the liberal and national movements of nineteenth-century Europe," Robert Freedman (ed.), *World Politics and the Arab-Israeli Conflict* (New York: Pergamon Press, 1979), p. 5.

38. Brecher, *op. cit.*, p. 143.

39. Goldman, *op. cit.*, pp. 136–139.

3

The Arab System: Opportunities, Constraints, and Pressures

Paul C. Noble

INTRODUCTION

The foreign policy of states is shaped by domestic conditions, by the values and perceptions of policy-makers, and by the global and regional environments in which they exist.[1] National concerns influence what governments would *like* to do, but the environment determines what they are *able* to do.[2] There are two ways in which systemic conditions shape state behavior. In the first place, systemic conditions either provide a set of opportunities, or, more commonly, serve as a set of constraints, permitting states a certain range of possible action. Second, systemic conditions generate forces that push or pull states in certain directions. Furthermore, even if the system does not have a significant impact on the initial formation of a state's policies, it has a decisive effect on whether those policies succeed or fail. These results are generally not lost on policy-makers and shape their subsequent behavior.

This chapter focuses on the regional system, particularly the Arab system.[3] The analysis is divided into two parts. The first part will examine the system's setting: the domestic and regional conditions that confront most system members and affect their policies and relationships. The second part deals with the characteristics of the system proper: i.e., the changing patterns of behavior and relations among Arab states.

PROPERTIES OF THE SETTING

Two sets of conditions will be examined here: the internal environment of Arab countries (domestic setting), and the transnational linkages between Arab societies (Arab setting).

41

The Domestic Setting

A single state's internal conditions are not normally considered as a system property. However, when similar domestic conditions prevail among system members and when these conditions influence international positions and behavior, they require examination. An important characteristic of Arab countries has been their experience of extensive social change. For much of the population, substantial alterations in the conditions of life have occurred due to urbanization, increased access to education, exposure to mass media,[4] and the emergence of new social forces and sets of values.[5] As a result, Arab states have experienced a rapid increase in the number of people with some degree of political awareness and a substantial enlargement of the political arena.

These developments had two major consequences for domestic politics during the 1950s and 1960s. To begin with, they generated serious domestic political instability. Traditional elites and regimes were severely shaken, and regimes were overthrown in Egypt, Syria, and Iraq. The ruling elites of Jordan, Morocco, and Saudi Arabia felt insecure and suffered serious disturbances as well as periodic coup and assassination attempts.[6] New Arab regimes experienced difficulties in establishing their authority and legitimacy. This was particularly evident in Syria, where forcible or irregular changes of government occurred in 1949 (three), 1952, 1954, 1958, 1961, 1963, 1966, and 1970, in addition to numerous unsuccessful coup attempts.[7] Neighboring Iraq had similar problems although to a lesser degree, with its government changing in February and November of 1963 and again in 1968.[8] The only exception to this widespread instability was Egypt, where Nasser emerged as an unchallenged ruler enjoying extensive popular support.[9]

A second major consequence of the far-reaching social and political changes was an increasing focus on ideological issues and the emergence of sharp ideological cleavages within Arab societies.[10] The old social order, previously accepted as legitimate, was seriously questioned. The new regimes headed in radically new directions to justify their existence and generate popular support. The remaining traditional regimes felt increasingly threatened by the combined pressure of new social forces within their own countries and the challenge posed by the transformation of the political and social order in other Arab countries.

These domestic conditions altered the international position and behavior of members of the Arab system. Internal instability seriously weakened the position of a number of key states, and the constant concern for political survival obliged most Arab governments to devote much of their attention and energy to staying in power. This made it difficult for them to engage in any sustained activity in support of foreign policy goals within the region. Furthermore, strong linkages between Arab societies exposed the unstable states to extensive penetration and intervention by other Arab governments. When conflicts occurred within the system, most Arab governments were exposed both to traditional forms of pressure and to externally generated subversive pressures as well. The simultaneous weakening of several states as a result of internal instability was an important factor contributing to the emergence, in the decade after 1955, of a highly unbalanced, virtually one-power system, dominated by Egypt.

Apart from shaping the pattern of power in the system, the widespread internal instability also affected the behavior of system members. It contributed to rigidity in policy, as insecure governments were unwilling to deviate from established approaches, particularly with regard to long-standing opponents such as Israel and, in many cases, the Western powers. Contrary to the widely held view that insecurity of tenure leads to external assertiveness and adventurism, Arab states that were relatively weak or had conservative or moderate governments (e.g., Jordan, Lebanon, and Saudi Arabia) became introverted in the face of domestic instability.[11] By adopting this posture they sought to avoid antagonizing stronger Arab states and thus to minimize outside pressure and external intervention. Among unstable Arab states, only those that were relatively stronger or led by reformist or radical governments (e.g., Syria and Iraq) tended to be assertive.[12] The most assertive of all the Arab states during this period, however, was also the most stable: Egypt.

Finally, the transformation of the political and social order within several Arab states, which began in the early 1950s, added a whole new ideological dimension to Arab foreign policy and relationships.[13] Ideological considerations began to color the perceptions and to some extent, shape the objectives of Arab policy-makers. Because most Arab governments were engaged in intense ideological conflict domestically, they became suspicious and intolerant of divergent regimes. They could not help but see these regimes and their own domestic opposition in the same light. These attitudes were intensified by the realization that the stability and even the survival of the government were at stake. Some made an effort to reshape other societies in accordance with their own beliefs and values through a variety of propaganda and subversive activities. Naturally, this ideological revisionism increased the insecurity of most elites in the system.

Because of the prominence of ideological issues, much of the conflict within the Arab system after 1955 centered on questions of legitimacy. This is not to say that the triumph of certain basic values and ideas was the sole or even the primary motivation of policy-makers. In fact, ideological issues were very often used as instruments in a struggle for status and power. Whatever the motivations of policy-makers, however, legitimacy was a major stake in inter-Arab politics. Any regime that neglected this issue did so at its own peril. A further consequence of the focus on ideological issues was the emergence of sharp divisions between regimes espousing different value systems. This reduced the flexibility of the system and consequently the options of policy-makers.

During most of the 1970s, domestic instability declined. After the unsettled conditions of the 1960s, Saudi Arabia enjoyed a period of relative tranquillity for much of the decade,[14] largely because of the tremendous influx of oil wealth. Under King Faisal the regime moved to provide both employment opportunities and some degree of responsibility to the burgeoning new middle class, thereby defusing a major source of potential opposition. Moreover, the position of the regime was enhanced by its activities in support of the Arab cause against Israel. This, together with Saudi Arabia's substantial financial aid to other Arab countries, led to a virtual halt in external propaganda and subversive pressures from Arab sources.

The most dramatic improvement in domestic conditions occurred in the Fertile Crescent area, particularly in Syria.[15] General Hafiz Al-Asad remained in power throughout the decade, far longer than any previous Syrian ruler. A similar trend occurred in neighboring Iraq, where after a decade of instability following the overthrow of the monarchy in 1958, the Ba'thist regime of Hassan Al-Bakr and Saddam Hussein was able to maintain effective control over the country throughout the 1970s.[16] The improvement in the domestic situation within Jordan was equally striking.[17] After nearly two decades of turbulence, culminating in a full-scale war with the Palestinian guerrilla movements in 1970, King Hussein was able to reassert his control over the country. The major exception to this trend in the Fertile Crescent area was Lebanon, where the whole fabric of the state and society broke down completely after 1975, when the country plunged into a prolonged and bitter civil war.[18]

Improvement in the domestic political situations of key states had two main effects. First, it strengthened the position of these states in the regional arena. They became far less vulnerable to externally initiated propaganda and subversive pressures and consequently, less on the defensive within the Arab system. Saudi Arabia, Syria, and Iraq, for example, were able to engage in more energetic and sustained foreign policy activity and to play more important roles in their immediate region as well as in the affairs of the system as a whole. The stronger positions of these key actors contributed to the increasing diffusion of power that occurred in the Arab system during the 1970s. Greater domestic stability also permitted these states greater flexibility in policy. Governments—particularly in Syria and Iraq—modified previously rigid policies toward the United States and Israel and toward other Arab states.[19]

Another change in the domestic setting during the 1970s was the declining importance of ideology to the leadership of several key states,[20] e.g., Egypt and Syria after the change of leadership in 1970. The seriousness of the territorial, military-security, and economic problems confronting these countries after 1967 made these issues the paramount concerns of the leadership. Moreover, the failure of growth rates to meet expectations led to some disenchantment with the socialist experiment. Sadat and Asad concluded that some scope and incentives for private entrepreneurial activity were necessary to achieve higher rates of economic growth.[21] Besides, as newly established leaders, Sadat and Asad were anxious to expand their power base and develop new sources of support. They saw measures of economic liberalization as helpful in building bridges to the local bourgeoisie. This overall trend, evident in Egypt and Syria in the early 1970s, also developed in Iraq in the late 1970s.

A decline in the importance of ideology was much less noticeable in Saudi Arabia, under King Faisal[22] the leading conservative regime. Sensitive to the existence of radical forces both inside and outside the kingdom, Faisal's intense desire to contain, weaken, and ultimately eliminate these forces continued to shape Saudi policy. Nevertheless, in response to signs of moderation from the leading progressive regimes, the Saudi regime became more flexible. After Faisal's death in 1975 and the emergence of Prince Fahd as the strong man of the regime, this tendency became more pronounced.

As a result of these developments, Arab foreign policies in the 1970s became more pragmatic, with tangible national interests prevailing over ideological considerations.[23] This pragmatic approach reduced the insecurity of regimes and opened a broader range of options for policymakers. Greater flexibility led to the development of working relationships across previously rigid ideological divisions. A de-emphasis on ideology and the predominance of national interest considerations were evident in the policies of the progressive regimes toward the major powers. In spite of socialist orientations, these regimes became, in general, more open to the Western powers during the 1970s. In the economic sphere, important trade and aid links with the West developed in the mid-1970s. In the political sphere, Egypt undertook a fundamental reorientation of its foreign policy that resulted in close ties with the West. Syria and Iraq made periodic—although tentative—efforts to open a dialogue with the United States. By the end of the 1970s, however, it became questionable whether these trends within the Arab domestic setting would persist. A return to conditions resembling those of the 1950s and 1960s occurred to some extent.

The principal development was *the return of a substantial level of domestic instability*.[24] This was most noticeable in Syria, Egypt, Saudi Arabia, and Iraq. In Syria, the Asad regime faced strong opposition from several quarters,[25] including dissident Ba'thists and other leftist and nationalist elements. More important, the majority Sunni community was increasingly dissatisfied with the dominant position enjoyed by members of the minority Alawi community. This dissatisfaction, combined with the secular orientation of the ruling Ba'thist movement, led to increasingly violent activity by Islamic fundamentalist groups. Economic difficulties, alleged corruption, and intensified repressive activity fed the growth of popular disenchantment with the regime.

In Iraq, the government of Saddam Hussein faced serious problems after the advent, in neighboring Iran, of Khomeini's Islamic fundamentalist regime.[26] The new Iranian authorities denounced Iraq's secular Ba'thist regime and exhorted both the underprivileged Shi'i majority and the religiously inclined Sunni elements to replace it with a regime based on Islamic precepts. The government appeared even more threatened in the wake of subsequent Iranian military successes against Iraqi forces.

Other major Arab states suffered in varying degrees from internal instability in the late 1970s. In Saudi Arabia, accelerated modernization generated a backlash from conservative religious elements, who felt that the Islamic character of the society was being seriously eroded.[27] This reaction was compounded by increased social inequality and corruption as well as by the growing Western presence and influence that accompanied modernization. The problem was exacerbated by propaganda and subversive pressures directed at Saudi Arabia and other Gulf states (e.g., Bahrain) by the Iranian regime.[28]

By the late 1970s, Egypt was experiencing internal difficulties,[29] which culminated in the assassination of President Sadat in October 1981. Although opposition activity has been less apparent under President Hosni Mubarak, most of the sources of discontent remain and could cause renewed instability.[30]

The 1970s were also characterized by the persistence of ideology as an element in Arab societies, even though its importance had declined at the leadership level. In effect, the Arab world was still in a period of transition. Although the old political and social order had been swept away or was being seriously questioned in most Arab countries, there was no consensus within these societies on what to replace it with. Consequently, although the ideological debate died down for a period, it flared up again in a new form in the late 1970s. The previous fervor for socialism gave way to a debate over the role of Islam in Arab society.[31] The resurgence of Islamic fundamentalism refocused the ideological debate within Arab societies,[32] and the Iranian revolution intensified it, particularly in the Gulf area. These developments were of major concern to Arab governments. If fundamentalist elements were to achieve a significant influence within one Arab state, the potential for a renewed ideological cold war would be substantial.[33]

The Arab Setting

The domestic setting of the Arab system differs only *in degree* from that of other systems of developing states, but the relations between Arab societies differ *in kind* from those elsewhere. This has important implications for policy-making in the Arab world. Linguistic and cultural homogeneity among the peoples of the Arab world has generated *strong linkages between Arab societies*. One manifestation of this has been an extensive movement of persons: short-term visitors, students, and many Arabs who take up residence in other Arab countries on a short- or long-term basis. The most striking example is provided by the more than 2 million Palestinians who have migrated to various parts of the

Arab world since the late 1940s.[34] Since the oil boom of the 1970s, more teachers, professionals, clerical personnel, and skilled and unskilled workers from the less well-off Arab countries (Egypt, Jordan, Syria, and North Yemen) have migrated to the more prosperous countries (Saudi Arabia, the Gulf states, Libya, and Lebanon).[35]

Similarities of language and culture have contributed to the development of other types of societal links. They have encouraged the growth of transnational professional, intellectual, and trade union associations. Most important, with the development of the communications media, the shared language of Arabic has made possible an extensive flow of information, ideas, and opinions among the people of the Arab world. Radio has been the main instrument of the diffusion of information and ideas, particularly among the mass public,[36] and it has been supplemented by the flow of printed materials. These channels of contact have carried a great deal of social communication across state frontiers in the Arab world.

The linguistic and cultural homogeneity of the Arab world has also contributed to the development of links *between political systems*. The population of the area has a sense of Arab identity that transcends individual nationalities[37] and encourages a sense of kinship. It has created awareness of an interest in political developments in other Arab states among the attentive and mass publics of most Arab countries. Furthermore, not only transplanted residents but also many members of the indigenous populations of Arab countries have developed an identification with, and responsiveness to, leaders and political movements in other Arab states. The classic example of this phenomenon is Nasser's tremendous appeal throughout the Arab world from the mid-1950s until his death in 1970.[38]

In particular, the sense of belonging to a larger Arab community has reduced psychological inhibitions about developing ties with political movements in other Arab states. Throughout its history, the Arab system has been characterized by a variety of cross-frontier alliances between the government of one Arab state and individuals or groups in others. This form of political link has been utilized by all regimes.

Cross-frontier alliances have fostered the development of political or quasi-political movements with branches in several Arab states. These have generally operated in opposition to existing governments, although occasionally one of the branches of a movement has come to power and provided support to the others. Transnational movements of this kind include the Ba'th party, various Nasserite groups, the Arab nationalist movement, and the Popular Front for the Liberation of Oman and the Arabian Gulf (PFLOAG), which was centered in the Gulf area.[39] The Moslem Brotherhood probably also falls in this category.[40]

Because of these links, the political systems of Arab states have been closely interconnected and permeable. In some ways, the Arab system has resembled a vast sound chamber in which information, ideas, and opinions have resonated with little regard for state frontiers. Political developments and changes in one segment of the system have set off reverberations in other segments, altering the local balance of forces and generating new momentum and assertiveness on the part of some of the contending elements.[41] These reverberations have frequently been accompanied by a substantial penetration of political systems as leaders and groups in some states activated cross-frontier alliances or transnational movements to manipulate the internal politics of others.

Thus, the Arab system of the 1950s and 1960s differed substantially from the billiard-ball model of a state system in which states come in contact only at their hard outer shell and domestic systems are relatively insulated from external influences. Instead, it resembled a set of interconnected organisms separated only by porous membranes or, to put it another way, a single large-scale political system divided into compartments of varying degrees of permeability.[42]

These conditions have had several important implications for policymakers in the Arab world. First, the homogeneity and ensuing sense of kinship means that the policies and behavior of member states have been scrutinized more closely, and reacted to more sharply, than has been the case in other state systems. Differences over basic direction and policies are treated not as a simple divergence in views but rather as behavior harmful to the interests of the community. The intensity of reaction has tended to magnify the level of conflict in the system.

Second, the sense of membership in a larger family has led to pressures for Arab solidarity when any segment of the community is in conflict with a non-Arab actor. Besides individual national issues, Arab governments therefore faced a number of *Arab core issues* (the Palestinian issue, the Arab-Israeli conflict in general, and pressures from the major powers).[43] In the 1950s and 1960s, the demands for commitment and conformity on these issues were extremely strong. A government's acceptability and status within the system depended on its response. In particular, governments that aspired to play a prominent role in the system were obliged to take up general Arab causes to satisfy the larger Arab constituency.

Third, the belief in a common Arab identity gave rise to the view that political unity was a desirable objective for the Arab world. This has in turn led to periodic pressures for mergers between various Arab states as a step toward overall Arab unity. This climate of opinion constitutes a permanent challenge to the legitimacy of existing states, and the pressure to merge has generated considerable insecurity on the part of those states that have been directly involved.[44]

Finally, linkages among Arab societies and political systems have created a strong sense of vulnerability in most Arab policy-makers. Due to the larger sense of Arab identity among their people and the identification or direct affiliation of some parts of their population with leaders or political movements in other Arab states, policy-makers have felt that their political systems were exposed to external manipulation. In addition to the status or the independence of states, the very existence of governments has been at stake. Overall, the Arab system has been a major area of concern and activity for Arab governments. For some, these conditions provided an excellent opportunity to extend their influence, but for most, they constituted both a source of pressure and a major constraint on policy.

Although many features of the Arab setting persisted into the 1970s, some did not. The modifications that did occur stemmed largely from a decline in the primacy of pan-Arab sentiments among political elites and publics alike.[45] The most obvious manifestation of this trend was a sharp reduction in pressures for political union. Emphasis was placed instead on functional cooperation between Arab states through the formation of diplomatic common fronts and military alliances, and through economic cooperation. As a result, the elites of many Arab countries felt less threatened, and the state and territorial framework of the system acquired greater legitimacy.[46] A declining sense of solidarity and responsiveness to Arab core concerns also reflected diminished pan-Arab sentiment. National and group interests were asserted to the detriment of community interests.

In earlier periods, lack of solidarity was evidenced by failure to provide tangible support to other segments of the community engaged in conflict with outsiders. This lack of positive commitment was very much in evidence in the latter part of the 1970s. In addition, various Arab actors disregarded the most minimal systemic commitments by breaking ranks and cooperating with outside powers, even with those engaged in conflict with other Arab states.

The most striking example of this was Egypt. After the 1967 war, Egypt's leadership was weakened. Devoting the bulk of its energy and resources to the conflict with Israel, Egypt ceased to be a driving force for solidarity in the system.[47] Furthermore, by the late 1970s, because of the costs of the continuing confrontation with Israel, President Sadat decided to break ranks and come to terms with Israel. He did so with little regard for the interests of other front-line states, who were left in a more vulnerable position vis-à-vis Israel.

The reduced appeal of Arab solidarity was also evident in the behavior of Saudi Arabia and other conservative oil-producing Gulf states in the late 1970s. The rapidly developing economic and financial ties between these countries and the Western world created relationships of interdependence that they were loath to damage in support of Arab causes.[48] Furthermore, after 1979 these governments were increasingly preoccupied with the threat posed by the new Islamic fundamentalist regime in Iran. Concerned about their vulnerability, they were less able to devote attention and energies to the problems of other Arab states, and were unwilling to exert any serious pressure on the United States on behalf of other system members.

Other examples of the declining force of pan-Arabism were found in Lebanon and Syria. In Lebanon, much of the Christian community felt sufficiently threatened to abandon the Arab fold and develop open ties with Israel.[49] In Syria, hostility toward the Iraqi government became so great by the late 1970s that the Syrian regime was prepared to align with an outside power, Iran, even though Iran posed a serious threat to several other members of the Arab system.[50]

Despite these events, Arab societies remain interconnected. Important segments of the population maintain a sense of attachment to the larger Arab community and continue to identify with Arab core concerns.[51] One question in this regard, however, concerns the attitudes of the emerging middle classes in the wealthy modernizing societies of the Arabian Peninsula. Will they become preoccupied with class concerns as well as with the problems, both domestic and foreign, of their societies? Or will the sense of Arab identity gain strength, increasing responsiveness to pan-Arab concerns?

In either case, it is premature to predict an end to the permeability of Arab states through the apparent decline of the pan-Arab mystique. The substantial potential for transnational responsiveness that remains could be reactivated by new leaders who successfully articulate the ideals and aspirations of the Arab community. Alternatively, a *new* basis for transnational solidarity might emerge within the Arab world. The Islamic factor appears to have the greatest potential. If a movement with a pronounced Islamic character were to achieve a breakthrough in a key Arab state, this could very well have substantial repercussions for other Arab states. The problem of vulnerability to cross-frontier political pressures would return.

PROPERTIES OF THE SYSTEM

We turn now to the characteristics of the Arab system proper, the patterns of behavior and relationships between Arab states at the governmental level. The principal systemic properties examined here are the basic structure and distribution of power, the sources and level of conflict, and the patterns of conflict and alignment.

The Bases and Distribution of Power

In the Arab system of the *1950s and 1960s*, the *bases of power* were quite different from those usually found in state systems. In other systems, military and economic capabilities have been extremely important and have generally been employed coercively to achieve state objectives. In the Arab system, however, there were constraints on the use of these traditional instruments of statecraft. Arab states possessed modest military capabilities and had little or no ability to project military power beyond their borders. Even the strongest Arab military power, Egypt, had only a limited ability to employ force against other members of the system; principally because of the absence of land links between itself and the Arab states of southwest Asia. Among the important extrasystemic constraints, the most compelling was the likelihood of Israeli military action in the event of armed force being used against states in its immediate vicinity.[52] There was also a strong possibility of action by the western powers in response to military pressure against any of their Arab allies or associates.[53] For these reasons, conventional military operations were unlikely except in peripheral areas of the system such as North Africa (e.g., the Algerian-Moroccan War of 1963) and the rimlands of the Arabian Peninsula (e.g., the Yemen War of 1962–1967).

Although military capabilities were of limited value as an instrument of coercion within the system, they could contribute to a state's standing in other ways. If an Arab state's armed forces met its own external and internal security needs, it avoided dependence on others. Moreover, states with greater capabilities were able to assist others who faced serious internal or external pressures and to claim a position of leadership in any joint defense efforts or collective military structures,[54] such as the joint command established in the mid-1960s.

Nor were economic capabilities extremely important during the 1950s and 1960s. In general, the military and economic needs of Arab states were nowhere near as extensive or costly as they later became. Hence, the financial resources of states were not as crucial to their international position. Furthermore, the low level of economic development limited economic interaction.[55] There were few bilateral relationships of consequence and they involved mainly transit facilities (e.g., the use of Syrian territory for the shipment of Lebanese or Jordanian goods and for the export of Iraqi and Saudi Arabian oil). Opportunities to manipulate economic transactions coercively to influence the behavior of other states were limited. Finally, none of the Arab states possessed sufficient financial resources to provide a level of aid or investment that would permit the development of influence relationships.[56] Financial assistance was scarce and generally took the form of payments to individuals or groups in other states who were willing to work informally with the donor government.

If the traditional instruments of statecraft were not widely used in the Arab system during the 1950s and 1960s, the instruments of political warfare—propaganda, cross-frontier alliances, and subversion—were.[57] Conditions favoring the widespread use and effectiveness of such techniques prevailed within the Arab world. These included serious internal cleavages, political instability, the extensive permeability of Arab societies, and numerous crises of legitimacy.

In these circumstances, the *political capabilities* of governments were important in two ways. One factor was the degree of domestic support that a government enjoyed. Any government in a weak position domestically would be extremely vulnerable to external propaganda and

TABLE 3.1
Demographic Capabilities, Eastern Arab World, Early 1960s[a]

Countries	Total Population (millions)	%	Literate Population (millions)	%	Secondary School Enrollment (thousands)	%	Overall %
Egypt	28.3	50.0	7.1	52.0	812.0	58.0	53.0
Iraq	7.7	13.5	1.8	13.0	220.0	16.0	14.0
Syria	5.1	9.0	1.9	14.0	161.0	11.5	11.5
Lebanon	2.3	4.0	1.6	11.5	72.0	5.0	7.0
Saudi Arabia	6.5	11.5	0.3	2.0	22.0	1.5	5.0
Jordan	1.9	3.0	0.6	4.5	89.0	6.0	4.5
Yemen	4.8	8.5	0.2	1.5	1.8	--	3.5
Kuwait	0.4	0.5	0.2	1.5	25.0	2.0	1.5
TOTAL	57.0	100.0[b]	13.7	100.0[b]	1,402.8	100.0[b]	100.0[b]

Sources: UN Demographic Yearbook 1970 (New York: United Nations, 1971); *UNESCO Statistical Yearbook 1976* (Paris: UNESCO, 1977); and *UN Statistical Yearbook,* 1964, 1967, 1968 (New York: United Nations).

[a]The figures represent an average of the relevant data for the years 1962 and 1965. The percentages indicate each country's proportion of the total for the eastern Arab World.

[b]Figures may not add up due to rounding.

subversive pressures and unable to act in a vigorous and sustained manner in the regional arena. Second, the attractiveness of the leadership and policies of governments in other Arab states was significant because of the uncertain stage through which Arab societies were passing. The people of the Arab world were searching for new directions, new models, new leadership. In this context, any leader or regime providing emotionally satisfying answers to the central issues confronting Arab societies could attract a following. Cross-frontier appeal could be translated into influence through propaganda and subversive activities designed to create internal pressures on governments to alter their policies or risk being overthrown. In short, political capabilities were probably the most important determinants of influence in the Arab system during the 1950s and 1960s.

During this period, the Arab system was also distinguished by the *pattern of power,* characterized by the predominance of Egypt. This concentration of power stemmed from Egypt's vast superiority in material capabilities. As can be seen from the accompanying tables, in all but one area, Egypt accounted for half or more of the capabilities of the eastern Arab world. Egyptian superiority was most pronounced in the softer forms of material capabilities. Demographic capabilities was one such area (see Table 3.1). Demographics concerns the quantity and quality of available manpower as measured by overall population size; the size of the literate population; and the size of the secondary school population. Although human resources are not a direct instrument of influence, they are the basis for most other forms of material capability.

TABLE 3.2
Cultural and Communications Capabilities, Eastern Arab World, Early 1960s[a]

Countries	Higher Education Enrollment (thousands)	%	Book Production (units)	%	Radio Transmitter Facilities (kw)	%	Overall %
Egypt	160.0	69.5	3,325	68.0	3,770	53.5	63.5
Iraq	21.0	9.0	250	5.0	1,125	16.0	10.0
Syria	29.0	12.5	375	8.0	650	9.0	10.0
Lebanon	15.7	7.0	390	8.0	310	4.5	6.5
Saudi Arabia	1.9	1.0	300	6.0	415	6.0	4.5
Jordan	2.3	1.0	105	2.0	525	7.5	3.5
Kuwait	0.2	--	140	3.0	220	3.0	2.0
Yemen	--	--	--	--	40	0.5	--
TOTAL	230.1	100.0[b]	4,885	100.0[b]	7,055	100.0[b]	100.0[b]

Sources: UN Statistical Yearbook, 1964, 1967, 1968 (New York: United Nations);
UNESCO Statistical Yearbook, 1964, 1965, 1966, 1967 (Paris: UNESCO).

[a]The figures represent an average of the relevant data for the years 1962 and 1965.
[b]Figures may not add up due to rounding.

Egypt accounted for approximately half the population of the eastern Arab world, with over half of the literate population—more than all the rest of the countries combined. Iraq, the next most populous country, had less than a third as many people as Egypt.

Cultural and communications capabilities (Table 3.2) were another soft form of material resource. Although these factors are not normally included in analyses of power, certain features of the Arab setting rendered them particularly important. The linguistic and cultural homogeneity that made possible the strong links between Arab societies ensured that states with developed cultural facilities—higher education facilities and a developed publishing industry, for example—would be attractive to educated elements of the population in other Arab countries. Similarly, the permeability of Arab societies and their reliance on political capabilities made communications a valuable instrument of influence. The development of electronic communications media was critical. Egypt's predominance in the cultural and communications spheres was striking, amounting to an overwhelming one-power pattern. Egypt enjoyed a large margin of superiority over its nearest rivals (Iraq and Syria) and surpassed the resources of all the states of the eastern Arab world combined. Superiority in higher education and communications facilities was readily translated into influence. Egypt's universities attracted large numbers of students from other Arab countries, who returned home filled with ideas of Nasserism. The same universities turned out Egyptian teachers and professionals who filled posts in less-developed parts of the Arab system, where they had opportunities to influence opinion. The most powerful instrument for shaping opinion, however, was Egyp-

TABLE 3.3
Military Capabilities, Eastern Arab World, Mid-1960s[a]

Countries	Armed Forces (thousands)	%	Tanks (units)	%	Planes (units)	%	Overall %
Egypt	180	43.0	860	42.5	370	60.0	48.5
Iraq	82	19.5	535	26.5	80	13.0	19.5
Syria	60	14.5	350	17.5	94	15.5	15.5
Jordan	45	11.0	150	7.5	30	5.0	8.0
Saudi Arabia	20	5.0	30[b]	1.5	16	2.5	3.0
Lebanon	13	3.0	42	2.0	14	2.5	2.5
Yemen	10	2.5	30[b]	1.5	--	--	1.5
Kuwait	7	1.5	25	1.0	10	1.5	1.5
TOTAL	417	100.0[c]	2,022	100.0[c]	614	100.0[c]	100.0[c]

Sources: J. Hurewitz, *Middle East Politics: The Military Dimension* (New York: Praeger, 1969); N. Safran, *From War to War* (New York: Pegasus, 1969); and J. Sutton and G. Kemp, *Arms to Developing Countries 1945-1965* (London: International Institute for Strategic Studies, 1966).

[a]The figures represent an average of the relevant data for the years 1962 and 1965.

[b]Rough estimates.

[c]Figures may not add up due to rounding.

tian radio, which carried the appealing message of Nasserism directly to the whole Arab world.

The situation in regard to the traditional yardsticks of power was less clearcut, although the pattern for military capabilities closely followed the distribution of communications facilities and population, as Table 3.3 makes clear. Egypt possessed almost half the military capabilities of the whole eastern Arab world, with more than a 2 : 1 advantage over its closest competitor, Iraq.

The pattern of economic indicators was quite different. In Table 3.4, the overall productive level of the societies is indicated by the gross domestic product; the level of economic modernization is measured by electricity production; and the general level of material well-being is indicated by per capita income. The financial capacity of countries to engage in foreign policy activity can be measured by foreign exchange reserves. Economic power in the Arab East was more diffused than were other resources. Egypt's large population had the second lowest per capita income in the eastern Arab world, and a lower level of reserves than Saudi Arabia, Iraq, and Lebanon. The inconsistencies in the rankings of Egypt and the other major actors on different indicators reveal the unbalanced, and hence tenuous, economies in these states.

In short, with respect to hard material capabilities, the Arab system in the 1950s and 1960s stood between that of an unbalanced multipower system and a one-power system, although it more closely resembled the latter. Egypt's ability to exploit its advantage and use its hard material capabilities coercively was checked by political and physical constraints

TABLE 3.4
Economic Capabilities, Eastern Arab World, Early 1960s[a]

Countries	National Income (billions US$)	%	Per Capita Income (US$)	%	Electricity Production (millions kwh)	%	Financial Reserves (millions US$)	%	Overall %
Egypt	3.90	38.0	140	3.0	4,790	60.5	205	14.5	29.0
Kuwait	1.30	13.0	3,439	72.0	610	7.5	110	8.0	25.0
Saudi Arabia	1.40	13.5	225	5.0	160	2.0	500	35.5	14.0
Iraq	1.40	13.5	192	4.0	1 000	13.0	210	15.0	11.5
Lebanon	0.86	8.5	378	8.0	660	8.5	230	16.5	10.5
Syria	0.81	8.0	164	3.0	560	7.0	45	3.0	5.0
Jordan	0.34	3.0	189	4.0	130	1.5	100	7.0	4.0
Yemen	0.26	2.5	55	1.0	2	--	5	0.5	1.0
TOTAL	10.27	100.0[b]	4,782	100.0[b]	7,912	100.0[b]	1,405	100.0[b]	100.0[b]

Sources: UN Yearbook of National Accounts Statistics 1969, Vol. 2 (New York: United Nations, 1970); *UN Statistical Yearbook*, 1963, 1969, 1972 (New York: United Nations).

[a]The figures for national income and per capita income are for 1963. The figures for electricity production and financial reserves represent an average of the relevant data for 1962 and 1965.

[b]Figures may not add up due to rounding.

on the use of Egyptian military strength within the system and by the absence of Egyptian economic leverage.

Although Egypt's military and economic capabilities provided a dubious basis of power, its political capabilities were enviable. They increased phenomenally during this period, becoming a highly effective instrument of influence. The Egyptian regime was extremely strong domestically, and Nasser's policies and accomplishments had tremendous appeal among the attentive and mass publics of most Arab states, enabling him to exert considerable pressure on other Arab governments. Its overwhelming political superiority allowed Egypt to achieve a position of commanding influence in the 1950s and 1960s. However, this was not expanded to total dominance because Egypt had difficulty using its material resources to reinforce its political appeal. Nasser's hegemonic ambitions antagonized those who might otherwise have been his allies.

During the *1970s*, important changes took place in both the bases and distribution of power in the Arab system. These changes affected the position of individual states and the pattern of relations within the system. With regard to the *bases of power*, there was a marked increase in the importance of material—particularly economic—capabilities. This can be traced to three factors, of which the first was a dramatic growth in the economic needs of the Arab states as a result of rapid population growth and the intensified drive for modernization.

The second factor was the rapidly expanding financial resources of the Arab oil-producing states. The large pool of surplus capital that developed in the region led the poorer states to turn increasingly to the wealthy oil-producing states for assistance. The result was a substantial expansion of economic links and consequently, a greater potential for economic strength as an instrument of influence.[58] Third, the importance of Arab oil, capital, and markets for the Western world gave the oil-producing countries, particularly Saudi Arabia, more leverage within the international system. The newly developed capacity to exert pressure on the Western powers in support of Arab interests further strengthened the influence of these states.

By contrast, the change in the role of military capabilities was relatively limited. Admittedly, the growing seriousness of the military-security problems facing the Arab world (as represented by Israel and later Iran) enhanced the importance of military capabilities. The more serious military pressures became, the more affected states depended on others for support, augmenting the leverage of those who could make a military contribution. However, no system member except Egypt had sufficient military strength to contribute effectively to the security of others vis-à-vis Israel and Iran. The possibilities for the coercive use of military power within the core area also remained severely restricted.

While economic capabilities were becoming more significant as a basis of power during the 1970s, political capabilities declined in importance. The Arab public had become less responsive to transnational ideological appeals. After Nasser's death, there was no leader who epitomized the ideals and aspirations of the Arab world and thus could effectively galvanize Arab opinion.[59] Furthermore, the rallying cries of Arab nationalism and socialism had lost some of their appeal.[60] Despite the growing preoccupation of Arab elites and publics alike with tangible national concerns, and the declining role of transnational political influence during the 1970s, it would nevertheless be a mistake to under-estimate the possibility of a resurgence in the 1980s. Arguments about legitimacy continue to be important in inter-Arab politics, and Arab leaders disregard them at their peril. The *potential* for transnational responsiveness is still substantial and new bases of appeal could emerge.

Along with this shift in the *bases of power*, a major change also occurred in the *pattern of power*. During the 1950s and 1960s, the concentration of capabilities and influence approached but never quite reached a one-power situation. After 1970, however, capabilities and influence were distributed more evenly, creating a more competitive multipower situation.[61]

This diffusion of power reflected a decline in the material and political strength of Egypt. Egypt's limited economic and financial resources were further strained by the continuing conflict with Israel, while its military strength suffered from strained relations with its principal arms supplier, the Soviet Union. The overwhelming defeat in 1967, the death of Nasser in 1970, and the major reorientation of Egypt's foreign and domestic policies thereafter all lessened Egypt's prestige and attractiveness, and seriously reduced its ability to shape opinion and mobilize support in other Arab countries.

While Egypt's capabilities were declining, those of other Arab states were on the rise. Spectacular changes occurred in the oil-producing states. Their financial wealth and their increased leverage with the Western powers endowed the oil-producing states with important new instruments of influence. The greatest beneficiary of these developments was Saudi Arabia.[62] Because it had the highest production levels and largest reserves, its financial position was much stronger and its leverage over Western oil-consuming nations much greater than the others. Saudi Arabia became particularly important to the Arab front-line states in their confrontation with Israel. Other major beneficiaries included Iraq and Algeria, although each suffered from certain liabilities (Iraq's intense internal war with the Kurds and its conflict with Iran, Algeria's preoccupation with the Maghreb and with the struggle for the New International Economic Order).

Apart from the oil-producing states, Syria experienced the greatest improvement in status. Although it lacked the economic resources of the oil-producing states, Syria occupied a key geopolitical position, bordering Lebanon and Jordan as well as Israel. It built up its armed forces to become the second-largest military power in the Arab world. Furthermore, Asad established substantial political stability within Syria for much of the 1970s. Benefiting from this solid internal base, from the declining influence of Egypt, and from the continuing confrontation with Israel, the Syrian government was able, through slow, painstaking effort, to exercise undeniable influence in the region of Greater Syria.

The more competitive multipower situation of the mid-1970s is reflected in Tables 3.5–3.8. With respect to the softer forms of material resources (see Tables 3.5 and 3.6), the basic pattern remained unchanged. Egypt continued to enjoy a dominant position in terms of human, education, and communications resources. The situation was rather different in regard to the harder capabilities (see Tables 3.7 and 3.8).[63] The economic indicators show an unbalanced multipower pattern, with Saudi Arabia clearly the leading actor in terms of national income and financial reserves. In the military sphere, there was also greater diffusion of power. Egyptian strength accounted for one-third of the strength of the eastern Arab world as a whole, down from one-half, and its lead over the second-ranked power, Syria, was relatively small.

This shift in the pattern of power had important implications for individual states and for the overall pattern of relationships in the system. To begin with, the relative weakening of Egyptian capabilities, particularly its political and economic strength, reduced Egypt's opportunities and options within the system. The decline in Egyptian activity and influence throughout the area lessened or removed the major source of systemic pressure. Other Arab governments had more latitude to decide policy. Moreover, Egyptian inability to dominate events provided opportunities for other major Arab states to play a greater role in the affairs of the system and to develop their own local spheres of influence. This was

TABLE 3.5
Demographic Capabilities, Eastern Arab World, Mid 1970s[a]

Countries	Total Population (millions)	%	Literate Population (millions)	%	Secondary School Enrollment (thousands)	%	Overall %
Egypt	37.2	46.0	14.00	53.0	1,710.0	54.0	51.0
Iraq	11.1	14.0	2.80	10.5	405.0	13.0	12.5
Syria	7.3	9.0	2.90	11.0	408.0	13.0	11.0
Lebanon	3.3	4.0	2.30	9.0	175.0	6.0	6.5
Saudi Arabia	9.0	11.0	1.30	5.0	149.0	4.5	7.0
North Yemen	6.7	8.5	0.40	1.5	14.0	0.5	3.5
Jordan	1.9	2.5	1.20	4.5	126.0	4.0	3.5
Kuwait	1.0	1.0	0.60	2.5	90.0	3.0	2.0
South Yemen	1.7	2.0	0.50	2.0	31.0	1.0	1.5
Oman	0.8	1.0	0.08	0.5	0.5	--	0.5
United Arab Emirates	0.2	0.5	0.04	--	22.0	0.5	--
Bahrain	0.2	0.5	0.08	0.5	17.0	0.5	0.5
Qatar	0.1	--	0.01	--	7.0	--	--
TOTAL	80.5	100.0[b]	26.21	100.0[b]	3,154.5	100.0[b]	100.0[b]

Sources: *UN Demographic Yearbook 1975* (New York: United Nations, 1976); *UNESCO Statistical Yearbook*, 1980, 1982 (Paris: UNESCO, 1980, 1982); and *UN Statistical Yearbook 1975* (New York: United Nations, 1976).

[a]In this table, the population data are for 1975; the literacy data are for the early 1970s; the data for secondary school enrollment are for 1973 or 1975.

[b]Figures may not add up due to rounding.

TABLE 3.6
Cultural and Communications Capabilities, Eastern Arab World, Mid 1970s[a]

Countries	Higher Education Enrollment (thousands)	%	Book Production (units)	%	Radio Transmitter Facilities (kw)	%	Overall %
Egypt	351.0	65.0	2,400	54.0	4,886	33.0	50.5
Iraq	65.0	12.0	620	14.0	3,140	21.5	16.0
Syria	52.0	9.5	460	10.5	1,340	9.0	9.5
Lebanon	44.0	8.0	650	14.5	237	1.5	8.0
Kuwait	5.0	1.0	140	3.0	2,476	17.0	7.0
Saudi Arabia	15.0	3.0	80	2.0	1,805	12.5	6.0
Jordan	8.0	1.5	90	2.0	318	2.0	2.0
North Yemen	1.0	--	--	--	170	1.0	0.5
Qatar	--	--	--	--	162	1.0	0.5
South Yemen	0.4	--	--	--	64	0.5	--
Bahrain	0.6	--	--	--	35	--	--
United Arab Emirates	--	--	--	--	75[b]	0.5	--
Oman	--	--	--	--	50[b]	0.5	--
TOTAL	542.0	100.0[c]	4,440	100.0[c]	14,758	100.0[c]	100.0[c]

Sources: *UN Statistical Yearbook 1975* (New York: United Nations, 1976); *UNESCO Statistical Yearbook*, 1974, 1975 (Paris: UNESCO, 1974, 1975).

[a]The data here are for 1972 and 1973.

[b]Rough estimates.

[c]Figures may not add up due to rounding.

TABLE 3.7
Economic Capabilities, Eastern Arab World, Mid-1970s[a]

Countries	National Income (billions US$)	%	Per Capita Income (US$)	%	Electricity Production (millions kwh)	%	Financial Reserves (millions US$	%	Overall %
Saudi Arabia	39.1	41.0	4,370	10.0	1,474	7.0	23,300	71.0	32.5
Kuwait	11.4	12.0	11,400	26.0	4,000	19.0	1,600	5.0	15.5
Egypt	11.5	12.0	310	1.0	8,200	38.5	294	1.0	13.0
United Arab Emirates	6.9	7.0	10,500	24.0	400[b]	2.0	989	3.0	9.0
Iraq	12.9	13.5	1,160	2.5	2,500	12.0	2,700	8.5	9.0
Qatar	1.7	2.0	8,440	19.5	325[b]	1.5	104	--	6.0
Lebanon	3.2	3.5	1,110	2.5	1,975	9.0	1,600	5.0	5.0
Syria	5.1	5.0	700	1.5	1,366	6.0	735	2.0	3.5
Bahrain	0.7	0.5	2,850	7.0	390	2.0	296	1.0	2.5
Oman	1.5	1.5	1,980	4.5	200	1.0	300	1.0	2.0
Jordan	0.9	1.0	460	1.0	310	1.5	492	1.5	1.5
North Yemen	1.1	1.0	170	0.5	29	--	337	1.0	0.5
South Yemen	0.2	--	140	--	174	0.5	55	--	--
TOTAL	96.2	100.0[c]	43,590	100.0[c]	21,343	100.0[c]	32,802	100.0[c]	100.0[c]

Sources: *Yearbook of National Accounts Statistics 1978*, Vol. 2 (New York: United Nations, 1979); *UN Statistical Yearbook 1975* (New York: United Nations, 1976); and *International Financial Statistics*, July 1977, (Washington, D.C.: International Monetary Fund, 1977).

[a]The data are for 1975 with the exception of electricity production, for which 1974 statistics have been used.

[b]Rough estimates.

[c]Figures may not add up due to rounding.

particularly true in the Arabian Peninsula, where through financial assistance, cross-frontier alliances, and religious ties, Saudi Arabia surfaced as the predominant power.[64] In the western Fertile Crescent area (Syria, Lebanon, Jordan, and the Palestinians) Syria was successful for a time in establishing a modified sphere of influence.[65] It faced competition, however, particularly from Saudi Arabia, Iraq, and Libya. The main beneficiaries of the shifting pattern of power were the second-ranking powers; the main loser was Egypt.

A second consequence of the diffusion of power was the increased fragmentation of the system. In the years before 1967, when Egypt enjoyed a position of commanding influence, Nasser was a focal point for cohesion within the system although he also antagonized governments and created disruptions. His widespread appeal, and the respect and fear it engendered among other Arab governments, usually helped him to mobilize a number of Arab states in a common front against outsiders. Without the unifying pressure that Nasser had applied, there was a strong tendency for system members to go their own ways. The cohesion of the system suffered accordingly.

TABLE 3.8
Military Capabilities, Eastern Arab World, Mid-1970s[a]

Countries	Armed Forces (thousands)	%	Tanks (units)	%	Planes (units)	%	Overall %
Egypt	343.0	35.5	1,975	28.0	700	39.0	34.0
Syria	227.0	23.5	2,400	34.0	440	24.5	27.5
Iraq	158.0	16.0	1,400	19.5	300	17.0	17.5
Jordan	68.0	7.0	500	7.0	66	3.5	6.0
Saudi Arabia	51.5	5.5	385	5.5	97	5.5	5.5
North Yemen	39.3	4.0	30	--	28	1.5	2.0
South Yemen	21.3	2.0	200	3.0	27	1.5	2.0
Lebanon	18.2	2.0	100	1.5	27	1.5	1.5
Kuwait	9.7	1.0	100	1.5	33	2.0	1.5
Oman	14.0	1.5	--	--	44	2.5	1.5
United Arab Emirates	21.4	2.0	27	--	26	1.5	1.0
Qatar	2.2	--	--	--	4	--	--
Bahrain	1.6	--	--	--	--	--	--
TOTAL	975.2	100.0[b]	7,117	100.0[b]	1,792	100.0[b]	100.0[b]

Source: International Institute of Strategic Studies, *The Military Balance 1976-1977* (London: IISS, 1976), pp. 32-39.

[a]The data here are for 1976.

[b]Figures may not add up due to rounding.

The Sources and Level of Conflict

A second basic feature of any state system is the level of conflict and consequently the degree of pressure and threat to which system members are exposed. During the 1950s and 1960s, the Arab world constituted a *revolutionary international system*. The policies of the major actors were extensively revisionist;[66] they promoted significant changes in the basic orientation and position of other system members. Consequently, inter-Arab politics was characterized by a high level of conflict.

The system's revolutionary character was reflected first of all in the *objectives* of the member states. To begin with, *directional* issues (i.e., questions of principle or basic orientation) were a source of deep division and revisionism during this period.[67] These directional issues included both *foreign policy issues* concerning the proper stance toward outside powers and the *ideological issue* of what constituted a legitimate domestic political, economic, and social order.

Two main factors were responsible for the prominence of directional issues from the mid-1950s on. The first was the extensive intrusion of outside actors. The bitter Arab experience of Western colonial rule and the continuing pressures to which the Arab states were subject made relations with the major powers emotionally charged from the outset. From the mid-1950s on, the differences between Arab states over these relations intensified as the Western powers sought to strengthen their presence and influence in the face of growing Soviet involvement in the Middle East. Saudi Arabia, Jordan, and (initially) Iraq aligned themselves more closely to the West, while Egypt, Syria, and (after 1958) Iraq vehemently opposed such ties. Egypt mounted a major offensive, an almost constant attack on the pro-Western governments.

Although policy toward Israel was also a very sensitive issue, it was not as divisive as the question of relations with the major powers. All members of the system, through conviction or through fear of the political consequences, abided by the basic norm: no accommodation with or recognition of Israel. Difficulties did arise periodically over what further action, if any, to take, and the inclination to engage in competitive posturing was strong. This posturing was particularly evident in the period preceding the Suez War, during the Jordan Waters dispute (1964–1965) and again just before the 1967 war. Second-ranking actors such as Syria and Iraq frequently challenged Egypt to adopt a tougher stand. The ensuing struggle generated considerable pressure on other Arab states to respond.

The second factor accounting for conflict over directional issues was the unsettled stage through which most Arab societies were passing. There were sharp ideological cleavages both within and between Arab states about the direction their societies should take internally as well as externally. The contending regimes found themselves locked in a struggle to promote or even impose their views. Egypt in particular embarked on a sustained campaign to transform the political, economic, and social order throughout the Arab world.

There was also extensive revisionism in regard to *distributional* issues (i.e., the allocation of tangible "values"). One subject of dispute was *the state and territorial framework*. As in most of the Third World, the shallow roots and questionable origins of many boundaries and state units, together with the existence of serious cleavages within societies, encouraged periodic challenges to the status quo. But the Arab world, unlike some Third World regions, was also characterized by a widespread sense of common identity and a historical legacy of unity. In the 1940s and early 1950s, this led to efforts to bring about the merger of various states (e.g., a Fertile Crescent union, Greater Syrian union, Jordanian-Palestinian union, and an Egyptian-Sudanese union). Pressures became particularly intense within the Fertile Crescent area in the late 1950s. The establishment of the United Arab Republic (Egypt and Syria) in 1958 appeared to pose a threat to the autonomy of Iraq, Jordan, and even Lebanon. For several years after the breakup of the UAR in 1961, Syria was under intense pressure from Egypt to reestablish the union. Attempts to revive it were broadened to include Iraq in 1963. Finally, in 1961, Iraq openly challenged the legitimacy of Kuwaiti independence and called for its annexation.

Status and influence questions were also an acute and pervasive source of conflict during this period. Several features of the system stimulated revisionism by encouraging the belief that substantial modifications to the power structure could be achieved relatively quickly. The small number of actors in the system meant that one or two alliances could significantly improve a state's power position. Widespread internal instability allowed governments to enhance their influence by helping friendly forces to come to power in neighboring states. Furthermore, the modest level of capabilities in the system provided tempting opportunities for states to improve their position considerably through aid from outside sources.

The distribution of capabilities and the geopolitical structure of the system provided further temptations to revisionism. A concentration of capabilities encouraged Egyptian governments to believe not only that Egypt was entitled to a dominant position in the system but also that this position was readily attainable. This perception led to a persistent Egyptian quest for power, which varied only in the degree of superiority sought and the nature of the methods used. Furthermore, the geopolitical structure was such that the small and medium actors in southwest Asia were separated from Egypt by water and by Israel. Hence, lesser actors saw opportunities to enhance their position and to rival Egypt through alliance with, or control over, neighboring states.

Although some of the second-ranking actors (i.e., Iraq and later Saudi Arabia) held revisionist views at certain points during the 1950s and 1960s, Egypt was by far the greatest source of disturbance on status and influence questions. From 1955 on, Nasser openly sought Egyptian hegemony, in part to impose his views on directional issues and in part because he believed it was Egypt's due. Most Arab governments could accept Egypt's claim to leadership. However, they disagreed sharply with Nasser on just how much influence Egypt was to have and how it was to be exercised. In any case, Egypt's drive for dominance and its intervention in the international and domestic affairs of other states provoked anxious insecurity on the part of other system members and led to bitter conflicts.

The revolutionary character of the system was reflected not only in the objectives of system members but also in their *techniques*.[68] Except among aligned states, little effort was made to shape the behavior of other governments through persuasion and influence, diplomacy, or economic and other inducements. When differences arose, Arab governments relied on unconventional coercive techniques. Instead of trying to influence one another directly, Arab governments sought to mobilize domestic opposition within each other's society. Egypt in particular campaigned to destabilize and overthrow opposing governments. Many Arab regimes, therefore, faced a serious challenge to their basic direction and policies, to important national interests, and to their very survival politically.

In short, during the 1950s and 1960s the Arab world was characterized by a high level of revisionism, which threatened the basic interests and values of system members. Egypt's attempts to bring about sweeping changes in the policies and positions of other Arab states made the situation even more threatening. The sense of insecurity among Arab regimes and the ensuing cold war climate seriously weakened the Arab world to outside challenges.

During the 1970s, the Arab system became distinctly *less revolutionary* in several respects. Conflict over previously contentious *directional* issues eased, particularly in regard to *ideological* questions. Egypt and Syria, which had both been highly revisionist in the past, were forced to reconsider their policies as a result of the dramatic change in their situations after the 1967 war. Both were faced with pressing territorial, military-security, and economic problems, and both were aware that the conservative regimes could be of considerable assistance in dealing with, if not resolving, these problems. To obtain support they began, in the early 1970s, to play down ideological differences and halt political attacks as well as subversive pressures on these states.[69] However, the objective differences between regimes remained as great as ever. The de-emphasis of ideology was carried further after the 1973 war when Egypt, and to a lesser extent Syria, instituted measures of economic liberalization that narrowed the differences somewhat. The Saudi regime continued its efforts to weaken and ultimately defeat leftist and radical forces, but in response to signs of moderation from the Egyptian and Syrian regimes, it too became more flexible in its approach.[70]

During the 1970s, the level of revisionism over ideological issues declined among the major states of the eastern Arab world. The main exception was the Ba'th regime in Iraq, which continued its ideological attacks on Gulf conservative regimes and on its fellow Ba'th regime in Syria for most of the decade. By the late 1970s, however, the Iraqi regime also began to de-emphasize ideological issues as it sought to develop ties with the Gulf states and to gain support in its conflict with Iran. During this period, lesser actors (e.g., Libya, South Yemen, and elements of the PLO) became the main sources of conflict over ideological issues.

There was somewhat less attenuation of discord over *relationships with the major powers*. In the early 1970s, the differences in policies on this matter remained sharp, as the progressive regimes maintained a strong anti-Western posture and the conservative regimes remained closely associated with the Western powers. However, in view of the possible benefits to be derived from an improvement in relations with the conservative regimes, the Egyptian government abandoned and the Syrian government toned down criticism of these regimes over ties with the West,[71] and the climate of inter-Arab relations improved.

After the war in 1973, this process was carried farther as the leading progressive regimes modified their policies toward the Western powers. Egypt, which had given earlier indications of its softening position, now sought eagerly to develop close relations with the United States.[72] This brought Egyptian policy into line with that of Saudi Arabia and other conservative states. In the mid-1970s, Syria modified its policy slightly. Besides expanding economic links with the West, the Syrian government cautiously explored the possibilities for improved relations with the United States, hoping to encourage a more evenhanded U.S. posture toward the Arab-Israeli conflict.[73] When these attempts proved unsuccessful, Syria reverted to denunciations of U.S. policy. Although some effort was made to limit the spillover effect on inter-Arab relations, Syrian pressures for Saudi Arabian action against the United States contributed to a deterioration of relations. During most of this period, Iraq maintained its strong opposition both to the United States and to those Arab states that were aligned with it. However, in the late 1970s Iraq began to play down the issue of policies toward the superpowers in the interests of a rapprochement with the conservative Gulf states. This was soon followed by cautious overtures to the United States in the wake of the Iranian revolution.[74] On the whole, although pronounced differences remained regarding relations with the superpowers, the issue generated less conflict than it had in the 1950s and 1960s.

While these two directional issues declined in importance, another— *policy toward Israel*—was so contentious that it became the principal directional issue during the 1970s.[75] Israel's sweeping victory in the 1967 war, its continuing occupation of portions of the territory of neighboring Arab states, and the emergence of a strong Palestinian national movement combined to place Israel at the top of the Arab foreign policy agenda. These events helped build a stronger sense of involvement in the conflict as well as a new mood of realism toward Israel among both the front-line states and the conservative oil-producing states. The new mood crystallized gradually and guardedly in a willingness to reach an honorable settlement. As some governments departed from the previous rigid policy of no negotiations, no recognition, and no peace with Israel, the potential for conflict in the system grew. However, prior to 1973 the evolution in policy took place quietly and was limited to Jordan and Egypt. Moreover, an inflexible Israeli policy and the relative passivity of the United States severely restricted possibilities for movement. Hence conflict over this issue remained latent for the most part.

After 1973, the situation changed substantially. The shock of the war spurred the United States to press more actively for a resolution of conflict and induced Israel to display some flexibility, at least toward Egypt.[76] Although the balance of forces among the front-line states, and in the Arab world generally, appeared to tilt in favor of an honorable settlement, serious divisions remained. Some actors (Iraq, Libya, South Yemen, Algeria, and the Rejectionist Front within the PLO) continued to oppose any settlement with Israel in principle and sharply attacked those who were willing to move in this direction. More importantly, even among those who leaned toward a settlement, there were differences in approach to the resolution of the conflict. This was particularly true among front-line actors (Egypt, Jordan, Syria, and the mainstream of the PLO), whose divisions were encouraged by Israeli variations in policy toward them. Sadat believed that Egypt stood a reasonable chance of satisfying its own purely national concerns, and he was ready to take initiatives and make concessions without receiving anything immediate in return.[77] Syria and the PLO were highly suspicious of Israeli aims and consequently, were extremely cautious and even inflexible in their bargaining positions, insisting on assurances that their basic national claims would be satisfied before they made any commitments or entered negotiations.[78] They were also fearful that Egypt would go its own way and leave them more exposed than before to Israeli attacks and expansionist aims. As a result, inter-Arab dissension intensified after the signing of the Camp David agreements (September 1979) and the Egyptian-Israeli peace treaty (March 1979). Thus, although conflict concerning directional issues declined overall, important divisions remained.

There was also a reduction in conflict over *distributional* issues. For one thing, *the state and territorial framework* was challenged much less than it had been in the 1950s and 1960s.[79] The pressures that did occur were limited in scope. In the early 1970s, Iraq renewed certain claims to Kuwait, but these amounted to a border issue rather than a challenge to Kuwait's independence.[80] The dispute soon faded into the background. Fears about the viability of other small Gulf states also proved unfounded as they took steps to consolidate their position. In the course of the Lebanese conflict (from 1970 onwards) questions were raised about Syria's objectives regarding Lebanon, but no moves toward annexation ensued.[81] This decline in serious challenges to the state and territorial framework was partially due to the increased acceptance it had gained with the passage of time. Stability owed more, however, to the failure of earlier attempts at union and to the decline of the pan-Arab mystique— events that greatly reduced popular and elite enthusiasm for political union. States began to emphasize arrangements for functional cooperation rather than outright mergers. Even when agreements were portrayed as involving political unification (e.g., the Egyptian-Syrian-Libyan and Egyptian-Libyan unions of the early 1970s, and the Syrian-Iraqi and Syrian-Libyan unions of the late 1970s), they never amounted to more than institutionalized cooperation.

Previously, Egypt's drive for dominance and involvement in the international and domestic politics of all areas of the system had caused much insecurity in other Arab states. By 1970, the situation had changed considerably. In view of the territorial, military-security, and economic problems confronting Egypt, Sadat decided to shift priorities. Egypt concentrated its attention and energies on immediate national problems and on the mobilization of support within the Arab world to cope with them. To this end, Sadat dropped his hegemonial aspirations and accepted a more modest definition of Egypt's status and influence in the system. This shift in Egyptian policy relieved pressure on other Arab governments.

It also provided an opportunity for some hitherto second-ranking powers to acquire a larger say in the affairs of the system or—as with Saudi Arabia and Syria—to establish local spheres of influence. To some extent, these states thereby satisfied their aspirations for status and influence.

New sources of disturbance and conflict over power questions emerged. In attempting to dominate the western Fertile Crescent, Syria threatened other local actors. In particular, its efforts to control developments in Lebanon with one hand and to bring the Palestinian resistance movement under Syrian tutelage with the other led to serious conflict with key Lebanese groups and elements of the PLO.[82] Syrian pressures on Jordan (1970–1972 and from 1980 on) produced similar results.[83] Saudi Arabia's greater assertiveness within the Arabian Peninsula occasioned some conflict, particularly with South Yemen,[84] but on the whole, Saudi activities in the peninsula were less disruptive than Syria's actions to the north.

Certain Arab states whose opportunities for establishing a local sphere of influence were blocked by rivals furnished another source of conflict over questions of status and influence. Iraq found itself blocked by Saudi Arabia and Iran in the Gulf area and by Syria in the western Fertile Crescent. Libya was hindered by Egypt in the Nile Valley and was unable to make any real headway in North Africa. As a result, the Iraqi and Libyan governments tended to initiate or support disruptive activity within and outside their immediate regions, trying to secure a base for influence. Iraqi pressures on the Arab Gulf states halted in the late 1970s as Iraq sought to improve relations with these governments because of its difficulties with both Syria and Iran.[85]

The greater moderation of the Arab system in the 1970s was also reflected in the *methods* employed by system members. Less emphasis was placed on political warfare designed to destabilize or overthrow regimes. Instead, a greater effort was made to influence other governments directly through traditional techniques of statecraft, diplomacy, and economic rewards and pressures.

This trend was evident mainly in the behavior of Egypt and Saudi Arabia. Under Sadat, the emphasis on "Egypt-the-revolution" gave way to that of "Egypt-the-state."[86] Sadat concentrated on improving relations with Arab governments to obtain the maximum support for Egypt. Saudi Arabia, while continuing to cultivate conservative and religiously oriented elements in other Arab societies, also was disposed to develop working relationships with certain of the progressive regimes.[87] In particular, the Saudi government attempted, through financial inducements and the promise of diplomatic brokerage vis-à-vis the United States and the Western powers, to encourage further moderation among the progressive regimes. The transformation of these regimes came to be viewed more as a gradual process.

Syrian behavior was mixed. For most of the decade, it suspended political attacks and subversive pressures against the wealthy conservative regimes and Jordan. However, it engaged in intense political warfare with the rival Ba'th regime of Iraq and intervened pointedly in Lebanese domestic politics.[88] Iraq engaged in subversive activities vis-à-vis Syria, the Gulf states, and the PLO.[89] In the late 1970s, however, Iraq moderated its behavior toward the Gulf states and Saudi Arabia, thereby reducing conflict in this segment of the system.

During the 1970s, then, the Arab system was much less revolutionary than before. Egypt, the formerly dominant power and principal source of disturbance, was forced to concentrate its attention and energies on pressing national problems. For a while, it also regarded the cooperation of other Arab states as essential to the resolution of these problems. Hence it ceased, by and large, to engage in revisionist activity and reduced its involvement in the affairs of the system. By the late 1970s, the Egyptian government was so preoccupied with its own problems that it favored measures, such as a virtually separate peace with Israel, that risked its isolation within the Arab world. In the wake of this gradual Egyptian disengagement from the affairs of the system, other actors—notably Syria, Saudi Arabia, Iraq, and Libya—became more assertive. However, because of a more competitive multipower structure, none achieved a predominant position, and thus none spawned the amount of disturbance that Egypt had in the 1950s and 1960s. In short, the Arab setting became less threatening and policy-makers felt more secure.

The Pattern of Conflict and Alignment

The third major development during the 1970s was a change in the pattern of conflict and alignment among Arab states and in the balance between the contending forces they represented. For the decade prior to 1967, inter-Arab relations had been marked by acute conflicts between progressive regimes with a strong anti-Western bias (Egypt, Syria, Iraq, and later, Algeria and Yemen) and conservative regimes with close ties to the Western powers (Saudi Arabia, Jordan, Tunisia, Morocco, and to a lesser extent, Kuwait). This conflict created deep cleavages and rigidity, as there was little scope for developing relationships across directional lines.[90]

A secondary axis of conflict developed among the progressive regimes. Nasser required that other governments pursue the same basic direction and policies as Egypt. They had to be willing to follow Egypt's lead and in some cases, to place Nasser's local allies in positions of power within their governments. As a result of this overbearing behavior, first Qasem's Iraq (1958–1963) and then Ba'thist Syria (1963–)became involved in bitter conflict with Egypt.[91]

Hence, although the system was highly polarized in *directional* terms, it was by no means fully bipolar in *political-diplomatic* terms. The conservative regimes, apart from their basic similarities in direction and policies, did not really form a cohesive bloc. Saudi Arabia and Jordan did work together closely, but only at certain times (from 1961 to 1963 and from late 1965 to 1967).[92] Conflicts with Nasser ensured that there was always at least one major progressive regime that remained aloof from Egypt and conducted an independent policy. In 1966, just a year prior to the June 1967 war, a common front developed among the progressive regimes, creating a political-diplomatic bipolarity that paralleled the divisions in the directional sphere.[93] Notwithstanding their differences, the progressive, anti-Western regimes had the upper hand, and they kept the conservative pro-Western regimes on the defensive for most of the 1950s and 1960s. The only exception was the counterattack launched by Saudi Arabia in late 1965 and 1966, which focused on the proposal for an Islamic grouping.

By the early 1970s, changes were beginning to occur in this pattern of relationships. The two leading progressive states, Egypt and Syria, were faced with territorial, military-security, and economic problems as a result of the 1967 war, and they were ready for détente with other Arab states. With the advent of détente, polarization along directional lines waned. This introduced more flexibility into the system and created more options for policy-makers. In the early 1970s, Saudi Arabia attempted to capitalize on the shift in direction within Egypt to develop ties with the new Egyptian leadership.[94] Détente progressed to entente.

After the 1973 war, the evolution continued. Ideological and directional issues ceased to be a force for polarization within the system. Instead, a more complicated triadic pattern of conservative (Saudi Arabia, the smaller Gulf states, and Jordan), moderate progressive (Egypt and to some extent Syria), and radical progressive (Iraq, Libya, and Algeria) regimes emerged. Saudi Arabia tried to take advantage of developments in Egypt and Syria and use its own increased financial capabilities and prestige to construct a broad-based coalition of conservative and moderate elements. By creating a favorable balance of forces, the Saudi regime hoped to make the area safe for conservatism.

The Saudis started with a substantial base of support among conservative regimes. The smaller Gulf states were usually prepared to follow the Saudi lead. Kuwait was a partial exception, often preferring an independent stance on issues relating to Israel and the Palestinians due to the substantial Palestinian presence and other opposition pressures within the country. Jordan was dependent on Saudi Arabian aid. Saudi Arabia also had considerable influence among conservative elements in Lebanon, particularly on the Moslem side. In addition, the Saudis developed close ties with North Yemen and the Sudan.

From this initial base, Saudi Arabia acted to create a broader coalition. The Saudi-Egyptian entente was strengthened considerably in 1973 when King Faisal employed the oil weapon to provide crucial support to Sadat in the confrontation with Israel. This close Egyptian-Saudi alliance constituted an important development in inter-Arab relations, as it linked the militarily and politically strongest Arab state to the leading Arab financial power.[95] The axis was successful for a time in developing ties with the second military power in the Arab world, Syria.[96] Initially, Syria was more closely associated with Egypt. However, after 1973 and particularly after the second Egyptian-Israeli disengagement agreement in September 1975, relations between Egypt and Syria deteriorated.[97] At the same time, Saudi-Syrian relations improved as modifications to Syrian policies produced considerable Saudi financial assistance and some measure of Saudi influence over Syria. Syria remained associated with the Saudi-Egyptian axis for a time as a result of its links with Saudi Arabia.[98]

During the 1970s, then, a loose conservative-moderate coalition headed by Saudi Arabia and Egypt emerged as the leading force in the Arab system. It was opposed by several less influential actors, notably Iraq, Libya, Algeria, South Yemen, radical elements within the PLO, and leftist-nationalist forces in Lebanon.[99] Although these dissident actors were very clear about what they opposed, they were unable to act cohesively. Nevertheless, their combined opposition activities, even if not closely coordinated, were effective enough to hamper the initiatives of the influential conservative-moderate coalition.

The fortunes of this coalition largely depended on its capacity to influence or pressure the United States to bring about a comprehensive settlement of the Arab-Israeli conflict. Significant progress in this direction would have created incentives for front-line actors such as Syria and the PLO to soften their opposition to the United States and draw closer to the Saudi-Egyptian axis. This would have strengthened the position of the pro-Western coalition and made it the dominant force in the system. However, the rigidity of Israeli policy and U.S. unwillingness to do much to change it proved a stumbling block to the coalition's success. The inability of Saudi Arabia and Egypt to persuade the United States to pressure Israel into concluding an honorable settlement on all fronts seriously undermined their influence. Furthermore, the lack of progress toward a comprehensive settlement prompted Egypt to seek a quasi-separate peace with Israel. This split the coalition, as Saudi Arabia and many of the conservative governments were opposed to these moves.

Failure to achieve a comprehensive peace placed the conservative pro-Western forces on the defensive.[100] The hard-line anti-Western elements seized the initiative and called for action both against Egypt and its newfound ally, the United States. Under political pressure, Saudi Arabia and the other conservative governments agreed to diplomatic and economic sanctions against Egypt but declined to take action against the United States. After 1978, Egypt became a virtual outcast in the Arab world, and the other pro-Western governments remained largely on the defensive.

The Arab world had now split several ways over policy toward Israel. Egypt both favored a settlement and was prepared to act on its own to procure peace. The other members of the system opposed Egypt's initiative but disagreed among themselves on the proper approach to take toward Israel.[101] Some—Saudi Arabia, Jordan, and the other conservative regimes—clearly favored a settlement and were prepared to make initial concessions, but only in the context of a move toward a comprehensive peace. Others—Syria, the mainstream of the PLO, and later Iraq—appeared to be leaning toward a settlement, providing it was comprehensive. They were unwilling, however, to make concessions or to take steps without assurances from Israel or the United States that a satisfactory agreement could be worked out. Still others—Iraq, Libya, Algeria, South Yemen, and the Rejectionist Front within the PLO—rejected any settlement with Israel in principle. These splits were reinforced by disagreements over other issues, including policy toward the United States and toward Iran, as well as by local power struggles (e.g., between Iraq and Syria).[102]

By the late 1970s, therefore, efforts to create a dominant coalition had failed, but there was no one dominant conflict that polarized the system. Instead, there were multiple divisions. The Arab system was seriously fragmented at a time when it was facing its most serious challenges.

CONCLUSION

During the 1970s, a number of changes took place both in the Arab system and its setting. The previous concentration of power in one state gave way to a more competitive multipower pattern with no one dominant actor. The scope of revisionism declined as a more limited range of basic values, policies, and interests were challenged, and this shift was accompanied by a greater reliance on diplomacy and inducements rather than on coercive instruments of statecraft. As the system became less revolutionary, it also became seriously fragmented. The dominant conflict over directional issues and the role of Egypt that had characterized the Arab system in the 1950s and 1960s gave way to separate conflicts. This had harmful consequences, particularly for the cohesiveness of the system. Nevertheless, the softening of rigid lines of division and the ensuing multipolarity diminished pressures on states and provided policymakers with more diplomatic options and alignment opportunities.

While intra-systemic pressures were lessening for most Arab states during the 1970s, pressures from the larger regional setting intensified substantially. In the late 1970s, the countries on the western flank of the Arab East were confronted with an overtly expansionist Israel that was becoming increasingly aggressive and adventurist. Israeli policies and behavior not only endangered the territorial integrity, security, and even national integrity (e.g., in Lebanon) of these states, but also threatened to reduce them to a subordinate and dependent position. The countries on the eastern flank were faced with different but perhaps equally serious pressures. The activities of the new Islamic revolutionary government in Iran threatened the regimes and the social peace (i.e., the intersectarian relations) of these states. The situation was exacerbated by a resurgence of Iranian military strength and the growing disposition of the Iranian leadership to resort to it. In recent years, the states of the eastern Arab world have been acutely aware of their vulnerability. Faced with threats from different quarters, Arab governments remained divided in their preoccupations, indecisive in their behavior, and dependent on one of the two superpowers to cope with intensified regional pressures.

NOTES

1. Michael Brecher, *The Foreign Policy System of Israel* (London and New York: Oxford University Press, 1972), pp. 1–7.

2. For a discussion of the impact of systemic characteristics on state behavior, see Kenneth Waltz, *Theory of International Politics* (Reading, Mass.: Addison-Wesley, 1979), Chs. 4, 5; and Richard Rosecrance, *International Politics: Peace and War* (New York: McGraw-Hill, 1973), Ch. 4.

3. Specifically, this study deals with the eastern Arab world, which includes Egypt, Syria, Iraq, Jordan, Lebanon, the Palestinian community, Saudi Arabia, and the remaining states of the Arabian Peninsula. Previous studies include Leonard Binder, "The Middle East as a Subordinate International System," *World Politics* 10, 3 (1958); M. Brecher, "The Middle East Subordinate System," *International Studies Quarterly* 15, 2 (1969); Paul Noble, *Regionalism and Conflict Management: The Case of the Arab System,* (Ph.D. diss., McGill University, 1971); and Ali Dessouki, "The New Arab Political Order: Implications for the 1980s," in Malcolm H. Kerr and El Sayed Yassin (eds.), *Rich and Poor States in the Middle East: Egypt and the New Arab Order* (Boulder, Colo.: Westview Press, 1982).

4. Daniel Lerner, *The Passing of Traditional Society* (Glencoe, Ill.: Free Press, 1958). See also Michael Hudson, *Arab Politics* (New Haven, Conn.: Yale University Press, 1977), pp. 4–5, 11–13, 126–162.

5. Manfred Halpern, *The Politics of Social Change in the Middle East and North Africa* (Princeton, N.J.: Princeton University Press, 1963).

6. For details on the opposition in Saudi Arabia see Helen Lackner, *A House Built on Sand* (London: Ithaca Press, 1978), pp. 93–105; and David Holden and Richard Johns, *The House of Saud* (New York: Holt, Rinehart and Winston, 1982), Chs. 13–15. On Jordan, see Benjamin Shwadran, *Jordan, A State of Tension* (New York: Council for Middle Eastern Affairs Press, 1959); and A. H. Abidi, *Jordan, A Political Study* (Bombay: Asia Publishing House, 1965).

7. Patrick Seale, *The Struggle for Syria* (London: Oxford University Press, 1965); Tabitha Petran, *Syria* (London: Ernest Benn, 1972); Itamar Rabinovitch, *Syria Under the Ba'th 1963–1966* (New York: Halsted Press, 1972).

8. Majid Khadduri, *Republican Iraq* (London: Oxford University Press, 1969).

9. For domestic developments in Egypt see Robert Stephens, *Nasser* (New York: Allen Lane, dist. Penguin Press, 1971); Raymond W. Baker, *Egypt's Uncertain Revolution Under Nasser and Sadat* (Cambridge, Mass.: Harvard University Press, 1978).

10. For a discussion of the main ideological currents during the 1950s and 1960s, see Majid Khadduri, *Political Trends in the Arab World* (Baltimore, Md.: Johns Hopkins University Press, 1970); Leonard Binder, *The Ideological Revolution*

in the Middle East (New York: Wiley, 1964), Chs. 6, 7; Sami Hanna and George Gardner, *Arab Socialism* (Leiden, Netherlands: Brill, 1969); R. Stephen Humphreys, "Islam and Political Values in Saudi Arabia, Egypt and Syria," *Middle East Journal* 57, 2 (1978).

11. Shwadran, *op. cit.*, pp. 312–344; Abidi, *op. cit.*, pp. 129–141; *New York Times*, March 29 and April 24, 1963, and January 13, 1964 (Jordan); Holden and Johns, *op. cit.*, pp. 196–197, 204 (Saudi Arabia); Fahim Quabain, *Crisis in Lebanon* (Washington, D.C.: Middle East Institute, 1961), Ch. 10; Michael Hudson, *The Precarious Republic* (New York: Random House, 1968), pp. 42–46, 93–101; and Kama Salibi, *Crossroads to Civil War* (Delmar, N.Y.: Caravan Books, 1976), pp. 11–12, 14–16 (Lebanon).

12. The leadership tended to be assertive toward the Western powers and occasionally toward Israel as well. The Syrian government adopted a very strong stance during the Jordan Waters conflict, partly because of its shaky domestic position. Edouard Saab, *La Syria ou la révolution dans la rancoeur* (Paris: Julliard, 1968), pp. 171–172. Iraq's more assertive posture on the Palestinian question as well as its claims on Kuwait may have been shaped by similar concerns. Khadduri, *Republican Iraq*, pp. 168–187.

13. This was evident in the late 1950s and in the 1960s, after Nasser's espousal of socialism and the advent to power of the Ba'th in Syria. See Malcolm Kerr, *The Arab Cold War*, 3rd ed. (London: Oxford University Press, 1965), pp. 5–7, 26–33; Petran, *op. cit.*, pp. 172–184, 195–196.

14. Hudson, *Arab Politics*, pp. 175–181; William Quandt, *Saudi Arabia in the 1980s* (Washington, D.C.: Brookings Institution, 1981), p. 106.

15. Moshe Maoz, "Syria Under Hafiz al-Asad: New Domestic and Foreign Policies," Jerusalem Papers on Peace Problems (Jerusalem: Leonard Davis Institute for International Relations, 1975), pp. 9–11, and "Hafiz al-Asad: A Political Profile," *Jerusalem Quarterly* 8 (1978), pp. 17, 23–31.

16. Majid Khadduri, *Socialist Iraq* (Washington, D.C.: Middle East Institute, 1978), pp. 69–76, 97–101, 177–179.

17. For domestic developments in Jordan, see Marc Yared, "Les institutions consacrent la suprématie de la monarchie Hachemite," *Le Monde Diplomatique*, November 1977; Samir Kassir, "Jordanie: Le moindre mal," *Le Monde Diplomatique*, May 1982.

18. For an analysis of the deteriorating situation in Lebanon and the subsequent civil war, see Salibi, *op. cit.*, and Walid Khalidi, *Conflict and Violence in Lebanon* (Cambridge, Mass.: Harvard Center for International Affairs, 1979).

19. See infra, notes 71, 73, 74, 85, and 96.

20. Robert Owen, "The Arab Economies in the 1970s," *MERIP Reports* 100–101 (1981); Malcolm Kerr, "Rich and Poor in the New Arab Order," *Journal of Arab Affairs* 1 (1981), pp. 6, 8–9.

21. For a discussion of changes in the Egyptian economic system and the decline of socialist ideology under Sadat, see John Waterbury, *Egypt: Burdens of the Past, Options for the Future* (Hanover, N.H.: American University Field Staff, 1972–1976), Part 3, Chs. 1, 2, and 5; Mark Cooper, *The Transformation of Egypt* (Baltimore: Johns Hopkins University Press, 1982), pp. 88–125. For economic liberation in Syria and its attendant problems, see Elisabeth Picard, "Le Syrie des militaires," *Le Monde Diplomatique*, April 1978; and Elisabeth Longuenesse, "The Class Nature of the State in Syria," *MERIP Reports* 77 (1979), pp. 7–8.

22. Adeed I. Dawisha, *Saudi Arabia's Search for Security*, Adelphi Paper No. 158 (London: Institute of Strategic Studies, 1979), pp. 1, 6–8, 10.

23. Dessouki, *op. cit.*, pp. 326–327.

24. See Saad Eddin Ibrahim, *The New Arab Social Order: A Study of the Social Impact of Oil Wealth* (Boulder, Colo.: Westview Press, 1982), Ch. 7, for a discussion of socioeconomic factors contributing to instability in the Arab countries.

25. For the growth of domestic opposition in Syria in the late 1970s, see S. F. Reed III, "Dateline Syria: Fin de Regime," *Foreign Policy* 39 (1980); "Vague d'agitation confessionnelle en Syrie," *Le Monde Diplomatique*, October 1979; P. Maler, "La société Syrienne contre son etat," *Le Monde Diplomatique*, April 1980; and A. Drysdale, "The Asad Regime and Its Troubles," *MERIP Reports* 110 (1982).

26. Hanna Batatu, "Iraq's Underground Shi'a Movements," *Middle East Journal* 34, 4 (1981); A. Faroughy, "Laicité et theocratie au Proche-Orient," *Le Monde Diplomatique*, November 1980; C. Kutschera, "Les vicissitudes de l'opposition democratique Irakienne," *Le Monde Diplomatique*, May 1982.

27. For a discussion of the religiously based opposition to the Saudi regime and the Mecca uprising see Holden and Johns, *op. cit.*, pp. 511–532; W. Ochsenwald, "Saudi Arabia and the Islamic Revival," *International Journal of Middle East Studies* 13, 3 (1981); J. Paul, "Insurrection at Mecca," *MERIP Reports* 91 (1980).

28. Selim Turquie, "Les inquietudes de l'Arabie Saoudite et des Emirats," *Le Monde Diplomatique*, January 1980, and "Dans les pays du Golfe," *Le Monde Diplomatique*, February 1980.

29. For an analysis of the 1977 riots and the factors that contributed to them, see Cooper, *op. cit.*, pp. 235–245.

30. See Malcolm Kerr, "Egypt and the Arabs in the Future," in Kerr and Yassin, *op. cit.*, for three scenarios regarding developments in Egypt.

31. For analyses of the role of Islam in contemporary Arab society, both generally and in particular countries, see Ali Dessouki (ed.), *Islamic Resurgence in the Arab World* (New York: Praeger Publishers, 1982) and J. Esposito (ed.), *Islam and Development* (Syracuse, N.Y.: Syracuse University Press, 1980).

32. Fouad Ajami, "The Struggle for Egypt's Soul," *Foreign Policy* 35 (1979), pp. 24–25.

33. See Kerr, "Egypt and the Arabs," pp. 468–472, for a scenario based on the advent of an Islamic fundamentalist regime in Saudi Arabia.

34. See Khalil Nakhleh and Elia Zureik (eds.), *The Sociology of the Palestinians* (New York: St. Martin's Press, 1980).

35. Ibrahim, *op. cit.*, Ch. 3.

36. The foremost example of this was Egypt's Voice of the Arabs in the 1950s and 1960s. See Lackner, *op. cit.*, pp. 85–86, for an indication of its audience in Saudi Arabia during this period.

37. Charles Cremeans, *The Arabs and the World* (New York: Praeger Publishers, 1963), pp. 84–85.

38. Peter Mansfield, *Nasser's Egypt* (Harmondsworth, Eng.: Penguin Books, 1965), pp. 55–60. See Seale, *op. cit.*, pp. 253–262, 309–315; and Hudson, *Precarious Republic*, pp. 95–96, for examples of Nasser's appeal in Syria and Lebanon respectively; see also Lackner, *op. cit.*, pp. 60–61, 99–100, 109; and Holden and Johns, *op. cit.*, pp. 188–189 on the popularity of Nasser and his ideas within Saudi Arabia.

39. See John F. Devlin, *The Ba'th Party* (Stanford, Calif.: Hoover Institution Press, 1976), Chs. 7, 10–15, on the Ba'th party; Walid Kazziha, *Revolutionary Transformation in the Arab World* (London: Charles Knight and Co., 1975) on

the Arab nationalist movement; Fred Halliday, *Arabia Without Sultans* (Harmondsworth, Eng.: Penguin Books, 1974), Ch. 11, especially pp. 386–390, on the PFLOAG.

40. Ishaq M. Husaini, *The Moslem Brethren* (Beirut: Khayat, 1956), Ch. 7; "Vague d'agitation," *op. cit.*

41. Noble, *op. cit.*, pp. 272–274.

42. K. Boals, "The Concept-Subordinate International System: A Critique," in R. Falk and S. Mendlovitz (eds.), *Regional Politics and World Order* (San Francisco: W. H. Freeman and Co., 1973), pp. 408–410.

43. Hudson, *Arab Politics*, pp. 5–7.

44. Fouad Ajami, "The End of Pan-Arabism," *Foreign Affairs*, 1978, pp. 355–356.

45. For an excellent discussion of this phenomenon, see *ibid.*, pp. 357–369.

46. *Ibid.*, p. 365.

47. *Ibid.*, pp. 358–360.

48. For a concise analysis of the economic and military relationship between Saudi Arabia and the United States see Joe Stork, "Saudi Arabia and the U.S.," *MERIP Reports* 91 (1980).

49. For an analysis of the development of Maronite "nationalism" see Tewfik Khalaf, "The Phalange and the Maronite Community: From Lebanonism to Maronitism," in Roger Owen (ed.), *Essays on the Crisis in Lebanon* (London: Ithaca Press, 1976).

50. Alan Taylor, *The Arab Balance of Power* (Syracuse, N.Y.: Syracuse University Press, 1982), pp. 93–94.

51. Citing opinion surveys taken in various Arab countries, Ibrahim maintains that the sense of Arab identity remains strong in the Arab world. Ibrahim, *op. cit.*, pp. 123–125. Ajami contends, however, that an opinion survey taken among students from various Arab countries studying at Kuwait University reveals a predominance of Islamic sentiment and of patriotism associated with independent Arab states. Ajami, "End of Pan-Arabism," p. 364.

52. This was particularly true of any military move against Jordan; see Shwadran, *op. cit.*, pp. 339–340; Abidi, *op. cit.*, p. 167; John Marlowe, *Arab Nationalism and British Imperialism* (London: Cresset Press, 1963), pp. 175–176.

53. On actual and potential Western intervention in the event of military moves, or even internal upheaval, affecting these states during this period, see Shwadran, *op. cit.*, p. 355; Nadav Safran, *From War to War* (New York: Pegasus, 1969), pp. 117–118; Humphrey Trevelyan, *The Middle East in Revolution* (London: Macmillan, 1970), pp. 190–194; Dana Adams Schmidt, *Yemen: The Unknown War* (London: Bodley Head, 1969), pp. 167–168, 186, 192.

54. Noble, *op. cit.*, p. 323, footnotes 107, 109; Adeed I. Dawisha, *Egypt in the Arab World* (London: Macmillan, 1976), pp. 88–89; Seale, *op. cit.*, pp. 196–198, 203–211.

55. For economic interaction within the Arab world in the 1960s, see A. G. Musrey, *An Arab Common Market* (New York: Praeger Publishers, 1969), Appendix, Tables 2–11.

56. See Table 3.4.

57. For the importance of propaganda as a technique of statecraft in the 1950s and 1960s, see Dawisha, *Egypt*, pp. 171–177. For cross-frontier alliances and subversion, see Seale, *op. cit.*

58. Kerr, "Egypt and the Arabs," p. 2; Ibrahim, *op. cit.*, pp. 154–159.

59. Ajami, "End of Pan-Arabism," pp. 359, 368.

60. *Ibid.*; Dawisha, *Egypt,* p. 173.

61. Dessouki, "New Arab Order," p. 329; Kerr, "Rich and Poor," p. 23.

62. For an analysis of Saudi Arabia's rising status in the global system, see Bahgat Korany, "Petro-puissance et système mondial: Le cas de l'Arabie Saoudite," *Etudes Internationales* 10, 4 (1979), p. 797. See, however, Ali Dessouki's warning about the "fragility" of Saudi Arabian power, "New Arab Order," p. 330.

63. For an original and perceptive treatment of stratification in the Arab system, see Ibrahim, *op. cit.,* pp. 132–148.

64. For a discussion of Saudi Arabian activities and influence within the Arabian Peninsula during this period, see Dawisha, *Saudi Arabia's Search,* pp. 19–21; Quandt, *op. cit.,* pp. 23–28, 34; and Holden and Johns, *op. cit.,* pp. 426–427, 446–448, 474–476.

65. For an outline of Syria's efforts to create a sphere of influence in geographic Syria during the mid-1970s, see Daniel Dishon, "The Web of Inter-Arab Relations," *Jerusalem Quarterly* 2 (Winter 1977), pp. 52–54; Itamar Rabinovitch, "The Limits of Military Power: Syria's Role," in P. Edward Haley and Lewis Snider, *Lebanon in Crisis* (Syracuse, N.Y.: Syracuse University Press, 1979), pp. 57–59.

66. Binder, "The Middle East."

67. For a fuller explanation of the concepts and events, see Noble, *op. cit.,* Chs. 7–8.

68. See *ibid.,* pp. 315–324, on the techniques of statecraft.

69. Dessouki, "New Arab Order," pp. 326–327; Taylor, *op. cit.,* pp. 51–53.

70. Quandt, *op. cit.,* pp. 66–67.

71. See Holden and Johns, *op. cit.,* pp. 291–297, for a discussion of the Saudi-Egyptian rapprochement and of Saudi activities as an intermediary between Egypt and the United States in the early 1970s.

72. For an outline of Egypt's developing political relations with the United States see Anwar Sadat, *In Search of Identity* (New York: Harper & Row, 1977), pp. 276–305. For the development of military relations, see Joe Stork, "The Carter Doctrine and U.S. Bases in the Middle East," *MERIP Reports* 90 (1980), pp. 7–9.

73. Galia Golan and Itamar Rabinovitch, "The Soviet Union and Syria: The Limits of Cooperation," in Yaacov Ro'i (ed.), *The Limits of Power* (New York: St. Martin's Press, 1979), pp. 216, 220–223.

74. Adeed I. Dawisha, "Iraq Changes Course," *Middle East International,* May 23, 1980.

75. Dishon, *op. cit.,* p. 46; L. Snider, "Inter-Arab Relations," in Haley and Snider, *op. cit.,* pp. 192–193.

76. William Quandt, *Decade of Decisions* (Berkeley: University of California Press, 1977), pp. 200–286; Harvey Sicherman, *Broker or Advocate* (Philadelphia: Foreign Policy Research Institute, 1978). For Israeli policy toward Egypt under the Begin government, see Moshe Dayan, *Breakthrough* (New York: Alfred A. Knopf, 1981); and Ezer Weizmann, *The Battle For Peace* (New York: Bantam Books, 1981).

77. In February 1971, Sadat indicated his willingness to conclude a peace agreement with Israel without any indications that Israel was prepared to return Egyptian territory captured in the 1967 war. In June 1975, he announced his willingness to reopen the Suez Canal even though the proposed second stage disengagement agreement had fallen through in March. In November 1977 he took the dramatic initiative of visiting Jerusalem and thus effectively recognizing Israel before any satisfactory peace agreement had been worked out. See Joe

Stork, "Sadat's Desperate Mission," *MERIP Reports* 64 (1978), and Sadat, *op. cit.*, pp. 273–274, 279–280, 302–312.

78. Asad had stated as early as March 1973 that he was prepared to accept UN Resolution 242 with the proviso that Palestinian rights be recognized. Maoz, *Syria Under Hafiz al-Asad*, p. 15. For the evolution of PLO policy toward Israel after the 1973 war, as well as some references to Syrian policy, see Sameer Abraham, "The P.L.O. at the Crossroads," *MERIP Reports* 80 (1979).

79. Ajami, "End of Pan-Arabism," p. 365. Dawisha emphasizes the prevalence of territorial issues in the Arab system. Adeed I. Dawisha, "The Middle East," in Christopher Clapham (ed.), *Foreign Policy-Making in Developing States* (New York: Praeger Publishers, 1977), pp. 52–53. This point would seem to be primarily applicable to the 1950s and 1960s.

80. Khadduri, *Socialist Iraq*, pp. 153–159.

81. For a discussion of Syrian objectives in Lebanon, see Khalidi, *op. cit.*, pp. 82–84, 110, 116–117, 150–152; and Rabinovitch in Haley and Snider, *op. cit.*, pp. 56–60, 67–73.

82. Adeed I. Dawisha, *Syria and the Lebanese Crisis* (New York: St. Martin's Press, 1980), pp. 109, 124–139, 157–166, 185–193; *Arab World Weekly* (Beirut: Arab World Press Agency), October 2, 1976, pp. 8–9, and October 16, 1976, pp. 5–6; and *Middle East Reporter Weekly* (Beirut: Press Services and Documentation Bureau), July 28, 1979, pp. 13–15.

83. Petran, *op. cit.*, pp. 247–248, 253–254; Adeed I. Dawisha, "Much Smoke, Little Fire," *Middle East International*, February 27, 1981.

84. Holden and Johns, *op. cit.*, pp. 272–282, 487–488, 501–502.

85. For the rapprochement between Iraq and Saudi Arabia since 1978, see *ibid.*, pp. 488–489; Dawisha, *Saudi Arabia's Search*, pp. 21–22; and Taylor, *op. cit.*, pp. 81–88.

86. See Kerr, "Rich and Poor," pp. 28–30; and Dawisha, *Egypt*, pp. 146–147, for the distinction between the two approaches. See Dawisha, p. 200, note 69, for the "deradicalization" of Egyptian foreign policy.

87. Dawisha, *Saudi Arabia's Search*, p. 1.

88. For Syrian political warfare activities directed against Iraq, see *Arab World Weekly*, July 31, 1976, p. 13; *Middle East Reporter Weekly*, August 18, 1979, pp. 8–10, August 23, 1980, pp. 8–9, December 6, 1980, pp. 15–18, and April 17, 1982, pp. 12–14. For a detailed study of Syrian involvement in Lebanon since 1975, see Dawisha, *Syria and the Lebanese Crisis*, and Khalidi, *op. cit.*

89. For Iraqi activities against Syria, see *Arab World Weekly*, April 12, 1975, p. 3, October 2, 1976, p. 5, and December 11, 1976, pp. 7–8; *Middle East Reporter Weekly*, January 13, 1979, p. 9, April 5, 1980, pp. 18–19, and April 7, 1982, pp. 12–14.

90. Kerr, *Arab Cold War*, *op. cit.*, pp. 5–6, 25–33, 40, 106, 110–117, 126.

91. *Ibid.*, pp. 17–18, 85–91, 102.

92. *New York Times*, August 30, 1962; Edgar O'Ballance, *The War in the Yemen* (London: Faber and Faber, 1971), pp. 86–88; Kerr, *Arab Cold War*, pp. 106, 114, 126.

93. Kerr, *Arab Cold War*, pp. 117, 121–125.

94. On the developing entente between Egypt and Saudi Arabia in the early 1970s, see Holden and Johns, *op. cit.*, pp. 291–297. On the improvement in Saudi Arabian–Syrian relations in the same period, see pp. 298–299, and Petran, *op. cit.*, pp. 252–253.

95. Paul Jabber, "Oil, Arms and Regional Diplomacy," in Kerr and Yassin, *op. cit.*, pp. 430–439.

96. Taylor, *op. cit.*, pp. 51–53; Fouad Ajami, "Stress in the Arab Triangle," *Foreign Policy* 29 (1977/1978), pp. 92–99.

97. Dishon, *op. cit.*, pp. 47–51; Holden and Johns, *op. cit.*, pp. 422–423.

98. For Saudi attempts to reconcile Egypt and Syria, see M. Graeme Bannerman, "Saudi Arabia," in Haley and Snider, *op. cit.*, pp. 119–129.

99. Taylor, *op. cit.*, pp. 55, 59.

100. Holden and Johns, *op. cit.*, pp. 481–506; Quandt, *Saudi Arabia*, pp. 16–17, 113–116; and Taylor, *op. cit.*, pp. 73–81.

101. Taylor, *op. cit.*, pp. 73–81.

102. *Ibid.*, pp. 81–94.

Algeria

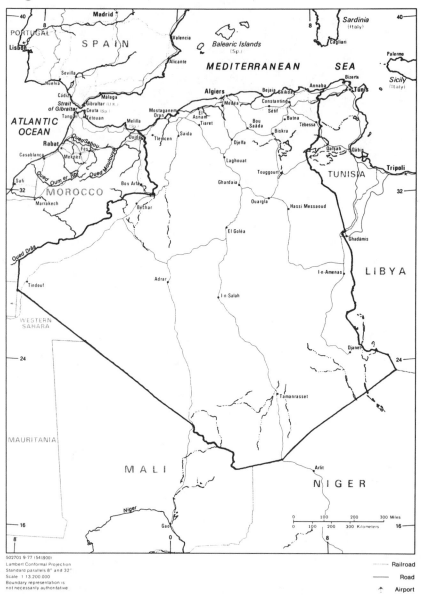

502701 9-77 (541900)
Lambert Conformal Projection
Standard parallels 8° and 32°
Scale 1 13,200.000
Boundary representation is
not necessarily authoritative

------- Railroad

――――― Road

⬥ Airport

4

Third Worldism and Pragmatic Radicalism: The Foreign Policy of Algeria

Bahgat Korany

INTRODUCTION: A THIRD WORLD SHOWPIECE

Algeria is an important gas and oil producer, with a comparatively large and rapidly growing market, and is engaged in an active and accelerated development process. The crude indicator of gross national product (GNP) ranks Algeria high among Mediterranean and developing countries: just below Spain, on a par with Yugoslavia and Turkey, and above Greece, Portugal, Morocco, and Egypt.[1]

As a foreign policy actor, Algeria holds a key diplomatic position. It is located at the crossroads of Europe, Africa, and the Arab world. For many Third World countries, it represents a model national liberation movement. It paid "one million martyrs" to gain real independence whereas other countries in French-speaking Africa were "granted so-called independence." Indeed, when Frantz Fanon, the psychoanalyst from Martinique and the "Third World Marx," aimed at elaborating a theory of Third World national liberation, he took Algeria as his frame of reference.[2]

Algeria's revolutionary élan continued after independence not only with the ideology of its first president, Ahmed Ben Bella (1962–1965), but also with the pragmatism of President Boumedienne (1965–1978). It was, after all, in Boumedienne's Algeria that the Group of 77 first met (October 1967) and established the charter that governs the Third World position in North/South negotiations. When the nonaligned movement seemed in disarray, its fourth summit (Algiers, September 1973) marked its renewal and its reorientation. It was Boumedienne, as the mandated head of the Third World, who addressed the 1974 special session of the UN General Assembly, the assembly that enunciated the concept of the New International Economic Order. One could cite many other examples of Algeria as "la montreuse de conduite" (the exemplar of behavior) in its desire to restructure international relations.

Yet it is the United States, the "height of world imperialism" and the guardian of the "anachronistic status quo," that was Algeria's chief commercial partner during the 1970s. Algeria's graduate students, i.e., its future managers and governing elite, flock in increasing numbers to North American universities. In 1970, there were 46 Algerians in North American graduate programs; in 1978, there were 1,720. Does this reveal a contradiction or inconsistency in Algeria's foreign policy between "say" and "do"? If so, is this inconsistency merely tactical, i.e., partial, limited, and probably temporary; or is it strategic, i.e., basic, comprehensive, and structural? How can this inconsistency be measured and explained?

The first section of this chapter deals with the bases of foreign policy, emphasizing the impact of the colonial legacy on social structure and exploring the linkage between developmental needs and foreign policy. Section 2 concentrates on Algeria's critique of the contemporary global system and its demand for international restructuring through Third World coalition-building. The third section focuses on the decision-making process, analyzing the participation of both institutions and elites. The fourth examines Algeria's practice of foreign policy at the superpower, Third World, and regional Arab-African levels. The chapter concludes with an investigation of the principles and the actual conduct of foreign policy in the bid to free U.S. hostages in Iran in January 1981. Due to space limitations, the chapter does not emphasize those aspects of Algeria's foreign policy that the standard literature has already treated in detail (e.g., relations with France).

1. THE DOMESTIC ENVIRONMENT

A review of the literature on Algeria published in French or English between 1965 and 1975 reveals some points of agreement among authors in the field.[3] The factors most frequently cited as determinants of Algeria's foreign policy were—in descending order of importance—ideology, internal politics, the state of the economy, and relations with France. Somewhat less important were leadership personality and membership in the African subsystem—which received more attention than membership in the Third World, the Middle East, and the Mediterranean subsystem. Relations with the superpowers were practically ignored, as was participation in nonregional organizations such as OPEC.

Geography, Population, and Social Structure

For the Algerians, the formation of foreign policy is first and foremost linked to Algeria's very special colonial legacy. For France, Algeria was not a colony, but a part of France, another *département* or province. Geography played an important role in this special colonial relationship. The relative proximity of Algeria and France had two major effects: it incited France to frenchify Algeria, and it encouraged hundreds of thousands of Algerians to seek jobs in France. After independence, these workers became an element of contention and heated negotiations between France and Algeria. Not only were these migrant workers a source of needed foreign currency for Algeria's gigantic development program, but the Algerian economy could not have absorbed their massive repatriation.

Of the 2.4 million square kilometers that constitute Algeria's surface, four-fifths is desert. The result is that 90% of Algeria's 20 million people are concentrated in the fertile and narrow littoral of hills and plains in the north by the Mediterranean. The Mitidja Plains, which extend 100 km westwards from Algiers, are highly urbanized and are under increasing pressure from immigrants from the rural areas and the hinterland.

The Sahara, however, provides Algeria with its natural resources. It was on the question of the Sahara that the last stages of Algerian-French negotiations for independence were broken off in 1961. France wanted a special status for the Sahara, a status that the Algerian negotiators adamantly refused. The Sahara, moreover, gives Algeria its African depth. Extending 1,500 km to its common frontiers with Niger and Mali, the Sahara puts Algeria in direct contact with Black Africa. Rather than accept that this vast stretch constituted a barrier between "Black" and "White" Africa, Algeria has made of the Sahara an African bridge by developing the trans-Saharan route and other means of transport. In this way, Algeria's role on the African political scene is facilitated.[4]

Proximity to France and the Saharan stretch have both left their imprint on Algeria's population and social structure. The pre-1830 Ottoman Algerian society was typical of other precolonial societies. It possessed a marked segmentation between Arabs and Berbers, nomadic herdsmen and subsistence farmers; its social organization—especially in the rural areas—reflected kinship ties. The influx of European settlers brought a new element to the existing social diversity.[5] Given the big differences in economic status and social values between the colonists and the local populations, the most important distinction in Algeria became that between "Europeans" and "Moslems." The discrimination and disabilities that Moslems suffered in France's drive to Europeanize Algeria created a strong bond of unity within the local population.

In relative terms, however, the 132 years of colonization were not as cataclysmic for Algeria's basic social organization as the 8-year War of Independence (1954–1962). For despite efforts at Europeanization and economic disruption, the rural inhabitants had managed to keep intact most of their social values, kinship organization, and traditional family ties. The War of Independence was to strike at precisely these elements:

> Individuals developed new perceptions of themselves, their abilities, and their roles through wartime activities. Women, accustomed to the sheltered

and segregated life traditional in Muslim countries, found themselves suddenly thrown into revolutionary militancy. . . . Many young people struck out independently of their families and elders, and new leaders emerged, chosen more for personal traits than for social position.[6]

France's policy of resettlement of 2 to 3 million Algerians during the war (the regroupment centers) further disrupted traditional ties and created instead bonds and solidarity networks based on shared identity as Moslems and Algerians. Three results followed from the situation of fast social change initiated by the War of Independence.

First, efforts to redress the disruptions and inequities of the colonial structure still take up a large proportion of government resources and permeate educational and cultural life. Even though segregated schooling of French and Moslem children had been abolished in 1949, Moslem schools were still in an inferior position on the eve of independence in 1962. The Europe-oriented curricula were taught exclusively in French; less than 30% of Moslem children were enrolled in the primary schools; and less than 10% of Moslem students reached the university level. Immediately after independence, the massive European exodus added to the problems. The educational system was in disarray and enrollment in schools at all levels fell to 850,000. A big push was needed: teachers were hastily recruited and trained, expatriate teachers were brought back, and classrooms were improvised in the homes vacated by French residents who had left. By 1967, school attendance had climbed to 1.5 million; in 1975 it reached nearly 3 million.[7] Between 1960 and 1979, the number of students enrolled in primary schools (expressed as a percentage of the age group) rose from 46% to 98%, secondary schools enrollment jumped from 8% to 31%; and the adult literacy rate rose from 10% to 31%.[8]

Even though this crisis is over, developing and putting the educational system in order is still a priority for Algeria. Between 1973 and 1977, Algeria contracted three education loans from the World Bank totaling $101.5 million. Of the 36,000 university students in 1975, some 25,000 were recipients of government fellowships, and an additional 1,800 fellowships were awarded for study abroad.[9] In 1978, 27% of the total budget was allocated to education. The task includes the development and the revision of the educational system, which, Moslem religion schools apart, had been conducted in a foreign language by foreign teachers. The revision of curricula and the development of new textbooks was necessary for the expression of Algeria's Arab-Moslem identity.

Second, the mobilization of the people during the war released mass energies and whetted rising expectations that were not completely satisfied with the advent of independence. Because the nascent political system was incapable of meeting these expectations in toto and immediately, dissatisfaction developed among the population. This dissatisfaction is ready raw material for political conflict and domestic turmoil. In such a context, social issues (e.g., neofundamentalist movements and Berber cultural demands) are quickly politicized.

For instance, though very few doubt the finality of the arabization program, its application has caused conflict among elites and social groups representing diverse cultural backgrounds. On the one hand are those educated in the French cultural tradition, who are in some cases more familiar with the French than with the classical Arabic heritage. Indeed, many prominent leaders of the War of Independence found it easier to speak in French, and many are still active in FLN (Front de liberation nationale) cultural and party activities. On the other hand are the religious scholars who enjoy great prestige from their knowledge of Islam's sacred texts. With them are graduates of prestigious centers of Islamic learning, and other elements of the population increasingly familiar with, or interested in, the contemporary Arab renaissance.

What makes these issues central to Algeria's social scene is that even the discussion of technicalities takes place within the context of a focus on cultural identity, the status of the French language, and the place of Islamic principles in a fast-moving, industrializing society. These issues are of course related to the status and role of the social groups espousing the different positions. Thus in his speech of November 29, 1971, in the conference of the nation's cadres, Boumedienne tried to reassure those whose position might be hurt by arabization: "after all," he said, "people are not responsible for their exclusive French formation."[10]

The third major concern of the government is reducing the effects of social cleavages and promoting the society's integration. Algeria's political orientation and behavior—domestic and international—has to satisfy "basic needs," both material and spiritual. Thus the constitution insists that Algeria is a Moslem country, that its socialism is an Islamic socialism, that Algeria is part of the Arab-Moslem world, and that it supports the continuation of the anticolonial revolution. Politics are at the center of Algerian society, and this brings us to the discussion of political structure.

Political Structure

At the political-administrative level, Algeria is divided into 31 *wilayat* (provinces or *départements*), 91 *daïrates* (counties or *arrondissements*), and 676 districts or *communes*.[11] Ultimate political authority resides in the FLN, Algeria's only official political party (established in 1954), and the National Assembly. For the major period of Algeria's independence, the assembly's function was assumed by the Council of the Revolution (1965–1977), which Boumedienne established following the "Adjustment Revolution" that overthrew Ben Bella in June 1965. However, the description of this formal structure in no way reveals how Algeria's corporatist state actually works. To understand the system's functioning, one must keep in mind, first, Algeria's colonial legacy and the effects of the War of Independence on the structure of political elites, and second, the primacy of development and industrialization.

As a result of the national liberation war, the government, the party, and the parliament of Algeria were created before the state itself was established. In 1956, a 17-member protoparliament—the National Council of the Algerian Revolution[12] (CNRA: Conseil national de la révolution algérienne)—was established as the ultimate wartime authority of the party, the FLN. In 1958, the National Council established in its turn Algeria's Provisional Government (GPRA: Gouvernement provisoire de la république algérienne).[13] What made the creation of these institutions both necessary and credible was the launching of the liberation war by the guerrilla army—the *maquisards*—in November 1954. This institutional development explains both the status and the role of the different social groups—especially the army—in the postindependence period.

Following the conclusion of the 1962 Evian Agreements, elections were to take place for the first time in independent Algeria in August 1962, but the elections were put off because of infighting among the Algerian leaders. There were two major divisions in this power struggle.

The first division was between the politicians and the military. Members of the Provisional Government felt they had the legitimacy to run the country; the military felt that as they had won the war that made independence possible, they deserved political recognition of their primary role. However, neither the politicians nor the military represented a neatly demarcated or monolithic group. Consequently, there was a second cleavage, between internals and externals. Within the military were two groups: the rurally oriented *wilaya* guerrillas (the internal army), and the professional army, concentrated in neighboring countries during the war (the external army). The internal army was disbanded as a distinct entity after independence, whereas the external army became the basis of the ANP (Armée nationale populaire).

To constitute the first postindependence government, the prestigious leader Ahmed Ben Bella (a politician, external), supported by Colonel Boumedienne (also an external), urged the FLN to replace the Provisional Government by the Political Bureau,[14] where he was strong.

> Although never formally approved by the CNRA [the National Council], the Political Bureau soon eclipsed the authority of the GPRA. By September [1962] dissident regional guerrilla commanders had also accepted the authority of the Political Bureau, which then prepared electoral lists for the National Assembly envisioned in the Evian Agreements. It drew heavily from Ben Bella's supporters and political unknowns in the process.[15]

On September 26, 1962, the assembly—itself elected only six days earlier—gave its legitimizing stamp to the de facto power of the Ben Bella–Boumedienne team. Ben Bella became the head of the first post-independence government[16] and Boumedienne became minister of defense.

This victory, however, did not put an end to the elite infighting. The drafting of the constitution and its approval a year after independence caused further dissension. A small group of the Political Bureau drafted the document and presented it first to the FLN conference. In protest against being bypassed, National Assembly president and ex-head of the GPRA Ferhat Abbas resigned in August 1963.

The constitution (approved in a referendum on September 8, 1963) instituted the *formal* supremacy of the FLN, which became the only political organization in Algeria. In reality, however, the constitution legitimized the political role of the army and consolidated the role of the president as both head of state and government and commander of the armed forces. The president appointed all high civil and military officials, and had almost no legislative check on his authority. Moreover, he could dissolve the National Assembly, but the assembly could not dislodge the president, whose mandate came to an end only through death or voluntary resignation.[17]

President Ben Bella was, however, removed in June 1965 by a military coup headed by his minister of defense and former ally, Colonel Boumedienne. Ben Bella was accused of monopolizing power, of manipulating divisions to reinforce the party against the army, and within the army itself of attempting to turn "internals" against "externals" so as to exclude Boumedienne and his supporters. For a transitional period— which in fact continued for almost twelve years and ended a year before Boumedienne's death—the new leader eliminated the Political Bureau and the National Assembly, thus further weakening the FLN. Instead, the country was run by two institutions: the twenty-six-member, all-powerful CNR,[18] which was the real policy-making body, composed mainly of the military plus some members of the defunct Political Bureau; and the Council of Ministers,[19] an executive body that ran the daily affairs of the country. Though the 1963 constitution was never formally abolished, the decree of July 10, 1965, transferred its power to the CNRA, "the depository of sovereign authority." Thus Boumedienne's 1965 "Correction" or "Adjustment Revolution" enhanced further the power of both the president and the military.

The 199 articles of the 1976 constitution, which was based on the National Charter of 1976, did not change these two characteristics of the political system.[20] As the single candidate nominated, Boumedienne was elected president on December 10, 1976, by 95.8% of the registered electorate, including emigrants abroad. Up until his death two years later, Boumedienne had no vice-president and he continued as both prime minister and minister of defense. When he fell seriously ill, effective and legal rule was transferred, on November 22, 1978, to colonels Chadli Bendjedid and Abdallah Belhouchet, commanders of the second and first military regions respectively.

With Boumedienne's death in December 1978, there were serious attempts to modify the one-man presidential pattern, but in retrospect it appears that the system was not drastically changed. With the support of the 640 army delegates Bendjedid emerged from the February 1979

FLN congress as the winner against his two rivals, Abdel-Aziz Bouteflika and Mohamed Yahiaoui, to replace Boumedienne. The party congress, however, favored the principle of collective leadership, and it redistributed the five posts previously concentrated in Boumedienne's hands. Thus, Colonel Mohamed Abdelghani—former military commander of Oran and Constantine and former member of the CNR—was appointed prime minister and also interior minister. Constitutional amendments passed on June 30, 1979, and January 7, 1980, aimed at reducing the president's powers, stating that the president must appoint a prime minister and has the right to appoint a vice-president. Moreover, the National Assembly was given the power to remove the president in the case of incapacitation due to ill health.

However, the powers of personnel and institutions outside the presidential center were still limited. Though it attempted to strengthen the FLN's position, the February 1979 party congress failed to separate the post of the FLN secretary-general from that of the president. In 1979, a decree defined the functions of the prime minister as "to help the President of the Republic with the coordination of government activities and implementation of the resolutions adopted by the Council of Ministers."[21] Moreover, his "organizational powers [are] delegated to him by the President."[22]

In the end, Bendjedid—who never relinquished the post of defense minister—emerged as the leader of both government and party institutions. He reduced the membership of the Political Bureau from seventeen to seven, took the position of interior minister from the prime minister and gave it to an ally, and curtailed the powers of both Bouteflika and Yahiaoui, his former rivals to the presidency. Bendjedid finally "completed the replacement of the allies of Belaid Abdesselam, Czar of the centralized heavy industry," during the reign of Boumedienne.[23]

The reference to Abdesselam indicates the presence of other influential groups outside the military. Prime emphasis on development, with the aim of "industrializing industry," led to the creation of two separate ministries for industry alone, and the formation of a growing technocratic elite with a policy-making role.[24] This brings us to the issue of development and economic capabilities.

Economic Capabilities and the Primacy
of Accelerated Industrialization

During Algeria's twenty years of independence, its economic policy has influenced its foreign policy in two major ways. Increasing state interventionism has caused the swelling of a technocratic or managerial elite with a policy-making role; and the increasing role of the hydrocarbons sector in the development plans enhanced Algeria's need both to find foreign economic partners and to develop sufficient credibility to borrow easily on international markets.

Though Algeria inherited a relatively good infrastructure (roads, airports), its economy at the time of independence was heavily distorted; it had been organized to function as part of France's economy and not as the economy of an independent country. An example is the concentration on vineyards and wine in a Moslem country. Economic dependence on the French market[25] put Algeria in a difficult position during the negotiations for independence and in the early years of the new state.

During those early years, the economy was also burdened with problems resulting from the War of Independence: considerable internal migration, the destruction of crops, the havoc wreaked on roads and transportation, the reduction in investments, and the deterioration of manufacturing and agricultural equipment. Moreover, the sudden departure of many French and European managers and owners[26] at the time of independence resulted in much waste and inefficiency. These conditions explain why Boumedienne's 1965 Adjustment Revolution turned inward to emphasize a nationalist form of socialism, accelerated industrialization, and hence growing state interventionism.

Development planning started in earnest with the three-year plan for 1967–1969, but the state had already been active in the economic sector. The departure of Europeans caused more than 700 factories to fall by default to the state[27] and to worker self-management. In 1966, the government nationalized major portions of the mining sector; in 1968, the large-scale manufacturing firms, and in 1970 and 1971, the hydrocarbon industry. Moreover, some private firms that either had difficulty with their workers or did not see eye to eye with the government were also nationalized. Though adequate compensation was paid, these nationalizations affected Algeria's foreign relations, particularly relations with France in 1970 and 1971.[28]

This last case is important for the economic capabilities–foreign policy linkage. Given the legacy of relations with a colonizing power and the need for nationalization and economic restructuring, Algerian-French relations were bound to suffer. Algerian policy-makers had to find other economic partners in order to increase their overall bargaining power and to pursue their development objectives much more freely: hence the rising importance of the United States in Algeria's economic relations. This aspect of the linkage between economic capabilities and foreign policy becomes even clearer when we consider the hydrocarbon sector.

Compared to many developing countries, Algeria had a piece of good luck at the time of independence: its hydrocarbon sector had been developed by private French firms with the help of the French government. As a result, Algeria escaped the hardship of immediate postindependence balance-of-payment deficits. On the negative side, however, this sector was not under Algeria's control and hence could not be properly integrated into the development plans. To remedy this situation, a national corporation was established in the last days of 1963: SONATRACH (Société nationale de transport et de commercialisation des hydrocarbures). By 1965, SONATRACH had redefined relations with foreign oil companies and made concessions subject to review every five years.

By the time of the first review, two new developments had occurred: the rise of OPEC and the acceleration of Algeria's socialist transformation. Thus, in February and April 1971, the Algerian government nationalized up to 51% of every petroleum exploration and production facility, and 100% of all natural gas and oil pipelines and other transport facilities. Foreign interests were to operate as junior partners or on a contract basis with SONATRACH. Thus between 1966 and 1972 the government considerably increased its control over the hydrocarbon sector: in exploitation areas, from 12% to 100%; in oil production, from 11.5% to 77%; in natural gas reserves, from 18% to 100%; in pipeline transport, from 38% to 100%; in refining, from 20.4% to 100%; and in distribution within Algeria, from 0 to 100%.[29] By 1978, SONATRACH had become the tenth largest oil company in the world.[30] Its managers are bound to influence the economic policy / foreign policy linkage in the future because of the primacy of industrial development and the vital role played by hydrocarbons in attaining this objective.

In 1978, a joint study by SONATRACH and the huge multinational Bechtel Corporation, entitled "Hydrocarbon Development Plan of Algeria, Financial Projections 1976–2005," was made public. This plan set the background for future development in the country.[31] As Chadli Bendjedid put it in an interview with Le Monde on November 1, 1979: "We have a global development strategy based on industrialization. . . . There is no question of going back on this path. . . . On the contrary, we have to maintain and improve the implementation of our policies while correcting inadequacies."[32] The sale of a large portion of the hydrocarbon reserves was the means of creating Algeria's large and integrated industrial base.

Indeed, reviewing Algeria's economic performance during the 1970s, one sees that it has been closely correlated with performance in the hydrocarbon sector. The revenue of this sector has risen considerably, from $1 million in 1958 to $1,050 million in 1973 and $4,100 million in 1974. The economy's growth rate followed closely. Thus when the value added in the export-oriented hydrocarbon sector was at an annual average of 4.9% during the 1973–1978 period, the gross domestic product (GDP) growth rate for 1974–1977 was 6.4%. When the hydrocarbon growth rate accelerated to 10% in 1978, the GDP growth rate increased as well, reaching the high point of 10.8% in 1978.[33]

Both the GDP and the hydrocarbon sector growth rates are crucial for Algeria's international status and its credibility in world financial markets. In early 1980, the Banque nationale d'Algérie was able to sign the best deal ever for an Algerian borrower on the international money markets: $200 million for ten years with five years grace at an annual interest rate of 0.875% above LIBOR (London Interbank Offered Rate). Earlier deals had averaged spreads of more than 1% above LIBOR.

This standing in international financial markets is important because Algeria borrows heavily to meet investment and development needs. In 1978, SONATRACH's international borrowing reached more than $3,200 million in loans and bonds. Algeria's external debt had reached just under $20 billion by early 1980. However, increased (hydrocarbon) revenue had allowed the debt-service ratio to decrease from 25% to 22.7% of the total debt by the beginning of 1980.[34] The world oil glut of the early 1980s and Algeria's efforts at oil conservation are expected to reduce revenue and increase borrowing if the 1980–1984 development plan (whose projected investments total four times those of the 1974–1977 plan) is to be respected. If we add to these financial needs the $33.4 billion (with more than 50% in foreign financing) required to carry out the above-mentioned SONATRACH-Bechtel Hydrocarbon Development Plan, the necessity for Algeria to continue its pragmatic radicalism to maintain its credibility and increase its borrowing facilities in international financial markets is clear.

The linkage between the state of the economy and foreign policy involves the impact of the SONATRACH-Bechtel Hydrocarbon Development Plan in another way—in the extension of pipelines to Europe, pipelines that have to go through the territories of neighboring countries. The pipeline to Italy must run through Tunisia, and the project was nearly abandoned in early 1977 because of Tunisian reluctance to have the pipeline cross its territory. But in 1977, Italy—not Algeria—signed the agreement for the construction of the Tunisian section, and on June 16, 1979, Bendjedid officially inaugurated work for the 2,498-km gas pipeline, Transmed.[35] This effect of petroleum on foreign policy is not unrelated to the 1982–1983 Algerian-Tunisian high-level visits that led to the conclusion of the twenty-year "Treaty of Brotherhood and Concord" between the two countries.[36] Similarly, the route of the planned gas pipeline to Spain was changed in June 1979. Instead of the planned Oued-Al-Malah/Almeria route, it will now be moved further from the Moroccan border, running from Oran to Cartagena.[37] The February 1983 meeting between King Hassan II and President Bendjedid at the Algerian-Moroccan border was arranged not only to stop the escalation toward direct military confrontation over the Western Sahara question, but also to discuss each country's economic considerations.[38]

Military Capabilities

The record is ambiguous on Algeria's military capabilities at the time of independence. Some elements of military training were provided during the period of colonization. For instance, Algerian recruits were used within French "pacification forces" during the 132-year colonial domination. Similarly, during World War II 200,000 Algerians provided needed military manpower for the French army, and they fought with valor against the Germans from France's trenches.

The army formed after independence was completely different in outlook, for it was based on the militants who launched the 1954 revolution. Boumedienne's task was to convert the guerrilla force into a modern military institution. To attain this objective, he had to find the means to acquire sophisticated weapons, train personnel, and build sectors such as the air force and the navy from scratch.

Given the heterogeneity of the ALN (Armée de liberation nationale), the task of putting an end to factionalism and of building the professional ANP proved difficult. From 1962 to 1968, factionalism led to abortive rebellions or *wilayism* (narrow *wilaya* or province-oriented power) every year except in 1966.[39] In 1967, the ANP squashed an attempted coup d'état. By the end of the 1960s, however, the task of building an army seemed to have been successful. Boumedienne stated in October 1969:

> The edification of the state, in its broadest sense, requires the simultaneous constitution of an armed force. This operation has proceeded according to our plans. The army of peasants and workers, the army of the poor, is each being transformed into a modern army equipped with the most recent techniques and composed of dozens, if not hundreds, of engineers and technicians. Although carried out in silence, without vain publicity, this action has nonetheless met our expectations.[40]

What type of individuals is this army composed of, and what are the soldiers' patterns of political socialization, their political beliefs, their values? According to a study published by the American University in Washington, D.C., this was the prototype of the Algerian career soldier in 1978:

> [He] was the son of a peasant or an urban laborer. He had the reputation of being tough, hardy, and amenable to discipline. He had a strong sense of national pride and military loyalty deriving from the accomplishments of the country's revolutionary fighters, some of whom were still in the ranks with him or among his senior officers. Moreover, he had been thoroughly indoctrinated in the nationalist and socialist goals of the continuing revolution.[41]

The army—whether the external professional group or the internal *mujahiddin* (warriors) group—has been the basis of the nationalist policy of Arab-Moslem Algeria. Did not Boumedienne say to Mohamed Heikal, *Al-Ahram's* editor-in-chief, "We are above all militants"?[42] Thus when the third Arab-Israeli war erupted in June 1967, Algeria immediately sent to Egypt a battalion-size combat team of infantry and artillery and about 100 MiG planes; on June 25, 1967, Algeria made conscription compulsory. But this involvement was not allowed to divert funds from the development sector toward the army. From 1965 to 1973 the military budget grew by only a third, and in relation to the overall budget, its share declined from 15% to only 8%.[43]

The worsening of the Western Sahara conflict with Morocco from the mid-1970s on revived bad memories of the earlier 1963–1964 military conflict, when the Algerian army did not fare well. The pattern of Algerian troop concentrations was altered, and a sixth military region, centered on Tindouf near the Moroccan frontier, was mentioned for the first time in the press in January 1976. Military expenditure also rose: from 1 billion Algerian dinars ($285 million) in 1975 to 3.9 billion ($856.8 million) in 1982, an increase of just under 400%, compared to a 40% rise between 1965 and 1973, from 484 million to 611 million Algerian dinars. As for arms purchases, the Stockholm International Peace Research Institute (SIPRI) has shown only five agreements for the period 1970–1975, whereas the period 1976–1981 produced fifteen agreements.[44]

Moreover, the evidence suggests that Algeria's military expenditures have exceeded budget figures substantially in some years, with funds being allocated from other accounts in the national fiscal plan.[45] The difference is usually drawn from Soviet credits for armaments (as was the case in both 1967 and 1974 to make up for the arms Algeria sent to the battlefront in the Mashreq). This brings us to the effects of arms purchases on foreign policy.

As early as 1967, and despite the continued use of some French material by the rural gendarmerie, the bulk of Algeria's equipment inventory was Soviet material, and the proportion had increased by 1980. Moreover, the army has internalized the Soviet liking for large numbers and size in both equipment and organization. Indeed, the closest relations between Algeria and the Eastern bloc members and other "radical" regimes are in the military field.[46]

The Algerian air force grew from a force of 1,000 at its establishment in 1963 to 12,000 or so by 1981. Pilot trainees were sent initially to Egypt and Syria in the 1960s, and afterwards increasingly to the USSR. By 1965, more than 1,000 ANP members had received training in the Eastern bloc, and by 1976 this number had risen to 2,200.[47] Though rumors of a Soviet base at Mers-el-Kebir seem to be groundless, about 1,000 Soviet advisers help ANP personnel master the use of increasingly sophisticated weapons. Moreover, all naval vessels of the 6,000-man navy are of Soviet origin.[48] Despite some reports in the mid-1970s of Soviet advice to adopt a moderate position on the Western Sahara question and even of Soviet warnings against the use of Soviet military equipment by Polisario, by December 1978 Soviet and East German technicians had arrived at Tindouf to work with Polisario to set up a helicopter base.[49] Was this the result of Cuban intervention on the side of Algeria?

The great mutual admiration between Algeria and Cuba is long-standing. Even before independence, Algeria condemned the 1961 U.S. Bay of Pigs invasion in the strongest terms. Cuban military advisers, for their part, conducted commando-guerrilla training in Algeria for the

ANP, and for Palestinian and various African liberation movements. This mutual support and political-military coordination continued in the 1970s. When Fidel Castro visited Algeria in March 1976, he reiterated to the press that "We are in favor of self-determination. We consider there is absolute majority among the Saharans for self-determination." He even had talks in Algiers with the prime minister of SADR—the Sahrawi Arab Democratic Republic, which Polisario seeks to establish in the former Spanish Sahara. In March 1977, Castro returned to Algeria. In May, the vice-president of the Cuban State Council delivered a message to Boumedienne from Castro. In August, it was the turn of Cuba's minister for armed forces, Raoul Castro, to travel to Algiers and to meet with the defense minister of SADR.[50] Algeria and Cuba felt they were defending the same world view, and military means were harnessed to this effect. This world view constitutes Algeria's role conception or foreign policy orientation.

2. FOREIGN POLICY ORIENTATION: INTERNATIONAL RESTRUCTURING AND THE THIRD WORLD

In an analysis of 175 speeches delivered by Boumedienne between June 1965 and June 1970 both inside and outside Algeria, the concept "revolution" ranked first and occurred 1,698 times; the concept "national" ranked second and occurred less than half as often, only 757 times.[51] This insistence on political change—both national and international—is consistently expressed in Algeria's foreign policy objectives and strategy.

In 1975, on the occasion of the tenth anniversary of Boumedienne's Adjustment Revolution, a book published by the army specified Algeria's foreign policy objectives. Put succinctly, they are: defense of national independence; restoration of national identity; refusal of any form of foreign intervention; elimination of foreign bases and refusal of the policy of blocs and military alliances; active solidarity with national liberation movements and democratic and progressive forces; effective participation in the struggle against underdevelopment and foreign economic exploitation and domination.[52]

Although the degree of emphasis and phraseology vary, all of Algeria's official documents—from those of the GPRA to those of the postindependence governments—have been consistent in upholding these objectives. As ambassador to the UN, Algerian scholar Mohamed Bedjaoui described his country's policy orientation as "a fixation on national independence and worship of [Third World] cooperation."[53] Al-Moudjahid—Algeria's major newspaper—put this in a wider historical context: "Algeria's attachment to its national independence is proportionate to the heavy price it paid to get it. In this sense, one can say that colonialism has constituted for Algeria's independence a strong driving force."[54] The preindependence Tripoli declaration, the 1976 National Charter, and Algeria's two constitutions, of 1963 and 1976, all go in the same direction.

In this respect, the National Charter is the culmination of the different official documents enunciating the country's foreign policy objectives. The whole of Chapter 5 of the charter is devoted to foreign policy. The single concept that dominates this chapter is at the core of the charter's spirit, and it acts as a link between its different parts. This is the concept of political change, national and international: "the great progress of the world economy, the continued expansion of the technological-scientific revolution, the irresistible developments of movements of national and social liberation, create all the time new situations, new ways of thinking, unknown imbalances, and processes in constant evolution."[55]

Concerning the international system, the underlying idea is that its structure is outdated. Article 86 of the 1976 constitution (which codifies the principles of the National Charter) is quite remarkable in its unconventional formulation. The article affirms Algeria's respect for "the principles and objectives of the charters of the UN, of the Organization of African Unity [OAU] and of the Arab League." This original formulation was preferred, after some discussion among Algerian legislators, to the more standard one of respect for "the general rules of international law." The reason for this change in formulation was the Algerian legislators' view that the present corpus of international law preceded the emergence of Third World states and was thus elaborated without their participation. Consequently, it is neither progressive enough nor adapted to the present international context. As Bedjaoui, in his new capacity as Algeria's representative in the International Court of Justice, put it:

International law has remained oligarchic. It has been dictated to the whole world by one or two groups of dominant states, especially the European powers who historically projected on the international level their pattern of domination and their own norms. This is why Algeria prefers the international law of participation, *i.e.*, the set of international norms based on the participation of all states.[56]

Boumedienne emphasized the same idea in his opening speech to the Fourth Summit of Nonaligned Countries (Algiers, September 1973). He asked rhetorically: "Isn't it time to restructure the rules of international law in order to reflect the new realities of the contemporary world?"

The need for international change was occasioned by the rise of the Third World, whose members have the prime responsibility in realizing the international restructuring. This restructuring is not primarily concerned with relations among the great powers, but rather between great powers and the small ones, for the basic international incompatibility is between small and big powers. This is the global system's number one defect.

This scale of priorities colors Algeria's judgment of East-West détente. Although welcome in principle, this détente is criticized as being concerned only with a few actors and dimensions of international relations: "Algeria is not ready to accept a restrictive interpretation of détente which will limit it to relations between developed countries, while leaving the rest of the world, *i.e.*, the overwhelming majority of mankind, to suffer under the yoke of exploitation, insecurity and war."[57]

As a result, East-West détente, which was motivated by a desire for nuclear balance, has not been correlated with peace and security in the rest of the global system. Yet, as Algeria's charter explicitly states, "it is increasingly in Africa, Asia and Latin America that the wars, the plots and the coups d'état organized from the outside take place, and where the battle is raging to guarantee hegemony at the level of the planet."[58] If détente is to be worthwhile, it has to be global. Global détente cannot reflect only the wishes of the closed club of a few great powers. On the contrary, it implies "a democratization of international relations and presupposes a sincere desire of real and equitable adjustment of relations between industrialized and Third World countries."[59]

The prime responsibility for bringing about this international restructuring falls on the Third World, whose members must protect their national independence and work together to overcome resistance to change. The first five pages of Chapter 5 of the charter use the expression "Third World" or an equivalent (not counting labels of partial conglomerations such as Africa or the Arab world) twenty-seven times—more than five times per page. This fixation on the Third World underlies Algeria's belief that Third World unity is a prerequisite for international change: "Imperialism uses formidable and varied means of pressure to subject to its own interests and strategic vision the newly emancipated countries. This is why these latter have to elaborate a platform of appropriate action and promote their solidarity in order to frustrate all attempts at domination."[60]

This Third World unity is to be based on a policy of nonalignment: "Third World solidarity constitutes an essential component of our foreign policy of nonalignment."[61] But nonalignment is not at all a policy of fence-sitting or the equivalent of Swiss-type neutrality. Nonalignment is not limited to political independence, but goes beyond it to insist on "the exercise of full and complete sovereignty over natural resources"[62] and the elaboration of a new international order.

To achieve this general level of Third World unity for international restructuring, Algeria's world view insists on some areas of special interest: the Maghreb, the Arab world, and Africa. These three foci of attention are an integral part of general Third World unity, and they are linked among themselves by mutual interests. For instance, the Maghreb is a part of the Arab nation, and consequently its unity is a first step on the road to pan-Arab unity. Similarly, African and Arab countries overlap, not only geographically, but also in their common objectives and interests. Moreover, Algeria's integration in all three areas is not a matter of choice or of a passing context: on the contrary, it is based on the "solidarity of struggle between all the peoples"[63] of these areas.

The word and concept "peoples" is basic for Algeria's policy-makers. When dealing with Maghrebi or Arab unity, official documents emphasize the primacy of "peoples' unity" over "states' unity."[64] To be durable, unity is not to be the simple result of agreements between governments and still less a product of a passing political context. If "peoples' unity" is not followed, the cause of Arab unity will not advance, and the end result will be a serious disappointment. This is why social and economic transformations, with their political concomitants at the mass level, are crucial for the realization of this "historical endeavor."

Algeria still supports the existing "pan" institutions, whether they be the OAU or the Arab League. However, its attitude differs toward each. Algeria emphasizes its role in the creation of the OAU and the elaboration of its charter. Concerning the Arab League, the emphasis is much more on the league's lagging behind. For this institution to be effective, its charter has to be adapted to the present regional and global context: "Only the revision of its Charter and the remaking of its structures would permit the Arab League to be in keeping with the present international context and play at the same time a more effective role in the realization of the aspirations of the Arab peoples toward unity and progress."[65]

Thus, whether at the macro level of the global system, at the level of Third World politics, or at the much more specific regional level, Algeria's world view shows consistency among its various components:

1. The emphasis all along is on the primacy of political change and international restructuring. Repeatedly and insistently, Algeria preaches the democratization of international relations, an "international law of participation."
2. If a bipolarity does exist, it is primarily between "imperialist" and Third World states, between developed and developing countries. The latter have to work together incessantly, inside and outside the UN, to stop the process of exploitation and bring about international restructuring.
3. Blueprints for unity (Maghrebi or all-Arab) have to be between peoples rather than between governments. Prior social and economic transformation within these countries would put them on the right political path and make the "unity of peoples" more easily attainable.

The verbalization of Algeria's role conception shows neither hesitation nor contradiction. The tone is assertive and the different parts of the policy-makers' "speech" are concordant, cumulative, and generally convincing.[66] These general foreign policy objectives stem from the similar frame of reference for both masses and elite: Algeria's colonial history, its War of Independence, and the primacy of development as both a complement and a basis of this independence. In the chapter devoted to foreign policy in the National Charter, the first sentence affirms this association: "Algeria's foreign policy," it asserts, "is a reflection of its internal policy. . . . Our option for a socialist society based on national independence, on social justice, on equality between citizens, and on the promotion of man and of his struggle against underdevelopment, determine the conception of our foreign policy."[67]

3. THE DECISION-MAKING PROCESS

The interaction between different factors, and its impact on foreign policy, is best revealed in the decision-making process. The analysis of this process must take into account the role of both participant institutions and the persons that represent them. Institutions are the official and— in principle—enduring participants. The persons that act as representatives of their will and interests change much more rapidly. This duality is reflected in Algeria's pattern of decision-making, which has exhibited three major characteristics: the dominance of the presidential center: the president, his staff, and his trusted companions; the primacy of the military; and the growing importance of the managerial or technocratic elite.

The Declining Role of Institutions

At the institutional level, the period before Boumedienne's 1965 Adjustment Revolution contrasts sharply with the period of his presidency (1965–1978). The pre-Boumedienne regime was characterized by plurality and rapid change in the decision-making organs. There were the various political leaders (*les chefs historiques*) who had decided to launch the revolution on November 1, 1954. Once the revolution had begun, military leaders had to be consulted as they were in direct contact with the situation on the terrain. This nascent influence of the military was, however, balanced by the decision-making organs that enjoyed political legitimacy and autonomy: the 1956–National Council of the Algerian Revolution and the 1958–GPRA. The Provisional Government was the organ that planned and conducted Algeria's foreign relations through the equivalent of ministries of foreign affairs, information, economy, and defense. The GPRA was also in charge of offices in foreign countries, the equivalent of embassies, which sent periodic reports and waited for guidelines.

During this period the decision-making pattern involved different levels and issue areas, a multiplicity of organs, and dozens of persons in different fields of specialization. Because of this decentralization, the decision-making pattern did not conform to the psychologistic hypothesis or the "great men" theory of history so dominant among theoretical approaches to Third World decision-making. Indeed, at the time, Algeria's decision-making pattern came nearest to the bureaucratic politics model with its emphasis on a multiplicity of participants and their bargaining.[68]

All participants, however, rallied behind the objective of political independence and the FLN as the most legitimate vehicle to attain it.

With independence, the FLN's objective was attained, but the party found it difficult to adapt to the postindependence context. Moreover, during the Ben Bella era (1962–1965) there was a concerted attempt to make the decision-making process more centralized. In retrospect, this period appears as a transition phase toward the presidentialism and primacy of the military so evident in the Boumedienne and Bendjedid eras.

Ben Bella, the first president and prime minister of independent Algeria, had little say in the decision-making of the preceding GPRA,[69] whose power he defeated with the help of Boumedienne and the army. As early as August 1962, Ben Bella was pushing for more centralized decision-making by strengthening the FLN's Political Bureau (in which his supporters were concentrated), which eclipsed, in practice if not in theory, the other decision-making organs: the CNRA and the GPRA. In the National Assembly elected on September 20, 1962, the military— still Ben Bella's ally at this time—got the highest number of votes (18%).[70] Ironically enough, it was the military that finally put an end to Ben Bella's drive toward a monopoly over decision-making by overthrowing him.

By launching his 1965 Adjustment Revolution from a strong military base, Boumedienne found it easier to accelerate the centralization of power. All decision-making organs except the Council of Ministers were put to sleep. The locus of power was transferred to the new Council of the Revolution, composed of trustees under Boumedienne's direct command. The 1963 constitution was abolished in practice, if not officially, and its jurisdiction was transferred to the newly established council, which legislated by decree. Moreover, the already disorganized FLN was further weakened; it functioned only at the subnational level through the *wilayat*, which did not play a direct role in "high politics" or foreign policy.

To fill this institutional vacuum, Boumedienne announced in his June 1975 speech (commemorating the tenth anniversary of his Adjustment Revolution) plans for the National Charter (published and debated in 1976), for a new constitution (also in 1976), and for the election of a new Popular National Assembly (convened in 1977). In April 1977, the newly elected president for a five-year term, Boumedienne carried out the first major reshuffle of the Council of Ministers since he had come to power twelve years earlier. Over half of the council was replaced by members who came from the military, internal security, or from Boumedienne's personal staff.[71] The new constitution and new assembly notwithstanding, this change in the Council of Ministers was interpreted as a further consolidation of power by Boumedienne. The actual decision-making pattern, based on presidentialism and the primacy of the military, remained intact despite institutional modification.

This pattern was confirmed with the president's death the following year. When Boumedienne went into a coma in November 1978 from a rare blood disease, the responsibilities of the president were transferred—not to Rabih Bitat, the head of the Popular National Assembly, as the constitution decreed—but rather to colonels Bendjedid and Belhouchet.

Moreover, the votes of the 640 army delegates to the February 1979 FLN congress were the prerequisite for Bendjedid's election as president. Attempts at collective leadership notwithstanding, Bendjedid emerged—after a short transition period—as *the* leader, combining the posts of president, defense minister, and FLN secretary-general, and eliminating from power his earlier rivals to the presidency, Bouteflika and Yahiaoui. The foreign minister, Ahmed Taleb Ibrahimi, a close collaborator of Bendjedid, came to the Foreign Ministry directly from the presidential staff.

Thus since independence, the decision-making process has become increasingly centralized, notwithstanding the reactivation of institutions a year before Boumedienne's death.

The Role of the Elite

In terms of the *elite*, centralization is less pronounced, but the structural characteristics of the primacy of presidentialism and of the military are clear. At this level too, the pattern follows the institutional evolution of the four Algerian regimes.

The GPRA (1958–1962). This phase was dominated by the "historic chiefs" (*chefs historiques*) who were old hands at political action (e.g., Ferhat Abbas),[72] or had the prestige of having launched the November 1954 revolution. Their average age at the time of independence was around forty, and they represented, par excellence, the liberally oriented, Western-educated political elites so prevalent in Third World regimes at the time of independence. At the time of Boumedienne's death in 1978, one member of this generation—Rabih Bitat (born 1925)—was the head of the Popular National Assembly.

The Ben Bella Period (1962–1965). This was the transition stage toward the centralized and personalized decision-making pattern that developed after Ben Bella was overthrown. Ben Bella (born 1919) was one of the nine historic chiefs, but he allied himself with the army and overthrew the GPRA. During his presidency he attempted to centralize decision-making around the presidency and its intellectuals by curtailing the influence of the military and their supporters within his government, and by seeking to reinforce the FLN. He was overthrown by Boumedienne and the army before he could succeed.

The Boumedienne Era (1965–1978). The arrival of Boumedienne marked a change in the elite and in the pattern of decision-making. Instead of the factionalism that had characterized the GPRA and Ben Bella regimes, Boumedienne (born 1932) pushed toward centralization under his control. Under his leadership, the primacy of presidentialism and the military were combined. The military supplied the direct decision-makers in the only decision-making organ, the 1965 Council of the Revolution. Of the 26 council members, 12 held military positions under Ben Bella, another 3 were members of the General Staff (Etat Major General) under Boumedienne just prior to independence, and yet another 3 were members of the famous Oujda group.

The creation of the Oujda group and of the General Staff dates back to the late 1950s and early 1960s. They were initiated by Mohamed Bou Kharouba, whose war name was Boumedienne. A graduate of the most prestigious Islamic university, Cairo's Al-Azhar, Boumedienne joined the ALN after the start of hostilities. He was promoted colonel of the Wilaya V in 1957, then commander of the western region (Oujda, on the frontiers with Morocco) in April 1958, and then head of the General Staff of the frontier army (the "externals" of the western and eastern regions) in 1960.

One of Boumedienne's aspirations was to form a military core and shape the army according to his specific views. With the support of the Oujda group (Bouteflika, Cherif Belkacem, and Mohamed Medeghri) guaranteed, he formed another military core in the eastern region (Ghardimaou, frontier command with Tunisia) around Ali Mendjli and Ahmed Kaid, with whom he formed the Ghardimaou Triumvirate. When the army was restructured and the General Staff was formed after the constitution of the GPRA was established, Boumedienne was already in a strong position to eliminate his rivals and separate the army from the "politicians," thus keeping the army tightly under his control.

On the basis of his consolidated authority and dedicated supporters, Boumedienne started to transform the lower levels of the military. He established a sort of military academy that not only taught soldiers how to harass the enemy, but also provided political education and thus trained the political cadre of tomorrow's Algeria. A few trustworthy and competent officers who had received training in the French army (e.g., Abdallah Belhouchet, Mohamed Bencherif, Bensalem, Moulay Abdel Kader named Chabou, and Souffi, who later all became members of the Council of the Revolution) were responsible for the army's technical reorganization. The reorganized military provided Boumedienne with a strong base from which to exercise pressure on the GPRA "politicians" even before independence was achieved.

During the negotiations for the 1962 Evian Agreements, the General Staff criticized the GPRA's "soft" position and its negotiating strategy. When Mohamed Ben Khedda, head of the GPRA, went to discuss the Evian Agreements with the ALN personnel in Morocco, he was met by determined protestors. ALN spokesman Bouteflika, who was then only twenty-five years old, denounced the future agreements as "a compromise paving the way for neo-colonial manoeuvers" and "a deliberate attempt to freeze the Revolution."[73] Bouteflika went so far as to threaten to impose the army's will "by military means" against the GPRA "embourgeoisie." These differences with the GPRA convinced the highest echelons of the army to throw their weight behind the Ben Bella team to unseat the GPRA.

While factionalism and intra-elite cleavages continued during the Ben Bella presidency, Boumedienne concentrated on the army to achieve some of his objectives. He resisted attempts to involve the army in the politicians' clans, worked hard to dispense with the *wilayat's* former guerrillas, the "internal" army, by either disbanding them or bringing them under his control, and generally pushed toward the consolidation of a strong, modern army.

During the 1964 FLN congress, Boumedienne came out strongly and publicly in favor of a political role for the army, and defended the army's autonomy and his own sovereignty against interference by the "Marxist Ben Bellists" and their attempts to exploit divisions between "internals" and "externals" within the army. Bouteflika—then a civilian minister in the Ben Bella government—defended his old friends and colleagues in the army and joined the 200 army delegates who constituted a solid bloc among the 1,500 civilian participants. When Ben Bella (on the eve of the Afro-Asian conference to be convened in Algiers) planned to get rid of Bouteflika, the latter's former army colleagues, headed by Boumedienne, overthrew him.

The military thus assumed direct decision-making power through the Council of the Revolution, whose members included old army colleagues of Oujda or of the General Staff. The council members who had already left the army and become "civilianized" as ministers or FLN Political Bureau participants under Ben Bella still kept close contacts and maintained a solid coalition based on their common experience in the army.

In 1968, the military were joined as top decision-makers by a rising elite: the managers or technocrats. They came from government or state-run companies such as SONATRACH (oil and gas), SNS (iron and steel), SONAREM (mining), SONACOME (heavy industry), SN METAL (metallurgy), SONEL-GAZ (gas and electricity), SNIC (chemicals), SON-ITEX (textiles), SNMC (building industries), SNCF (railroads), CNAN (shipping), and Air Algerie.[74]

This administrative and technocratic elite did not have the same decision-making power as the military or their spokesmen, who remained the top decision-makers. But with Boumedienne's increasing emphasis on accelerated development and the growing role of gas and oil in the functioning of the economy, the administrative-technocratic elite were implementing major national decisions. They wielded significant power in their own areas of administrative and economic decision-making, and they increasingly made their influence felt on the top policy-makers, as the previously cited data on economic capabilities indicate. Consequently, "as a group the technocrats were second only to the military in power and influence, and in social status they may have been the most prestigious."[75]

The Bendjedid Presidency (1979-). The end of the Boumedienne era and the succession in 1979 of Chadli Bendjedid (born 1929) do not seem to have affected the established threefold pattern of decision-making (presidentialism, primacy of the military, and growing importance of the administrative-technocratic elite). Boumedienne was replaced by another active military man, an old associate, who was in fact the most senior man in the army.[76] Presidentialism and the military continue as close partners in the top decision-making. The outcome of the leadership rivalry in which Bendjedid triumphed, and the new president's accumulation of different posts in the country's highest political institutions, show that the centralized pattern of decision-making is still in effect. As a very well informed Tunisian journalist, Bechir Ben Yahmed, said more than twenty years ago: "Tomorrow's Algeria will be what the ALN would really like it to be."[77]

The Role of the Foreign Ministry

According to the constitution, the president is responsible for foreign policy, and he is to be assisted by the foreign minister, whom he appoints. The foreign minister himself is assisted by the secretary-general of the Ministry of Foreign Affairs. The ministry itself was reorganized in March 1977. As a result, the special French Directorate, which had heretofore reflected the importance of Algeria's relations with France, was integrated into the Directorate of Western Europe and North America. The structure of the ministry is pyramidal, going from the five general directorates to the ten regional directorates, to the multiple subdirectorates and bureaus.[78]

In the conduct of foreign relations, Algerian diplomats are professional, competent, and well-respected at the international level. They usually arrive at meetings with well-prepared position papers and thus guarantee Algeria's success in Third World coalition-building. That does not mean that the Foreign Ministry personnel are among the top decision-makers, yet they are essential for the conduct of the country's international behavior and thus belong to the 500 to 600 members of the general political elite. This elite includes the Central Committee members of the FLN, the 31 *wilaya* governors, the 261 members of the National Assembly, the general secretaries of ministries, presidents and directors of the fifteen or so major state-owned industries, the presidents and executive councils of the five national organizations (of workers, peasants, students or youth, women, and veterans), and heads of the numerous professional associations (lawyers, doctors, teachers, etc.).[79] The influence of the top ambassadorial and diplomatic corps varies, of course, according to the issue area and also according to the personnel's connections with the top decision-makers, the core elite.

The minister of foreign affairs has until recently been part of this limited group of top decision-makers. The minister's influence, however, was much less a function of his administrative position as head of the

Foreign Ministry than it was the result of his connection with the very top decision-maker, the president. Nothing illustrates this better than the position of Abdel-Aziz Bouteflika, who probably had the longest term as foreign minister in any Third World country. In a system plagued by factionalism and rivalry, Bouteflika was foreign minister from the second Ben Bella government (September 1963) until Boumedienne's death in December 1978.

Bouteflika had the reputation of being one of the youngest foreign ministers in the Third World. He was born in March 1937 in Tlemcen, in the western part of Algeria near the Moroccan frontier.[80] In the 1950s he became an activist within the "Morocco section" of the General Union of Algerian Moslem Students in France, an organization that worked closely with the FLN. After finishing his secondary school education, Bouteflika joined the ALN rather than pursue a university education. He was sent to the western region at Oujda, where Boumedienne was the commander. Their ensuing friendship meant that with the rise of Boumedienne, Bouteflika's responsibilities and influence also grew, and he was entrusted with delicate missions. An example was his selection for a three-man delegation to study the possibilities of opening a southern front against the French army and of contacting Algeria's neighbors to the south, Guinea and Mali. Along with his military experience Bouteflika was thus initiated into political-diplomatic activities.

In the last stages of the Evian negotiations, the French government permitted contacts with the FLN "historic chiefs" detained in France, the *prisonniers d'honneur*, Ben Bella and his colleagues, who were kept at the Chateau d'Aulnoy. As one of the GPRA delegates to these consultations, Bouteflika impressed Ben Bella. When Ben Bella was in conflict with the GPRA, Bouteflika served as a privileged link between him and the Oujda group whose support assured Ben Bella's political victory. In the first Ben Bella government Bouteflika became minister of youth and sports (at the age of twenty-five); a year later he became foreign minister, replacing the assassinated Khemisti, a close Ben Bella ally.

Soon, however, differences arose concerning jurisdiction in decision-making. Ben Bella and Boumedienne differed on the army's role in decision-making, and Bouteflika took Boumedienne's side. Then Ben Bella, who followed a Gaullist concept of the state and foreign policy—making, clashed with Bouteflika, who refused to play a subordinate role in foreign policy decision-making. This conflict ended in Ben Bella's overthrow.

From the beginning of the Boumedienne era, Bouteflika was a pillar of the regime. He sat on the twenty-six member Council of the Revolution and continued as foreign minister. His influence over foreign policy increased as Boumedienne devoted most of his time in the early years to the domestic front. From the late 1960s and early 1970s, however,

Boumedienne and the presidential center became increasingly active in foreign affairs, and rumor revealed a latent tension between the president and the foreign minister. Friction between the two men did not, however, lead to a public break, as both agreed on the bases of Algerian foreign policy orientation and behavior. When Boumedienne died, Bouteflika was among the three candidates to the presidency. He lost to Bendjedid, the army man. He also lost his position as foreign minister and after a few months, his membership in the FLN Political Bureau.

Former finance minister Mohamed Benyahia replaced Bouteflika as foreign minister. When Benyahia died in 1981 in a plane crash while on a mission to mediate the Iraq-Iran war, Ahmed Taleb Ibrahimi, a presidential aid to Bendjedid, replaced him. Thus the pattern of decision-making, with its emphasis on the president and the military, continues. The conduct of foreign policy is left to the Foreign Ministry with its qualified personnel. This brings us to the analysis of Algeria's foreign policy behavior.

4. FOREIGN POLICY BEHAVIOR

The basic key to Algeria's role performance is the concept of nonalignment, which is viewed as an active and assertive international behavior promoting international change, as Boumedienne stated in 1969.[81] In this sense, the convening of the fourth nonaligned summit in Algiers in September 1973 was a watershed that renewed the movement and enhanced Algeria's role as a Third World leader. As the movement's president for the following three years, Boumedienne stressed the economic and dynamic content of nonalignment and left Algeria's imprint on the movement's evolution.

The renewal of the nonaligned movement was due in great part to Algeria's leadership. Algeria's efforts, however, were helped by the global context: the 1973 oil embargo, the rise of OPEC, and the effects of newly acquired Third World capabilities such as oil power on the structure of relations between developed and developing countries. Algeria summoned the sixth special UN session (1974) to discuss the problems of primary products and development; and Boumedienne—as president of the nonaligned group and thus the Third World spokesman—addressed the UN General Assembly in 1974. Moreover, the Twenty-ninth Session of the UN (1974–1975), chaired by Bouteflika, approved the basic document on the restructuring of international economic relations: the Charter of Basic Rights and Obligations of States.

At the same time, Algeria used OPEC's rising power to show what the Third World could do to hasten international change and accelerate the strengthening of relations between Third World countries. Some examples: the June 1975 Dakar conference on raw materials, the March 1975 OPEC summit in Algiers, the creation of various development funds by oil-producing countries, and success in convening the First

Summit of Afro-Arab Cooperation (Arab League headquarters, Cairo, 1977).

Nonalignment and Relations with the Superpowers

The United States. Given the two countries' diametrically opposed views of the international system, one might expect Algeria's relations with the United States to be pure conflict. Conflict does exist, but so does cooperation, especially in the gas and oil sector and in the education of Algerian students at U.S. universities.

Washington recognized Algeria on September 29, 1962, and William Porter, the U.S. consul, was promoted to the rank of ambassador in Algiers in December of the same year.[82] Algeria's ambassador to Washington, however, did not arrive until almost a year later, in September 1963. Diplomatic relations were cut off in August 1967 following the Six-Day War and were not reestablished until November 1974. Strangely enough, it was during this absence of diplomatic relations that Algeria's relations with Washington developed quickly. U.S. consulates in Oran and Constantine remained open, Kissinger stopped in Algiers in October and December 1973 during the initial stages of his Middle East shuttle diplomacy, and Boumedienne met Nixon on April 11, 1974, during the UN Special Session on Primary Products.

It was relations in the petrol and gas sector that reinforced Algeria's connections with the United States. By the end of the 1970s, the United States became Algeria's foremost partner in this sector. Boumedienne himself had to intervene publicly by early 1971 to explain this "anomaly of relations with the biggest imperialist power," and to insist that Algeria was determined to follow its own militant foreign policy and did not need lessons from anybody in its business or political relations.[83] Thus Algeria continued to sign contracts with U.S. companies—especially with El-Paso, committing itself to deliver between 35 and 40 billion cubic meters of gas in a twenty-year period beginning in 1969. By the late 1970s, 50% of Algerian petrol and gas went to the United States, comprising about 9% of U.S. imports of crude. The big refining complex at Arzwo port, built with direct U.S. participation in 1978, is evidence of the intensity of these relations.

Algeria developed its economic relations with other Western countries, too. SONATRACH signed several agreements with both the Federal Republic of Germany and Belgium. Between 1973 and 1979, the percentage of Algeria's trade with the West (or with developed market economies, according to UN usage) rose from 87.1% to 88.9%, and the percentage with the East (the centrally planned economies) declined from 6.2% to 4.7%.[84]

The Soviet Union. One could easily imagine that Algeria's relations with the USSR would be close in all fields. The two countries share an anti-imperialist ideology and an emphasis on socialist transformation as the road to development. Other elements, however—divergent views on the solution of the Middle East conflict and on the place of Israel in the region, and different perceptions of East-West détente—intervene to disrupt the image of complete political concordance.

Despite its ideological commitment to the anti-imperialist struggle, Moscow's support for Algeria's independence in the 1950s and early 1960s was influenced by Soviet involvement in the East-West conflict and especially by Moscow's interest in President Charles de Gaulle's disengagement policies toward the North Atlantic Treaty Organization (NATO). Consequently, the USSR initially seemed favorable to an Algerian-French rapprochement. Moreover, although the GPRA representatives were received in Moscow in September 1960, Soviet de jure recognition came only in March 1962, *after* the Evian Agreements.[85]

As for Algeria, its development pattern is indeed based on a rejection of the capitalist model, but its socialism—as the charter and other declarations repeat—is very specific in its linkage to Islam[86] and its maintenance of "nonexploitive" private property. Nevertheless, the general ideological affinities of anti-imperialism and anticapitalism drew the two countries together, especially in the fields of economic cooperation, economic organization, and military collaboration and arms purchases. Three years after Algeria's independence, there were 3,500 Soviet technicians in Algeria, and by 1972 Soviet economic aid had reached $421 million.[87] Soviet arms transfers between 1966 and 1974, worth $248 million, constituted 90% of Algeria's arms purchases.[88]

From 1974 to 1981, however, Algeria varied its military relations. The twenty arms purchase agreements[89] made during this period are equally divided between the USSR and Western countries (with the United States signing five agreements). This diversity of arms sources at the quantitative level notwithstanding, agreements with Moscow were more expensive, more varied, and included real combat weaponry—MiG-23s and even MiG-25s, T-72 tanks, and ship-to-ship and ground-to-air missiles. In its weaponry and training, then, the Algerian army is Soviet-oriented.

There is, however, no Algerian infatuation with Moscow. On the contrary, political differences loom large. First, at the global level, Soviet priorities are East-West détente and the prevention of a "nuclear accident." As we have seen, Algeria's priorities are system change and the conflict between the South and the North (which includes the USSR), as Boumedienne's opening speech to the fourth nonaligned summit illustrated.[90] Secondly, Algeria and the USSR have different perceptions of Israel's place in the Middle East. These differences collided head on following the 1967 Six-Day War. The minutes of Boumedienne's Moscow meeting with Soviet leaders to discuss the Arab-Israeli conflict reveal mutual accusations, the exchange of hard words, and finally a "dialogue de sourds."[91]

Third Worldism

Algerian policy behavior has involved three Third World arenas:[92] (1) the Afro-Asian group, in which Algeria's activities were short-lived because of the problems inherent in the movement itself and because of Boumedienne's coup d'état on the eve of the convening of the second Afro-Asian summit in Algiers; (2) the economic development group centered around the Group of 77: Algeria hosted the Group of 77's first meeting in October 1967 and worked toward the publication of its charter; and (3) the nonaligned group. Algeria was a founding member of this group even before its independence, and it worked to promote a militant anticolonial and economically oriented interpretation of non-alignment instead of the interpretation associated with Nehru and Tito, which emphasized mediation in the East-West conflict. Three examples can be cited to demonstrate Algeria's behavioral involvement at this Third World level: the 1973 nonaligned conference in Algiers, the 1974 call for the New International Economic Order, and work within OPEC to heighten Third World unity and to restructure relations between developing and developed countries.

The choice of Algiers as a site for the fourth nonaligned summit was a recognition of Algeria's international status and a consolidation of its views of the concept of nonalignment. Algeria made the conference a success both for the movement and for itself.[93] In the summer of 1973, Algeria established an organizational committee to guarantee the largest participation. In July a few ambassadors were sent around the world to encourage attendance at the highest level. A month later, Algeria's ministers were sent on similar missions throughout the nonaligned group. As a result, seventy-five countries attended (compared to fifty-four at the third summit at Lusaka three years earlier) and as many as sixty delegations were led by their heads of state.[94]

With characteristic vigor, Algeria also summoned the 1974 UN special session that issued the Declaration on the Establishment of a New International Economic Order. As chairman of the nonaligned group and as an active link with the deliberations of the 1973 Algiers summit, Boumedienne delivered the opening speech on April 10, 1974.[95] A comparison between Boumedienne's speech and the UN declaration indicates Algeria's success: text of the UN document reflected Algeria's views as expressed in the opening speech (see Table 4.1).

Algeria profited from the global context of the mid-1970s and the rise of OPEC power in implementing its integrated and coherent approach to development, the "priority of priorities," as Boumedienne put it in his UN speech. This resulted in a confrontation with the United States, which following the panic of the 1973 oil embargo wanted to limit discussions to the problems between consumers and producers of oil.[96] Algeria objected to the 1975 Washington conference on the grounds that it attempted to form a bloc of developed countries against oil producers. Instead, Algeria insisted on dealing with oil as yet another

TABLE 4.1
Boumedienne's Speech to the April 1974 UN Special Session and the May 1974 UN Declaration
on the Establishment of a New International Economic Order

Boumedienne's Speech	The UN NIEO Document
The present world system is as "unjust and outmoded as the colonial order from which it originated."	"The gap between the developed and the developing countries continues to widen in a system which was established at a time when most of the developing countries did not even exist as independent states and which perpetuates inequality."
"The prevailing system on international power relations" is condemned for reducing to "a passive role . . . the immense majority of peoples."	Measures should be taken to insure "more effective participation by developing countries . . . in the decision-making process" in the competent international organs "through the establishment of a more equitable pattern of voting rights."
The measures needed to promote a world development strategy are:	
"Mastery by the developing country over natural resources and control of their price mechanism."	"All efforts should be made . . . to defeat attempts to prevent the free and effective exercise of the rights of every State to full and permanent sovereignty over its natural resources.
"An integrated and coherent development is based on the exploitation of the agricultural and industrial potential of the developing country and the transformation of mineral or agricultural resources on the spot."	"All efforts should be made by the international community to . . . encourage the industrialization of the developing countries, and to this end . . . contribute to setting up new industrial capacities including raw materials and commodity-transforming facilities as a matter of priority in developing countries that produce those raw materials and commodities."
"Mobilization of international sources of financial, technological, and commercial aid from rich and developed countries to developing countries."	"Extension of active assistance . . . free of any political or military conditions; increase in the official component of the net amount of financial resource transfers. All efforts should be made" to carry out seven specific measures that assure "transfer of technology."
"Elaboration and implementation of a special program to guarantee more aid for peoples considered by the UN community as most seriously affected by unfavorable economic conditions."	"The General Assembly adopts the following Specific Program, including particularly emergency measures to mitigate the difficulties of the developing countries most seriously affected by economic crisis, bearing in mind the particular problem of the least developed and land-locked countries."

Sources: The text of Boumedienne's speech (in French) can be found in Paul Balta and Claudine Rulleau, *La Stratégie de Boumediène* (Paris: Sindbad, 1978), pp. 316-329. This translation is by Bahgat Korany. The text of the UN NIEO document is taken from Edwin Reubens (ed.), *The Challenge of the New International Economic Order* (Boulder, Colorado: Westview Press, 1981), pp. 19-37.

raw material and discussing it within the general context of North-South economic relations. Algeria deployed its efforts to overcome hesitation among pro-Western oil producers, convening an OPEC summit in Algiers in March 1975. Boumedienne's opening speech set the criteria of an OPEC united front. Moreover, the OPEC summit referred explicitly on three occasions to the sixth special UN session and its resolutions as the relevant framework for coming to grips with the problems of the international economy. Nobody needed reminding that Algeria was the leading actor in both initiatives.

After abortive attempts to hold a conference on energy problems alone (thereby dividing the Third World between oil producers and oil consumers), Kissinger had to give in. He declared in Paris in May 1975 that "the dialogue between the producers and consumers will not progress unless it is broadened to include the general issue of the relationship between developing and developed countries."[97] As Bouteflika said jubilantly on another occasion, "the Third World is finally being heard"— that is, the Third World as represented by Algeria. The election of Bouteflika as president of the 1974 session of the UN General Assembly was further confirmation of Algeria's leading position.

The 1975 Paris conference on international cooperation (attended by nineteen developing and eight developed countries) set up committees on raw materials, energy, development, and financial issues to deal with the world economic situation. Each committee was cochaired by a developing and a developed country—a manifestation of Algeria's success in insisting on "effective participation" by the Third World at the decision-making level. Algeria participated in the committees on energy and on development, acting as cochair (with the EEC) of the latter committee.[98]

Algeria's Behavior at the Regional Level: Africa and the Arab World

Algeria is an active and full member of both Africa and the Arab world,[99] but does one region take precedence for the policy-makers? The preindependence Tripoli declaration and the National Charter, written fourteen years later, talk of the Arab world (of which Algeria is an "integral part"), the Maghreb, and Africa, in that order of importance. The amount of space the charter devotes to each region confirms this ranking: they merit ten, eight, and five paragraphs respectively.

These admittedly convenient indicators should be interpreted with caution for three reasons. First, Algerian policy-makers refuse to accept a clearcut separation between the three regions; they point out that the Maghreb is both Arab and African, and that 70% of all Arabs live in Africa, where they constitute 25% of the continent's total population. Second, although Algeria is tied to the Arab world by common culture and language, pan-Arab ideology has traditionally evolved in the Mashreq through Nasserism and Ba'thism, and thus Algeria's chances to lead or even to make its influence effectively felt on the main front more than a thousand miles away are slim. Other indicators of behavior show, finally, that Algeria has been heavily involved in Sub-Saharan Africa.

As both Etienne[100] and Algerian scholar Chikh[101] affirm, Africa constitutes the base of Algeria's Third World policy[102] and its prime field of action. Algeria was one of the very few African countries to carry out the 1965–OAU ministerial resolution to break off diplomatic relations with London following Rhodesia's unilateral declaration of independence. Algeria has hosted several OAU summits and ministerial meetings, as well as pan-African nongovernmental conferences such as the First Pan-

African Cultural Festival, held in 1969. It has been an active member of the OAU Liberation Committee since its establishment, and has been the headquarters of a dozen liberation movements. Indeed, the Algerian government established a special section—the Department of International Studies—to coordinate aid to these movements. This section, in principle part of the FLN, is in fact directly linked to the presidency. Relations between Algiers and many of the African governments were thus established well ahead of their independence.

After independence, bilateral agreements were concluded to consolidate cooperation. Thus the total of Algeria's bilateral agreements with Sub-Saharan African countries for the sample years 1970, 1973, 1975, 1977, and 1978 amounts to thirty-seven agreements (twenty-five in the economic area, eleven in the cultural-technical area, and one—with Mali—in the diplomatic sphere).[103] Moreover, even though Algeria's trade with Sub-Saharan Africa is less than 1% of its total trade (with the trade balance usually against Algeria), Algeria still signs agreements to maintain direct contact. Between 1972 and 1976, fifteen agreements for air and maritime communication were concluded with ten African countries.[104] In contrast to communication lines with Europe or with the Arab world, the ones with Sub-Saharan Africa are run at a financial loss.

In such cases, purely economic calculations have been subordinated to political objectives. Algerian universities receive an increasing number of African students, i.e., the future governing elite of Africa. The total from twenty African countries was 286 students for the academic year 1975-1976, 371 for 1976-1977, and 451 for 1977-1978.[105]

Sub-Saharan African countries have responded to Algeria's interest in the continent. The rising level of regular diplomatic representation in Algiers from these countries is impressive. The following scale measures the level and directness of regular diplomatic representation:

Resident ambassador . . . . 5 points
Nonresident ambassador. . . . . 4 points
Resident chargé d'affaires . . . . 3 points
Nonresident chargé d'affaires . . . . 2 points
Unidentified diplomatic representative . . . . 1 point

In 1970, Algeria accredited diplomatic representatives from nine Sub-Saharan African countries, with a total value of 41 points (six countries sent resident ambassadors; two, nonresident ambassadors; and one, a resident chargé d'affaires). This is a high level of representation given the limited financial capacities of most of these countries. Yet by 1982, the number of African countries represented in Algiers rose to thirty, with a total value of 111 points.

With the aim of reconciling its Arab character and its African involvement, Algeria attempted the institutionalization of the Arab-African dialogue.[106] To initiate an institutional structure, the sixth session of the

Arab summit (Algiers, November 26–28, 1973) invited non-Arab Africa to send representatives, and President Mobutu of Zaire attended. The Arab summit decided on the convening of an Afro-Arab summit (which took place in the Arab League headquarters in March 1977)[107] and on the creation of a number of basic institutions: the Arab Bank for Economic Development in Africa, with capital amounting to $738 million in 1977; the Arab Special Fund for Africa, with an initial fund of $210 million; and the Arab Fund for Technical Assistance to Arab and African Countries, with a modest initial capital of $15 million, later increased to $25 million.[108]

CONCLUSION: MAKING THE BEST OF GLOBAL ODDS

Despite its success, an analyst can still pinpoint some incoherent aspects in Algeria's foreign policy projects. Although it insists on international system change, Algeria's business dealings are most advanced with the United States—the stronghold of the status quo. Moreover, while adopting an economically oriented concept of international relations, emphasizing the transnational dimension, and preaching the necessity of a new system, Algeria's policy and declarations still adhere to the nineteenth-century concept of an international system based on the outdated notion of state sovereignty.

The Algerian policy-maker might consider these criticisms rather academic. They do not allow for Algeria's particular dilemmas nor for the necessary limits of a Third World country's foreign policy. A Third World country comes to independent statehood burdened with a historical legacy of societal disorganization and economic underdevelopment. It faces a hegemonic system that has developed across centuries and cannot be changed overnight. Even when a country challenges the system, it has to be ready to pay the price. It must therefore sort out secondary policy objectives, which can be sacrificed if necessary, from those that must be defended at all costs. Algeria has emphasized its national independence and mastery over its own natural resources, the primacy of an integrated and attainable development project, and international restructuring through unified action by the Third World. Occasional inconsistencies and deficiencies notwithstanding, Algeria's foreign policy has narrowed the characteristic gap between a Third World country's grandiose objectives and its limited capabilities. It has reduced incompatibilities among the components of its foreign policy orientation and between its foreign policy orientation and behavior. Given domestic and global constraints, the balance sheet is positive. A good demonstration of this positive balance sheet is Algeria's successful mediation to free the U.S. hostages in Iran in January 1981.[109] This mediation provides a microcosm of Algeria's foreign policy orientation and behavior, and gives a glimpse of the actual daily conduct of its diplomatic personnel.

U.S. relations with the former shah, the absence of diplomatic relations between the United States and Iran, the revolutionary orientation of the new Iranian elite and the problems it faced in establishing control: all of these factors seriously complicated the hostage issue. The outbreak of the Iran-Iraq war in September 1980 only added to the problems.

In the United States, the hostage issue became the dominant daily question, and the U.S. government was hard pressed to find a way out. As no direct official channels existed with the new Iranian regime, Washington had no choice but to work through third parties. When attempts to work through Germany (September 9–16, 1980) failed, Washington seized the opportunity of the Iranian prime minister's October 1980 visit to the UN in New York (to defend Iran's case against Iraq) to ask for the good offices of both the UN secretary-general and the Algerian delegation in New York. On November 2, 1980, Iran's Majlis stated conditions for the diplomats' release and solicited Algeria's help in reaching an agreement. Algeria was thus the only third party accepted by the two opponents.[110]

The United States preferred Algeria for three reasons: (1) despite "philosophical divergences," relations were good between the two countries and communication was smooth; (2) Algeria had kept a posture of neutrality during the hostage crisis. Without condemning anyone publicly, it showed in a semiofficial way that it did not condone what had happened; and (3) Algeria's humanitarian and diplomatic behavior since the beginning of the crisis in November 1979 was appreciated by the United States. At the human level, A. Gheraieb, Algeria's ambassador to Teheran, was the first diplomat to meet the American hostages; Cardinal Duval, archbishop of Algiers, was one of three religious figures to meet the hostages in March 1980. At the diplomatic level, Mohamed Bedjaoui, Algeria's UN representative, was a member of the UN mission sent to Teheran to mediate the crisis.

The Islamic Republic of Iran also had three reasons to favor Algeria's mediation: (1) both Algeria and the new Iran had similar international sensibilities and believed in an active Third World role; (2) the two countries were linked by a common Islamic ethos; and (3) despite the different sources of their revolutionary orientation, both countries opposed the "ancien régime" nationally and internationally, and sought authentic development based on independent identity. These affinities motivated Iran's new regime to ask Algeria to represent Iranian interests in Washington when diplomatic relations were broken off with the United States. Contacts between Algeria and Iran had been intense since the arrival of the new regime. In February 1979, Bendjedid sent a personal message to Ayatollah Khomeini; in March, Algeria sent an official delegation to Iran; and in July Algeria's first ambassador to the Islamic Republic of Iran presented his credentials. In November 1979, Iran sent an official delegation to participate in the celebrations of the twenty-fifth anniversary of the Algerian Revolution.

If Algeria's policy *orientation* ensured its acceptance as mediator by both opponents, Algeria's actual foreign policy *behavior* in conducting the negotiations guaranteed the successful denouement of the hostage crisis. Three personalities in Algeria's negotiating team were directly responsible for the conduct of this complicated process of international bargaining: A. Gheraieb, Algeria's ambassador to Teheran; Reda Malek, ambassador to the United States; and Mostefaï, director of Algeria's Central Bank. In addition, the Ministry of Foreign Affairs acted as an efficient clearinghouse throughout the negotiations, collecting and transmitting information for both sides. Because continuous residence in Algiers of high-level representatives of the two countries was not possible for an extended period, and because a continual shuttle was not feasible either, most of the basic work fell on the shoulders of the Algerians. The team of experts constituted by the Algerian government traveled to Teheran and Washington whenever necessary. Between November 1980 and January 1981, the Algerian team received the head of the U.S. delegation, Christopher Warren, three times, but made a total of five trips themselves, to Washington and Teheran.

The two phases (from moderator to mediator) of Algeria's behavior in the negotiations are also significant. Starting as merely a moderator, Algeria did not produce a full-fledged plan to be implemented by both sides. Instead, Algeria aimed at this stage to overcome obstacles and keep the negotiations from breaking down. At times, it used its influence to eliminate stumbling blocks and to help each of the parties reformulate propositions in terms more acceptable to the other side.

Algeria began by making an inventory of points of agreement and disagreement and sorting out "easy" and "difficult" points to be negotiated. A study was made of Iran's four conditions for the release of the hostages as expressed in Khomeini's September 1980 speech: U.S. nonintervention in Iran's internal affairs; unfreezing of Iranian assets in the United States; withdrawal of claims before U.S. courts; and return of royal assets. The first two demands were accepted by the United States. Hence real negotiations were to center on the last two, and to prevent breakdown in negotiating these difficult issues, Algeria helped each party to see the constraints of the other and to reformulate its demands in such a way as to avoid a categorical refusal.

For instance, the U.S. government did not know how much the royal assets amounted to or where they were located. Even if it had known, it could not simply return them without due process of U.S. law. Algerian negotiators helped the Iranians to see these constraints and thus reformulate their demand differently. Iran then asked for an inventory of the assets and their sequestration until they could be returned according to correct legal procedure.

When stalemate risked driving the two sides even further apart, Algeria saved the negotiations by carrying out the second, mediatory phase of its third-party role. On December 20, 1980, Teheran declared that the assets to be returned by the United States amounted to $24 billion. This figure had a disastrous effect on Washington, and some people started talking about blackmail.[111] In agreement with the United States the Algerians thus left the exact figure aside and worked instead on a procedure to assess the sum. It was in this context that the Algerians offered for the first time to issue an "Algerian declaration" instead of a bilateral agreement between Washington and Algiers. The Iranians were very receptive to this idea and a few days later their claims had been reduced to a total of $9 billion.

When the Air Algerie plane had finally transferred the hostages from Teheran, some people remarked that this was the greatest deal ever negotiated without direct contact between the parties. According to the head of the U.S. negotiating team, Christopher Warren, its success could not have been achieved without "the Algerian government, its Foreign Ministry, its negotiating team, and its diplomats." It was Warren who likened the Iranian and U.S. negotiators to two tennis players playing a match in two different courts.[112] The Algerians brought the players to the same court and umpired the match through to the end.

NOTES

1. Paul Balta and Claudine Rulleau (with the collaboration of Mireille Duteuil), *L'Algérie des Algériens: Vingt ans après* (Paris: Les Editions Ouvrières, 1981), Part 2.

2. Frantz Fanon, *Les damnés de la terre* (Paris: Maspero, 1964). Fanon was appointed Algeria's first ambassador to Ghana.

3. The review covered eleven articles published in well-known periodicals such as *Foreign Policy* (1972, pp. 108–131), *International Affairs* (1967, pp. 678–698), *Polity* (1973, pp. 477–488), *Revue Française de Science Politique* (1972, pp. 1276–1307), and *Chronique de Politique Etrangère* (1972, pp. 199–212). The article in the last-mentioned journal is by A. Bouteflika—a close companion of President Boumedienne since preindependence days who headed the Ministry of Foreign Affairs from 1963 until Boumedienne's death in 1978.

4. Slimane Chikh, "La politique Africaine de l'Algérie," in Chikh et al. (ed.), *Le Maghreb et l'Afrique subsaharienne* (Paris: Foundation National de Recherche Scientifique, 1980), pp. 1–54.

5. "In the late 1970s, the Roman Catholic population had been reduced to about 45,000. In addition there were a few thousand Protestants, including members of Protestant missions. . . . The Jewish community had numbered well in excess of 100,000 before the Algerian revolutionary period, but at independence in 1962 their number had been reduced to 4,000 and to about 1,000 by 1967. Because the Cremieux Decrees of 1870 had granted them French citizenship, most of the Jews went to France." *Algeria: A Country Study* (Washington, D.C.: American University, Foreign Area Studies, 1979), p. 116.

6. *Ibid.*, p. 92.

7. *Ibid.*, p. 117.

8. World Bank, *World Development Report 1982* (New York: Oxford University Press for the World Bank, 1982), p. 111.

9. *Algeria, op. cit.*, p. 118.

10. *El-Moudjahid*, December 1, 1971, as quoted in Bernard Cubertafond, "Reflexions sur la pratique politique Algérienne," *Maghreb-Mashreq* 69 (1975), p. 31.

11. Mohamed Dahmani, *L'Algérie: Légitimité historique et continuité politique* (Paris: Le Sycomore, 1979), p. 83.

12. For the names, see William Quandt, *Revolution and Political Leadership: Algeria 1954-1968* (Cambridge, Mass.: MIT Press, 1969), p. 288.

13. For the names of members in the three cabinet shuffles, see *ibid.*, p. 289.

14. The number of Political Bureau members rose from five in August 1962 to sixteen in April 1964. For names and characteristics, see *ibid.*, pp. 227, 293.

15. *Algeria, op. cit.*, p. 192.

16. For names and data on Ben Bella's three cabinets, see Quandt, *op. cit.*, pp. 232, 291-292; and Lhachmi Berrady et al., *La formation des élites politiques Maghrebines* (Paris: Librairie Générale de Droit et de Jurisprudence, 1973), pp. 109-111.

17. Jean Leca and Jean-Claude Vatin, "Le système politique Algérian 1976-1978: Idéologie, institutions et changement social," in Jean Leca et al., *Developpements politiques au Maghreb* (Paris: Centre National de la Recherche Scientifique, 1979), pp. 19-31.

18. Dahmani (*op. cit.*, p. 83) mentions only twenty-four members. For the names and career patterns of the twenty-six members, see Quandt, *op. cit.*, pp. 244-245.

19. For the names and characteristics of council members, see *ibid.*, p. 247, and Berrady et al., *op. cit.*, p. 113.

20. For more details, see *Algeria*, p. 196.

21. "Algeria," in Colin Legum (ed.), *Africa Contemporary Record*, 1979-1980 (London: Holmes and Meier, 1981), pp. B3-27.

22. *Ibid.*, pp. B3-27.

23. Legum, *Africa Contemporary Record*, 1980-1981, pp. B3-17. (Hereafter referred to as *Africa Record*.)

24. I. William Zartman, "Algeria: A Post-Revolutionary Elite," in Frank Tachau (ed.), *Political Elites and Political Development in the Middle East* (Cambridge, Mass.: Schenkman Publishing, 1975), p. 276.

25. So important is this phenomenon for understanding the present policies of Algeria that a standard book on Arab economies begins its chapter on Algeria by linking the country's economy to the historical colonial relationship. See Yusif A. Sayigh, *The Economies of the Arab World* (London: Croom Helm, 1978), pp. 514, 521.

26. *Ibid.*, p. 532; and Robert Merle, *Ahmed Ben Bella* (Paris: Gallimard, 1965), pp. 161-184.

27. *Algeria*, p. 149.

28. Balta and Ralleau, *op. cit.*, pp. 202-214.

29. Sayigh, *op. cit.*, p. 553.

30. *Algeria*, p. 152.

31. *Ibid.*, p. 157.

32. Legum, *Africa Record*, 1979-1980, p. B17.

33. Legum, *Africa Record*, 1980-1981, p. B13.

34. *Ibid.*

35. Legum, *Africa Record*, 1979-1980, p. B21.

36. For the text of the treaty, see *Le Lien* (Algerian Embassy, Ottawa) 5 (March 1983).

37. Legum, *Africa Record*, 1979-1980, p. B21.

38. *Le Monde*, March 1, 1983. The state of the economy/foreign policy linkage can work the other way, too, with foreign policy influencing domestic economic

choices. Following the 1973 oil embargo, some developed countries talked of using the "food weapon." In order to avoid "starvation," some Third World countries worked to develop their agricultural sectors. In April 1979, at a meeting with the national secretary of the Peasants Union (UNPA), Bendjedid reiterated that the government's objective was "the realization of the highest level of self-sufficiency possible in terms of food and agricultural products and, in consequence, the consolidation of national independence." Food imports in 1978 represented a third of domestic consumption and cost $750 million. Legum, *Africa Record*, 1979-1980, pp. 19–20.

39. *Algeria*, p. 264.

40. *Ibid.*, p. 260.

41. *Ibid.*, p. 269.

42. I. William Zartman, "The Algerian Army in Politics," in I. William Zartman (ed.), *Man, State and Society in the Contemporary Maghreb* (New York: Praeger Publishers, 1973), p. 217.

43. *Algeria*, p. 272.

44. *SIPRI Yearbook*, 1980-1981 (London: Taylor and Francis for SIPRI, 1981).

45. *Algeria*, p. 272.

46. See *ibid.*, for figures, p. 284.

47. *Ibid.*, p. 286.

48. *Ibid.*

49. *Ibid.*, p. 285. "Polisario" is the name used by the People's Liberation Front for Sagui El Hamra and Rio de Oro. The group seeks to establish an independent state—the Sahrawi Arab Democratic Republic—in what was formerly Spanish Sahara.

50. *Ibid.*, pp. 287–288.

51. Josiano Criscuelo, *Armée et nation dans les discours du Colonel Boumedienne* (Doctoral diss., Université Paul Valéry, 1975), Figure VIII.

52. *Dix ans d'efforts* (Alger: Les Presses des Editions Populaires de l'Armée, 1975), p. 57.

53. Mohamed Bedjaoui, "Aspects internationaux de la constitution Algérienne," *Annuaire Français du Droit International* 23 (1977), pp. 75–94.

54. As quoted in *ibid.*, pp. 75–94.

55. Charte Nationale du Peuple Algérien, edited and presented in Robert Lambotte, *Algérie, naissance d'une société nouvelle* (Paris: Editions Sociales, 1976), p. 225.

56. Bedjaoui, *op. cit.*

57. Charte, in Lambotte, *op. cit.*, pp. 213–227.

58. *Ibid.*, p. 214.

59. *Ibid.*, p. 215.

60. *Ibid.*, pp. 216–217.

61. *Ibid.*, p. 217.

62. *Ibid.*, p. 215.

63. *Ibid.*, p. 225.

64. Paul Balta and Claudine Rulleau, *La stratégie de Boumedienne* (Paris: Sindbad, 1978), p. 226.

65. Charte, in Lambotte, *op. cit.*, p. 218.

66. Balta and Rulleau, *La stratégie*, pp. 226–227.

67. Charte, in Lambotte, *op. cit.*, p. 213.

68. The standard application of this approach in foreign policy decision-making analysis is in Graham T. Allison, *Essence of Decision: Explaining the Cuban Missile Crisis* (Boston: Little, Brown and Co., 1972).

69. Ben Bella describes his meeting with GPRA members after his release from prison in 1962 as "a bitter experience." For details, see Merle, *op. cit.*, p. 133.

70. Quandt, *op. cit.*, p. 180.

71. *Algeria*, p. 198.

72. Ferhat Abbas, *Autopsie d'une guerre* (Paris: Garnier, 1980), pp. 271–294.

73. Ali Haouchine, *L'Etat et les travailleurs*, M.S. diss., University of Montreal, 1983, p. 218.

74. John P. Entelis, "Algeria: Technocratic Rule, Military Power," in I. William Zartman et al., *Political Elites in Arab North Africa* (New York and London: Longman, 1981), p. 108.

75. *Algeria*, p. 127.

76. Jean-Louis Buchet, "Qui est réellement le nouveau président?" *Jeune Afrique* 945 (February 14, 1979), pp. 28; Balta and Rulleau, *L'Algérie*, pp. 48–51, for a synthesis of information available on Bendjedid.

77. As quoted in Hamza Kaidi, "Une armée fortement politisée," *Jeune Afrique* 945 (February 14, 1979), p. 29.

78. For a chart on the ministry's organizational structure, see *Algeria*, pp. 234–236.

79. Entelis, *op. cit.*, pp. 101–102.

80. Albert-Paul Lentin, "Les hommes: Abdelaziz Bouteflika," *Maghreb-Mashreq* 52 (July-August 1972), pp. 7–10.

81. For the text of his speech to the meeting of Algerian ambassadors in Algiers, see Balta and Rulleau, *La stratégie*, p. 231.

82. Claude Roosens, "L'Algérie entre les deux grands," *Studia Diplomatica*, 34 (1981), pp. 591–608.

83. See Balta and Rulleau, *La stratégie*, pp. 255–256, for the text of his speech.

84. United Nations, *Yearbook of International Trade Statistics 1980* (New York: United Nations, 1981), p. 66.

85. Roosens, *op. cit.* France reacted to this by reducing its diplomatic representation in Moscow to the level of chargé d'affaires from March 25 to July 26, 1962.

86. The National Charter affirms that Algeria's socialism "does not emanate from any materialist metaphysics, and is not attached to any dogmatic conception alien to our national genius." It is a socialism "in accordance with the fulfillment of our Islamic values." Charte, in Lambotte, *op. cit.*, pp. 86–87. Of the 412 submissions to *Al-Moudjahid* on the National Charter during the public debate in May and June of 1976, 13 insisted on the protection of Islam, and emphasized compatibility between Islam and socialism. See the excellent paper by John Nellis, *The Algerian National Charter of 1976*, Center for Contemporary Studies Occasional Paper No. 2, 1980, pp. 25–27.

87. Roosens, *op. cit.*, p. 603.

88. *The Middle East and North Africa, 1977-1978* (London: Europa Publications, 1978).

89. Data are extracted from *The Military Balance 1979–1981* (London: International Institute of Strategic Studies) and *SIPRI Yearbook*, 1970–1981.

90. Robert A. Mortimer, "Algeria and the Politics of International Economic Reform," *Orbis* 21 (1977), pp. 671–700.

91. Abdel-Majid Farid, *From the Minutes of Nasser's Meetings* (Beirut: Institution of Arab Research, 1979), pp. 46–78 (in Arabic).

92. For greater detail, see Mortimer, *op. cit.*

93. For more details on the "economization of nonalignment as a movement," see Bahgat Korany, "From the Politics to the Economics of Nonalignment," Paper presented to the Twelfth Congress of the International Political Science Association, Rio de Janeiro, Brazil, August 1982.

94. Mortimer, *op. cit.*; and Peter Willetts, *The Nonaligned Movement* (London: Frances Pinter, 1979), pp. 254–259.

95. For the text, see Balta and Rulleau, *La stratégie*, pp. 315–330.

96. Henry Kissinger, *Years of Upheaval* (Boston: Little, Brown and Co., 1982), pp. 911–920.

97. Mortimer, *op. cit.*

98. For a detailed analysis of the Paris conference by an Algerian scholar who also represented his country in North-South and OPEC meetings, see Abdelkader Sid-Ahmed, *Nord-Sud: Les enjeux* (Paris: Publisud, 1981), pp. 99–141.

99. For a treatment of relations between these two regions in the context of inter-Arab relations, see Nicole Grimaud: "Maghreb et péninsule Arabe: De la réserve à la rivalité ou à la coopération," *Defense Nationale* 37 (1981), pp. 95–110; for a preliminary but rigorous attempt to compare the foreign policies of Algeria and Saudi Arabia, see Bocar E. Dia, "Etude comparative du comportement international de l'Algérie et de l'Arabie Saoudite de 1970 à 1977," M.S. thesis, University of Montreal, 1980.

100. Bruno Etienne, *L'Algérie, culture et révolution* (Paris: Seuil, 1977), p. 227.

101. Chikh, *op. cit.*, p. 4.

102. Balta and Rulleau also adopt this view in *La stratégie*, their excellent collection and classification of Boumedienne's speeches. They deal with "The Arab Homeland" in Chapter 10, and Chapter 11, entitled "From Africa to the Three Continents," includes speeches related to both Africa and the Third World in general.

103. Based on data in the excellent *Annuaire de l'Afrique du Nord*, 1970–1981 (Aix en Province: Centre de recherche et d'étude sur les sociétés méditerranéennes) [CRESM]. For different data and years, see Chikh, *op. cit.* Both sources, however, confirm Algeria's concentration on French-speaking Africa.

104. Adapted from Chikh, *op. cit.*, p. 35.

105. Adapted from *ibid.*, p. 28.

106. For a recent reconstruction and analysis of the different phases of this dialogue, see Magdi Hamad, "The Role of the Arab League in the Arab-African Dialogue," in *The Arab League: Reality and Ambition* (Beirut: Center for Arab Unity Studies, 1983), pp. 509–574 (in Arabic).

107. For documents of this conference and other relevant material, see the white paper published by Egypt's Ministry of Foreign Affairs, *Afro-Arab Cooperation 1977–1978* (Cairo: State Information Service, 1980).

108. *The Arab League*, pp. 509–574.

109. My reconstruction of events is based on data mentioned by *Keesings Contemporary Archives*, September 18, 1981, pp. 31081–31086; the chronologies of *Maghreb-Mashreq* and *Middle East Journal*; and the excellent analysis of Patrick Juillard, "Le rôle joué par la République Populaire et Démocratique d'Algérie dans le règlement du contentieux entre les Etats-Unis d'Amérique et la République Islamique d'Iran," *Annuaire Français de Droit International* 27 (1981), pp. 19–45.

110. Algeria had its own "national interest" reasons for accepting this mediatory role. The new regime was eager to retain international credibility after Boumedienne's death, and also to promote Algeria's style of conflict resolution, as demonstrated during the 1975 mediation between Iran and Iraq. Some analysts emphasize Algeria's expectations of a "U.S. sympathetic under-standing" concerning the Western Sahara conflict or the economic deals with El-Paso. See Jonathan C. Randal, "Algerians Angered by U.S. Moves Since Hostage Deal," *International Herald Tribune*, March 27, 1981, p. 4.

111. It is interesting that the Algerian team did not communicate the Iranian calculations to Washington in person, but just sent the document through their embassy, either to dissociate themselves from Teheran's figure or to spare their efforts for another round on a more workable basis.

112. As quoted in Juillard, *op. cit.*

5

The Primacy of Economics: The Foreign Policy of Egypt

Ali E. Hillal Dessouki

INTRODUCTION

In the 1970s, Egypt restructured its foreign policy orientation, and this restructuring reflected a trade-off between economic and political objectives as perceived by Egypt's primary decision-maker, President Anwar Al-Sadat. Foreign policy restructuring entails a major alteration or break-up in the orientation of an actor in *favor of* establishing a new set of commitments and alliances. It is more than a change in tactics or instruments of policy implementation; it also goes beyond the fluctuations and oscillations of foreign policy behavior of developing countries. It involves a basic reconsideration of an actor's perceptions of the global or regional system and of the country's role within that framework. Indicators of the restructuring of foreign policy orientation include patterns of diplomatic, commercial, military, and cultural relations between the country and the outside world.[1]

In the 1970s Sadat managed to change the name of Egypt (from the United Arab Republic to the Arab Republic of Egypt), its flag, and its national anthem. Economically, Egypt moved away from Nasser's Arab socialism and toward liberalization of the economy and the encouragement of private capital. Egypt's one-party political system, which had existed since 1953, was gradually replaced by a form of controlled political pluralism. At the regional level, the country changed its alliances in 1971–1973 and forged a close relation with pro-Western, conservative oil-producing states, particularly Saudi Arabia. As a result of Sadat's visit to Jerusalem in November 1977, Egypt was expelled from all Arab and Islamic councils. At the global level, Egypt moved from an essentially pro-Soviet position that included the granting of naval and air facilities to a virtual strategic alliance with the United States.

This chapter examines the sources, dynamics, and contradictions of Egypt's restructuring of its foreign policy orientation. The analysis underlines issues such as the role of domestic economic factors in foreign

120

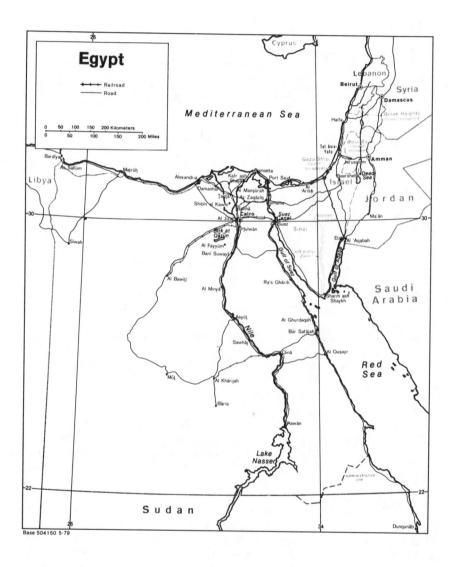

Egypt

+—+—+ Railroad
——— Road

0   50   100   150   200 Kilometers
0   50   100   150   200 Miles

Mediterranean Sea

Cyprus

Lebanon
Beirut
Syria
Damascus
Golan Heights
(Israeli occupied)

Haifa

Tel Aviv-Yafa
West Bank
(Israeli occupied)
Gaza Strip
(Israeli occupied)
Jerusalem
Amman
Beersheba
Dead Sea

Bardiya
As Sallūm
Maţrūḥ
Alexandria
Damanhūr
Kafr ash Shaykh
Ţanţā
Shibīn al Kawm
Banhā
Al Jīzah
Cairo
Birk at Qārūn
Hulwān
Al Fayyūm
Banī Suwayf
Al Manşūrah
Az Zaqāzīq
Ismailia
Suez Canal
Suez
Al 'Arīsh
Port Said
Damietta
Israel
Jordan
Ma'ān

Libya

Siwah

Sinai

Ela El 'Aqabah

UN Buffer Zone

Al Bawīţī
Al Minyā
Ra's Ghārib
Gulf of Suez
Gulf of Aqaba
Sharm ash Shaykh
Saudi Arabia

Asyūţ
Nile
Al Ghurdaqah
Būr Safājah
Sawhāj
Qinā
Al Quşayr
Red Sea

Mūţ
Al Khārijah
Bāris

Aswān

Lake Nasser

administrative line

Sudan
Dunqunāb

Base 504150 5-79

policy change, the perception of foreign policy as a resource mobilization activity, the strain resulting from the divergence between role conceptions developed in the 1950s and 1960s and the new environment that Egypt had to deal with, and the dilemma of maintaining a balance between reliance on foreign aid and assistance and protection of the country's independence.[2]

Comparative studies of foreign policy restructuring or alliance switching show that change occurs for various reasons: security considerations, perceptions of gross external dependency and asymmetrical vulnerabilities, ideological disputes, and nationalism. In Egypt's case, there are three crucial variables to be considered.[3] The first concerns relations between the superpowers. In breaking with one superpower, the timing of the small country is essential. The alternate superpower has to be both able and willing to assume the role instead. Thus, alliance switching is more easily accomplished in a cold war situation or at least in a situation of strong competition between the superpowers.

A second variable is the personality traits of the leadership. This variable is particularly important in Third World countries characterized by low political institutionalization. We should not, however, overstate the importance of personal attributes, for leaders do not act in a vacuum, and they are not entirely free to indulge their biases and idiosyncrasies. On the contrary, structural conditions—global, regional, and domestic—determine the environment in which individual leaders must operate. Domestic conditions, including the internal balance of political groups and the degree of political stability or instability, are particularly important for their impact on foreign policy.

The third variable is the dialectical interaction of any close relationship or alliance involving unequal states in the global stratification system. For a while, a small state may feel profound gratitude for the military and economic help coming from a superpower, but soon it may also resent the dependent relationship. The breakup of this patron-client type of relationship is to a certain extent predictable. The necessary conditions form a pattern: sufficient motivation (feeling of dependence), the existence of an alternative (the other superpower), and perception of potential benefits from a breakup.

THE DOMESTIC ENVIRONMENT

Geography

Some authors treat the geography of Egypt as an independent variable, postulating a sort of geographic determinism. In a two-volume book of more than 1,500 pages, the eminent Egyptian geographer Gamal Hamdan views the history of Egypt as an interaction between the Nile and the desert, and draws from this a number of conclusions about Egypt's national interest and policy.[4] The problem with this perspective is its static bias, its assumption of certain unchanging geographic effects of foreign policy. As was explained in Chapter 1, the effects of geography depend upon the *interaction* between geographic factors and how a particular elite or leader perceives their significance.

Egypt, a land of broad cultural and social homogeneity, is a distinct geographical and historical entity. Egypt's geographical data are simple but extremely significant. The country occupies the northeastern corner of Africa with an extension across the Gulf of Suez into the Sinai Peninsula in Asia. It is bordered by the Mediterranean Sea to the north, the Sudan to the south, the Red Sea to the east, and Libya to the west. Egypt consists of three regions: (1) the Nile Valley and Nile Delta (a little less than 4% of the total area), which extend from the Sudan northward to the Mediterranean; (2) the eastern desert and the eastern gate to Egypt—the Sinai Peninsula (28%), which extends from the Nile Valley to the Red Sea east of the Suez Canal; and (3) the western desert (68%), which stretches from the Nile Valley westwards to Libya. Briefly stated, Egypt is a line of water and verdure that runs between two deserts and widens near the Mediterranean Sea.

Two important conclusions emerge from this description. First, Egypt's geographic position made it an easy country to control and to rule. Two main features of the Egyptian society and polity are centralized rule and the absence of long-standing regional allegiances. Dependence on the Nile for irrigation called for central administration and enabled the government to extend its authority to the distant parts of the land. Because the territory is mostly desert, 96% of Egyptians live on less than 4% of the total area of their country.

Egypt's geographic position lends itself to two different perceptions and therefore, two different foreign policy objectives. Some view the relative physical isolation of the valley as the most important factor in Egypt's situation: it sets the country apart from its neighbors. In the twentieth century, this perception gave rise to tendencies toward isolationism, Swiss-type neutrality, and the advocacy of an "Egypt first" policy. Others see Egypt's geographic position primarily as a bridgehead, a linking point, a crossroads between Africa and Asia and between the eastern and western parts of the Arab world. Adherents of this school advocate an active foreign policy in the Arab world and Africa. Egypt's eastern, Arab policy is justified in terms of Arab nationalism and security; its southern, African policy rests on the need to protect the Nile waters, the lifeline of Egypt. Nasser embraced the activist view throughout most of his rule, but Sadat gradually emphasized Egyptian patriotism and the urgency of concentrating on Egypt's domestic economic problems. In the war of words that followed the Camp David Accords Sadat openly accused the Arabs of being dwarfs, uncivilized and unfit to understand the complexities of the modern world. Because of its wars with Israel, Egypt had become the poorest Arab state, Sadat frequently reminded the Egyptians.

Population and Social Structure

Egypt's population is characterized by social cohesiveness and since the 1950s, a baby boom. Historically, Egypt is one of the oldest continuously settled communities in the world. Egyptians long ago acquired the sense of being one people. All Egyptians speak Arabic, with the exception of the Nubians (less than 1%) and an insignificant number of isolated Berber-speaking groups in the western desert. More than 90% of the population are Moslems, and Islam is the state religion. The indigenous Copts form the largest of the other religious groups. Estimates of their numbers vary between 2.3 and 4 million. The Copts speak Arabic, and hardly any racial or ethnic differences exist between them and the Moslems. In 1983, the population of Egypt reached 45 million, and was increasing by 1 million every ten months. The population growth rate between 1966 and 1976 was about 65,000 persons each month, or 2,141 every day and one every 41 seconds.[5]

A direct consequence of the population explosion is the youthfulness of Egypt's population. Almost one-half of Egyptians are under twenty years of age; two-thirds are under thirty. Another consequence is the high dependency ratio, or the large number of dependents supported by working adults, a situation that put severe constraints on the economy in the 1970s. The government is increasingly incapable of meeting the demands for food, education, and work opportunities. A third consequence is the migration of some 3 million Egyptians in search of work to other Arab countries, particularly the oil-producing states.

In contrast to the situation in most developing countries, the population in Egypt shows a high degree of social and national integration. Both Nasser and Sadat spoke proudly of Egypt's national unity. There are no fundamental minority cleavages to constrain foreign policy–makers and limit their options. The one major area of anxiety is the Copts' concern about the implementing of Islamic law in Egypt and the status of Copts in an Islamic state. Sadat used to contrast Egypt's deep-seated unity with the sectarian, familial, and communal fragmentation of most Arab countries. According to Sadat, this unity allowed Egypt to pursue a purposeful foreign policy and to make hard decisions (e.g., peace with Israel) impossible for most Arab countries because of their domestic fragmentation. The population of Egypt constitutes a relatively large human resource pool. It allowed the government to mobilize an army of about 1 million in 1973. Egyptians working abroad provide another positive resource: their remittances reached $2.7 billion in 1982 and constituted the single largest source of Egypt's hard currency.

Notwithstanding these positive aspects, population growth has had an adverse impact and has limited Egypt's developmental efforts. The population explosion has aggravated unemployment problems, increased the dependency ratio, augmented rural migration to urban centers, and led to the diversion of resources from investment to consumption needs.[6] Egypt is a prime example of structural imbalance between population and material resources. Population is increasing at a rate far beyond the growth in arable cropped land, far beyond educational and industrial development. The per capita cropped area declined from 0.73 feddans per person in 1882 to 0.33 feddans per person in 1970 (a feddan equals 0.42 ha or 1.04 acres). Thus, despite the fact that the cropped area almost doubled during this period, population growth absorbed and surpassed the increase. In the 1970s Egypt had to use its limited hard currency to import foodstuffs. This made the country more dependent on the outside world and more vulnerable to the fluctuations of world food market prices. The extent and consequences of food dependency are likely to be major policy concerns in Egypt for years to come.

Economic Capability

In the 1970s economic factors played a crucial role in the determination of Egypt's foreign policy objectives. By 1980, inflation was running at nearly 30% a year, debts reached a total of $17 billion, and the GNP per capita was $580. Sadat's decision to visit Israel was largely motivated by economic considerations: the reduction of defense expenditures (37% of the GNP in 1977), the encouragement of foreign private capital, and the need for more U.S. aid. Even before this step, Sadat's Arab policy and his forging of a Cairo-Riyadh alliance had also been predicated on expected economic gains.

Since the Second World War, Egypt has had a balance-of-payments deficit that had had to be filled from other sources. From 1948 to 1958 it was filled from existing Egyptian reserves; from 1958 to 1964 Egypt received foreign aid from Eastern and Western sources; from 1965 to 1971 the USSR shouldered most of the deficit; from 1971 to 1977 the aid was Arab money; and since 1978 it has been U.S. money. In 1981 Egypt received $2.2 billion in Western aid, of which half came from the United States. In the 1970s Egyptian debts increased by a yearly average of 28%, compared with the 13% in the 1960s.

Thus, Egyptian foreign policy has faced the important task of mobilizing external resources to ease the growing population-resources gap. Because of its important strategic-political position and role, Egypt has successfully managed to find aid to bail the country out, but this is a tragic success, as it proves the failure of Egypt's developmental plans.

The Egyptian record in the 1970s demonstrates the tensions resulting from a limited resource base, the pursuit of an activist foreign policy, and increasing economic troubles at home. Economic difficulties contributed to the evolution of a more inward-looking and less activist foreign policy. The failure of the government's development efforts to meet the needs of the country's population resulted in growing numbers of shantytowns and the potential for political instability. This led the Egyptian leadership increasingly to seek external help to resolve the country's difficult economic situation. The era of revolutionary zeal and enthusiasm (1955–1965), which had witnessed the ascendency of Egypt and a number of other Third World states in international politics, was gradually replaced by more sober behavior in the 1970s. One important factor was the limited success of development plans in these countries and the subsequent surfacing of serious internal social and economic problems. In Egypt, ideological and political considerations were overshadowed by more immediate economic concerns, and as John Waterbury wrote, "the primacy of economics has become undisputed in Egypt of 1975."[7] Thus, the balance between external and domestic concerns was greatly affected by Egypt's poor economic performance in the face of an ever-expanding population.

In 1974 Sadat inaugurated *Al-Infitah*, the open door economic policy (ODEP), to lure foreign investment into Egypt. He justified the *Infitah* on the following grounds: (1) the failure of Nasser's socialist experience; (2) the availability of Arab capital from the oil-producing countries; and (3) the international context of détente. From an economic standpoint, the two essential purposes of ODEP were, first, to attract export-oriented foreign enterprises by the establishment of duty-free zones, and second, to attract foreign capital through a liberal investment policy. However, the ultimate goal of the policy was to set the stage for the development of the Egyptian economy through joint ventures and projects bringing together Egyptian labor, Arab capital, and Western technology and management expertise.[8]

A full analysis of ODEP is beyond the scope of this chapter. What is of interest to us here is how ODEP was motivated by foreign policy considerations and what its impact on them was. Divorcing the analysis of policy-making processes in developing countries from their foreign environment can only lead to erroneous and misleading conclusions. Given their low degree of political institutionalization, their high level of political and social instability, the general structure of their international economic relations, and most importantly, their dependence upon the outside world for almost everything from food to armaments, developing countries are highly susceptible to external influences.

Little has been written on the role of external factors in the formulation of ODEP; yet these factors greatly influenced Egyptian officials, and they may become ingrained in the logic of any "open door" policy. When a ruling elite decides to pursue a development strategy based on foreign aid and capital, it follows that all necessary steps will be taken to attract and reassure its creditors. And the more dependent it is on others, the more vulnerable a country becomes to their pressure. This is especially true in developing countries whose leadership fails to produce coherent development strategies. In the case of Egypt, the initial vagueness of ODEP's goals, and the lack of consensus on its content among the ruling elite, allowed external factors to play a more crucial role.

The World Bank, the International Monetary Fund (IMF), private financial institutions, and the oil-producing Arab states have all played a role in influencing Egypt's economic policy.[9] The crux of the matter is that for two years (1975 and 1976) international financial institutions and Arab and Western creditors pressured Egypt to make its economy more acceptable and accessible to the world capitalist market by curbing subsidies and devaluing the Egyptian pound. For two years Egyptian officials resisted, mainly because the subsidies and the currency supports were what allowed the lower middle and lower classes to maintain an already low standard of living. By the fall of 1976, oil-producing Arab states joined the United States and the IMF in pressing Egypt for additional fundamental changes. They refused to give Egypt more than a limited amount of money until the government agreed to the "reforms" proposed by the IMF. Egypt's requests for loans from the IMF and United States banks were delayed in the face of a $1.25 billion deficit for the second half of 1976. Western countries provided short-term loans to finance their exports to Egypt, but the big money needed to meet debt obligations and the balance-of-payment deficit was not forthcoming.

In January 1977 the government announced price increases for a number of basic commodities such as rice, sugar, gas, cigarettes, and household cooking gas. Almost immediately, violent demonstrations erupted in major cities, leaving an official death toll of about 70. An estimated 800 people were injured, and 1,270 were arrested. Economic decisions were suspended, a curfew was imposed, and the army was called in to maintain law and order. The January riots underlined the political explosiveness of the subsidy issue. Immediately after the riots, the United States and the oil-producing Arab states came to the rescue.

Thus, the impact of economic factors can be summarized as follows: first, Egypt's limited resources put a constraint on its government's ability to pursue an activist foreign policy and encouraged it to reach a modus vivendi with conservative rich Arab states; second, the economic troubles made Egypt more dependent on foreign aid and therefore more vulnerable to external influence.

Military Capability

In the 1970s, Egypt's arms arsenal was considerably weakened by (1) the failure of the Soviet Union to resupply the army adequately after the war of 1973 and the eventual severance of the Soviet military link in 1976; (2) the time needed to shift procurement needs from the Soviet Union to the West and to forge a new link with the United States; and (3) the economic costs of massive rearmament. From 1967 to 1975, according to official estimates, Egypt spent $25 billion for military purposes, and this was matched by an equal amount in war-related losses. During the same period, Egypt received less than $900 million from Arab states.[10]

Of particular interest in this regard is the experience of the Arab military armaments organization (AMIO), founded in 1975 as a joint venture by Egypt, Saudi Arabia, the United Arab Emirates, and Qatar.

AMIO was endowed with more than $1.4 billion in an effort to combine oil money with Egypt's skilled labor force. By 1978 the groundwork was laid for the establishment of a basic Arab defense industry located mainly in Egypt. Contacts were initiated with American Motors Corporation to assemble jeeps, with the Ryan Teledyne Corporation to produce high-altitude Drones (pilotless planes equipped with light and infrared sensors), and with Lockheed Aircraft Industries to build C-130 military transports.[11] Contacts were also made with Westland of Britain to construct 50 Lynx helicopters and the Swingfire antitank missile.[12] This project was reduced by half in May 1979 in protest over the Egyptian-Israeli treaty, and the other three Arab partners decided to terminate the venture as of July 1, 1979. Egypt rejected the decision and instead transformed AMIO into a fully Egyptian enterprise. In 1981, Egypt produced $40 million worth of arms, and in 1983 it assembled the new French Alpha jets. Increasingly, Egyptian arms deals are made on the basis of coproduction, with an Egyptian role in assembly and parts production.[13]

The relative erosion of Egyptian military power put a constraint on the use of the military instrument in conducting foreign policy. This is not to suggest that the military role vanished altogether. Egypt still has one of the best-trained and most highly skilled armies in the region, and Egyptian armed forces number well over 300,000, making Egypt's military the largest in the Arab world and Africa. Since the late 1970s, Egypt has embraced an ambitious program for the modernization of its armed forces, ordering more than $4 billion worth of equipment from the United States and another $1 billion from Britain and France. U.S. military aid to Egypt is around $1.3 billion a year. Thus, Egyptian decision-makers still emphasize the readiness of their country to help other Arab states militarily. Egypt has provided arms, ammunition, and logistical aid to Iraq in its war with Iran.

Political Structure

From 1952 to 1970 the basic characteristics of the political regime in Egypt were absence of political competitiveness, centralization of power, emphasis on mobilization rather than participation, supremacy of the executive over the legislative branch, and repression of political dissent. A clear imbalance existed between politics and administration; output institutions (bureaucracy, police, and army) far outgrew input institutions (interest groups and political organizations). Whenever possible, the government attempted to penetrate and dominate intermediary associations and groups such as trade unions, professional associations, religious institutions, and universities, bringing them under its legal and financial control. The political system gave its leaders, Nasser and Sadat, an almost free hand in the conduct of foreign policy. The leader was not accountable to either a free press, opposition parties, or an independent strong parliament. The regime controlled both the mass media and the legislature and could mobilize their support for its objectives.

In the 1970s two important processes took place: increasing civilianization of the ruling elite and the development of a limited political pluralism. Sadat followed a policy of professionalizing the army, disengaging it from current political affairs and placing more reliance on civilians in high posts. For the first time since 1952, civilians assumed the posts of vice-president (Mahmoud Fawzi) and prime minister (Aziz Sidky, Fawzi, Abdel-Aziz Hegazi, and Mustafa Khalil). In the realm of foreign policy, Ismail Fahmy, a career diplomat, became the minister of foreign affairs for five years, 1973–1977, till his resignation in protest over Sadat's Jerusalem visit. In 1977, Boutros Ghali, a professor of political science at Cairo University, became the state minister for foreign affairs.

The second development was the gradual democratization of the political structure, leading in 1976–1977 to the establishment of a controlled multiparty system. The democratization process was inspired in part by foreign policy considerations: Sadat's rapprochement with the United States and his desire to project the image of a stable, democratic Egypt. In 1980, opposition political parties included the Labor Socialist party (LSP), led by Ibrahim Shukry; the National Progressive Unionist party (NPUP), led by Khaled Mohie Al-Din, and the Liberal Socialist party, led by Mustafa Kamel Murad. The opposition had a weak parliamentary following (20 seats out of 390), but they exercised a far greater influence through their newspapers and publications. Foreign policy was a major bone of contention between the regime and the opposition. The LSP and the NPUP attacked Sadat's pro-Western policy, Egypt's increasing dependency on the United States, Sadat's policy toward Israel, and the break with Arab countries. The Moslem Brotherhood's journal, the monthly *Al-Da'wa* (The Call), also voiced most of these concerns, and its writers condemned governmental policies.

The government could have viewed these criticisms as a justification for stiffening its negotiating position toward Israel. Sadat, however, perceived them as signs of vulnerability, weakness, and the erosion of his personal stature, an interpretation that led to political polarization and the confrontation of September–October 1981, the arrest of 1,963 persons in September, and Sadat's assassination in October.

FOREIGN POLICY ORIENTATION

President Sadat assumed office in October 1970 under circumstances that obliged him to emphasize continuity with his predecessor's policies. Nasser's sudden death as a hero restrained Sadat's freedom to deviate from Nasser's domestic and foreign policies. In a meeting of Parliament on November 19, 1970, he presented a ten-point program for national action that included "working for Arab unity, playing a role in the nonaligned movement and in the Third World revolutionary movement."[14] In an essay entitled "Where Egypt Stands," published in *Foreign Affairs* in 1972, Sadat reiterated the basic tenets of Nasser's foreign policy: nonalignment and Arab unity.[15] Sadat lived in Nasser's shadow until 1973, when he acquired legitimacy in his own right through success in the October War. The new legitimacy allowed him to pursue domestic and foreign policies different from Nasser's.

Egyptian general foreign policy objectives in the 1970s, as articulated and acted upon by Sadat, were as follows: (1) the restoration, preferably by negotiation, of Egyptian territories occupied by Israel since 1967 (As a consequence, when Sadat's February 1971 peace plan failed, the only option left was war.); (2) the termination of the war with Israel, as the economic costs had become unbearable; (3) the improvement of relations with Washington, as the United States was the only country that could influence Israel; (4) the rejuvenation and modernization of the economy through the import of modern Western technology and private capital; and finally (5) the modification of Egypt's global and regional policies in order to better pursue these objectives.

Sadat's decision to seek better relations with the United States was influenced by his mistrust of and political hostility toward the Soviets and by his belief that the United States would help solve Egypt's pressing economic problems. Sadat was a pragmatist, a realist with little attachment to grand theories and ideologies. He was essentially anti-Communist and anti-Soviet. East-West détente gave him the chance of a lifetime. Sadat saw détente and explained it to the Egyptians as the alliance between the two superpowers and their agreement on international issues. The Arabic word used to describe détente, *wifaq*, is actually the equivalent of "entente."

In 1971 and 1972 Sadat viewed the delay in Soviet arms deliveries as a pressure on Egypt. He clearly saw in it an agreement between the two superpowers to prevent a new major war in the area, and interpreted the inclusion in the U.S.-Soviet communique of May 1972 of the expression "military relaxation" in reference to the Middle East as justification for his suspicions. It follows that Sadat saw no difference between the United States and the Soviet Union insofar as their position toward the Middle East was concerned. This made the shift from one superpower to another less difficult.

Sadat's attitude toward the Soviet Union was primarily one of mistrust and hostility. In his speeches on the Soviet Union one detects a feeling of humiliation, frustration, and violated dignity. Sadat spoke of the many promises that were given and never fulfilled, the many messages from Cairo that went unanswered. He once described the Soviets as "crude and tasteless people."[16] By the late 1970s, Sadat became a publicly avowed anti-Soviet; he cautioned the United States against underestimating the Soviet threat and pointed out that U.S. influence in the region was on the wane.[17] Sadat volunteered the services of the Egyptian army and territory to combat the Soviet threat. Egyptian officials spoke of the Soviet encirclement of the Middle East through surrogate states with the objective of destabilizing and overthrowing moderate pro-Western Arab regimes, particularly Egypt. In September 1981, Egypt's minister of defense stated: "Egypt is now in a very critical situation because of the threat surrounding it on the West and from the South."[18]

Sadat's strategy concerning the United States was designed to achieve three objectives: first, to outbid Israel and secure U.S. support in the peace negotiations; second, to obtain U.S. military and economic aid at an increasing rate; and third, to assure pro-Western Arab governments that their opposition to Egypt's relationship with Israel would lead nowhere and that Egypt remained the centerpiece in U.S. strategy in the region.

As early as November 1973, in his first meeting with Henry Kissinger, Sadat talked about common strategy between Egypt and the U.S. to remove Soviet influence from the Middle East. He expanded his strategic vision to encompass a local triangular hegemony in the Middle East, an axis of the three predominant anti-Communist powers: Egypt, Saudi Arabia, and Iran.[19]

Sadat believed in the importance of close economic and strategic links with Western countries, particularly with the United States. Anti-imperialism, Afro-Asian solidarity, and similar clichés were out of date and no longer useful to Egypt. Sadat was attracted to the American way of life, the consumer society, and the capitalist path of development. Politically, the United States held "the key to peace" in the area, "99% of the cards of the game," he frequently stated. This was because the United States was the only country that could exert influence on Israel. Sadat's view of the superpowers was reinforced by his desire to cement his relations with oil-rich conservative Arab countries whom he perceived as a vital source of economic aid.

Contrary to Nasser, who saw the Arab world as Egypt's natural sphere of influence and leadership and as the main arena for an active foreign policy, Sadat saw Egypt's leadership position as a structural property, not a behavioral attribute, as a property that could not be challenged or taken away. Consequently, he did not feel the need to pursue an activist Arab policy to maintain this leadership. For instance, as early as 1974–1975 Egypt dismantled its apparatus of influence in Lebanon, which had included financial support to friendly political groups, subsidies for newspapers, strong intelligence presence, and close contacts with local politicians. In Sadat's mind, the costs of that leadership style overshadowed its dividends.

As generally argued, leadership is a two-way process, involving influence as well as responsibility. The credibility of a regional power depends on its ability to support friendly states. Thus, the resources of a state and its readiness to translate them into effective instruments of foreign policy are major factors in the determination of regional leadership.

For Sadat, the ultimate constraint was the unavailability of resources to pursue an active Arab foreign policy and to compete with countries with immense financial resources such as Saudi Arabia and Iraq. This view was reinforced by his desire in the early 1970s to develop a broad Arab consensus against Israel in preparation for the war. Consequently, Egypt followed a policy of coexistence with other Arab regimes, primarily those that had oil wealth and happened to be conservative. He was ready to praise and court the Saudis in public and by 1973 the Cairo-Riyadh axis became paramount in inter-Arab politics.[20] Moreover, he was ready to develop closer relations with the shah of Iran and to find a role for Iran in the region.

Sadat emphasized the need for greater Arab cooperation and solidarity. What was important, he kept saying, was not legal and constitutional formulae, but the ability of the Arabs to coordinate and act jointly and effectively. According to Sadat, Arab states must recognize the differences existing between them and the fact that there could be no total or permanent convergence between their interests. He attacked his critics as ignorant dwarfs and stooges of foreign powers, namely the USSR, motivated by malice and locked into the same rotten mentality that had existed for thirty years.[21]

THE DECISION-MAKING PROCESS

Under Nasser and Sadat, foreign policy was the *domaine privé* of the president and his close associates. Although the two leaders differed in their styles and orientations, both centralized and personalized the foreign policy–making process, limiting the role of institutions. The influence of different individuals upon the process depended not on their position in the cabinet or the bureaucracy but rather on their personal relations and access to the president. Thus, for instance, when the responsibilities of Ismail Fahmy, minister of foreign affairs from 1973 to 1977, were increased, it reflected Sadat's confidence in Fahmy and not a change in the functions of the ministry as an institution.

Although this picture is essentially accurate, the dynamics of the decision-making process are more complex. Presidents and kings, however authoritarian and unaccountable, do not make decisions in a vacuum but rather in a specific institutional context. The context affects the behavior of individuals, the formulation of options, and the way choices are made. Compared with other Arab countries, Egypt is an organizationally developed and intellectually diversified society. Consequently the leader, notwithstanding his immense power, has to assume the various roles of arbiter, mediator, and lobbyist at one time or another.

Egypt's foreign policy decision-making process comes closest to the "leader-staff group" or the "presidential center" type.[22] This type of process involves an authoritative decision-maker who can act alone, with little or no consultation with other people or institutions except for a small group of subordinate advisors. These advisors are appointed by the leader and have no autonomous power base.

The leader-staff type of decision-making results in a highly personalized diplomacy. It is also characterized by the ability to respond quickly and to adopt nontraditional behavior. On July 8, 1972, upon the receipt of an unsatisfactory message from the Soviet Union, Sadat informed the Soviet ambassador immediately of his decision to dismiss Soviet advisors. He announced the decision ten days later. To understand leader-staff policy-making, we must take a closer look at the leader, President Sadat.

President Sadat (1918–1981) had a colorful and controversial political background before the revolution of 1952. He graduated from military college in 1939, mixed with different political groups, and in the 1940s was engaged in several intrigues against the government and the British. He was sacked from the army, and worked then as a journalist, a truck driver, and at a lot of petty jobs. After 1952, he held a number of prestigious titles, including vice-president and speaker of the Parliament, but Sadat's power was more nominal than real. All through this period, however, he was able to watch Nasser decide and act, and the valuable experience he gained was useful to him when he assumed the presidency in October 1970.

Sadat's political style was characterized by initiative, surprise moves, unexpectedness and shock treatments; he described it as one of "electric shocks." He used to surprise his own associates as well. For example, Mustafa Khalil, the prime minister, was taken by complete surprise when President Jimmy Carter, after his private meeting with Sadat at Cairo Airport in March 1979, announced that Sadat had agreed to Israeli terms on the peace treaty. Also, contradicting a statement Boutros Ghali, state minister of foreign affairs, made in May 1979—that Egyptian-Israeli borders would not be open before the official date for the normalization of relations, Sadat promised Begin a week later that borders would open once the Sinai capital had been handed over to Egypt.[23]

Another feature of Sadat's style was personalization. He spoke of *my* people, *my* army, *my* initiative, *my* foreign policy, and he viewed relations between states as a function of the relations between their leaders. In many speeches he referred to other leaders as personal friends of his; the list includes Carter, Faisal, Ford, D'Estaing, and a host of others.[24] In his analysis of Egyptian-Soviet relations he emphasized the personal mistreatment he had been subjected to. Finally, Sadat related that when he was considering the visit to Jerusalem his primary concern centered on Begin: "Was he a strong man, was he capable of making hard decisions?" In another instance he said that he studied Begin's personality and character as boxers do with their adversaries.[25]

Sadat had the ability to attract the media and use it to further his objectives. He managed, perhaps to a degree unmatched by any Third World leader, to remain a center of Western media attraction. Major

Western newspapers and radio and television stations established permanent offices in Cairo, or increased existing ones. Sadat was conscious of the importance of the media, and kept himself surrounded by its representatives. To succeed, Sadat had to say what would be interesting and attractive to them. The role of the media was crucial in the few days preceding his visit to Jerusalem. Indeed, the media, particularly the television media, played an important role in promoting the visit. In November and December of 1977, Sadat met 1,500 media representatives and appeared on the cover of some 143 magazines.[26]

To sum up, Sadat was a man of constant action; "I prefer action to reaction," he stated once in 1975.[27] One of his favorite expressions in relation to the peace negotiations was the necessity of "keeping the momentum" and "the process going on." He was a master of adaptation and survival, ready to change strategy quickly in the course of his political maneuvers. For some, Sadat represented the perfect diplomat, the professional politician—a fox whose political skills enabled him to manipulate conditions for his own objectives. Others saw him as an unprincipled man who sought international recognition and fame and was ready to say or do whatever would keep the media interested.

In addition to the president, the decision-making process includes presidential aides, the National Security Council, the Ministry of Foreign Affairs, and other ministries.

Presidential Aides

The president's aides form a diverse group of individuals whose titles and jobs have differed over time. Chief among them are:

- *Vice-president:* From his appointment in April 1975 until October 1981, Hosni Mubarak acted in a number of foreign policy missions; he mediated inter-Arab disputes (the Algerian-Moroccan Sahara conflict), attended conferences, and conveyed important political messages.
- *Presidential Staff:* In the early 1970s Ashraf Marwan, presidential secretary of information and later for foreign relations, was crucial in the implementation of foreign policy. He traveled extensively in the Arab world, particularly to Saudi Arabia. Marwan attended the OPEC ministerial meeting in March 1974 and called for the removal of the oil embargo on the United States.[28] In 1972 Sadat appointed Hafez Ismail, formerly an officer, undersecretary for foreign affairs, and ambassador to London, as national security advisor. Ismail became involved in the early stages of dialogue with the United States and visited Washington in February 1973. Hassan Al-Tohami, former officer and a presidential aide with the rank of vice–prime minister, twice met Moshe Dayan in Morocco in 1977 before Sadat's visit to Israel. This group also included Mahmoud Fawzi, presidential advisor for political affairs; Hassan Sabri Al-Kholi, personal representative of the president; Osama Al-Baz, under-

secretary of foreign affairs; and Tahseen Basheer, presidential press affairs advisor.

• *Presidential Assistants:* In the 1970s a number of senior politicians assumed this job: Aziz Sidky, Mamduh Salem (both former prime ministers), and Sayed Marie (former speaker of Parliament). The president assigned these assistants specific foreign policy missions. In March 1973, Sadat asked Marie to visit the Sudan, Libya, and Saudi Arabia in preparation for the October War. Marie traveled again on October 7, visiting Saudi Arabia, Kuwait, and other Gulf states.[29] In August 1980 Sadat sent Mamduh Salem to a number of African states to offset Arab attempts to suspend Egypt's membership in the Organization of African Unity.

National Security Council

The National Security Council, established in 1969, is the highest organ for strategic planning and national security issues. Its membership includes, among others, the president, the vice-president, the ministers of foreign affairs and defense, and the head of intelligence. The council has no definite jurisdiction and meets upon the invitation of the president. Sadat convened the council on major issues only. He called a meeting of the council for September 30, 1973, to discuss options of war, but he did not inform its members of the exact date of the battle, which began six days later.[30] He also convened the council in October 1977 to discuss the idea of visiting Israel.[31] In 1981 and 1982, President Mubarak convened the council only once.

Ministry of Foreign Affairs

Egypt's Foreign Ministry has a history that goes as far back as 1837, when it was established as a *diwan* (department) during Mohamed Ali's reign. It was abolished on December 17, 1914, with the proclamation of Egypt as a British protectorate, and it was reinstated in 1922 after independence.

In the 1970s the job of foreign minister was assumed by several men: Mahmoud Riad, 1971 (former officer involved in diplomacy since the late 1940s); Murad Ghaleb, 1971–1972 (M.D. and former ambassador to Moscow); Mohamed Hassan Al-Zayyat, 1972–1973; Ismail Fahmy, 1973–1977; Ibrahim Kamel, 1977–1978 (all career diplomats); Mustafa Khalil, 1978–1980 (engineer); and Kamal Hassan Ali, 1980– (former officer, intelligence chief, and minister of defense). Murad Ghaleb, Mohamed Riad, and Boutros Ghali were state ministers for foreign affairs.

The role of the ministry was naturally overshadowed by the presidency, and the foreign minister acted mainly as a presidential advisor. He did not attend all the president's meetings with foreign officials. For example, some of the most crucial sessions in the Egyptian-Israeli negotiations were confined to Sadat. In his visits to Egypt in November 1973 and January 1974, Kissinger primarily conferred with Sadat alone. Messages were exchanged directly between the president and other countries without the knowledge of the ministry, and Egyptian ambassadors to Arab capitals were not informed about the many visits Ashraf Marwan made to these countries in the early 1970s.[32]

In contrast to Hermann's notion of "positive reinforcement," according to which staff members tend to sympathize with their leader's wishes and demands,[33] in 1977–1978 three successive Egyptian foreign ministers resigned in protest over presidential policy. When the stakes are high and the dangers great, even staff members who are totally dependent on the president may take independent positions.

Other Ministries

These include the Ministries of Defense (formerly called the War Ministry), Economy, and Investment. They maintain official representation in key capitals of the world.

FOREIGN POLICY BEHAVIOR

In this section we will deal primarily with Egypt's changing relationship with the two superpowers and with regional Arab policy.

Egyptian-Soviet Relations

For a long time Egypt was the cornerstone of Soviet Arab and Middle Eastern policy, and Egyptian-Soviet relations were thought of as a model of cooperation between the Soviet Union and a non-Communist Third World country. Ironically, since 1967 Soviet influence and prestige have correlated adversely with the fortunes of Egypt. The 1967 defeat greatly enhanced the Soviet presence, and the success of 1973 contributed to its waning. In the post-1973 era, relations were primarily characterized by mutual mistrust and hostility. Disagreement between the two countries covered a broad range of issues: political-diplomatic (renewed relations with the United States as a means of resolving the Arab-Israeli conflict); military (armament, compensation for weapons lost in the war, and Egypt's decision in 1975 to diversify its sources of supply); and economic (rescheduling the debt).[34]

Sadat's relations with the Soviet Union were strained most of the time. In May 1971 he removed from office the group that was perceived as pro-Moscow. The Soviets were so worried that they rushed a high-level delegation headed by Podgornyi to sign a friendship and cooperation treaty with Egypt. Sadat found the timing inappropriate because the treaty would appear to be a reaction of the purge of "Soviet friends." He suggested postponing it till the celebrations of July two months later, but the Soviets insisted, and the treaty was signed on May 27, 1971, less than two weeks after the purge of this group.

On July 19, a Communist coup in Sudan was crushed with Egyptian help. Against Soviet advice to recognize the new regime, Sadat ordered the Egyptian air force to transport back to Khartoum a Sudanese paratroop brigade that was stationed in Egypt. The brigade was instrumental in the countercoup of July 22–23.[35] The Soviet Union also obviously mistrusted Sadat's intentions and his attempts to build bridges with Saudi Arabia and the United States. Military, economic, and political issues were bones of contention between the two countries.

Political-Diplomatic Relations. As early as November 1973, it seemed that Sadat was ready to put the U.S. option into effect. He saw what limited help the Soviet Union could provide in a peaceful resolution of the Arab-Israeli conflict. The Soviets officially cochaired the Geneva conference held in December with the United States, but Heikal reports that "they were relegated to the role of spectators."[36]

The Soviets felt uneasy about the developing Egyptian-U.S. relations. They did not like Kissinger's monopoly, with Egyptian consent, of the negotiation process, which resulted in the first disengagement agreement between Egyptian and Israeli forces on January 20, 1974. Diplomatic relations between Egypt and the United States were resumed in March, followed by Richard Nixon's visit in June. The Soviet Union expressed grave concern and Egypt's foreign minister, Ismail Fahmy, was dispatched to Moscow to discuss Soviet-Egyptian relations.

The culmination of these events was on March 14, 1976, when Sadat, in a speech to the Parliament, unilaterally abrogated the Soviet-Egyptian treaty of 1971. He gave five reasons for his action: (1) the Soviet Union showed no desire for peace in the Middle East; (2) the Soviet Union opposed Egypt's new economic policy; (3) the Soviet Union refused to reschedule Egypt's debts and demanded interest on military debts; (4) the Soviet Union not only refused to overhaul Egyptian aircraft and provide spare parts—a clear violation of Article 8 of the treaty: it also forbade other countries (India) to do so; and finally (5) the Soviet Union had a hand in Ali Sabri's plot to overthrow Sadat.

According to Sadat, it was also a matter of upholding Egyptian independence and sovereignty. In the same speech he said: "The Soviets thought at one time that they had Egypt in their pocket, and the world has come to think of the Soviet Union as our guardian. I wanted to tell the Russians that the will of Egypt was entirely Egyptian; I wanted to tell the whole world that we are always our own master. Whoever wished to talk to us would come over and do it, rather than approach the Soviet Union."[37]

Egyptian-Soviet relations suffered another setback in August 1976, when the Soviet Union supported Libya in its dispute with Egypt. In July 1977 three Soviet technicians were reportedly killed during an Egyptian bombing raid on a Libyan radar station. This resulted in condemnation from Moscow and Egyptian countercharges of Soviet involvement in Libya. In December 1977, in the aftermath of Sadat's visit to Israel, the Soviet consulates in Alexandria, Port Said, and Aswan were closed. Egyptian-Soviet relations came almost to a complete halt.

The Soviet Union opposed Egypt's policy toward Israel on the basis that it would not lead to a comprehensive peace in the area. Sadat escalated his anti-Soviet and anti-Communist remarks; he also criticized the U.S. "Vietnam complex" and asked for a more active U.S. role.

In September 1981 the Soviet embassy in Cairo was accused of being involved in harmful spying activities and the Soviet ambassador and a number of diplomats were asked to leave the country.

Military Relations. The military dimension of the Egyptian-Soviet rift is complex. It includes problems of arms supplies, economic costs of the weapons, and interpersonal conflicts between Egyptian and Soviet officers. First there was the problem of Soviet reluctance to respond to Egyptian demands for arms. Lt. General Saad Al-Shazly, chief of staff of Egyptian forces (1971–1973), writes: "As a monopoly supplier the Soviets could and did control their release of arms to us: the weapons, the amounts, and their dates of delivery."[38] Throughout 1971 and 1972, little in the way of arms reached Egypt. Gradually a reconciliation was effected and by the beginning of April 1973, Sadat was able to declare: "The Russians are providing us now with everything that's possible for them to supply and I am quite satisfied."[39]

In the aftermath of October 1973, the problem surfaced again. Egypt requested Soviet compensation for the arms lost in the war, just as the United States had compensated Israel and the Soviet Union had done for Syria. For months to follow Egypt's requests met with rejection. In June 1975, Sadat declared that if the Soviet Union continued to ignore Egypt's demands and took no notice of its economic situation, he would have to do something about it. In particular, Sadat was critical of the Soviet massive armament of Libya, whose relations with Egypt were deteriorating. He perceived this as an avenue of Soviet penetration in the area and a potential threat to Egypt.

Another dimension of the military rift was the result of interpersonal conflicts between Egyptian and Soviet officers before 1972, which left a legacy throughout the 1970s. Shazly, who worked closely with senior Soviet officers, says: "The Russians have many qualities, but concern for human feelings is not among them. They are brusque, harsh, frequently arrogant and usually unwilling to believe that anyone has anything to teach them."[40]

Soviet facilities in Egypt presented another touchy issue for the Egyptian military. The Soviets had exclusive control over a number of airfields that provided air cover for the Soviet fleet. Soviet ships obtained facilities in several ports—Alexandria, Port Said, and Al-Salloum.[41] During the years 1974 to 1976 Sadat continually reminded his people of the Soviet legacy in Egypt. He played on the sentiments of the military by reminding them that Soviet "bases" were a breach of Egyptian sovereignty, and commentators emphasized the theme of liberating Egypt from Soviet influence and domination.

A third dimension of military relations was financial. Although the famous 1955 arms deal was largely a barter agreement, hard currency was increasingly the required medium of payment for Soviet weapons and personnel. In a December 1971 interview, Sadat told Arnaud de Borchgrave of *Newsweek* that "all the Soviet officers and men [are] paid in hard currency, not Egyptian money. We are paying through the nose for the maintenance of these Soviet Sam crews in Egypt."[42] By 1972, Shazly reports that the Soviet Union "was demanding payment in full and hard currency" for all new equipment.[43] Sadat was to cite this frequently in his speeches to show that the Soviets were not the true friends they claimed to be.

Economic Relations. In December 1975 Egypt's nonmilitary debt to the Soviet Union was $4 billion; its military debt totalled $7 billion. Despite repeated requests, the Soviet Union refused to reschedule the debt, and on December 14, 1975, Sadat announced that Egypt would not sign the trade protocol with the Soviet Union for 1976. When Egypt was ready to sign in January 1976, the Soviets postponed the signing. The protocol was finally signed on April 28, 1976, but at $640 million, it provided for $160 million less in trade than the figure negotiated the previous December.[44] In August 1977 Sadat suspended cotton exports to the Soviet Union and two months later announced that debt repayments would be suspended for ten years beginning January 1978.

Economic and trade relations decreased during this period. Economic aid agreements with Egypt declined from $1 billion in 1955–1964 to $440 million in 1965–1975, and then to zero in 1975–1979.[45] Trade relations also declined after the cotton embargo and Egypt's refusal to maintain the large trade surplus used to service its debt. The Soviet share of Egyptian exports fell from 50% in 1970–1975 to less than 15% in 1975. Egyptian imports from the Soviet Union also dropped from about 25% of Egypt's total imports to around 10%. Soviet exports to Egypt dwindled from 301 million rubles in 1974 (about $4 million) to 200 million rubles in 1976, to 148 million in 1978, and to 127 million in 1979. Soviet imports from Egypt decreased as well, from 427 million rubles in 1974, to 331 million in 1976, and to 198 million in 1978 and 1979.[46] By 1979 a few Soviet technicians and a limited volume of trade were the remnants of a once flourishing relationship. In the political crisis of September 1981, when the Soviet embassy in Cairo was accused of helping some communist elements and indulging in spying activities, most of those technicians were ordered to leave the country.

Egyptian-U.S. Relations

In the 1970s, the United States made a dramatic return to Egypt and the Arab world. U.S. diplomacy could contain, outmaneuver, and sometimes expel Soviet influence from the area. Even with "radical" Arab states such as Algeria or Syria, the United States maintained flourishing commercial and economic relations. The big success story, however, is that of U.S.-Egyptian relations. In 1970 there were no diplomatic relations between the two countries; they were resumed in March 1974. Within four to five years, Egypt developed special relations with the United States. Since 1978, the United States has become a "partner" in Egyptian-Israeli relations, the major supplier of arms, and the primary donor of economic assistance to Egypt.

Political-Diplomatic Relations. In the first three years of Sadat's rule, 1970–1973, the United States continued its policy of total support to Israel. The Israeli occupation seemed stable and the Arab states appeared incapable of launching a new war. The United States, on the other hand, was busy ending its Vietnam involvement, opening new inroads to China, and inaugurating a decade of détente.

In February 1971, Sadat proposed opening the Suez Canal and signing a peace treaty with Israel, but nothing much came from this proposal. The expulsion of Soviet advisors from Egypt in July 1972 provided a new opportunity for the United States. It seems that Egyptian-U.S. contacts were initiated at that time. Heikal reports that talks were conducted through two channels, the diplomatic channel of foreign ministries and also a quiet one suggested by Nixon—the U.S. Central Intelligence Agency (CIA).[47] In addition, a third avenue was provided by Saudi Arabia, whose dignitaries communicated messages between Washington and Cairo. All efforts, however, including National Security Advisor Hafez Ismail's visit to the United States in 1973, led nowhere. It took the war of 1973 to finally bring the seriousness of the situation to Washington's attention. It became clear that Egypt and the Arabs could act and take the initiative; they could coordinate an attack and harm Israel. The use of oil as a weapon showed that U.S. interests in the area could be threatened.

Through his famous "shuttle diplomacy," Kissinger monopolized the indirect negotiation process that took place after the war, resulting in the first disengagement agreements between Egypt, Syria, and Israel in 1974. The oil embargo was lifted, and in June 1975 the Suez Canal was opened. Egypt signed the second Sinai agreement in September 1975, a step that created a rift in the Arab world because of the failure of Syria and Israel to achieve a similar agreement. In 1977–1978 Sadat became more emphatic about the importance of the U.S. role. The United States was not just a mediator, but a full partner in the peace process. Thus, Sadat concentrated on American public opinion, he spent endless hours with media people, senators and congressmen, and leaders of the Jewish community. And he did make an impact on them. One is tempted to argue that the target of his visit to Jerusalem was not only the Israelis but equally the American people. He made the visit in front of television cameras, and well-established news stars such as Walter Cronkite and Barbara Walters accompanied him. The visit was a media event, an exercise in television diplomacy, and Sadat captured the imagination of millions in the West. He definitely improved the image of Egypt and its leadership, but his other more subtle objective—political disengagement between Israel and the United States—did not materialize, and strong U.S. pressure on Israel was not forthcoming. U.S.-Egyptian relations were closely related to the negotiations with Israel. Carter's decision to take an active role in 1978 resulted in the signing of the Camp David framework and the Egyptian-Israeli treaty in 1979. The treaty opened the door for much closer economic and military relations.

Military Relations. Military cooperation between the two countries has taken various forms: arms supplies, transfer of military technology, provision of military facilities, and joint training and maneuvers. In 1975, Sadat emphasized the need to diversify Egypt's sources of arms. Egypt acquired some British and French jet fighters, helicopters, and air-to-surface missiles, and U.S. arms came slowly and gradually. In 1975, after the signature of the second disengagement agreement, Egypt bought six C-130 transport airplanes. In the summer of 1977, fourteen additional C-130s were provided. Military relations developed at an unprecedented rate after the visit to Jerusalem. Arms sales from the United States to Egypt jumped from $68.4 million in 1976 to $937.3 million in 1978.[48] In 1979 Egypt was offered further U.S. military credits, making the United States Egypt's major arms supplier.

Military relations between Egypt and the United States also included the licensing and coproduction of arms. After the collapse of AMIO in October 1979, Egypt and the United States agreed to cooperate in the manufacturing and assembling of armored vehicles and electronic equipment. As another form of cooperation, Egypt offered the U.S. "temporary limited access" to airfields near Cairo (Cairo West) and in Ras Banes on the Red Sea. Though separated from the Gulf by Saudi Arabia, Ras Banes is still a strategic point in relation to the Suez Canal and the Mediterranean. It is all the more important as more oil is shipped through Saudi Arabia by pipeline and up to the Red Sea, through the Suez Canal to the Mediterranean.[49]

The United States hoped to convince Sadat to sign an agreement making the Ras Banes base available to the U.S. Army. Secretary Alexander Haig discussed this during his visit to the region in April 1981, but with no success. Egypt resisted the idea of signing a formal agreement with the United States guaranteeing access to military facilities.[50] Sadat's formal position was that Egypt would make the facilities available to the United States in response to a request by any member of the Arab League. This commitment was reiterated by President Mubarak.

The United States and Egypt also collaborated in joint training and maneuvers. On January 1, 1980, two U.S. AWACS (Airborne Warning and Control System) planes flew to Qena Air Base in Upper Egypt with 250 air force personnel to "practice contingencies such as directing fighter bombers to targets."[51] It was acknowledged that the exercise was aimed in part as a response to events in Iran and Afghanistan. Another objective was to test the capability of the planes to use the Qena base.[52] In July, five C-141s and twenty-eight C-5s airlifted equipment, supplies, and some U.S. Air Force personnel to Cairo West. Also in July a squadron of twelve F-4E Phantom fighter bombers landed in Cairo West after a nonstop thirteen-hour flight. The squadron spent three months in operation "Proud Phantom," which involved air combat exercises with the Egyptian air force.

In November, U.S. rapid deployment forces—including approximately 1,400 troops and eight A-7 tactical ground-support planes, participated in a two-week exercise in Egypt. The exercises, called "Bright Star," gave the rapid deployment forces their first taste of duty in Middle Eastern deserts and brought to attention a number of problems in both operations and equipment.[53] Similar exercises were conducted in 1981 and 1983.

Economic Relations. In the last three decades, Egypt has been a major recipient of foreign aid in the Third World. Thirty-seven percent of total investments in development and 36% of total imports between 1952 and 1975 were financed by foreign aid. As for the United States, between 1946 and 1980 U.S. economic aid totaled $7.2 billion, most of which ($6.8 billion or 94%) was given in the late 1970s. The increase in economic aid coincided with the shift in Egypt's domestic and foreign policies. The political underpinnings of the aid were articulated in a 1981 AID (Agency for International Development) document as follows: "Our high level of aid to Egypt is premised on the belief that President Sadat's peace initiatives are crucial to that objective and that these efforts will be supported and enhanced by a vigorous and growing economy."[54]

The aid covers a broad range of needs: food, infrastructure improvement, the upgrading of social services, technical assistance, agricultural and industrial projects, and loans to help Egypt's balance of payments. This last item, called general economic support, is the largest single item of aid. From 1975 to 1980, it amounted to $3.2 billion, or 47% of total U.S. aid to Egypt, and included commodity-import programs and payment for PL 480 food-for-peace shipments. Payments for food is another major item. Wheat and flour deliveries amounted to nearly $1.22 billion between 1975 and 1980, about 20% of the total aid. Food aid allowed Egypt to keep wheat prices low and maintain its massive food subsidy program. It also released government resources for other activities. Another major item (about $1.05 billion in 1975–1980) covered infrastructure projects—power, communications, urban water and sewerage, and transportation. A third item, commodity deliveries, amounted to $1.7 billion in the 1975–1980 period. This money was spent to import U.S.-made machinery, spare parts, buses, tractors, and raw materials for industry.

U.S.-Egyptian relations have thus changed drastically since 1973, from no diplomatic relations to very close political and military relations. The new pattern of relations does have its problems and contradictions. Egyptians have grown wary of the increasing dependence of their country on the United States and the decline of Egypt's image as a nonaligned country.

The Arab World

Egypt's Arab policy has been primarily motivated by two objectives: the need for a good Arab consensus to reach a comprehensive solution of the Arab-Israeli conflict, and the need to generate massive economic and financial aid. Egyptian tactics and positions have changed over time in pursuing these two objectives.

In the early 1970s Sadat ridiculed the distinction between revolutionary and conservative Arab states; the real criterion should be a country's position toward the Arab effort against Israel. "Egypt measures each Arab country by its relation and orientation to the Palestinian resistance," Sadat stated on October 15, 1972. He started to build a broad Arab front by reconciling differences between Arab regimes, advocating non-intervention in each other's internal affairs, and emphasizing the need for Arab solidarity. To achieve this, Sadat paid many visits to various Arab countries; he was the first Egyptian head of state ever to visit Iraq or Kuwait.

Sadat demonstrated his ability for swift action; in most cases he could outbid and outmaneuver his critics. The ups and downs of Egypt's relations with other Arab countries must be seen in the context of its search for an end to the Arab-Israeli conflict. Thus, for instance, the first public rift between Egypt and Syria centered around Egypt's second disengagement treaty and its acceptance of Kissinger's step-by-step approach. The major developments, however, took place after Sadat's visit to Israel in November 1977.

The decision to go to Israel was motivated by a number of factors: Sadat's frustration with Arab disunity, the feeling that Syria was not enthusiastic about an early resumption of the Geneva conference, increasing economic problems at home (the January food riots), and U.S. impatience with the push and pull of Arab politics.

The reactions of Arab states to the visit differed markedly. Morocco, Sudan, Somalia, and Oman supported the move; Algeria, Libya, Syria, Iraq, South Yemen, and the PLO condemned it in a meeting they held in Tripoli in December 1977. Sadat responded by severing diplomatic relations with the five Arab states. In the middle, Saudi Arabia, Jordan, and the Gulf states were neutral, giving Sadat the benefit of the doubt.

The Camp David Accords (1978) and the ensuing Egyptian-Israeli treaty (1979) were met by almost universal Arab rejection. In an Arab summit meeting in Baghdad, Arab states decided to break off diplomatic relations with Cairo, suspend Egypt's membership in the League of Arab States, transfer the headquarters of the league from Cairo to Tunis, and boycott any Egyptian company that would do business with Israel.

Certain Arab countries were engaged in special relations with Egypt. Chief among them was Saudi Arabia. As mentioned earlier, in the early 1970s there was a close alliance between the two countries. Egypt needed Saudi Arabian financial help and Faisal needed Sadat to sustain stability in the Arab East. He expected Sadat to diminish Nasser's revolutionary model of development, cut close relations with the Soviet Union and restrain radicals in Syria, Iraq, and the PLO. One story relates that President Richard Nixon urged Saudi Arabia in mid-June 1972 to pressure Egypt to get rid of the Soviet presence as a precondition to an active U.S. role.[55] Relations between the two countries were not affected by the visit to Israel. Indeed, Saudi Arabia agreed to represent Egyptian interests in Iraq, Syria, and South Yemen after the severing of diplomatic relations. Later Saudi Arabia went along with other Arab countries, breaking off diplomatic relations with Egypt and refusing to pay for the fifty U.S.-made F-5E fighter jets ordered by Egypt earlier.

Sadat accused Saudi Arabia of leading an anti-Egyptian campaign and using its financial clout to isolate Egypt in concert with Libya and Iraq. He ridiculed the Fahd-Saddam axis and advised the Saudi rulers to pay more attention to their growing domestic problems as manifested in the attack on the Grand Mosque of Mecca in November 1979.[56] Egypt's special relations with the PLO and with Syria are covered in Chapters 8 and 10 respectively.

CONCLUSION

In the 1970s Egypt was not the only state whose foreign policy experienced fundamental change. Somalia and also Sudan underwent similar major shifts in the same direction. Ethiopia moved in the opposite direction, from being a Western strategic asset to having close relations with the Soviet Union. Revolutionary Iran broke links with the United States and in the early 1980s both foreign and domestic policies were still in turmoil in Iran.

In the case of Egypt, the crucial factors in restructuring foreign policy orientation seem to have been: increased economic troubles and anticipated economic gains through change; the existence of the United States as an alternative ally due to the U.S.-Soviet competition in the Middle East; leadership orientation; and finally the dialectics of big state/small state relations.

Under President Mubarak, the main thrust of Egypt's foreign policy has been an attempt to rehabilitate the country's position in Arab, African, Islamic, and nonaligned councils, without introducing a sudden or major shift in its foreign policy orientation. On the one hand, Mubarak has emphasized the continuity of Sadat's basic policies: peace with Israel and special relations with the United States. On the other hand, he has stressed Egypt's nonaligned position. Mubarak attended the 1983 nonaligned summit meeting in New Delhi and has allowed the Egyptian press to criticize U.S. policy on a great number of issues involving its support of Israel. Vehement anti-Soviet attacks are no longer pronounced in Cairo, and relations with the Soviet Union have moved gradually to normalcy. A cultural and educational agreement between the two countries was signed in April 1983, and a trade protocol was signed in May, the first since 1976.

Regionally, Mubarak has condemned the Israeli invasion of Lebanon, withdrawn the Egyptian ambassador from Tel Aviv, and has refused to visit Jerusalem because its status as the capital of Israel is still a subject of negotiations. As for other Arab states, Egypt has terminated its war of words with them, increased its military support to Iraq, and coordinated its policies with Jordan and Lebanon. By July 1983, Mubarak had exchanged political notes with most Arab heads of state, and Cairo had developed close relations with Amman, Baghdad, and Beirut. Oman, Somalia, and Sudan had maintained cordial relations with Egypt all along. How long Mubarak will be able to maintain his foreign policy balancing act and which direction Egypt will eventually take are questions still to be answered.

NOTES

1. On the concept of foreign policy restructuring see K. J. Holsti, *Why Nations Realign: Foreign Policy Restructuring in the Post-War World* (London: George Allen and Unwin, 1982).

2. This issue was discussed in Franklin Weinstein, *Indonesian Foreign Policy and the Dilemma of Dependence* (Ithaca, N.Y.: Cornell University Press, 1976).

3. Ali E. Hillal Dessouki, *Egypt and the Great Powers 1973–1981* (Tokyo: Institute for Developing Economies, 1983).

4. Gamal Hamdan, *The Character of Egypt*, 2 vols. (Cairo: Maktabat Alam Al-Kutub, 1980 and 1982) (in Arabic).

5. *Al-Ahram Al-Iktisadi* [The Economist], May 1, 1977, pp. 8–9.

6. Robert Mabro and Samir Radwan, *The Industrialization of Egypt* (Oxford: Clarendon Press, 1976), p. 32.

7. John Waterbury, "Egypt: The Wages of Dependency," in A. L. Udovitch (ed.), *The Middle East: Oil, Politics and Hope* (Lexington, Mass.: Lexington Books, 1976), p. 293.

8. Ali E. Hillal Dessouki, "The Politics of Income Distribution in Egypt," in Gouda Abdel-Khalek and Robert Tignor (eds.), *The Political Economy of Income Distribution in Egypt* (New York: Holmes and Meier, 1982), pp. 55–87.

9. Ali E. Hillal Dessouki, "Policy-Making in Egypt: A Case Study of the Open Door Economic Policy," *Social Problems* 28, 4 (1981), pp. 410–416.

10. Interview with Egypt's Minister of Planning, *New York Times*, April 9, 1975.

11. *Christian Science Monitor*, February 8, 1978.

12. *Arabia and the Gulf*, September 18, 1978, p. 10.

13. Jim Paul, "The Egyptian Arms Industry," *Merip Reports* 112 (February 1983), pp. 26–28.

14. *Africa Diary* 10, p. 5262.

15. Anwar Sadat, "Where Egypt Stands," *Foreign Affairs* 51, 1 (1972), pp. 144–153.

16. *Time*, January 2, 1978, p. 19.

17. Interview with Joseph Kraft in the *Los Angeles Times*, April 14, 1980.

18. Interview with Field Marshal Abu Gazala in *Armed Forces Journal International*, September 1981, p. 49.

19. Edward Sheehan, *The Arabs, Israelis and Kissinger: A Secret History of American Diplomacy in the Middle East* (New York: Reader's Digest Press, 1976), p. 89.

20. On Egyptian-Saudi relations, see Ali E. Hillal Dessouki, "The New Arab Political Order: Implications for the 1980s," in Malcolm H. Kerr and El Sayed Yassin (eds.), *Rich and Poor States in the Middle East: Egypt and the New Arab Order* (Boulder, Colo.: Westview Press, 1982), pp. 330–336.

21. See Sadat's interviews (in Arabic) with the weekly *October*: No. 59, December 11, 1977; No. 70, February 26, 1978; No. 72, March 12, 1978; No. 74, March 26, 1978.

22. Charles Hermann, "Decision Structure and Process Influences on Foreign Policy," in Maurice A. East, S. Salmore, and C. Hermann (eds.), *Why Nations Act* (Beverly Hills, Calif.: Sage Publications, 1978), pp. 69–102.

23. *Middle East Reporter* 20, 531 (May 30, 1979), p. 11.

24. *October* 59, December 11, 1977.

25. *Ibid.*

26. *October* 60, December 18, 1977; and *Al-Ahram*, December 10, 1977, and November 21, 1978.

27. *Time*, June 9, 1975, p. 28.

28. Hamdy Fouad, *Diplomatic War Between Egypt and Israel* (Beirut: Dar Al-Qalam, 1980), p. 315.

29. Sayed Marie, *Political Papers*, Vol. 3 (Cairo: Al-Maktab Al-Misri Al-Hadith, 1978), pp. 690, 727 (in Arabic).

30. *Ibid.*, p. 704; and Fouad, *op. cit.*, p. 222.

31. Interview with Minister for Foreign Affairs Kamal Hassan Ali, in *Rose Al-Youssef*, April 19, 1982.

32. Hamdi Al-Taheri, *Five Years of Politics* (Cairo: Publisher not identified, 1982), pp. 21–23 (in Arabic).

33. Hermann, *op. cit.*

34. For a general survey of Soviet-Egyptian relations, see Karen Dawisha, *Soviet Foreign Policy Towards Egypt* (New York: St. Martin's Press, 1979), pp. 54–82.

35. Jon D. Glassman, *Arms for the Arabs: The Soviet Union and War in the Middle East* (Baltimore, Md.: Johns Hopkins University Press, 1975), p. 90.

36. Mohamed H. Heikal, *The Sphinx and the Commissar* (New York: Harper & Row, 1978), p. 219.

37. Speech on July 22, 1972, printed in *Al-Ahram*, July 23, 1972.

38. Saad Al-Shazly, *The Crossing of the Suez* (San Francisco: American Mideast Research, 1980), p. 49.

39. *Newsweek*, April 9, 1973, p. 46.

40. Shazly, *op. cit.*, p. 50.

41. Ammon Sella, *Soviet Political and Military Conduct in the Middle East* (London: Macmillan, 1981), p. 31.

42. *Newsweek*, December 13, 1971, p. 43.

43. Shazly, *op. cit.*, p. 70.

44. K. Dawisha, *op. cit.*, p. 76.

45. *Communist Aid Activities in Non-Communist Less Developed Countries, 1979* (Washington, D.C.: Foreign National Center, 1980), p. 7.

46. Alan H. Smith, "The Influence of Trade on Soviet Relations with the Middle East," in A. Dawisha and Karen Dawisha (eds.), *The Soviet Union and the Middle East* (London: Heinemann Educational Books, 1982), pp. 110–111.

47. Mohamed H. Heikal, *The Road to Ramadan* (Glasgow: William Collins and Co., 1975), p. 202.

48. Ibrahim Karawan, "Egypt and the Western Alliance: The Politics of Westomania," in Steven L. Speigel (ed.), *The Middle East and the Western Alliance* (London: George Allen and Unwin, 1982), pp. 174–175.

49. Christopher Madison, "U.S. Reducing Act in the Middle East," *National Journal* 28 (November 1981), p. 2107.

50. *Newsweek*, March 23, 1981, p. 35.

51. Joe Stork, "The Carter Doctrine and U.S. Bases in the Middle East," *MERIP Reports* 90 (1980), p. 8.

52. *Wall Street Journal*, January 9, 1980, and the *Washington Post*, January 9, 1980.

53. *Newsweek*, December 29, 1980, p. 23.

54. Quoted in Saad Eddin Ibrahim, "Superpowers in the Arab World," *Washington Quarterly* 4, 3 (Summer 1981), pp. 88–89.

55. *New York Times*, July 24, 1972.

56. See Sadat's speeches and interviews in the daily *Al-Ahram* of August 6, 13, 22, and 24, and October 2 and 11, 1979. See also *October*, September 23 and 30, 1979.

6

The Dialectics of Domestic Environment and Role Performance: The Foreign Policy of Iraq

Ahmad Yousef Ahmad

INTRODUCTION

Analyzing Iraqi foreign policy is important for a number of reasons. First of all, Iraq has played a significant role in inter-Arab politics. Second, in the 1970s Iraq adhered to a Ba'thist, pan-Arabist socialist ideology and projected itself as a model for Arab revolutionary countries. Third, Iraq is an active member of the nonaligned countries. And finally, Iraq has played a significant role as an oil-producing country advocating producers' demands.

Iraq provides a prime example of the salience of domestic factors as influences on foreign policy orientation and behavior. As we shall see, geography and population structure are crucial variables in the determination of Iraqi policies. Iraq also provides an example of the "unfulfilled leadership role." Although it possesses most of the ingredients of national power, circumstances have always diluted this potentiality; a gap has always existed between possibility and performance, between role conception and role enactment.

DOMESTIC ENVIRONMENT

This analysis of Iraq's domestic environment will deal with geography, population and social structure, economic and military capabilities, and political structure. Emphasis will be placed on the population and social structure variable because of its significance in Iraq's foreign policy.

147

148

Base 502879 1-76

Geography

The geography of Iraq presents more constraints than opportunities for the country's foreign policy. Located in the Gulf area, and possessing elements of national power such as population and wealth, Iraq has always been a potential leader in the area. Ironically, throughout history not only has Iraq been unable to fulfill that role; it has also suffered from the invasion of great powers and their overbearing influence. In fact, Iraq never achieved the capabilities inherent in its geographic position.

The geography of Iraq is distinguished by the number and identity of adjacent countries. Iraq is bounded by six countries: on the north by Turkey, on the east by Iran, on the south by Kuwait, on the southwest by Saudi Arabia and Jordan, and on the northwest by Syria. This maximizes Iraq's national security problems, particularly in the light of population structures and resource availability in the area. Bordered by deserts in the south and a multitude of passes in the north, Iraq is virtually without defense against invasion.[1]

Two examples of vulnerability are Iraq's borders with Iran and its sources of surface water supply. The southern portion of the frontier with Iran, below Basra, follows the course of the Shatt Al-Arab waterway and has been a subject of conflict between the two states for a long time. From 1936 to 1975 Iraq controlled the whole waterway, a situation that became increasingly unacceptable to Iran. In March 1975 the two countries signed an agreement in Algiers by which the border was restored to the pre-1936 Thalweg line, dividing the countries in the middle of the deepest shipping channel in the waterway.[2] For a variety of reasons to be discussed in the analysis of the Iraq-Iran war, Iraq unilaterally abrogated that agreement in September 1980, and the border dispute came to the fore again. As of late 1983, the two countries were still at war.

The other example concerns the water supply. Unlike the situation in other Arab oil-producing countries, the privotal role played by oil in the Iraqi economy has not diminished the importance of the agricultural sector. The central region around Baghdad and the southern area of Iraq constitute the principal agricultural zone of the country. Its two rivers, the Euphrates and the Tigris, are the only sources of water. The Euphrates, like the Tigris, rises in the Armenian mountains of Turkey, but unlike the Tigris (1,850 km), which enters Iraq directly from Turkey, the Euphrates (2,333 km) flows first through Syria (675 km) and then Iraq (1,200 km) till it joins the Tigris.[3] In this context, geography has been relatively unkind to Iraq in the sense that the country's political frontiers have left its vital sources of surface water supply in the hands of neighboring, and not always friendly states.[4]

Population and Social Structure

There is every evidence to suggest that understanding Iraqi foreign policy through population and social structure is a promising perspective.

The Iraqi population was estimated in 1977 to be 12 million.[5] In a 1982 speech President Saddam Hussein referred to the population as totaling 14 million.[6] On the whole, Iraq is underpopulated and could support a larger number of inhabitants.[7] This may explain the opposition of President Hussein to calls for birth control or reduction of the annual growth rate estimated at 3.2 percent in 1982.[8]

A relevant feature of Iraq's population composition in its age structure. The Iraqis are an exceptionally young people; by the late 1970s one in five was under ten years old, and two in three were under 25.[9] Another feature is the lack of skilled labor and managerial personnel. Particularly in the 1970s, there was a shortage of the skilled labor required to implement the vast schemes of agricultural and industrial development that were contemplated or in the process of execution.[10] The Iraq-Iran war aggravated the situation. More important, however, is the ethnic composition of the population. Steeped in the tradition of confessionalism and communal politics, Iraqi society remains a mosaic of religious, linguistic, and regional groups.[11]

From an ethnic perspective, in addition to the Arabs and the Kurds who together constitute about 95% of the population, there are other ethnic groups such as the Turkomans, the Persians, the Lurs, and the Armenians. With the exception of the Kurds and to a lesser degree the Persians, it could be said that these minority groups have practically no relevance to foreign policy.[12] The Kurds, who speak a language of Indo-European origin, account for about 15 to 20% of Iraq's population. They number over 1 million and may be approaching 2 million. Most Iraqi Kurds live in the north and northeast of Iraq—the region contiguous with the Kurdish zones of Turkey and Iran.[13]

Religiously speaking, Iraq has both Christian and Jewish minorities. However, the most politically relevant division is to be found within Iraq's Islamic majority itself. Since the days of Caliph Ali (656–661 A.D.) Moslems in general, and Iraqi Moslems in particular, have been divided into Shi'ites (the followers of Ali) and Sunnites (the followers of orthodox Islamic law). Iraqi Shi'ites make up 55 to 60% of the population.[14] In geographical terms, northern Iraq is largely Sunni; Baghdad itself is divided between Sunni and Shi'i Islam; and southern Iraq is under strong Shi'i influence.[15]

The two main cleavages in Iraqi population structure (i.e., the ethnic division between Arabs and Kurds, and the religious one between Sunnis and Shi'ites) are not mutually exclusive. Apart from some different religious practices from Sunni Arabs, Iraqi Kurds are Sunnis.[16] The Sunni-Shi'i division has some economic and social implications. Sunni Moslems are in general wealthier than the Shi'ites.[17]

The Kurdish issue represents one of the most important linkages between population structure and Iraq's foreign policy, especially at the regional level. Before World War I, the Kurds lived under two regimes, the Ottoman Empire and the Qajar dynasty of Iran. After the fall of the Ottoman Empire, and as a result of their cordial relations with the victorious European power, the Kurds were promised under the Treaty of Sèvres an autonomous Kurdistan and, "if they should show that they wanted it," the right to independence.[18] However, their hopes were short-lived and in 1923 the Treaty of Lausanne, which replaced that of Sèvres, divided Kurdistan between Turkey, Iran, Iraq, Syria, and the Soviet Union.[19]

The change of heart was dictated in large measure by international oil interests. The British and French were interested in seeing Iraq acquire the Mosul region because of their joint control of the Iraqi-based Turkish Petroleum Company. The United States also sided with the British and French because of the inclusion of United States oil interests in the Turkish Petroleum Company.[20]

Not only did oil interests directly cause the splintering of Kurdistan and the resultant Kurdish problem for Iraq; they continued to be a main source of conflict in the years to come. Among the few bonds that kept the Iraqi Kurds united were their continuous demands for an autonomous region including the oil-rich province of Kirkuk (which produces approximately 70% of Iraq's oil), and the sharing of oil revenues.[21]

Between 1919 and 1932 many tribal uprisings took place in Iraqi Kurdistan.[22] During the 1930s and 1940s, the Kurds, under the leadership of Mullah Mustafa Barzani, engaged the government forces in intermittent guerrilla warfare. In the mid-1940s, the situation took a rather dramatic turn. With Soviet encouragement and military support by troops stationed in northern Iran (1941–1946), the Kurds in Iran declared their independence and the establishment of the Republic of Mahabad. Barzani moved several thousand of his tribal troops from Iraq into the new republic, where he fought against the Iranian army. After the Soviets had withdrawn their troops from Iran, the republic came to an end. Barzani and the remnant of his army crossed over to the Soviet Union, where he stayed until 1959 when he was allowed to return to Iraq.[23]

Between the mid-1940s and the overthrow of the monarchy in Iraq in 1958, there were no major disturbances in the Kurdish area of Iraq. The Kurds hailed the 1958 revolution in the hope that the new regime would be more sympathetic to their cause. Indeed the revolutionary regime responded positively. Constitutionally, the Arabs and the Kurds were considered partners in the Iraqi fatherland and their national rights within the unity of Iraq were acknowledged. One of the three members of the "Sovereignty Council" established to undertake the responsibilities of the president was a Kurd, and another Kurd was included in the first cabinet. Moreover, all Kurdish political prisoners were released and Barzani and his followers were permitted to return from the Soviet Union.

A phase of cooperative relations between the government and the Kurds followed. This was best manifested when the Kurds formed for a while an important element of the power base of Abdel Karim Qasem's regime. In fact, the main reason for the cooperation between Qasem and the Kurds was their common opposition to Arab nationalist forces in Iraq. When the Kurds made demands that Qasem perceived as secessionist, he turned against them and in the spring of 1961, the Kurds renewed their revolt against the regime.[24]

Between 1961 and 1975 a pattern of stalemated civil war persisted despite several temporary truces, negotiations, and a number of changes in the regime. In 1975, however, the Iraqi army was able to achieve a major military victory over the Kurds. Although there were reports afterwards of renewed skirmishing, it was not serious enough to challenge the government's military achievement of 1975.[25]

It is not true, however, that the Kurdish conflict was stabilized only by military means. The revolt of 1961, which lasted fourteen years, and the military resistance of the Kurds made it inevitable to seek a political solution and to respond to Kurdish demands. Apart from the above-mentioned "oil demands," the Kurds pressed for a free hand in handling their own affairs. They argued that in order to preserve this freedom as well as their national identity, the Kurdish area should be granted autonomy, Kurdish should be made the official language, and only Kurds should be given government appointments in these areas.[26] Because of the high cost of the long war, both parties showed a readiness for compromise. The government moved gradually toward recognition of the national rights of the Kurds, and the Kurds were ready on more than one occasion to accept a formula that did not completely satisfy their demands.[27]

In March 1970, the Iraqi government reached an agreement with the Kurds. The agreement satisfied almost all apart from "oil demands."[28] The war continued after the agreement, and it was through a combination of diplomacy and force that the conflict was considerably stabilized in 1975. The crucial factor in terminating the war was Iraq's agreement with Iran whereby the latter, the Kurds' main source of supply and support, agreed to abandon that role.

The Kurdish problem has a negative impact on the economic and military capabilities of Iraq. It also influenced Iraqi policy towards the issue of Arab unity. Over the years the government of Iraq entered into a series of political and military agreements to achieve unity with several Arab states. However, the Kurdish issue acted as a constraint and this explains in part Iraq's failure to pursue an active unionist policy even when pro-union groups were in power.[29]

Kurdish opposition to Iraqi union with other Arab countries was both ideological and political. As early as 1960, the Kurds categorically rejected the idea that Iraq was part of the Arab world on the ground that historically, Kurdistan was never considered part of Arab lands. The Kurdish stance in this respect was that the "Iraqi Republic consists of a part of the Kurdish nation, whose country is Kurdistan, and a part of the Arab nation, whose country is the great Arab homeland." This

TABLE 6.1
Iraq's Oil Revenues, 1970-1980 (in millions US$)

Year	1970	1971	1972	1973	1974	1975	1976	1977	1978	1979	1980
Revenue	521	840	575	1,843	5,700	7,500	8,500	9,631	10,200	21,291	25,981

Source: Middle East Economic Survey 25, 1 (October 19, 1981), supplement, p. VII.

Kurdish ideological opposition continued even after the 1970 agreement. In other words, the autonomy promised the Kurds according to the agreement was not enough to make them abandon their ideological stance.[30]

The relevance of the Kurdish conflict to an understanding of Iraq's foreign policy was not limited to the Iraqi position in Arab affairs. It was also felt in the broader regional context. As in other civil war situations, the war against the Kurds created an environment for external intervention.[31] For its part, the Kurdish leadership saw increasing foreign involvement in the conflict as instrumental in forcing the Iraqi government to give more concessions. Most prominent as an interventionist power was Iran, which had more than one reason to involve itself. One was the Shatt Al-Arab issue. Another was the struggle for influence in the Gulf area. A third was to check Iraq's radical and revolutionary regional policies and to divert the attention of its leadership towards domestic issues.

Economic Capability

Oil is the principal source of wealth in Iraq. By the end of the 1970s, output from the oil sector (entirely owned by the state) was estimated to constitute about 60% of Iraq's GNP, and oil revenues accounted for four-fifths of the country's foreign exchange receipts. Income remained stable in the early 1960s at 120–135 million Iraqi dinars* (ID), but in the fiscal year ending March 31, 1972, oil revenues had risen to ID 354 million as a result of increased production and revised agreements with the oil companies. The improvement was halted for a short time by the nationalization of the Iraq Petroleum Company (IPC) in 1972, which led to a temporary loss of production. As a result of price increases since 1973, the volume of oil revenues[32] has increased correspondingly (see Table 6.1).

The future of Iraqi oil seems promising. A favorable factor was the discovery in 1975 of major new oil fields.[33] In terms of both proven and probable reserves, the published 1978 CIA estimate for Iraq was 36 billion barrels, a fraction of Saudi Arabia's 150 billion, and behind

---

*From September 1949 to August 1971 an Iraqi dinar equalled $2.80; between December 1971 and February 1973 it was worth $3.04; between 1974 and 1980, $3.38.

Kuwait's 71 billion, Iran's 60 billion, the Soviet Union's 40 billion, and the United States' 39 billion. However, in both Saudi Arabia and Iran old oil has been pumped faster than new oil has been found, whereas exploration activities in Iraq since 1977 have steadily expanded proven reserves and sustainable capacity levels. Senior Iraqi oil officials confirm no figures, but they are content not to dispute British estimates of potential reserves of 95 billion barrels.[34] In February 1981 an Iraqi diplomat stated that "The world is approaching a period of time when dependence on oil will increase. . . . If we recall that we have established the fact that Iraq is considered to be one of the strongest countries in terms of oil reserves, then we can conclude that the role of Iraq will increase in importance in the next two decades."[35]

One of the positive features of the Iraqi economy is the fact that Iraq is one of the few Arab countries with the potential for a balanced economic development. Roughly half of Iraq's 443,000 square kilometers is arable, and of this, only about one-fourth is under cultivation. If the agricultural sector were fully developed, it could feed twice the present population.[36] The Iraqi leadership has shown considerable awareness of the necessity to build a self-sustained economy. In 1978 Saddam Hussein stated that Iraqi strategy was to ensure that when oil lost its importance as a source of energy, or when it was exhausted, the Iraqi economy would be able to sustain the planned growth rate.[37] The relation between a balanced economy and an active foreign policy is clear in the mind of Saddam Hussein.[38]

Oil has provided Iraq with a considerable capability, especially since 1973. Oil revenue has made heavy increases in military expenditure possible and enhanced Iraqi bargaining power in arms purchases. The Iraqi government has been able to use grants and loans as instruments of foreign policy. The main source of weakness in the Iraqi economic situation is, of course, its dependence on oil, a dependence that Iraq plans to ease through an ambitious program of economic diversification.

Unfortunately, the war with Iran (1980-) has drastically affected these positive developments. Although Iraqi officials have tried to minimize the war's adverse effects on the economy, it is obvious that a protracted war lasting more than three years is bound to have a significant economic and political impact. As Adeed Dawisha puts it: "The Iranian bombing of Iraq's oil industry and infrastructure is bound to slow Iraq's massive efforts at industrialization and modernization. Given the damage to Iraq's oil industry, national income will be reduced drastically, and what is left will have to be used to re-equip the armed forces."[39] A senior official of the Iraqi Ministry of Planning admitted the government's inability to initiate new economic projects under the circumstances. He also admitted that the oil sector has been affected because of the halt in oil exports through the Gulf and Syria (as a result of the latter's support of Iran in the war).[40] Saddam Hussein stated in 1983 that the first two years of the war went without economic hardships. However, it was natural, according to Hussein, to make some adjustments in the third year of the war. All Iraqis were asked to adopt certain patterns of rational economic behavior with a view to protecting the national economy and coping with the requirements of war.[41]

Military Capability

The two main resources for Iraq's military capability are its large population and its oil revenues. In terms of population, Iraq ranks fifth in the Arab world (after Egypt, Morocco, Algeria, and Sudan) and seventh in the Middle East (if one adds Turkey and Iran). In 1980 Iraq had the third largest army in the Arab world (242,500 soldiers after Egypt's 367,000 and Syria's 247,500) and the fifth in the Middle East (if one adds Israel's 629,600 and Turkey's 567,000).[42] During most of the 1970s, oil revenues enabled Iraq to be third in military expenditures in the Arab world (after Egypt and Saudi Arabia) and sixth in the Middle East (if one adds Israel, Iran, and Turkey). Although experience in the Middle East shows that such figures may have nothing to do with real military power, they cannot be ignored.

An important aspect of Iraq's military power is the government's plan to establish a nuclear capability. Using the leverage of oil in 1976, an agreement with France was signed to supply Iraq with a nuclear research center containing two reactors and three years' supply of enriched uranium. Iraq also signed agreements with Brazil and Italy for the supply of uranium and nuclear technology. Although Iraqi leaders consistently denied any intention of using the nuclear reactors for military purposes,[43] Israel was unconvinced. On June 7, 1981, the Israeli air force destroyed the Iraqi nuclear reactor near Baghdad only three months before it was due to begin operations.[44] Although President Saddam Hussein has emphasized that Iraq will continue to pursue plans for its own nuclear capability,[45] it is unlikely that the country will be able to do so in view of the economic hardships resulting from the war with Iran.

The bombing of the Iraqi nuclear reactor raises the issue of constraints on Iraq's military capability. Israel is not the only constraint or even the most important one in this respect. An analysis of the regional use of the Iraqi army in the 1960s and the 1970s shows that both geography and population structure are unfavorable factors that seriously limit military strength.

For two decades the Kurdish conflict severely limited the use of the military as a means of conducting Iraqi foreign policy. For example, an anti-Kurdish general offensive in 1965 was estimated to include 40,000 to 50,000 troops. In 1974, the government dispatched—for the same reason—three army divisions totaling 48,000 troops, or nearly half of its armed forces. These divisions included Iraq's best armored units. At the beginning of August 1974 the government launched its biggest offensive, involving some 100,000 troops.[46]

Geography and population structure have been sources of conflict with Iran over the disputed Shatt Al-Arab, the Kurdish problem, and Sunni-Shi'ite relations. For the first time since the Second World War, these and other sources of conflict have recently led the two countries to a war that in 1983 had been going on for over three years. Whatever its result, the war will leave a marked economic and military impact on Iraq for years to come.[47] This will affect Iraq's Arab role, especially in the Arab-Israeli conflict. All available evidence leads to the conclusion that the 1980s are likely to bring more constraints on Iraq's military capability.

Political Structure

According to the 1970 Iraqi constitution and its 1973 amendments, the Revolutionary Command Council (RCC) is the supreme political organ and the highest legislative body. It oversees all foreign and domestic policies and elects (by two-thirds vote) one of its members as president of the RCC and the republic and another as vice-president. The RCC has the right to relieve any of its members or add new ones up to a maximum of twelve. Although the president is theoretically responsible to the RCC, the constitution makes no reference to his term of office or to the procedure for unseating him, except by resignation. The president is the chief executive and the commander-in-chief of the armed forces. He nominates members of the council of ministers.

The constitution also calls for a national assembly representing all political, economic, and social groups in the country. The assembly is responsible for considering bills proposed by the RCC or by one-fourth of the assembly members. In initiating legislation, the assembly may not deal with military matters or with issues of internal security. According to the constitution, when a difference of opinion takes place between the RCC and the National Assembly, it is resolved through a joint meeting of the two councils.[48] In actuality, the National Assembly was not even formed until June 1980. In that month, more than 7 million Iraqis elected 250 assembly members. With restricted powers and a war in progress with Iran, it is doubtful whether the assembly could play a significant role in Iraqi politics.

Since 1970, the Iraqi political system has been dominated by the socialist Arab Ba'th party. In theory, the Iraqi Ba'th party is a branch of the same party that rules Syria, but because of strong ideological and political differences, the two regimes are at odds with each other. In an attempt to broaden its political base in November 1971, the Ba'th party issued a National Action Charter and initiated negotiations with other political parties. In 1973 the Ba'th and the Communist party formed the National Progressive Front.[49]

President Saddam Hussein considered the front to be a first in the sense that the Ba'th had launched a revolution alone, assumed political power successfully, and then voluntarily invited other revolutionary political powers to share that responsibility.[50] However, the emphasis on the special role of the Ba'th in the front was a source of tension. The Ba'th leaders tended to minimize the role and strength of other political forces in the country, including their single partner in the front. In 1978 a group of Communists were executed after being convicted of conducting political activities inside the army, an act prohibited by law and by the front documents. The execution invited severe criticism by Communist countries, and Hussein took issue with this criticism.[51] In 1980 President Hussein acknowledged the problems within the front.[52]

During the second half of the 1970s Saddam Hussein had been the strongman of Iraq behind ex-president Hassan Al-Bakr. For several years he maintained a low profile as vice-president of the RCC; then, on July 17, 1979, Saddam Hussein assumed the presidency when Al-Bakr, on grounds of ill health, handed in his resignation.[53]

Until the eruption of war with Iran in 1980, there was strong evidence that Saddam Hussein had achieved a considerable degree of stability in Iraq. Although the internal security apparatus must have played an important role in this respect, the economic and social policies of the regime contributed a great deal as well. The continuing war with Iran represents a serious challenge to the regime. For the time being, there is apparently an Iraqi consensus that Saddam Hussein is the right man to lead the country in the war effort, but when the war comes to an end—depending, of course, on its outcome—he may face serious problems in maintaining the regime's stability.

FOREIGN POLICY ORIENTATION

In this section, Iraqi foreign policy orientation is presented through an analysis of Ba'th party ideology and the views of Saddam Hussein. Hussein's speeches reflect definite views on the global and regional systems and of Iraq's role in the world. Without underestimating the impact of the global system, Hussein maintains that the crucial factors in the making of Iraq's policies and priorities are primarily domestic and regional.[54] His writings and speeches reveal his awareness of a distinct Iraqi role in regional and global politics.

The Global System

The Iraqi president holds a consistent view of the current phase of the evolution of the global system. The two distinguishing elements in his world view are: (1) that the global order is moving from bipolarity to multipolarity, necessitating certain Iraqi and Arab roles to influence the process; and (2) that the impossibility of a direct war between the superpowers, because of its nuclear implications, had led to the proliferation of small wars by proxy between Third World countries. Saddam Hussein perceives the world as going through a process of fast and radical change, similar to the period during and immediately after the

Second World War. However, current global change is more basic and more comprehensive. It will lead in the coming twenty years to a multipolar world and to the emergence of new centers of global power and influence. These centers will include China, Western Europe, and Japan. This new multipolar system is perceived as a welcome development for Iraq and other Arab countries because it will increase their freedom of action. Enhancing this development requires an Iraqi and an Arab "role" to influence the process of change. Concretely, this would involve neutralizing or even securing the support of one or more of the new centers with regard to Arab strategic objectives such as achieving Arab unity and pursuing the conflict with Zionism. Arabs assume that they have a role to perform in the shaping of the new global system because, they believe, no superpower can afford to follow a policy that is opposed by a great number of small countries.[55]

Another dimension of the Iraqi president's perception of the global system is his understanding of the growing tensions and contradictions between the superpowers. Since the global balance of power does not allow direct wars between the superpowers, wars by proxy take place between pro-Eastern and pro-Western developing countries.[56] This situation does not favor the interests of Third World countries.

In addition to these two characteristic views, Hussein shares most of the views of revolutionary Third World leaders on colonialism, equality between nations, national liberation movements, and the need for a new international economic order. He also shares the view that the developed, industrialized countries are to be blamed for failing to establish that new order.[57]

For Saddam Hussein, the core of Iraq's foreign policy is nonalignment, considered to be the best strategy to deal with the changing global system. First of all, as an Arab nationalist, Hussein is not inclined to favor either of the two superpowers, and in his speeches he refers to them indiscriminately. Second, nonalignment is more necessary and possible in the context of mounting tension and increasing conflict between great powers than in a period of détente. Finally, the nonalignment movement has a special role and responsibility in building the New International Economic Order.[58]

The Regional System

The ideology of the Ba'th party is primarily a nationalist ideology based on the concept of the oneness of the Arab nation, a nation that has a glorious past and a mission to fulfill in the future. The Ba'th ideology underlines three historical goals for the Arab nation: (1) unification of the existing, artificially created Arab states into a larger Arab political entity; (2) freedom from all foreign influence and hegemony; and (3) socialism. Although Ba'thist writers do not dwell much on the implications of their ideology for foreign policy in general, they do direct their attention into inter-Arab and regional issues. To be a Ba'thist means that you hold an ideology perceived as valid for all Arab countries. It does not accept the legitimacy of existing political divisions and frontiers and seeks to change them. Thus, it is inherently a change-oriented ideology. Other implications follow. The order of priority given to Ba'thist objectives (unity, freedom, socialism) opens the way, for example, for collaboration with conservative Arab regimes. Adherence to the concept of the Arab nation leads Ba'thist leaders to sympathize with, if not directly support, the demands of groups of Arab origin living in non-Arab states—groups such as the Eritreans in Ethiopia.

Saddam Hussein's statements advocate an Iraqi regional role very similar to that of Nasser's Egypt in the 1950s and the 1960s. In June 1975 he openly espoused such a role, stating: "In brief, we want Iraq to play a leading role in the area and especially in the Arab homeland. We want Iraq to play a leading role in the consolidation of anti-imperialist policy at the international level."[59] In October 1979, a few months after assuming the presidency, he spoke of a historical role for Iraq. According to Hussein, for centuries Iraq and the Arab nation had been denied the congruent elements of national power: wealth, leadership, ideology, and organization. Arab states possessing one of these elements were sadly bereft of the others. Now, for the first time, Iraq had all of them; it had the credentials for a historical Arab role.[60]

FOREIGN POLICY DECISION-MAKING

As in many other Third World countries, sufficient and accurate data on the details of foreign policy decision-making in Iraq are simply not available. The existing literature on Iraq is confusing, gives contradictory information, and in many cases is obsolete.

We have already seen that according to the constitution, the RCC oversees all matters of foreign policy. It declares general mobilization and war, accepts armistice, and concludes peace (Article 43-B). It ratifies treaties and international agreements (Article 43-D). We have also seen that the president is entrusted with the responsibility of preserving the independence of the country and its territorial integrity (Articles 58-A and 58-G). The president appoints Iraq's diplomatic representatives abroad (Article 58-E). Although the constitutional amendment of 1973 created a council of ministers as a separate institution, this council is headed by the president (Article 60) and is primarily concerned with domestic issues (Article 61). Finally, our analysis has already disclosed the limited powers of the National Assembly and the unfavorable circumstances that followed its formation in June 1980. The assembly is headed by a member of the RCC.

We may conclude that foreign policy decision-making in Iraq is influenced by a very limited group. The president, Saddam Hussein, is the principal decision-maker because of his powerful constitutional position and because of his personality and style. In this context, three questions are in order: What is the role of the Ba'th party; what is the role of political institutions other than the RCC and the presidency; and what, if any, are the political and institutional constraints on the president?

As to the party: all members of the RCC, with the exception of the Kurdish vice-president, must belong to the Ba'th leadership.[61] However, there is no evidence that the party plays an influential role in foreign policy–making. Indeed, President Saddam made the point that it was not necessary to have total congruence between the party's positions and those of the state. Of course, both follow the same strategy, but the state has to adapt to changing circumstances and conduct day-to-day affairs; the party does not. Saddam illustrated this distinction with examples drawn from the foreign policy field, pointing out the need for the state to tolerate and deal with reactionary Arab regimes that are condemned by the party.[62]

As regards the role of political institutions, the decision-making process is without a doubt dominated by the RCC and the president. However, at a meeting with Iraqi ambassadors in Western Europe and Japan, Saddam Hussein emphasized the importance of accurate information for correct decision-making:

> One of the most essential conditions for a successful decision is the availability of accurate information. Hence, when headquarters or rear command wants to make a decision, it must rely on the data supplied by the front lines or the observation posts, as they say in the armed forces . . . ambassadors will be expected not only to transmit information but also to make a preliminary analysis. . . . Don't hesitate because of any thought that your information, opinions and analysis may not be needed by the center which has better information. The mind of the command and headquarters cannot function without the eyes and the minds of those in the front lines.[63]

Thus, Iraq, as does Egypt, comes closest to the leader-staff style of decision-making. The president is the center of the process, and other individuals and institutions participate as advisors.

In the matter of constraints, we have to distinguish between institutional-legal and social-political constraints. Although Saddam Hussein may be relatively free from institutional constraints, he is subject to a variety of internal constraints, determined by geography and population structure, that severely limit his freedom of action. Iraqi leaders cannot afford to take a serious step toward unity with another Arab country without taking the Kurdish reaction into account. The Shi'ites constitute another constraint. Saddam's decision to go to war was partly a reaction to revolutionary Islamic appeals to Iraqi Shi'ites.

FOREIGN POLICY BEHAVIOR

In this section, we review Iraq's foreign policy behavior at the global and regional levels. From a global standpoint, our analysis includes Iraq's relations with the superpowers, Western Europe, and Japan; its non-aligned status; and its oil policies. From a regional standpoint we will deal primarily with Iraq's policy toward other Arab countries and Iran.

The Global Level

Relations with the United States. Iraq's Ba'thist ideology creates a potential for conflict rather than cooperation with the United States because of U.S. support for Israel and because of the nature of U.S. interests in the Arab world, especially in oil. Iraqi-U.S. relations were mainly influenced by ideological considerations in the late 1960s and early 1970s, but practical necessities have affected these relations since the late 1970s.

Because of the United States' pro-Israeli policy in the war of 1967, a number of Arab countries, including Iraq, severed diplomatic relations with the United States. As of 1983, Iraq still had no diplomatic relations with the United States. According to a senior Iraqi diplomat, the Carter administration initiated contacts with Iraq to restore the relationship, and a number of emissaries were sent to that effect. In Baghdad they were told that as the United States had not changed its unconditional support of Israel, Iraq could find no adequate reason to restore diplomatic relations between the two countries.[64]

From the mid-1970s the deterioration of Soviet-Iraqi relations and the Iraqi rapprochement with prerevolutionary Iran created a new context for U.S.-Iraqi relations. Despite Iraq's leading role in mobilizing Arab states against the Camp David Accords and the Egyptian-Israeli treaty, Iraq and the United States later found common ground, albeit for different reasons, in their desire to contain, if not undermine, the impact of Khomeini's revolutionary Iran.

In the 1980s there was a gradual Iraqi rapprochement with the West. On April 14, 1980, National Security Advisor Zbigniew Brzezinski stated: "We see no fundamental incompatibility of interests between the United States and Iraq. . . . We do not feel that American-Iraqi relations need to be frozen in antagonism."[65] In 1981 President Saddam Hussein announced that Washington had submitted certain suggestions through its representative in Baghdad to strengthen the relations between the two countries. The Iraqi government approved some of these suggestions, granting the U.S. representative in Baghdad a sort of diplomatic status (the right to be informed of Iraqi positions and to meet Iraqi officials for consultations) and opening the possibility of exchanging visits or holding meetings between representatives of the two countries. The

Iraqi government also allowed U.S. representatives in Baghdad to have communications facilities similar to those of other embassies.[66]

This changing environment led to more consultations, including two meetings between the U.S. and Iraqi foreign ministers in 1983. Iraq's attitude towards restoring diplomatic relations became ambivalent. In 1982 Iraqi officials, including President Saddam Hussein, referred to having diplomatic relations with the United States as natural.[67] Iraqi statements no longer made a direct link between restoring the relations and U.S. support to Israel. In July 1983 Tarek Aziz, deputy prime minister and minister of foreign affairs, stated that "we have clearly informed the American side that the Iraqi leadership does not think well of restoring diplomatic relations while the war with Iran is still going on."[68] No reference to U.S. policy toward the Arab-Israeli conflict was mentioned in this context. Notwithstanding these developments, Iraqi-U.S. relations are still constrained by U.S. support to Israel, U.S. policy towards the Palestine problem, and Iraqi-Soviet relations. Another constraint is the absence of strong economic relations. In 1978 the United States came after Western European, Asian, and socialist countries as trade partners.[69] The ultimate constraint, however, is the prospect of Iranian-U.S. relations and the possibility entertained by the Iraqis of growing cooperation between the two countries.

Relations with the Soviet Union. Since the mid-1950s the Soviet Union has emerged as a global ally of Arab nationalist regimes. However, the nature of pan-Arabist ideologies has limited Soviet-Arab relations. One source of tension stemmed from differing views of the role of Arab Communists in the politics of their countries. This led to a rift with Egypt in the late 1950s and with Iraq in the 1970s. When the Ba'th party assumed power in July 1968, Iraqi-Soviet cooperation was already established, particularly in the economic field through Soviet participation in the development of the Iraqi oil industry. Relations reached a new height by the conclusion in April 1972 of a treaty of friendship and cooperation between the two countries. The treaty provided for full cooperation in political, economic, commercial, technical, cultural, and other fields, including regular consultations, defense support, and military cooperation.[70]

Thus Iraq was broadly perceived in the West as a Soviet satellite. In fact, sources of tension were gradually mounting. Internally, problems created by the Ba'thist-Communist front led in 1978 to the execution of some Iraqi Communists. At the regional level, there was considerable Iraqi dissatisfaction with the Soviet policy permitting Soviet Jews to emigrate to Israel,[71] and with the Soviet pro-Ethiopian policy against both Somalia and the Eritreans.[72] Since early 1980, Soviet intervention in Afghanistan has been officially condemned at the highest levels.[73]

However, the above symptoms of tension in Soviet-Iraqi relations appear minor when compared with their differing evaluations of the Iranian revolution. The Iraqi leadership perceives it as a "reactionary" movement; the Soviets view the Iranian revolution as essentially anti-imperialist. This perception has affected Soviet policy toward the war between Iraq and Iran, delaying the delivery of Soviet arms purchased by Iraq. From the second half of 1981 there were signs of easing tension and calculated improvement in the relations. The Iraqi president declared at the press conference held after the bombing of the Iraqi nuclear reactor in June 1981 that the Soviets had expressed a desire to continue and to develop relations with Iraq. Military cooperation was resumed in 1982. In July 1983, Foreign Minister Aziz related the improvement in relations to an increasing Soviet understanding of the Iraqi view of the conflict with Iran.[74]

Relations with Western Europe and Japan. In our analysis of Iraq's foreign policy orientation, we have seen that the Iraqi leadership expects the evolution of a multipolar world and that the new centers of power will include Western Europe and Japan. We have also seen that President Saddam Hussein referred to the need for an Iraqi and Arab role to influence this process.

This attitude was encouraged in the case of France by the French policy adopted, especially since de Gaulle, toward the Arab-Israeli conflict. This led from the early 1970s to a pattern of close cooperation between Iraq and France in economic and military fields. According to Iraqi figures, in 1978 France was Iraq's fourth largest trading partner.[75] Increasingly, France became a major arms exporter to Iraq and was crucial in building Iraq's nuclear facilities. Cooperation in the field of oil will be dealt with later in this chapter.

The Federal Republic of Germany also has special relations with Iraq. West Germany was Iraq's second largest trading partner in 1978 and its first in 1977. In both years Western Europe came first as a region.[76] Iraq has a positive attitude towards Euro-Arab dialogue. Even when the third economic agreement was concluded between the European Economic Community (EEC) and Israel in 1975, Saddam Hussein called for a "calculated" Arab reaction. He criticized those who proposed an end to the Euro-Arab dialogue. He implied that such an attitude would, in the final analysis, serve U.S. interests.[77]

Iraq's relations with West European countries have also encountered difficulties. Saddam Hussein once accused West German officials of trying to impose unequal relations and accused the German mass media of being hostile to Iraq.[78] He was also dissatisfied with the French reaction to the Israeli bombing of the French-built Iraqi nuclear reactor in June 1981.[79]

As for Japan, it became Iraq's number one trading partner in 1978.[80] In that year, the value of Iraqi-Japanese trade alone exceeded the value of Iraq's trade with all other Asian or socialist countries.

Nonalignment. Analysis of the Iraqi leadership's perception of the global system reveals the central position of nonalignment. Iraq played a distinctive role in nonaligned summit meetings in the 1970s, and especially at the Havana conference in 1979. At that conference, Iraq called for more institutionalization of the movement and for the establishment of an international fund to help Third World countries offset the effects of inflation.[81] This fund was to have been financed by industrially developed countries and Third World oil-producing countries. Iraq was to host the 1982 summit meeting in Baghdad and Saddam Hussein was to become the spokesman of the nonaligned movement for the following three years. Because of the war, however, the meeting was postponed for a year and moved to New Delhi.

Oil Policy. Traditionally, Iraq has been opposed to the foreign oil concessions awarded by the British to the Iraq Petroleum Company in 1925. However, the Qasem regime (1958–1963) rejected nationalization as impractical, pressing instead for higher shares of oil profits. This led in 1961 to serious strains in relations with oil companies, which were unable to reach a settlement with the regime. Consequently, the Iraqi government expropriated all IPC concessionary areas not yet under production (i.e., 99.5% of the area for which it held prospecting rights). The government then enacted a law that authorized a state-owned Iraqi National Oil Company (INOC) to exploit all resources throughout the country except in the areas already being developed by the IPC and its associates.

Iraqi oil policy worked as a catalyst in improving relations with some countries, especially the Soviet Union and France. Both a French state-owned group of companies and the Soviet Union expressed willingness to enter into agreements with INOC for oil prospecting and exploration. The French group became a contractor under INOC, which held all proprietary rights pertaining to oil and installations to be constructed in Iraq. However, it was agreed that the French agency would receive from INOC 50% of the oil discovered in commercial quantities. On the other hand, INOC acquired Soviet loans totaling $72 million to develop the North Rumeila oil fields. In addition, Iraq received promises of technical cooperation from the Soviet Union and East European countries.

Notwithstanding these developments, the Iraqi government still received a major proportion of its oil income from the Western oil companies operating in the country. In early 1972, either for purely commercial reasons (as the IPC and its affiliates claimed) or to put pressure on the government (as the Iraqi regime perceived it), the Western oil companies reduced oil production in Iraq. The Iraqi government reacted on June 1, 1972, by nationalizing all IPC assets in Iraq. Again, this was a catalyst in promoting relations with the USSR and France (among other countries). To overcome the difficulties related to oil transportation and distribution, the Soviet Union had agreed to lease tankers to INOC. On the other hand, Iraq concluded an agreement with France for the sale of oil from the nationalized fields. Contracts were also made with Spain, Italy, Greece, India, Japan, and Brazil. By the end of 1972, it was clear that Iraq was coping with the marketing problem.[82]

From 1973 onwards, Iraq became an influential "hawk" in pushing for higher prices at the meetings of OPEC. President Saddam Hussein viewed raising oil prices as a reaction to the rising inflation in industrialized countries.[83] Iraq has developed a policy of relating production to its developmental needs and also to the oil needs of friendly countries.[84]

The Regional Level

Inter-Arab Politics. In retrospect, the 1970s may be viewed as the decade most favorable to the fulfillment of Iraq's Arab role since the Second World War. This decade witnessed increasing political stability in Iraq and enhanced economic capability because of oil. The 1975 success in resolving the Kurdish problem and the signing of a new agreement with Iran concerning the Shatt Al-Arab were added favorable factors. With all these developments, the stage was set in the second half of the 1970s for an active Iraqi role in the Arab world. President Sadat provided the opportunity for Iraq to act by his conclusion of the Camp David Accords in September 1978. Traditionally, Iraq had followed an extremist line towards the Arab-Israeli conflict, and the Ba'thist regime opposed any kind of peaceful settlement. Iraq rejected Resolution 242, adopted in 1967, and all diplomatic initiatives based on it. Militarily, Iraq participated in the 1973 October War in support of Syria. The Camp David Accords were thus perceived by the Iraqi leadership as primarily serving the interests of Israel and diluting the potential for the Arab struggle against Israel in the next twenty years. With the emergence of more centers of global power and better Arab management of the conflict with Israel, Arabs would be able to achieve their goals, felt the Iraqi leaders. Hence the Camp David policy had to be contained and discredited.[85]

Opposition to the Camp David Accords took priority over all other Iraqi concerns. The Iraqis insisted that the Arabs unite against this grave threat, and Iraq led the formation of this united front. At the Baghdad Arab summit (November 1978), called to discuss concerted Arab action against Egypt, Iraq performed successfully in its new diplomatic role.[86] One outcome of the Baghdad summit was the improvement of Iraqi-Syrian relations. Iraq and Syria had been at odds with each other for a number of reasons. The first was a long-standing dispute over the distribution of the Euphrates water.[87] Then there was Iraqi dependence on the transit routes across Syrian territory to the eastern Mediterranean terminals and disagreements over oil royalties.[88] In the 1970s, the alleged manipulation of Iraq's Shi'ites by the Syrian Alawite rulers was another source of tension.[89]

This Iraqi-Syrian rapprochement at the Baghdad summit was perceived by many Arabs as a promising development in inter-Arab politics. It was hoped that through an Iraqi-Syrian alliance the strategic imbalance created by the Egyptian withdrawal from the military front with Israel would be redressed. However, relations soon became strained. Iraq accused Syria of supporting dissident elements and of following a policy that threatened Iraqi security and national integrity. Thus, it is not surprising that Syria chose to support Iran in its war with Iraq. Bearing out Iraqi accusations that Syria was involved indirectly in the war,[90] the Syrian government stopped the flow of Iraqi oil across its territory, inflicting considerable losses on Iraq.

It is interesting to observe the process of adaptation and change in Iraqi policy towards the Arab-Israeli conflict both during the Baghdad summit and afterwards. As Dawisha puts it:

> Iraq had a great stake in insuring the success of the Conference, but realized at an early stage the difficulties involved in reaching a position acceptable to all Arab states. . . . The Iraquis themselves were forced to temper their hitherto rigid revolutionary position. The Baghdad Summit appears to have given the Iraqi leaders a taste for diplomacy, as well as a greater awareness that moderate and pragmatic positions could prove far more effective than revolutionary orthodoxy in influencing Arab attitudes and policies.[91]

Iraq now accepts King Fahd's Fez formula, which provides a peaceful approach toward the settlement of the conflict with Israel and does not refer to the concept of a "secular, democratic Palestine." (The Fez formula is Fahd's Middle East plan, accepted in the Arab summit held in Fez in 1982.)

Saddam Hussein's proclamation, in February 1980, of an Arab National Charter emphasizing the strategy of national consensus was another sign of the new Iraqi moderation.[92] This strategy was suggested as the best way to deal with the Arab-Israeli conflict because no individual Arab country, regardless of its capabilities, could liberate Palestine alone.[93]

The war with Iran has been another important moderating influence, and this is particularly evident in the case of Iraqi-Egyptian relations. The war situation made Iraq dependent on Egyptian military support in terms of arms and ammunition. Under Sadat and Mubarak, Egypt took a position of unreserved support of Iraq. The present Iraqi leadership considers that the Egyptian absence from the Arab family has created a strategic imbalance that has been reflected in all Arab issues. It maintains that in 1983 circumstances in the Arab world are no longer what they were in 1978. Two new factors are the Iranian challenge and the threat of further Arab balkanization. The situation in Egypt is also different under Mubarak. These developments led to the reestablishment of contacts with Egypt, the restoration of economic relations, and an exchange of official visits. Neither Egypt nor the Arab countries would be asked to give up their current policies.[94] High-level officials in the two countries exchanged visits and met at an international conference in 1983. By the end of 1983, Egyptian-Iraqi relations had been strengthened considerably.

As regards economic issues, Iraq has adopted a position calling for optimum use of Arab oil revenues to satisfy the developmental needs of poor Arab countries.[95] Iraq has also adopted an Arab-oriented migration policy. Lack of skilled labor made Iraq a labor-importing country, and it allows any Arab into the country without an entry visa to look for a job. No differentiation in salaries exists.[96]

Conflict with Iran. Sources of conflict in Iraqi-Iranian relations were discussed earlier: geography, the contest for influence in the Gulf area, and population structure. Before 1958, these issues were overshadowed by a similarity in monarchical political regimes and by their common alignment with the West. The Iraqi revolution of 1958 brought the sources of conflict to the fore.

Iranian intervention in support of the Iraqi Kurds began soon after 1958 and continued in varying degrees, depending on the political climate. By the end of 1965, fighting occurred close to the Iraq-Iran border, leading to a number of frontier violations that engendered sharp tension between the two states during the first half of 1965. The Iranian army was even engaged on some occasions in actual combat against the Iraqi army.[97] When open hostilities between the Iraqi army and the Kurds broke out in October 1968, the Iraqi government claimed that the rebels were receiving aid from Iran. With the new round of fighting in March 1974, the shah of Iran, Mohamed Reza Pahlavi, escalated his assistance to the Iraqi Kurds. Not only did he begin to supply artillery, sophisticated antitank weapons, and ammunition: he also facilitated the flow of other foreign aid to the rebels.[98] In all, it seems that Iranian intervention was so effective that terminating it became a necessary condition for the Iraqi government to end the fighting. Unable to put an end to Iran's intervention militarily, the Iraqi regime was forced to reach a compromise with the Shah.

On March 6, 1975, at the OPEC meeting in Algeria, both countries agreed to end any infiltration of "subversive character." The price Iraq paid for this was its acceptance of the Iranian proposal that the Shatt Al-Arab waterway border be drawn down the center of the estuary, dividing it equally. As a consequence of this détente, the Iranian government ceased its financial and military help to the Kurds.

Iraqi-Iranian relations remained more or less cordial until the success of the Iranian Islamic revolution in 1979. From the very beginning, the Iraqi leadership perceived this as a "reactionary" development and did not see progressive prospects for the situation in Iran. The revolution was not led by workers or even the middle class. Its religious leaders represented the industrial, agricultural, and commercial bourgeoisie in Iran.[99] Later on, the Iraqi leadership accused the Iranian revolutionary regime of being faithful to the expansionist tradition of the "Persians" against the Arabs. In the perception of the Iraqi leadership, the Iranian threat is not confined to Iraq, but extends to the whole Gulf area. Iraq has a special role in defending the Gulf countries against this threat.[100]

Despite this perception, the Iraqi leadership initially maintained cordial relations with Iran. On more than one occasion Iraq expressed its sympathy toward the Iranian people in their struggle, its desire for close friendship with them, and its support of Iran's desire to join the nonalignment movement. However, traditional sources of conflict as well as the revolutionary zeal of the new leaders in Iran became paramount in influencing the relations between the two countries. The deterioration began with a war of words that soon developed into subversive activities, border clashes, and eventually total war.[101]

On September 17, 1980, President Saddam Hussein unilaterally abrogated the 1975 agreement. At the time, all indications suggested that Iranians were increasingly disillusioned with the factionalism and incompetence of the revolutionary government in Teheran, that the Iranian armed forces were demoralized, and that because of Iran's almost total international isolation, its army was lacking in essential spare parts. The Iraqi leadership concluded that militarily, the Iranians were no match for the Iraqi army.[102]

On September 22, the Iraqi army launched a full-fledged war against Iran. Quick and impressive victories were achieved by the Iraqis at the beginning.[103] However, the Iranians showed unexpectedly stiff resistance, and Iranian counterattacks eventually forced Iraqi troops to withdraw to Iraq's international borders with Iran (although it is too difficult now to specify which ones). By 1983, the Iraqi leadership was ready for a peaceful settlement based on a cease-fire and direct or indirect negotiations. Mutual nonintervention in internal affairs, respect by both parties of the sovereignty and territorial integrity of each country, and the exclusion of the use of force in relations between them must be the basis for any future settlement.[104]

Judging by the developments of the past three years, the war is at a stalemate and it is hard to imagine a classic military victory for either party unless the domestic situation changes drastically in either country. With no such change forthcoming, political settlement of the war is inevitable. Regardless of its outcome, the war has posed severe constraints on Iraq's foreign policy. For years to come, Iraq's freedom of action in the region will be limited by the consequences of that war.

CONCLUSION

One underlying theme of this chapter has been the influence of Iraq's domestic environment on its foreign policy. Although Iraqi policies were largely influenced in the 1970s by the preferences of Saddam Hussein, his choices were affected by the structural characteristics of Iraq's situation. This is not to suggest that external variables are irrelevant to Iraq's foreign policy. However, the most crucial external variables have exercised influence through domestic variables (the Kurdish conflict and the war with Iran).

Throughout the 1970s, it seemed that the Iraqi leadership had successfully managed Iraq's domestic environment and brought together the elements of national power to fulfill Iraq's potential as a regional leader. Iraq's economy was enhanced through a distinctive oil policy; oil revenues were skillfully used to diversify the economy and develop the military; the Kurdish conflict was resolved; and for the first time since the Second World War, Iraq enjoyed political stability. Iraq's relations with Iran improved considerably after 1975, and the Iraqi role against Egypt's peace with Israel led to moderation and a more pragmatic political line. By the late 1970s it seemed that Iraq was finally ready to fill the role of regional leader. At that very moment, the Iranian revolution occurred, and the new Iranian government started its appeals to Iraqi Shi'ites. War became inevitable.

It is perhaps an ironic twist of history that Iraq had to divert its resources, political and material, to the war situation. The war is likely to have an impact on Iraq for years to come. Iraq's moment of history has passed for the time being, and its potential leadership role must await some future date.

NOTES

1. David E. Long and John A. Hearty, "Republic of Iraq," in David E. Long and Bernard Reich (eds.), *The Government and Politics of the Middle East and North Africa* (Boulder, Colo.: Westview Press, 1980), p. 107.

2. W. B. Fisher, "Iraq," in *The Middle East and North Africa, 1979-1980* (London: Europa Publications, 1979), p. 386.

3. Zohurul Bari, "Syrian-Iraqi Dispute over the Euphrates Water," *International Studies* 16, 2 (1977), pp. 228–230.

4. Keith McLachlan, "Iraq, Problems of Regional Development," in Abbas Kelidar (ed.), *The Integration of Modern Iraq* (New York: St. Martin's Press, 1979), p. 137.

5. This figure excludes Iraqis living outside Iraq, estimated to number 29,000 in 1977. *Statistical Handbook for 1978* (Baghdad Ministry of Planning, 1978), p. 13 (in Arabic).

6. Saddam Hussein, *Iraq: A Mobilized Army* (Baghdad: Dar Al-Horriya, 1982), p. 15 (in Arabic).

7. Fisher, *op. cit.*, p. 387.

8. Saddam Hussein, *Our Own Way to Build Socialism*, 2d ed. (Baghdad: Dar Al-Horriya, 1980), p. 91 (in Arabic).

9. Claudia Wright, "Iraq, New Power in the Middle East," *Foreign Affairs* 58, 2 (1979–1980), pp. 269–270. For the implications of age distribution in calculating national power see Nazli Choucri, *Population Dynamics and International Violence* (Lexington, Mass.: Lexington Books, 1974), p. 71.

10. Fisher, *op. cit.*, p. 401. For greater detail on Iraqi population composition see Ali Fahmy, "The Basic Sociological Features of Iraq, A Simplified Sociological Map," *National Review of Social Sciences* (Cairo, Egypt) 18, 1–2 (1981), pp. 63–92.

11. R. D. McLaurin, Mohammed Mughisuddin, and Abraham Wagner, *Foreign Policy Making in the Middle East* (New York: Praeger Publishers, 1977), p. 108.

12. *Ibid.*, p. 109. There was an important Jewish community in Iraq, larger than in most Arab countries. After the establishment of Israel and Iraqi in-

volvement in the first Arab-Israeli war, there was considerable emigration of Jews from Iraq, especially in the years 1951 and 1952. The number of Iraqi Jews was estimated in 1976 to be about 2,500 (compared with 125,000 in 1947). See Fisher, *op. cit.,* pp. 387–394, and also by Fisher, "Ethnic and Religious Minorities in Egypt, Iraq, Jordan, Lebanon and Syria," *Middle East Review* 9 (Fall 1976), p. 61.

13. McLaurin, *op. cit.,* pp. 108–109.

14. *Ibid.,* p. 108.

15. Fisher, "Iraq," p. 391.

16. *Ibid.,* p. 419; McLaurin, *op. cit.,* pp. 108–109.

17. Fisher, "Iraq," p. 387.

18. McLaurin, *op. cit.,* p. 130.

19. Sa'ad N. Jawad, "The Kurdish Problem in Iraq," in Kelidar, *op. cit.,* p. 171.

20. Theodore Richard Nash, "The Effect of International Oil Interests Upon the Fate of Autonomous Kurdish Territory: A Perspective on the Conference at Sevres, August 10, 1920," *International Problems* 15, 1–2 (1976), pp. 119–120.

21. McLaurin, *op. cit.,* p. 109; Jawad, *op. cit.,* p. 180.

22. *Ibid.,* p. 171.

23. McLaurin, *op. cit.,* p. 131.

24. Omran Yahya Feili and Arlene R. Fromchuck, "The Kurdish Struggle for Independence," *Middle East Review* 9 (1976), p. 51.

25. Jawad, *op. cit.,* pp. 177–180; and McLaurin, *op. cit.,* pp. 133–139.

26. Jawad, *op. cit.,* p. 171.

27. McLaurin, *op. cit.,* pp. 133–134; Jawad, *op. cit.,* p. 178.

28. On the oil issue, the two sides argued that Kirkuk should not be included in the Kurdish autonomous region until a plebiscite was held. However, the plebiscite was postponed indefinitely, and the Kurds complained that the postponement was meant to give time for more Arabs to emigrate to the area. The March agreement provided for full recognition of Kurdish nationality, autonomy within a four-year period, and the appointment of a Kurdish vice-president. Kurdish was declared an official language and was to be taught, together with Arabic, all over Iraq. Moreover, Kurds were granted the right to form their own political and professional organizations, and a number of Kurdish forces were kept as border guards as part of the Iraqi armed forces. More important was the government declaration that the Kurds were part of the divided Kurdish people and Kurdistan, and that the Kurdish national movement was part of the general Iraqi national movement. See *ibid.,* pp. 179–180; and Honore M. Catudal, Jr., "The War in Kurdistan: End of Nationalist Struggle," *International Relations* 7, 3 (1976), pp. 133–134.

29. McLaurin, *op. cit.,* pp. 110–111.

30. The Sudanese experience is most relevant in this respect. See William H. Dorsey, "An Interview with Joseph Lagu, Anyana Leader," *Africa Report* 17, 9 (1972).

31. Evan Luard, "Civil Conflicts in Modern International Relations," in Evan Luard (ed.), *The International Regulation of Civil Wars* (London: Thames and Hudson, 1972), p. 7. For a full analysis of the internationalization of civil war situations, see James N. Rosenau (ed.), *International Aspects of Civil Strife* (Princeton, N.J.: Princeton University Press, 1964).

32. Fisher, "Iraq," p. 40; and McLaurin, *op. cit.,* p. 146. Also consult "Detente and the Arab Zionist Conflict," Interview of Saddam Hussein by Egyptian

journalist Sakina Al-Sadat in January 1977, in Saddam Hussein, *Social and Foreign Affairs in Iraq*, trans. Khalid Kishtainy (London: Croom Helm, 1979), pp. 90–91.

33. Fisher, "Iraq," p. 387.
34. Wright, *op. cit.*, p. 261.
35. Salah Al-Mukhtar (press counselor of the Iraqi mission to the UN), "The Role of Iraq in the Next Two Decades," Lecture delivered in Houston, Texas, February 1, 1981, pp. 16–18. Mimeo.
36. Long and Reich, *op. cit.*, p. 130.
37. Press conference of Comrade Saddam Hussein held on July 18, 1978 (Baghdad: Dar Al-Horriya, 1978), pp. 54–55 (in Arabic).
38. "Detente," in Hussein, *Social and Foreign Affairs*, pp. 87–88.
39. A. I. Dawisha, "Iraq: The West's Opportunity," *Foreign Policy* 41 (1980–1981), p. 147.
40. Interviews with Ismail Al-Delimy, Advisor of the Iraqi Ministry for Planning, in *Al-Hiwar Al-Arabi*, November 1982, pp. 108–112 (in Arabic).
41. Speech by President Saddam Hussein on the sixty-second anniversary of the establishment of the Iraqi army. Supplement, *Sout Al-Talaba Magazine* 167 (February 1983), pp. 29–32 (in Arabic).
42. "Strategic Statistics," *Arab Strategic Thought* 1 (1981), pp. 480–493 (in Arabic).
43. Dawisha, *op. cit.*, pp. 143–144; Wright, *op. cit.*, pp. 263–264.
44. See the excellent report by Mahmoud Azmy, "Strategic and Military Dimensions of the Bombing of the Iraqi Nuclear Reactor," in *Arab Strategic Thought* 1 (1981), pp. 399–416 (in Arabic).
45. Press conference of President Saddam Hussein held after the Israeli bombing of the Iraqi nuclear reactor (Baghdad: Dar Al-Horriya, 1981), pp. 9–12 (in Arabic).
46. Catudal, Jr., *op. cit.*, pp. 1024, 1029.
47. Dawisha, *op. cit.*, p. 148.
48. The provisional constitution of the Iraqi republic, issued on July 16, 1970, and amended in 1973. As Western sources on Iraq's political structure are full of inaccurate data, it is always advisable to consult Iraqi official documents.
49. Long and Reich, *op. cit.*, p. 122.
50. Press conference of Comrade Saddam Hussein, held on July 18, 1978, *op. cit.*, pp. 8–9.
51. *Ibid.*, p. 11.
52. Saddam Hussein, *One Ditch or Two Ditches?* (Baghdad: Dar Al-Horriya, 1981), pp. 4–5 (in Arabic).
53. Long and Reich, *op. cit.*, p. 117.
54. Saddam Hussein's statement to the Iraqi ambassadors to Western Europe and Japan, June 12, 1975, in Hussein, *Social and Foreign Affairs*, p. 78.
55. Speech given by Comrade Saddam Hussein at the general meeting of the National Progressive Front's committees on June 7, 1975 (Baghdad: Dar Al-Horriya, 2d ed., 1980), p. 7 (in Arabic).
56. Speech given by President Saddam Hussein at Al-Najaf Province on October 17, 1979 (Baghdad: Dar Al-Horriya, 1980), pp. 31–34 (in Arabic).
57. The analysis is based on several speeches by President Saddam Hussein in the years 1975 to 1977. Saddam Hussein, *Our Struggle and International Politics*, 2d ed. (Baghdad: Dar Al-Horriya, 1980), pp. 2–19, 54–57, and 85–86 (in Arabic).

58. Speech given by President Saddam Hussein on the thirteenth anniversary of the 1968 revolution (Baghdad: Dar Al-Horriya, 1981), pp. 46–47 (in Arabic).

59. Speech given by President Saddam Hussein at the Sixth Summit Conference of the Nonaligned Movement held in Havana, September 3–7, 1979 (Baghdad: Dar Al-Horriya, 2d ed., January 1980), p. 17 (in Arabic).

60. See Article 38-C of the Iraqi constitution and the interview with President Saddam Hussein in *Al-Majalla* 167 (December 4–10, 1982), p. 19 (in Arabic).

61. *Ibid.*

62. Speech given by comrade Saddam Hussein at the meeting of the regional and Iraqi leadership of the Ba'th party on December 26, 1977 (Baghdad: Dar Al-Horriya, 1978) (in Arabic).

63. Hussein, *Social and Foreign Affairs*, pp. 65–66.

64. Al-Mukhtar, *op. cit.*, pp. 8–13.

65. Cited in Dawisha, *op. cit.*, p. 149.

66. Press conference of President Saddam Hussein held after the Israeli bombing of the Iraqi nuclear reactor, *op. cit.*, pp. 83–85.

67. Interview with Hussein, *Al-Majalla, op. cit.*, p. 18.

68. Interview with Mr. Tarek Aziz, Iraqi deputy prime minister and minister for foreign affairs, in *Attadamon* 1, 14 (July 16, 1983), p. 7 (in Arabic).

69. *Statistical Handbook for 1978*, pp. 34–39.

70. Edith Penrose and E. F. Penrose, *Iraq: International Relations and National Development* (London: Ernest Benn, 1978), pp. 426–434.

71. Statement of Comrade Saddam Hussein to *Der Spiegel* (Baghdad: Dar Al-Horriya, 2d ed., 1980), p. 41 (in Arabic).

72. Press conference of Comrade Saddam Hussein held on July 18, 1978, *op. cit.*, p. 92.

73. Press conference of President Saddam Hussein held after the Israeli bombing of the Iraqi nuclear reactor, *op. cit.*, pp. 87–88. See also Dawisha, *op. cit.*, p. 137.

74. Interview with Hussein in *Al-Majalla, op. cit.*, p. 18. Interview with Tarek Aziz in *Attadamon, op. cit.*, p. 8.

75. See *Statistical Handbook for 1978*, pp. 34–39.

76. *Ibid.*

77. Hussein, *Social and Foreign Affairs*, pp. 82–83.

78. Statements of Comrade Saddam Hussein to *Der Spiegel, op. cit.*, p. 45.

79. Press conference of President Saddam Hussein held after the Israeli bombing of the Iraqi nuclear reactor, *op. cit.*, pp. 98–99.

80. *Statistical Handbook for 1978*, pp. 34–39.

81. Speech given by President Saddam Hussein at the Sixth Summit Conference of the Nonaligned Movement, *op. cit.*, p. 16.

82. Fisher, *op. cit.*, p. 398; McLaurin, *op. cit.*, pp. 148–150.

83. Press conference of Comrade Saddam Hussein held on July 18, 1978, *op. cit.*, pp. 52–54.

84. Statement of Comrade Saddam Hussein to *Der Spiegel, op. cit.*, p. 36. Press conference of President Saddam Hussein held after the Israeli bombing of the Iraqi nuclear reactor, *op. cit.*, p. 107.

85. See statement of Comrade Saddam Hussein to *Der Spiegel, op. cit.*, pp. 15–28.

86. Dawisha, *op. cit.*, p. 140.

87. For details see Bari, *op. cit.*, pp. 234–244.

88. Fisher, *op. cit.*, pp. 396–399.

89. *Ibid.*, p. 400; Wright, *op. cit.*, pp. 265–267.

90. Speech given by President Saddam Hussein on the occasion of the Iraqi army anniversary on January 6, 1981, pp. 25–26 (in Arabic).

91. Dawisha, *op. cit.*, pp. 144–145.

92. Speech given by President Saddam Hussein on the thirteenth anniversary of the 1968 revolution, *op. cit.*, pp. 32–33.

93. Press conference of President Saddam Hussein held after the Israeli bombing of the Iraqi nuclear reactor, *op. cit.*, pp. 66–78.

94. Interview with Mr. Tarek Aziz, in *Attadamon* 1, 13 (July 9, 1983), pp. 6–7 (in Arabic).

95. Speech given by President Saddam Hussein on the thirteenth anniversary of the 1968 revolution, *op. cit.*, pp. 33–38.

96. Mohsen Khalil Ibrahim, "About Iraq's Experience in Importing Labor," *Arab Future* 51 (May 1983), pp. 93–104 (in Arabic).

97. Feili and Fromchuck, *op. cit.*, p. 53.

98. Catudal, Jr., *op. cit.*, p. 1036.

99. Interview with Mr. Tarek Aziz, *Attadamon* 1, 14 (July 16, 1983), p. 8.

100. Speech given by President Saddam Hussein on the Iraqi-Iranian dispute at the third Islamic summit, January 25–28, 1981, pp. 8–15 (in Arabic). Saddam Hussein, "Iraq: A Mobilized Army," pp. 30–31. Speech by President Saddam Hussein on the sixty-second anniversary of the establishment of the Iraqi army, *op. cit.*, pp. 9–13.

101. For a full Iraqi official record of these developments, see the speech given by President Saddam Hussein on the Iraqi-Iranian dispute, *op. cit.*, pp. 25–30.

102. Dawisha, *op. cit.*, p. 146.

103. Speech given by President Saddam Hussein on the Iraqi-Iranian dispute, *op. cit.*, pp. 35–36.

104. Interview with President Saddam Hussein in *Al-Majalla*, *op. cit.*, p. 16.

174

Libya

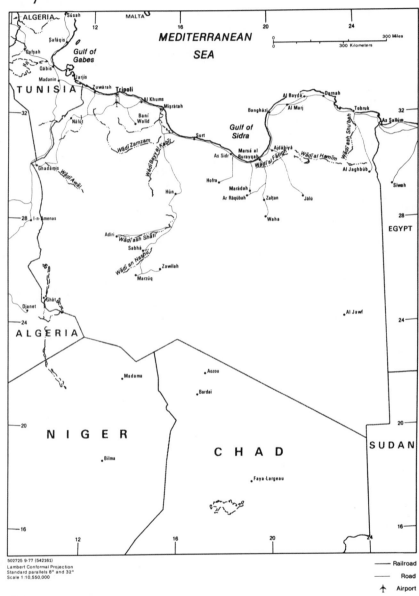

Railroad
Road
Airport

7

Heroic Politics:
The Foreign Policy of Libya

I. William Zartman
A. G. Kluge

INTRODUCTION

Since the military coup that overthrew the government of King Idris in 1969, the foreign policy of what is now formally called the Socialist People's Libyan Arab Jamahiriya has earned the country a reputation as an "Arab Prussia" and an "international gadfly."[1] Libyan leader Colonel Muammer Al-Qaddafi, generally recognized as the strongman behind the state's power, has been associated with international terrorism on a grand scale, from attempts to destabilize neighboring countries to the funding of radical groups such as the Irish Republican Army (IRA) and the Palestine Liberation Organization.[2] Libyan foreign policy, like Libya's leader, is widely perceived to be capricious. Egyptian president Anwar Al-Sadat even went so far as to call Qaddafi "crazy."[3] Such labels, however, do not serve to increase our understanding of Libya's leader or its foreign policy. It is a serious mistake to dismiss what initially may appear alien or incomprehensible. Or, as one scholar of Arab politics writes: "It is easier to judge but hard to understand the ghosts with which people and societies battle, the wounds and memories that drive them to do what they do. Even if we disagree with people's choice of allegiance, we must understand the reasons for their choice, the odds they fight against, the range of alternatives open to them."[4]

The task, then, is to convey the motives, opportunities, and constraints that influence Libyan state behavior. The unpredictability of human enterprises will not disappear, but from this perspective Libyan foreign policy emerges more clearly as a product of a particular cultural and historical context. It is against this backdrop that this chapter outlines the beginning of a framework for analyzing Libya's foreign policy as that of a rational, goal-oriented nation pursuing its professed revolutionary aims of "freedom, socialism, and unity."

DOMESTIC ENVIRONMENT

Historical Legacy

The conception of foreign policy as the "role" of a nation has deep grounding in Arab political tradition and is a powerful tool for understanding Libyan behavior in particular.[5] The language of heroism and historical role was used by the revolutionary new Egyptian premier, Gamal Abdel Nasser, in 1955 to describe his perception of the Arab world of his time:

> For some reason it seems to me that within the Arab circle there is a role, wandering aimlessly in search of a hero. And I do not know why it seems to me that this role, exhausted by its wanderings, has at last settled down, tired and weary, near the borders of our country and is beckoning to us to move, to take up its lines, to put on its costume, since no one else is qualified to play it.[6]

With the defiant seizure of the Suez Canal from British control in 1956, Nasser's Egypt became the center and symbol of Arab unity and assertiveness. For a time, it appeared that Egypt had successfully assumed the role "to spark this tremendous power latent" in the Arab world.[7]

To Qaddafi, listening to Radio Cairo's Voice of the Arabs and plotting to depose the Libyan monarchy, Nasser was a hero and example. Even after the Arab defeat of 1967 at the hands of the Israelis revealed the illusions of Nasser's pan-Arabism, Qaddafi remained loyal to the shattered dreams of his spiritual father, and the defeat spurred his coup against the Libyan monarchy two years later.

The content and heroic form of Nasser's aims continued to have a profound influence on Qaddafi's policies. Just after the Libyan coup in 1969, Qaddafi reported to Mohamed Heikal, then Egyptian minister of information and former editor of *Al-Ahram*: "Libya represents depth. We have hundreds of miles of Mediterranean coastline; we have the airfields; we have the money; we have everything: tell President Nasser we made this revolution for him. He can take everything of ours and add it to the rest of the Arab world's resources to be used for the battle."[8] The total identification of Libya with the goals of Nasser provoked Heikal to call Qaddafi "shockingly innocent—scandalously pure."[9] The incident nevertheless gives telling insight into Qaddafi and his perception of Libya as a geopolitical hinterland for the policies of Nasser.

On the rhetorical level at least, Qaddafi's espousal of Nasser's revolutionary goals of "freedom, socialism, and unity" has been remarkably consistent. Since the 1977 proclamation of the new Libyan constitution and "Jamahiriya" or "state of the masses," neither Qaddafi nor his former Revolutionary Command Council (RCC) insurrectionists hold official posts in the government. Qaddafi nevertheless remains the de facto head of the state and the chief architect of Libyan foreign policy. Qaddafi's frequent pronouncements on foreign policy, in the press and his widely publicized *Green Book*, represent both an adherence to and a unique elaboration of Nasserism.

Qaddafi's brand of neo-Nasserism is distinctive in several respects. Nasser's view of his nation's role was shaped by the Egyptian experience; he spoke with the prestige and worldly wisdom of Cairo and with the authority of Egypt's tens of millions of people. Qaddafi's vision of his country's role shares much with that of Nasser, but it also bears the marks of Libya's different cultural traditions and socioeconomic conditions. Heikal writes of Qaddafi:

> Two people and two backgrounds combined to make Qaddafi the man he was. The people were the Prophet Mohammed and Gamal Abdel Nasser. . . . His two backgrounds were the army and the desert. . . . Qaddafi's difficulty was that he lacked the resources and the experience to enable him to digest all the conflicting influences that operated on him. But the result of this conflict was a personality of fascinating complexity.[10]

Heikal saw Qaddafi as a complicated mix of Nasserism and Islam, but he also claimed, at least in the 1970s, that Qaddafi was "a simple puritan caught up in a complicated world full of intrigue and manoeuvre."[11]

Lastly, Qaddafi's loyalty is to the dreams of the charismatic and heroic Nasser of the days of Suez, rather than to the wiser man who survived the Arabs' crushing 1967 defeat. Many of Qaddafi's policies show the characteristics of heroic politics, betraying more aesthetic appeal than political wisdom. For example, Qaddafi continues to proselytize the unimpressive "Third International Theory" of his *Green Book*. In the typical wisdom of the *Green Book*, Qaddafi advocates direct political participation of the masses, stating: "Theoretically, this is the genuine democracy. But realistically, the strong always rule, i.e., the stronger part in the society is the one that rules."[12] Qaddafi vastly overestimates the applicability and importance of the grand schemes of the *Green Book*. In 1979, Qaddafi told a Western journalist: "The Green Book is the new gospel. . . . One of its words can destroy the world. Or save it . . . the third world only needs my Green Book. My word. One word and the whole world could blow up. The value of things could change. And their weight . . . everywhere and forever."[13]

There is indeed a very Sufi-sounding tone to this and many other of Qaddafi's statements that is quite different from Nasser's language.[14] For Qaddafi is neither a copy nor an imitation of Nasser but rather is inspired by his example, expressing similar goals in different ways. Here enters a second source of Qaddafi's views and behavior, the mystic and fundamentalist reformist of the Libyan desert. Alongside of the secular neo-Nasserism is the purifying religious movement of the Senussiya, established about 1843 in Cyrenaica.[15] Although centered in Libya and later headed by Idris Al-Senussi, who became Libya's first and last monarch, the Senussiya was an international movement calling for a return to basic revitalized Islam. As a reaction against the formalism and the corruption of urban practices of the time, the Senussiya represented one of the recurring waves of desert revivalism that Ibn Khaldun identified as a feature of the Arab world.[16] In all of the characteristics, the "Qaddafiya" is similar to its predecessor, the latest wave of austere fundamentalist revivalism, seeking to create solidarity across state boundaries.

Grand schemes, dramatic and irrevocable decisions appeal to Qaddafi. During the Israeli siege of Beirut in 1982 (to cite a recent example), Qaddafi urged PLO commander Yasser Arafat "to commit suicide rather than accept disgrace." "Your suicide will immortalize the cause of Palestine for future generations. . . . It is the road to victory. . . . It is the decision to die."[17] Martyrdom may be heroic, but in the context of the Arab-Israeli dispute it is hardly the most practical course.

Geography and Population

The second element in the domestic environment from which Qaddafi's foreign policy springs is the geographic and demographic "depth" that he offered to Nasser.[18] Libya is a big country (the fourth largest in Africa) with few people (3 million, ranking thirty-third in Africa and eleventh in the Arab world). The vast land area has little value other than its geostrategic location on the Mediterranean shore and the borders of four Arab and two Sahelian countries. Little of it is arable today, even though it was the breadbasket for Rome some fifteen centuries ago. Its meager population, a fifteenth the size of Egypt's, is concentrated in three areas, around Tripoli and Benghazi on the coast and along the Fezzan oases in the southwestern interior. Only Tripolitania has an urban tradition, and it is scarcely the cosmopolitan center one finds in most other Arab countries. The one thing of value the land holds is oil, in reserves estimated at the beginning of the 1980s at 25 billion barrels, enough to provide the small population with a per capita income of $9,000. Since Qaddafi's coup, this wealth has been used for an ambitious social welfare program (including extensive education facilities) and for equally ambitious foreign ventures (including extensive arms acquisitions far beyond Libya's own capabilities for use).[19] In sum, Libya's position is exactly the reverse of Egypt's: Libya has few people and much wealth in a peripheral position, whereas Egypt is burdened with a large population and few resources, situated in a central location in both the Arab and global strategic world.

The implications of this situation for foreign policy are straightforward. Libya has the means (oil) and the purpose (neo-Nasserism) that the Arabs need, but lacks the population and strategic location of other Arab states. The goal of Libyan policy is to unite the two, a goal that at the same time follows and leads to the neo-Nasserite purpose of Arab unity and anti-imperialism. Of course, other Arab countries have oil too, but they do not have a clear vision (or a vision at all) of the role that Qaddafi has seen, and so it becomes important to build popular Arab support and adherence to Qaddafi's policy, not just state support.[20]

Economic and Military Capabilities

Economic and military capabilities in relation to foreign policy are determined by population and geography. Except for its oil production and revenues, Libya has only a small national economy, and is highly dependent on outside sources of supply for both food and manufactured goods. Despite intensive efforts in the 1970s, Libyan agriculture has not given the nation the desired self-sufficiency. Nor is this likely to occur in the near future, in some measure because of poor management and planning.[21] Libya has no industrial base and no raw material to transform. There is no armaments industry and no possibility of developing self-sufficiency in armaments. Libya's military is limited by the small population and by its lack of a background in technical skills or in military traditions in general.

Libya's army stands at 53,000, the eighth largest in Africa and the eighth in the Arab world, about the size of Saudi Arabia's. It has been growing steadily since the military government came to power, with the largest jump in 1978, when it increased by two-thirds over the previous year. There is a high ratio of soldiers to civilians (18 : 1), much higher than in most other Arab states (except Syria, UAE, and Qatar) and in almost all other African states.[22] Still, the army depends on foreign training and even foreign operators, particularly in the air force. Soviets, North Koreans, Pakistanis, and Palestinians pilot Libyan planes.[23] The results have not been outstanding: the Libyan army was beaten by the Egyptians in the border war of July 1977, and its efforts on behalf of fallen governments in Uganda (1979) and Chad (1983) have not been successful. Libya's most impressive military activity has been its transport capability, notably demonstrated in the airlift and groundlift of tanks and troops to Chad in 1981, carried out with Soviet assistance. Libya is a party to three presumably active military assistance treaties, the 1975 Treaty of Hassi Mess'oud with Algeria, the 1981 Treaty of Aden with Ethiopia and South Yemen, and the 1980 unification agreement with Syria. The Hassi Mess'oud treaty has been a greater restraint on Algeria than on Libya and has not prevented military confrontations on the common border in 1981 and strains from policy differences. The Aden treaty has brought frequent consultations among the members, and specifically, Libyan financing for the Ethiopian invasion of Somalia in 1982–1983 (although Libya also financed the Ethiopian arms airlift in 1977–1978 before the treaty was signed). The Syrian treaty appears less operative.

Political Structure

By advocating both Islam and socialism, or social justice, Qaddafi has tried to monopolize the cultural symbols of legitimacy. In addition,

Qaddafi has taken a strong stance on what is perceived to be a powerful test of Arab nations: support for the Palestinian cause.

Libya has a long tradition of rebellious and powerful religious leaders. In recognition of the power of Islam, from genuine belief, or both, Qaddafi has attempted to give an Islamic cast to the Jamahiriya (people's state) by reviving the Qur'an as the basis of Libyan legislation.[24] Qaddafis' personal and modernist interpretation of Islam has alienated more traditional members of society, yet to Qaddafi Islamic society is a radically different and important alternative to Communist and Western models.

In practice, Qaddafi and his junta have been grappling with age-old questions of governance as they search for new and satisfying answers. The repeated attempt to find appropriate institutions for the revolution has taken forms that seek to be as inventive as the neologism "jamahiriya." Qaddafi's regime has tried to combine authority and participation, giving power to the people and at the same time completely reorienting the people's notions of what to do with power. Qaddafi's attempts have been serious, but in the end, his answers have not been new, and the outcome of his effort to reconcile conflicting values has been the classical response of authoritarianism and reorientation, under the label of popular power and participation.

The first round of institutions covered the first half of the 1970s, when authority was represented by the Revolutionary Control Council of the Free Officers, with participation by the people's committees and the Arab Socialist Union, all Nasserist bodies.[25] When each body failed to do its job, the reorganization of 1975 began, leading to the second round. The institutions were embodied in the current pyramid of "people's" bodies, with the People's General Congress as the surrogate legislature and the people's committees acting as participatory organs at all levels. Various secretaries were appointed as agents of authority and control. For further vigor and control, appointed revolutionary committees were gradually added, creating more disorder than revolutionary fervor. In 1978, a third phase of socialist austerity began, which in turn alienated the same growing middle class that the oil boom had favored. As dissatisfaction grew, so did repression. The conflict between authority and participation remains.

LIBYAN FOREIGN POLICY ORIENTATION: "FREEDOM"

In order to assess the success of Libya in playing out the neo-Nasserist role it has defined, at least rhetorically, for itself, it is necessary to examine the specifics of the state's official policy as well as its actual behavior. In the Nasserist slogan of "freedom, socialism, and unity," proclaimed in 1969 to be the guiding philosophy of the Libyan revolution, "freedom" deliberately is first. Though the definitions of the terms overlap in Libyan usage, "freedom" is closely related to "socialism" and is considered the essential means to the ultimate goal of Arab "unity."

In a speech in Tripoli shortly after the revolution, Qaddafi set forth the official interpretation of the Nasserist slogan. "Freedom . . . is the liberation of our dear land from all evil and intruders, from every imperialist and reactionary element, and also emancipation of the Arab homeland, in all its parts, from every intruder and guilty aggressor."[26] Qaddafi sees "freedom" as the elimination of imperialist and reactionary elements both from Libya and from the "Arab homeland," i.e., from the Arab states and Palestine.

From the very beginning of his regime, Qaddafi has been critical both of the "imperialist" camp (initially Israel, the United States, and the USSR; later only the first two) and of "reactionary" Arab states. Though Qaddafi asserts that Libya is an Islamic regime, he is nevertheless critical of Arab and Islamic regimes that are in his opinion reactionary. Heikal cites an interesting Qaddafi assessment of King Hassan of Morocco at the Rabat summit in December 1969. As the chief of the royal cabinet greeted King Hassan by kissing his hand, in keeping with Moroccan tradition, Qaddafi is "horrified," Heikal writes. Heikal notes Qaddafi's outburst: "Does hand kissing still go on in the Arab world? Do we still stick to these relics of feudalism and slavery? How are we ever going to liberate Palestine if we still kiss hands?"[27]

The example points to an important and continuing strain in Qaddafi's policy—his perception that a modernist stance (albeit Islamic) is necessary for freedom. This modernist inclination is an important factor in Qaddafi's relations with the conservative Arab states and in his relations with the Soviet Union and its client nations.

"Freedom" has an additional, related meaning in official Libyan ideology. In the same 1969 Tripoli speech Qaddafi stated: "Freedom also is the liberation of the individual from poverty, illness, ignorance, and injustice."[28] This internal freedom is closely related to what Qaddafi means by "socialism." Libyan socialism is used synonymously with the phrase "social justice" to distinguish it from a Marxist-atheistic socialism deemed incompatible with Islam. "The people who have long been deprived of social justice, and whose wealth and treasures have been robbed will accept no alternative for socialism. They will impose socialism by force and will fight for it until social justice has become an accomplished fact and until this people has ensured a sufficiency in production along with just distribution."[29] Clearly, beneath the martial rhetoric is an attempt to rally the people behind Qaddafi's aim. The goal of socialism, one gathers from the phrases, means a socially just distribution (apparently based on Islamic principles) and self-sufficiency. Qaddafi's vision of self-sufficiency implies an autarkic state.

Further elaborating foreign policy goals for his country, Qaddafi delineates a progressive or dynamic sequence of policies.

> In order to preserve this great and national unity which is a distinguishing mark of Libya, the door should be closed to partisanship. Regionalism should also on no account be allowed to grow after today. We must raise

the following slogans and proceed behind their banners, towards execution and application. We must raise the slogan of full evacuation, of positive neutralism and of non-alignment. We must raise the slogan of "being hostile to those who antagonize us, and being friends to those who befriend us." We must also raise the slogan of national unity as a first step along the road of all-embracing Arab unity.[30]

From this statement, we may discern important elements of Qaddafi's foreign policy.[31] First is his emphasis on Libyan unity. Second is his goal of full independence, i.e., no foreign military bases. Third are the broader goals of "positive neutralism and non-alignment" and of support for helping powers and enmity for hostile powers. And of course, true to the Nasserist tradition, Qaddafi claims his ultimate goal to be an "all-embracing Arab unity." It should be noted that the first and last goals are those of consolidation of power, perhaps Qaddafi's power.

As with most countries, one might expect to find various shifts and phases in Libyan foreign policy, perhaps corresponding to periods in Libyan domestic policy.[32] Indeed, for about the first five years of the regime, such periods can be noted: first a focus on recovering control of national assets (bases, oil prices, oil production) in 1969–1971; then (and slightly overlapping), the period of Arab unification, with Sudan, Syria, and Egypt, in 1970–1973, ending in isolation; and then a last attempt with Tunisia in 1974. Certainly, the time of isolation during the October War of 1973, corresponding with the time of domestic renewal in the Cultural Revolution, was a serious turning point in Libyan political behavior. It seems to have led to a new period of disenchantment with the Arab East and renewed attention to the Arab West and the Moslem south. The short-lived Libyan union with Tunisia was followed the next year by the Hassi Mess'oud treaty with Algeria; at the same time, Libya took on initial funding of the People's Liberation Front for Saguia Al Hamra and Rio de Oro (Polisario) in the Western Sahara, financial aid for Mauritania and then direct interference after the military coup of 1978, and growing support for dissident groups in Mali, Niger, and eventually Senegal. By the early 1980s Libya was providing support for military coups in Gambia, Ghana, and Upper Volta, and direct support for the rebellion in Chad after the conservative military coup in 1975 through the union attempt and military occupation of 1981. Close relations with the military government of Idi Amin in Uganda also covered the last half of the 1970s. After Sadat's visit to Jerusalem in 1977, Qaddafi helped found the Rejectionist Front and then the Steadfastness Front, remaining faithful to their principles (the three "no's" of the Arab summit resolution of Khartoum in 1967: "no" to direct negotiations with Israel, "no" to recognition of Israel, and "no" to peace with Israel) even after their collapse in 1982 at the Arab summit of Fez.

A closer look at dates blurs the phases. Qaddafi's interest in Mauritania dates from his visit there in 1972, when he discovered that Mauritanians speak the same Arabic dialect as his maternal home; that same year marks the visit of President Ngarta Tombalbaye to Libya and the Chadian "secret recognition" of Libyan rights over the 'Aouzou Strip of northern Chad. Official truces with Morocco and renouncement of all disputes with the monarchy in mid-1981 and mid-1983 may show a pattern of regularity, but this pattern was interrupted by the wreckage of the OAU summit over the Saharan and Chadian issues on two occasions in 1982 and the renewed intervention in Chad in mid-1983.

It appears that Libyan foreign policy is a policy of opportunity, conducted on the basis of rather constant principles as outlined above. When an opportunity presents itself, Libya acts. When opposition is too strong, Libya effects a strategic withdrawal, but not a change in goals. Ironically, this tactical flexibility no doubt contributes to Qaddafi's reputation as opportunistic and capricious and hides the consistency of his goals.

THE DECISION-MAKING PROCESS

The personalization of Libyan policy and the interchangeable usage of the leader for the country are not merely literary devices; Qaddafi is the personal policy chief of Libya, to an even greater extent in foreign than in domestic policy. He makes specific decisions of importance and establishes the ideological context within which they are made; Qaddafi is his own chief delegate and envoy as well as the leading foreign policy authority at home. Yet, without suffering any diminution, this personal primacy does operate within an institutional framework and under some political constraints.

The agency responsible for foreign relations in Libya is the Office of External Contacts (*Maktab Al-Itisal Al-Khariji*), which replaced the Foreign Ministry in 1980. The office is chaired by the secretary of the People's Committee for External Contacts; under the Jamahiriya system the people in a branch of service form a committee and choose their own manager. Overseas, the office is represented by Fraternity Offices (*Makatib Al-Ikhiwa*) in Arab and Moslem countries and People's Offices (*Makatib Al-Sha'biya*) in others. Again in theory, it is the Libyan community in these countries that constitutes these offices and chooses its leaders. In fact, however, the various offices in Libya and abroad are run as a diplomatic service, with offices posted as decided in Tripoli and officials appointed by Qaddafi or by diplomatic officials.

The actual operations within this structure or in the political circles outside are difficult to penetrate. Qaddafi's most visible and active lieutenants are External Contacts Secretary Abd El-Ati 'Obeidi and former foreign minister and then presidential advisor for foreign relations Abdel Salam Triki. On occasion the remaining Free Officers act as either emissaries or collegial decision-makers: Major Abdel-Salam Jallud, in charge of government affairs; General Abu Bakr Unis Jabr, in command of the army; General Mustafa Kharrubi, in charge of intelligence; and Major Khuwaildi Hamidi, in charge of the people's militia and chief of staff. Similarly, other presidential advisors besides Triki are sometimes involved in foreign affairs as they touch political matters (Omar Al-Osta) and security matters (Ahmed Keddaf Eddem).[33]

Apart from a few notable events, little is known about divisions of advice and opinion on foreign relations among these members of the foreign affairs group. The most serious of these events was the Meheishi affair in 1975, a major turning point in the direction of the junta.[34] Major Omar Al-Meheishi, one of the original Free Officers, sought to restrain the emerging radical orientation of the regime and to limit its foreign adventures and its heavy spending for Soviet arms at a time when oil revenues were in temporary decline. His planned coup was discovered and checked, and Meheishi fled to Egypt. Earlier there had been serious disagreement over related matters: the decision in late 1970 to push for union with Egypt over closer Maghrebi relations, the decision to pursue the union with Egypt despite a cool reception in July 1972 and March 1973, and the decision to come to a "medium high" rather than a "high high" settlement with the oil companies in the second Tripoli negotiations of March 1971.[35] On the Egyptian decisions, Qaddafi won, in the latter instances by threatening the opposing majority with his resignation; in the 1970 case, Free Officer Mohamed Najm was forced to resign as foreign minister. In the petroleum case, Jallud prevailed over Qaddafi in collegial decision-making. Since the Meheishi affair, however, decision-making has been less collegial among the military colleagues, the original junta has been reduced in size, and specific sectors of politics have been assigned. The remaining members of the foreign affairs group, with the exception of Jallud, are clearly advisors, not even lieutenants to Qaddafi.

FOREIGN POLICY BEHAVIOR

The Third International Theory of Qaddafi's *Green Book* suggests an alternative model of political, economic, and cultural development to those advocated by the Communist and Western blocs.

> The Third International Theory is offered as a substitute for communist and capitalist ideology, applicable specifically to Islamic countries but also offering useful principles to non-Islamic Third World states. Libya advocates nonalignment in general and positive neutrality in particular as alternatives to alignment with either East or West. Whereas nonalignment is based on merely the avoidance of ties with either of the two blocs, positive neutrality involves the aggressive pursuit of foreign policy goals that may include bilateral relations short of alignment with the East and the West.[36]

It is clear that Qaddafi does not pursue nonalignment as defined here, "the avoidance of ties with either bloc." As we have seen, however,

Qaddafi does endorse the goal of Libyan self-sufficiency. He is especially concerned with agricultural self-sufficiency, which is a high priority of the regime: "There is no independence for those who secure their food from abroad."[37]

Libya and the West

Rhetoric aside, Libya has fairly stable commercial relations with the West and continues to be dependent on the West for food, manufactured goods, and even some skilled labor. With the notable exception of military purchases, the pattern of Libyan imports has changed little from before the 1969 revolution to the present. A former Italian colony, in 1979 Libya imported approximately 26.4% of its general purchases from Italy (up from 21.6% in 1970). Germany (14.3%), France (8.2%), and Japan (8.9%) followed just behind Italy as sources of imports in 1979; this ranking has remained constant since 1971.[38]

Moreover, Libya continues to export far more heavily to Western Europe (and from 1975 to 1982, the United States) than to the Soviet bloc nations or other developing nations. In 1979 the United States was the Jamahiriya's single largest export recipient (36.1%, up from 2.7% in 1970). Italy followed, receiving 18% of Libyan exports (down from 25.9% in 1970).[39]

Ironically, until President Reagan's embargo on the U.S. purchase of Libyan crude in 1982, Libyan exports to the United States showed an inverse relation to the deteriorating political relations between the two countries. Libya succeeded in the early 1970s in taking majority control of most foreign oil companies on its soil.[40] Libya is still dependent on foreign technicians, however, to operate the petroleum plants. Since the exodus of U.S. workers in 1982, Libya has been successful in recruiting engineers from Canada, Iran, Algeria, Kuwait, and the United Arab Emirates.[41] In all sectors including the oil industry, Libya had 467,000 foreign workers at the end of 1981, a figure approaching half the native Libyan labor force.

Libya's foreign debts were reported to be $10 billion in 1983, "of which $2.3 [billion] is owed to foreign companies exporting to Libya and $6–7 [billion] to construction firms operating there."[42] Libya is reportedly making attempts to step up exports to Soviet bloc nations, in order to relieve international debts and to pay for arms purchases. With the world recession, the U.S. embargo is affecting Libyan development plans as well as Libyan military activity:

The world oil glut, coupled with the U.S. embargo, has greatly hampered the implementation of the $62.5bn five-year plan for 1981–1985, which was announced at the General People's Congress in January 1981. Libya's production of oil had fallen to 0.5m bpd, and income from oil exports was well below current expenditure. As a result, Colonel Qaddafi was forced to withdraw his troops from neighboring Chad, and sought to settle debts with trading partners such as Turkey, Greece, Sweden and East European countries.[43]

Prospects for the first half of the 1980s repeat the experience of the mid-1970s, when Libyan growth slowed in an overheated world economy. Although Libya's base figures are high, its growth in the decade of the 1970s was a negative 2.9%, the fourth lowest in all Africa after the war-torn economies of Angola, Mozambique, and Chad. Yet Libyan finances are expected to stabilize. One expert writes, "Even if the phasing of payments may cause occasional liquidity crises (as in 1977, when French arms deliveries were temporarily suspended due to Libya's falling into arrears on payment), the ability of the State to sustain this level of expenditure over the medium term is not in question."[44]

Whether or not the U.S. embargo and the world oil glut will have a long-term effect on the Libyan economy, it is nevertheless clear from Libya's trade patterns that Libya maintains close economic ties with the West. Moreover, Libya is reported to have sizable investments in European and NATO countries. A 1979 financial report states:

> Through the Libyan Arab Foreign Bank (LAFB), millions of petrodollars are being funneled to such economically weak and politically unstable European nations as Italy, Turkey, Spain, and Greece. No one knows how much money Libya has invested abroad, but in the last two years it has bought nearly 10% of Italy's Fiat, for $415 million; given a $300 million loan to Turkey to curb its slide into political chaos; and sent hundreds of millions of dollars to Spain, Greece, Tunisia, and Morocco.[45]

Libya's dependence on, and investment in, Western nations (not to mention Libya's significant dependence on the skilled labor of pro-Western allies, such as Egypt and Tunisia, in the Libyan work force) form one element in Libya's ambivalent relation with the West. "Despite its huge Soviet-supplied arsenal and an ideology vaguely evocative of Marxism, the country still leans economically toward the West, selling oil to the United States and its European allies and purchasing their technology. Libyan students go to universities in the United States, not the Soviet Union."[46] Another primary element of Libya's relation to the West is Qaddafi's opposition to Western "imperialism," which is responsible for his alliance with the Soviet Union and his support of international terrorism.

Qaddafi is alleged to be associated with international terrorism and national liberation movements of every sort. Terrorist organizations tend to be secretive about supporters and funding, hence Libyan backing is often difficult to prove. Qaddafi admits backing Uganda's dictator Idi Amin, the Italian Red Brigades, the IRA, and radical "rejectionist" factions of the PLO. Less clear is Qaddafi's involvement in several hijackings and the 1972 Munich Olympics massacre of Israeli athletes.[47] One scholar of Libyan politics, John Wright, asserts that there is evidence that Qaddafi pursues foreign adventures for the sake of international prestige or notoriety and that his actual monetary contributions are correspondingly exaggerated.[48] If this is true, then U.S. hysteria about Libyan threats to U.S. security and Libyan assassination attempts on President Reagan only contributes to Qaddafi's power.[49]

The last brutal irony is that even Qaddafi's orgies of subversion, terrorism, and violence—conveniently called "anti-imperialist," are indebted to the West. Not only did the U.S. Central Intelligence Agency (CIA) assist the Qaddafi regime after it seized power in 1969, but the extent of CIA involvement with its former agents Terpil and Wilson in training terrorists is as yet unclear.[50]

Libya and the Soviet Union

Though Libya is no more "free" in 1983 of dependency on Western goods and services than it was before the coup, Qaddafi has succeeded in changing the orientation of Libyan foreign policy. Under the Senussi monarchy of King Idris, Libya was timid and Western-oriented.[51] Under pressure from Qaddafi, the British and Americans agreed to evacuate their military bases in Libya. The withdrawals were complete in 1970.[52] In the years since, Qaddafi has given Libyan foreign policy a strident pan-Arabist voice and has shifted its primary military alliance to the Soviet Union.

At present, Libya's most important military ally is the Soviet Union. Although in 1978 Qaddafi threatened to join the Warsaw Pact, he has thus far been neither invited nor accepted. A friendship treaty was agreed on "in principle" in March 1983 but not signed. Qaddafi has overcome his initial antipathy to the atheistic Communism of the Soviet Union and to what he criticized in the early 1970s as Soviet "imperialist designs" in the Indo-Pakistani war.[53] From limited initial arms deals with France, Qaddafi turned to the Soviets to supply a new increase in armaments purchases. Until about 1973, the new Libyan regime purchased a generally balanced array of military supplies, but in 1974–1975, the Libyan regime began to purchase arms for apparent stockpile rather than use.[54]

Like everything else in the clandestine world of strategy and arms transfers, specific rationales for arms acquisitions seldom appear uncloaked in the press. Since the early 1970s Libya has acquired more weaponry than is warranted for the purpose of national defense:

> Libya, with fewer than 3,000,000 people and such unthreatening neighbours as Tunisia, Niger, Chad and Sudan, has the tenth largest force of medium tanks in the world. With the exception of Israel and Syria, all the other members of this select group with over 2,000 tanks have at least ten times Libya's population. Libya is the limiting case in that class of oil-rich, population-poor states whose defence expenditure is neither constrained by circumstances nor directed against recognisable military threats. Nor does it seem bound by an unimaginative adherence to traditional

military percepts: the ratio of tanks to artillery pieces in the Libyan army is of the order of 13 to 1.[55]

The Soviet Union is not forthcoming about its motives in supplying such massive arms to the Libyans. Soviet academician Anatoly Gromyko states, "the USSR and Africa's independent countries are closely cooperating to eliminate the vestiges of racism and colonialism and fight against neocolonialism, and that brings notable results and promotes closer relations between this country and the young African states."[56] At the same time, Gromyko asserts that the Soviet Union opposes the export of any kind of revolution and that it offers aid only to legitimate governments. Official Soviet statements about the provision of aid or arms to Africa are cloaked in the rhetoric of trade, cooperation, and of course, anti-imperialist liberation. Other analysts, however, offer more mundane reasons for the Soviet provision of arms to Africa and to Libya.

Analysts have pointed out that the Soviets began shipping arms to Libya in the mid-1970s not only because they were annoyed at being expelled from Egypt, but because they were seeking the hard currency that the Libyan oil revenues provide: "Particularly noteworthy among Soviet objectives is a familiar capitalist imperative—to acquire hard currency in order to meet balance of payments deficits resulting from trade with the United States and Western Europe. Interestingly, Soviet agreements with oil producing countries have almost always been concluded on a cash (hard currency) basis."[57]

On Libya's side, the rationales for armament are expressed in terms of the broadest foreign policy aims. In fact, Libyan press statements deal more often with mobilization against the Israeli and U.S. enemy than against Libya's more immediate neighbors. An example of the official Libyan preoccupation with Israel and the United States as military opponents, the following Libyan broadcast calls for the arming of the Libyan people.

> The leader [Qaddafi] explained that the transformation of the schools, institutions and colleges into military barracks will hasten the creation of an armed people as soon as possible, confirming that this was the real popular mobilization of the masses to confront the aggression to which the Arab nation is being subjected these days and to face the siege which imperialism is trying to lay around Libya.[58]

This illustrates the general tone of Qaddafi's foreign policy, that of militant anti-American pan-Arabism. Qaddafi clearly envisions Libya as surrounded by hostile "imperialist" nations bent on aggression.

Officially, Libyan military acquisitions and modernization are aimed primarily at the United States and "Zionist imperialism." One military analyst writes:

The armaments which the Libyan regime has been buying in ever-increasing amounts since 1970 are intended for the modernization of the armed forces, which in turn are officially stated to be intended for the sole purpose of destroying the Israeli presence in the Middle East. . . . In recent years these equipment acquisitions have clearly exceeded the ability of the Libyan armed forces to operate them even in terms of sheer manpower availability, and it must be assumed that a large proportion are destined for other Arab nations when they finally see the light and join Libya in one last victorious *jihad* against Israel.[59]

Even beyond its capability to absorb such weapons, Libya is buying and stockpiling arms for a holy war against Israel and U.S. imperialism. There is a more ominous note, however, in Libya's neo-Nasserist rhetoric. In October 1980, Libya's Qaddafi urged the "Arab people" to "embark on a counterattack, ignoring all regimes and boundaries." He continued: "We urge the Arab people from the Ocean to the Gulf to embark on counter-attacking U.S. bases, the U.S. presence and its main base in Palestine. Should the Arab regimes obstruct the counterattack of the Arab people, they must pay the price for this; they will be treated like the United States and the Israelis."[60] Qaddafi's inflammatory rhetoric has serious implications for the use of Libyan arms in the Middle East and North Africa. Under the cover of attacking "imperialism," Libyan equipment is to be directed against local regimes perceived to be sympathetic to the U.S. cause, or rather, obstructionist of the Libyan cause.

Despite the overlap of Libyan and Soviet interests, specifically anti-Americanism, the overlap is more apparent than real. Qaddafi sees regional and international issues as related, but for Qaddafi the cause of Arab unity is paramount. In 1979 Qaddafi told a Western journalist: "The Soviet Union is on the side of the Arabs against Israel. This we consider an anti-imperialist position. . . . I know that there are two great powers. . . . I also know the Soviets are our friends."[61] Because he needs Soviet training and arms, Qaddafi is willing to cooperate with them, so long as it suits his purpose.[62] Neither country is an agent of the other, neither agrees to the other's basic philosophy, but both are frequently on parallel courses and encourage, benefit from, and try to influence the other's foreign policy behavior.

Regional Goals

Officially, the Qaddafi regime echoes the Nasserist conceptions of three circles of concern: the Arab circle, the continent of Africa, and the worldwide Islamic circle.[63] In practice, these circles overlap, and Qaddafi divides his interest between the Moslem Arab Mashreq, the Moslem Arab Maghreb, and the rest of the African continent. Although Qaddafi depends both on the West (for food, goods, and services) and on the Soviet Union (for arms and training), his main interests are regional.

Qaddafi sports a checkered history both in the Maghreb, the Mashreq, and in Black Africa. In the early 1970s, Qaddafi sought to expand his territorial base and his prestige through unity with Egypt, Syria, Sudan, and later with Tunisia. These aborted attempts marked in each case deterioration of relations with Libya. In the 1980s, Libya made overtures to Chad and again to Syria. In addition, Qaddafi sought unity with Mauritania, Algeria, and the Polisario movement of the Western Sahara.[64]

In all of these cases, Qaddafi ostensibly sought the Nasserist goal of unity. Unlike his earlier successes in evacuating Western military bases, Qaddafi's attempts at unity failed miserably. Qaddafi's relations with Egypt broke down in 1977, culminating in what has been called a "major bloodletting" between the two countries.[65] After the collapse of Tunisian-Libyan unity talks, their relations deteriorated, and in 1980 Libyan guerrillas raided the Tunisian mining town of Gafsa; in 1982, the town of Kasserine; and in 1984, the pipeline at Henchir Al-Bassassa. The two nations have long disagreed over the ownership of oil in the Gulf of Gabès.[66] In conjunction with Algeria, with which its relations are generally good, Libya sponsored Polisario resistance against the Moroccan government, another cause of friction in North Africa.[67]

Libya offended Black Africa by its occupation of Chad's northern 'Aouzou Strip in 1973, by its announced intention to unite with Chad in 1981, and by its invasion of Chad in 1983. Libya supported the Transitional National Union Government (GUNT) under Goukouni Weddei, whom it helped bring to power, and continued to support Goukouni—to the point of blocking an OAU summit in 1982—even after he had lost control of Chad and had been evicted. Libya's policy in Chad was one of the reasons why Qaddafi was deprived by African states of his opportunity to be president of the OAU in 1982–1983.[68]

Unfortunately, examining the Libyan trail of violence and instability in its three circles of operation is a larger task than can be completed here. Qaddafi's Nasserist goal of unity has thus far eluded him. In fact, Qaddafi's actual role in regional relations is destabilizing. An Israeli general assessed the effectiveness of Qaddafi in uniting the Arabs against Israel thus:

> Look, in the long run, of course we have to take Qaddafi seriously. He is a man with a single purpose: the destruction of Israel. In the long run, he has the money, the arms, and the means to cause us all serious harm, including you in the West. In the medium and short runs, it's a different story. You might even say that for Israel, Qaddafi can be a kind of asset. Who else, in all his frantic attempts to unite the Arabs, is keeping them divided to the extent Qaddafi is? He is a strategic threat, but perhaps a tactical asset; an agent of division in the Arab World.[69]

Qaddafi has achieved his goal of pursuing "positive neutrality" to a large extent. Libya has no military bases of either the Western or Soviet bloc on its territory. The heavy military purchases from the Soviets are offset by Libya's close economic ties with the West. But Libya has failed miserably at attaining the most important goal of Arab unity. We may speculate that the difficulties lie more in the policy than in Qaddafi's particular personality, however "capricious" some may deem him. Writes George M. Haddad:

> Egypt nevertheless had its conspiracies and purges. . . . Moreover, while Nasser's Egypt kept its people and its officers under control, it was largely responsible for the instability of the other Arab countries by its revolutionary propaganda, its incitement to violence, its direct intervention and its subsidies to the dissident and mercenary elements. The mere example of the changes imposed by the officers in Egypt accompanied by the initial success of Nasser's challenges to the great powers and their Arab allies also produced an unsettling effect on the various Arab states.[70]

Thus, it is an irony of Arab history that in so closely emulating the revolutionary goals of freedom, socialism, and unity, Qaddafi has re-created the actual Nasserist role of a destabilizer, a catalyst of disunity.

CONCLUSIONS

Internally and externally, Qaddafi has tried to impose heroic politics of military mobilization for the Nasserist goal of Arab unity. Internally, Libya faces a double-edged legacy of violent reform. Qaddafi has tried to generate mass support, and to the extent that he has raised the standard of living of Libya's poor, he may well have succeeded. But as in every society, reforms engender resistance, and the severest threat comes from those with access to the means of violence, the military. Writes Ruth First:

> The coup is becoming conventional wisdom not only among Africa's army men, but among her young intellectuals. . . . Young aspirants for power, or social change, consider the making or unmaking of African governments in terms of their contacts within the Army. . . . Power lies in the hands of those who control the means of violence. It lies in the barrel of a gun, fired or silent.[71]

It is hard to predict the future, but for the moment it appears that Qaddafi controls enough guns in Libya to ensure the continuation of his policies.

Externally, it is likely Qaddafi will continue his policy of seeking unity through destabilization and force. Qaddafi's Nasserist dreams appear to be unrealizable visions for the aggrandizement of Libya and Qaddafi. Abdullah Al-Qusaymi writes: "The story of the big state and the big empire has never been the story or idea or hope of the masses. It has always been the story of men who wanted to be great men or tyrants by diminishing others."[72] Qaddafi's violent methods, and the difficulty of the quest itself, will likely continue to make his vision of

Arab unity unattainable, for Qaddafi preaches pan-Arab dreams and ideological designs to an Arab world that knows their failure all too well. The increasingly obvious reality of Arab disunity, amid the great gaps in the distribution of wealth, show much of Qaddafi's neo-Nasserism to be anachronistic. Fouad Ajami writes of Qaddafi and the Arabs:

> Neither the fire and passion of the Libyan revolution nor its money could turn history around and revive an exhausted idea. Here and there, a few writers and publicists—not to mention some troublemakers—prospered on Libyan money, repeating Qaddafi's slogans about his Third Theory or carrying out Qaddafi's wishes in Beirut and Cairo. But this was not to be Qaddafi's era. He was an anachronism: what he said and thought in the 1970s other Arabs had experienced and lived through in the 1950s and 1960s. . . . Qaddafi's arena is now Libya; his pan-Arab dreams have aborted. Qaddafi's conviction that the Arabs are one nation is no longer shared by a critical segment of Arabs—the students and the youth—who once gave pan-Arabism power in Arab life.[73]

The time of Nasser is past, and in trying to perform a Nasserist role in the international theater, Qaddafi's Libya finds itself in the embarassing position of playing to an audience that is not paying attention. The charismatic nation, like the charismatic figure, needs a following. Or, as Weber writes: "[The] charismatic claim breaks down if [the] mission is not recognized by those to whom [the bearer] feels [it] has been sent."[74]

There is another side to heroic foreign policy that students of heroes often miss. In seeking simple interpretations, in rejecting the ultrasophisticated conventions of the urbane diplomatic world, in denouncing imperialism and other perceived evils of the world, in acting like the Jeha or the Asterix or the Popeye of his world, Qaddafi often gets applause as a wily common-man folk hero, doing things people who know better would love to do (if they didn't know better), taking a poke at the big boys and getting away with it. This kind of behavior will not gather followers, but it does attract grudging admirers. In its language and goals, Libya only expresses—sometimes in extreme terms—ideas that are common to many parts of state and society in the Middle East. His style may be uncouth and his tactics may be ones less revisionist states avoid, but Qaddafi often expresses themes that are widely felt, and in ways regarded as daring. Sometimes the tactics draw disapproval, to be sure. But like a student revolt that turns passive onlookers into sympathizers when it can claim police brutality, Qaddafi can gather more sympathy for his ill treatment at the hands of the West than he can for his claim to leadership. In this sense, Libya has found a different role—not that of charismatic leadership, the man on a white horse, but that of the freelance outlaw, the folk hero, the desert raider admired for his exploits but having no seat at court. To his admirers, Qaddafi is not King Richard the Lion-Hearted or Salah Al-Din, but Robin Hood.

NOTES

1. John K. Cooley, *Libyan Sandstorm* (New York: Holt, Rinehart and Winston, 1982), p. 265. See also Robert Rinehart, "Historical Setting," *Libya: A Country Study*, Area Handbook Series (Washington, D.C.: American University, 1979), p. 50.

2. *Ibid.*, p. 186.

3. *Ibid.*, p. 115. See also Fouad Ajami, *The Arab Predicament* (Cambridge: Cambridge University Press, 1981), p. 126.

4. Ajami, *Predicament*, p. 198.

5. See for example Nadav Safran, *Egypt in Search of Political Community* (Cambridge, Mass.: Harvard University Press, 1961).

6. Gamal Abdel Nasser, *Egypt's Liberation: The Philosophy of the Revolution* (Washington, D.C.: Public Affairs Press, 1955), pp. 87–88.

7. *Ibid.*, p. 88.

8. Mohamed Heikal, *The Road to Ramadan* (New York: Times Book Co., 1975), p. 70.

9. *Ibid.*, p. 71.

10. *Ibid.*, p. 185.

11. *Ibid.*, p. 189.

12. Muammar Al-Qaddafi, *The Green Book*, 3 vols. (London: Martin Brian & O'Keeffe: 1976), 1:41.

13. Oriana Fallaci, "Iranians Are Our Brothers," *New York Times Magazine* (December 16, 1979), p. 123.

14. Cf. Martin Lings, *A Muslim Saint of the Twentieth Century* (New York: Macmillan, 1961), notably p. 156.

15. E. E. Evans-Pritchard, *The Senussi of Cyrenaica* (New York: Oxford University Press, 1963).

16. Ibn Khaldun, *The Muqaddimah*, trans. E. Rosenthal (Princeton, N.J.: Princeton University Press, 1958); see also A. G. Kluge, "The 'Objective' of Ibn Khaldun and Max Weber," Senior Honors Thesis in Social Studies, Harvard University, 1981.

17. Muammar Al-Qaddafi (Tripoli Voice of the Arab Homeland, July 3, 1982), quoted in Karen Dawisha, "The U.S.S.R. in the Middle East: Superpower in Eclipse?" *Foreign Affairs*, Winter 1982/1983, p. 438.

18. The best overall book on Libya is John Wright's *Libya: A Modern History* (Baltimore, Md.: Johns Hopkins University Press, 1982).

19. On the economy, see Yves Gazzo, "L'Economie Libyenne," *Maghreb-Mashreq* 93 (July 1981), pp. 56–57. On arms, see I. William Zartman, "Arms Imports: The Libya Experience," in *World Military Expenditures and Arms Transfers 1971–1980* (Washington, D.C.: U.S. Arms Control and Disarmament Agency, 1983), pp. 15–22.

20. Said Qaddafi in an interview with *Le Monde*, February 11, 1976, "Regimes don't interest me anymore; I address myself to the Arab masses." Cited in Wright, *Libya*, p. 206.

21. J. A. Allani, "Management of Agricultural Resources in Coastal Libya," *Maghreb Review*, September-December 1980, p. 113.

22. Figures from *World Military Expenditures 1971–1980*.

23. John Keegan, *World Armies* (London: Macmillan Press, 1979), p. 446; Michael Martin et al., "Les armées et la défense," *Annuaire de l'Afrique et du Moyen Orient* (Paris: Editions Jeune Afrique, 1981), p. 255.

24. See Ann Elizabeth Mayer, "Le droit musulman en Libye à l'age du livre vert"; Hervé Bleuchot, "Le livre vert: Contexte et signification," *Maghreb-Mashreq* 93 (July 1981), pp. 5–38; Lisa Anderson, "Qaddafi's Islam," in John Esposito (ed.), *Voices of Resurgent Islam* (New York: Oxford University Press, 1983).

25. On Libyan domestic governance, see Raymond A. Hinnebusch, "Libya: Personalistic Leadership of a Populist Revolution," in I. William Zartman et al., *Political Elites in Arab North Africa* (New York: Longman, 1981), pp. 177–222; Remy Leveau, "Le système politique libyen," in Maurice Flory (ed.), *La Libye nouvelle* (Paris: CNRS, 1975), pp. 83–100; Wright, *Libya*; Omar Fathaly, Monte Palmer, and Richard Chakerian, *Political Development and Bureaucracy in Libya* (Lexington, Mass.: D. C. Heath & Co., 1977); Omar Fathaly and Monte Palmer, *Political Development and Social Change in Libya* (Lexington, Mass.: D. C. Heath & Co., 1978); Marius Deeb and Mary Jane Deeb, *Libya Since the Revolution* (New York: Praeger Publishers, 1982); Ruth First, *Libya: The Elusive Revolution* (Baltimore, Md.: Penguin Books, 1974); Jacques Roumani, "From Republic to Jamahiriya: Libya's Search for Political Community," *Middle East Journal* 37, 2 (Spring 1983), pp. 151–168; *Maghreb-Mashreq* 93, Special issue, *Libye 1978–81* (July 1981); E.G.H. Joffe and K. S. McLachlan (eds.), *Social and Economic Development of Libya* (Boulder, Colo.: Westview Press, 1983).

26. Muammar Al-Qaddafi (Tripoli Radio, October 16, 1969), cited by Meredith O. Ansell and Ibrahim Massaud Al-Arif, *The Libyan Revolution: A Sourcebook of Legal and Historical Documents* (New York: Oleander Press, 1972), p. 88.

27. Heikal, *Ramadan*, p. 79.

28. Qaddafi, Tripoli Radio, October 16, 1969.

29. *Ibid.*, p. 89.

30. *Ibid.*, p. 92.

31. See "The Libyan Revolution in the Words of Its Leaders," *Middle East Journal* 24, 2 (Spring 1970), pp. 203–219.

32. On Libyan foreign policy, see I. William Zartman and Aureniano Buendia, "La politique étrangère Libyenne," in Flory, *La Libye*; Lisa Anderson, "Libya and American Foreign Policy," *Middle East Journal* 36, 4 (Autumn 1982); Nathan Alexander [pseud.], "The Foreign Policy of Libya," *Orbis* 24, 4 (Winter 1981), pp. 819–846; René Otayek, "La Libye révolutionnaire au sud du Sahara," *Maghreb-Mashreq* 94 (October 1981), pp. 5–35.

33. See *Jeune Afrique* 1110 (April 4, 1982), p. 32.

34. On the Meheishi affair, see Writhe, *Libya*, pp. 186, 196, 252, 276; Cooley, *Sandstorm*, p. 166; and *Jeune Afrique* 770 (October 10, 1975), pp. 26–27.

35. On these various events, see Leveau, "Le système politique," p. 93; Wright, *Libya*, p. 187; G. Henry M. Schuler, "The International Oil Negotiations," in I. William Zartman (ed.), *The 50% Solution* (New York: Doubleday & Co., 1976, and New Haven, Conn.: Yale University Press, 1984), pp. 124–207.

36. William A. Mussen, Jr., "Government and Politics," in *Libya: A Country Study*, p. 214.

37. Muammar Al-Qaddafi, cited in Allani, "Agricultural Resouces," p. 108.

38. "Libyan Arab Jamahiriya," *1980 Yearbook of International Trade Statistics* (New York: United Nations, 1981), 1:592. See also Zartman and Buendia, "La politique," p. 108.

39. "Libyan Arab Jamahiriya."

40. Cooley, *Sandstorm*, p. 75.

41. *Al-Fajr Al-Jadid*, October 28, 1981; see also *Maghreb-Mashreq* 95 (January 1982), p. 79; *Jeune Afrique* 1105 (March 10, 1982), p. 23; *Arabia*, April 1983.

42. *Arabia,* April 1983.

43. *Ibid.*

44. John Keegan, *World Armies,* p. 442.

45. "Libya's Quiet Investments in NATO Countries," *Business Week,* March 26, 1979.

46. Christopher S. Wren, "Libya's Identity Blurred by Ties with East, West and Terrorism," *New York Times,* October 14, 1979.

47. Cooley, *Sandstorm,* p. 186.

48. Wright, *Libya,* p. 173.

49. "Washington Steps up Pressure on Qaddafi," *Arabia: The Islamic World Review,* April 1982.

50. Cooley, *Sandstorm,* pp. 189–192.

51. Alexander, "Foreign Policy of Libya," p. 823.

52. Zartman and Buendia, "La politique," p. 105.

53. Cooley, *Sandstorm,* p. 83; *Le Monde,* March 22, 1983.

54. Keegan, *Armies,* p. 441.

55. *Ibid.,* p. 437.

56. Anatoly Gromyko, "Soviet Foreign Policy and Africa," *International Affairs,* February 1982, p. 33.

57. William H. Lewis, "Arms Transfers and the Third World," in *World Military Expenditures, 1970–1979,* p. 31.

58. Muammar Al-Qaddafi, Foreign Broadcast Information Service (FBIS), November 13, 1980.

59. Keegan, *Armies,* p. 439.

60. Muammar Al-Qaddafi, FBIS, October 8, 1980.

61. Fallaci, "Iranians."

62. Zartman, "Arms Imports."

63. Nasser, *Egypt's Liberation,* pp. 109–111.

64. Zartman, "Arms Imports," p. 18.

65. Cooley, *Sandstorm,* p. 118.

66. Alexander, "Foreign Policy of Libya," p. 835; *Jeune Afrique* 1105 (March 10, 1982), pp. 24–25.

67. *Ibid.,* p. 738.

68. "Libya," *Middle East Journal* 36, 2 (Spring 1982), p. 230. See also I. William Zartman and Yassin El-Ayouti (eds.), *O.A.U. After 20 Years* (New York: Praeger Publishers, 1984).

69. Cooley, *Sandstorm,* p. 100.

70. George M. Haddad, *Revolutions and Military Rule in the Middle East: The Arab States, Part II: Egypt, the Sudan, Yemen and Libya* (New York: Robert Speller and Sons, 1973), p. 392.

71. Ruth First, *The Barrel of a Gun* (London: Penguin Press, 1970), p. 6.

72. Abdullah Al-Qusaymi, "So that Harun al Rashid Would Not Return," *Mawaqif* 1 (October-November 1968), pp. 24–40, as cited in Ajami, *Predicament,* p. 38.

73. Ajami, *Predicament,* p. 126.

74. Max Weber, *From Max Weber,* Translated, edited, and with an introduction by H. H. Gerth and C. Wright Mills (New York: Oxford University Press, 1946; reprint 1975), p. 246.

8

The Survival of a Nonstate Actor: The Foreign Policy of the Palestine Liberation Organization

Mohamed E. Selim

INTRODUCTION

Among all foreign policy actors analyzed in this book, the Palestine Liberation Organization (PLO) is the only nonstate actor. Foreign policy analysts have traditionally excluded nonstate actors from their studies. For them, a foreign policy actor must possess the legal quality of sovereignty; consequently, only states qualify for this role. However, the new realities of international politics, especially the emergence of powerful transnational and transgovernmental organizations and the obvious structural weakness of some states, have led growing numbers of foreign policy analysts to shift away from this state-centric paradigm. In the new view, the defining characteristic of a foreign policy actor is the behavioral attribute of autonomy. Autonomy in this sense means the ability to behave in ways that have consequences in international politics and cannot be predicted entirely by reference to other actors.[1] According to this definition, a wide variety of nonstate actors can be classified as foreign policy actors, including multinational business enterprises, revolutionary movements, trade unions and scientific networks, international organizations, and powerful domestic groups.[2] By virtue of its undeniable impact upon the international politics of the Middle East, its international status, its elaborate linkages with the Palestinian people, and finally, its internal dynamics, the PLO, though not a state, is a major Arab actor.

When they formulate foreign policies and operate in the international system, nonstate actors confront certain problems that state actors do not usually experience. Nonstate actors, especially when they take the form of a regional revolutionary movement aspiring to alter the territorial status quo, lack territorial political symbols to draw upon as a basis for defining foreign policy. They confront problems of control and legitimacy, factionalism, visibility, durability, and maneuverability.[3] Lacking a territorial base and the conventional means of conferring legitimacy, these actors find the legitimacy of their representation to be always in question. They must be concerned with the issue of being heard, perceived, and recognized by nation-states and international organizations. The visibility of nonstate actors brings to the forefront the issues of durability and maneuverability. As the nonstate actors become more visible and draw more international support, they run the risk of being portrayed by their adversaries as mavericks threatening international legitimacy. Allies may also become a source of threat. Supporters of nonstate actors expect a higher level of compliance from them than they expect from their state clients.

In this chapter, we will analyze the interplay of these problems in the making of the foreign policy of the PLO. The choice of the PLO as the actor representing the Palestinian dimension in Arab politics is justified by the PLO's status as the only representative acceptable to the Palestinian people. At the inter-Arab level, according to a resolution issued by the Arab summit held in Rabat in 1974, the PLO is recognized by all Arab countries as the sole legitimate representative of the Palestinian people. The PLO represents Palestine in the League of Arab States, and the United Nations has granted the PLO an observer status. The PLO is also recognized by 112 countries as the representative of the Palestinian people, sometimes with full diplomatic status, and maintains official bureaus in almost 90 countries. Since 1976, the PLO is a full member of the nonaligned group.

DOMESTIC ENVIRONMENT

Historical Legacy: The Origins of the PLO

The establishment of the PLO in 1964 was a function of two converging trends: the resurgence of Palestinian national feelings in the 1960s and the inter-Arab consensus to draft a common strategy against Israel. The breakup of the Egyptian-Syrian union in 1961 and the failure of the 1963 unity talks between Egypt, Syria, and Iraq shook the faith of the Palestinians in the eventual realization of Arab unity, earlier viewed as a prerequisite for the restoration of Palestine. The 1962 victory of the Algerian revolution convinced the Palestinians that self-reliance would be a more viable strategy for achieving their goals. As a result, they began to form their own organizations. By 1965, about forty such organizations existed.[4] In response to this increasing Palestinian militancy, the first Arab summit, held in Cairo in January 1964, decided inter alia to organize the Palestinians to enable them to carry out their role in liberating their homeland. The summit further asked Ahmed Al-Shukairy, the representative of Palestine in the League of Arab States at the time, to study the feasibility of establishing a Palestinian entity.[5]

The idea of a Palestinian entity received mixed reactions in the Arab world.[6] Reservations came from Jordan, Saudi Arabia, Syria, and some Palestinian resistance organizations. On the other hand, this proposal was fully supported by most radical Arab regimes, especially Egypt, Iraq, and Algeria.

Shukairy invited 422 Palestinians representing the various Palestinian groups (excluding Palestinians who lived in Israel) to attend the first Palestine National Council (PNC) in May 1964. It was at this meeting that the PLO was proclaimed. The council drew up a national charter and a fundamental law as the basic constitution of the PLO. The second Arab summit, held in Alexandria in September 1964, endorsed the establishment of the PLO and gave it the pan-Arab stamp of legitimacy.

An examination of the subsequent evolution of the PLO reveals certain elements of change and continuity that have played a crucial role in PLO foreign policy. The PLO underwent three basic changes: the shift of its leadership from traditionalism to radicalism, the shift from individual membership to organizational representation, and the shift from a leader-staff pattern of decision-making to a collective pattern of interorganizational bargaining.

During the first five years of its existence, the PLO was dominated by traditional Palestinian elements, especially local notables, businessmen, bankers, and mayors. This resulted in a pattern of membership that was heavily traditional and strictly individual. Individuals sat on the various political structures of the PLO in their own capacity and not as representatives of other organizations. Further, the PLO failed to set its own program of military and political action to achieve its objectives. Its leadership attempted to duplicate the operations of Palestinian resistance organizations that had declined to enter the PLO. This tarnished the PLO image and incited an increasing number of members to call for a change. In December 1967, the Executive Committee of the PLO (EXCOM) forced Shukairy to resign; Yehia Hammouda replaced him.

The new chairman approached resistance organizations to coordinate their activities with PLO actions. This policy resulted in the convening of a new session of the Palestinian National Council in Cairo in July 1968; the session was attended by resistance organizations for the first time. From this point on, PLO membership counted an increasing number of representatives from various organizations. It was only a matter of time before formal PLO leadership was transferred to commando organizations as well. In the next session of the PNC, held in February

1969, Yasser Arafat, the leader of the Palestine National Liberation Movement (Fateh), was elected chairman of the PLO. The membership of commando organizations in the PLO required the adoption of a new Palestinian Patriotic Charter in 1968. This replaced the Palestinian National Charter of 1964.[7] Since then, the PLO has emerged as the focal point for Palestinian loyalties and actions. It has developed an overall strategy of political and military action, established extensive political links with the Palestinians living in Palestine, and begun to play a mediating role between various Palestinian organizations. Finally, when the guerrilla organizations joined the PLO this caused a shift in the decision-making process. Under Shukairy (chairman from 1964 to 1967), the PLO chairman enjoyed tremendous powers. He chaired both the Executive Committee and the Palestine National Council and chose the members of the Executive Committee at his own discretion. Subsequently, the EXCOM and PNC chairmanships were separated, and the powers of the PLO chairman were reduced to brokerage between various PLO commando organizations.

Two basic elements of the PLO historical legacy continued to influence its functioning, namely intra-Palestinian rivalries and the intervention of Arab governments. Shukairy recalls that during his consultations to establish the PLO, he rarely found two Palestinians agreeing on anything.[8] Once the PLO accepted organizational membership, interorganizational conflicts and differences in strategies and ideologies between Palestinian resistance groups were indelibly imprinted on PLO politics. The problem of organizational unity became one of the nagging issues that has plagued the PLO ever since.

By virtue of the very nature of its creation, the PLO was highly vulnerable to the manipulation and intervention of Arab governments. As soon as the PLO was established, it became embroiled in the Arab cold war of the 1960s. The PLO aligned itself with Arab radicals, especially with Nasser's regime. Jordan and Saudi Arabia almost forbade PLO mobilizational activities within their territories. In the early 1970s, the PLO aligned itself with the Egyptian-Syrian-Saudi axis, and by the end of the decade it became part of the "Steadfastness Front" that set out to reject the Egyptian-Israeli treaty. Moreover, Arab governments established their own individual guerrilla organizations. As these organizations entered the PLO, they injected into its politics the policies of their respective patrons. In a sense, the PLO became a microcosm of inter-Arab politics.

Population:
The Geographical Dispersion of the Palestinians

The total population of Palestine is almost 4.5 million. The Palestinians do not live in a single territory under the control of one political authority. They are geographically dispersed in various countries and territories, as Table 8.1 indicates. Almost 58% of the Palestinians live

TABLE 8.1
Geographical Distribution of the Palestinian People in 1970 and 1981

Location	1970		1981	
	Population	%	Population	%
West Bank	670,000	22.7	833,000	18.7
Gaza Strip	364,000	12.4	451,400	10.0
Israel	340,000	11.5	550,800	12.4
Jordan	900,000	30.5	1,148,334	25.9
Lebanon	240,000	8.1	358,207	8.0
Kuwait	140,000	4.8	299,710	6.7
Syria	180,000	6.1	222,525	5.0
Saudi Arabia	20,000	0.7	136,779	3.0
Egypt	33,000	1.1	45,605	1.2
Gulf States	15,000	0.5	60,737	1.4
Libya	5,000	0.2	23,769	0.6
Iraq	14,000	0.5	20,604	0.5
Other Arab Countries			50,706	1.1
United States	7,000	0.2	104,856	2.3
Other Countries	20,000	0.7	140,116	3.1
TOTAL	2,948,000	100.0	4,447,148	100.0

Sources: The 1970 statistics are taken from Ibrahim Abu-Lughod, "Educating a Community in Exile: The Palestinian Experience," *Journal of Palestine Studies* 2, 3 (1973), p. 97. The 1981 statistics are taken from *Compendium of Palestinian Statistics for 1981* (Damascus: Central Statistics Office of the PLO, 1982), p. 30 (in Arabic).

outside the territory of mandatory Palestine. According to the 1948 statistics, the total number of the Palestinians was 1,474,500; almost 20.2% of them became refugees in the West Bank, Gaza, and various Arab countries. In the wake of the June 1967 war and by the end of 1967, about 178,000 West Bank Palestinians and almost 127,000 Gaza residents had been forced to leave their homes.[9] The geographical dispersal of the Palestinians set in motion four basic processes affecting the Arab-Israeli conflict and PLO policy.

The Demographic Shift. The dispersal of the Palestinians tilted the Palestinian-Israeli demographic balance in favor of Israel. If one projects the Arab population of the West Bank and Gaza in 1952, which was about 1.06 million, at an estimated natural growth rate of 3.3%, one would expect it to have reached 2.76 million by now. If one adds the Palestinians who live in Israel (550,800), the figure comes to 3.3 million. The total number of Palestinians who now reside within the boundaries of mandatory Palestine is only 56% of this figure.

Social Mobilization and National Identity. The fragmentation of the Palestinians triggered a process of social mobilization and led to the development of a well-defined Palestinian national identity. The Palestinians underwent three basic processes: depeasantization and semiproletarianization, increased education, and the emergence of a new national leadership. A 1973 study of the West Bank and Gaza revealed that almost 50% of the active population were wage workers, almost 77% of them were employed in industry, and only 23% were in agriculture.[10] Parallel to the shift in the work force, the Palestinians' educational status improved remarkably. According to the 1975 statistics, almost 22% of the Palestinians are enrolled in educational institutions, with almost 1.2% in institutes of higher education. This ratio goes as high as 3% among West Bankers and 5.5% among Palestinians in the Diaspora.[11] Mar'i attributes this "Palestinian phenomenon" to the dispersion of the Palestinian community,[12] and Davies cites the value of education for a displaced community as the major factor behind this phenomenon. For Palestinians, education has proven to be a means of survival and insurance against future uncertainties. For these uprooted, displaced, and dispossessed people, education is a portable and transferable commodity.[13]

Finally, the geographical fragmentation of the Palestinians resulted in the decline of the old family groups and parties that had dominated the political and social life of Palestinian society during the British mandate. As a result of urbanization and increased education, a new and modern professional and nationalist leadership emerged. It is this leadership that controls the PLO and other member resistance organizations. The new Palestinian is more educated, revolutionary, and ideologically inclined.[14] The influence of the new leadership on the Palestinian community surpasses that of the old traditional one. In a survey study of the Palestinian refugees living in Lebanon, Bassam Sirhan found that the influence of the old feudal leadership has declined considerably. He also concluded that the political leadership among camp refugees rests firmly in the hands of the vanguard of the resistance movement.[15]

The interplay of these factors led inter alia to the social and political mobilization of the Palestinians and to the sharpening of their national consciousness and sense of identity.[16] The basic components of this identity can be summarized as follows: (1) the theme of resistance, and the refusal to accept expulsion and statelessness, (2) emphasis on the land of Palestine as a potent symbol of Palestinian identity, (3) emphasis on the common origins of the Palestinians and on Palestinian traditions as intrinsically good, (4) distinction between the specific Palestinian identity and the general Arab identity, and (5) emphasis on the ability of sustained struggle to restore Palestine.[17] A sample survey of the Palestinians who live in the Shatilla refugee camp in Lebanon came to several conclusions concerning the components of the Palestinian national identity.[18] At the cognitive level, almost 69% of the respondents were aware of the history, geography, national leaders, and other national symbols of Palestine. Almost 80% of the respondents identified themselves as Palestinian Arabs or Arab Palestinians, whereas 3.5% identified themselves as just Arabs. At the affective level, almost 88% displayed a strong feeling of belonging to Palestine and 94% preferred to marry only fellow Palestinians. At the behavioral level, almost 80% of the respondents expressed willingness to let their children join resistance organizations in the future. One of the most revealing findings is that these conclusions apply to the 1948 exodus generation as well as to the post-1948 generation. The only exception was that the new generation is more militant than the old generation. Whereas only 49% of the old generation rejected the 1947 Partition Resolution, almost 71% of the new generation rejected it.[19]

Various factors account for the tenacity and intensification of Palestinian identity. Social mobilization was found to be a crucial factor in the process of national differentiation.[20] The conditions in which the Palestinians lived, whether in Palestine or in the Diaspora, inadvertently led to the same outcome. Prominent among these conditions are the limited socioeconomic absorptive capacity of Arab countries and the discrimination directed against the refugees by governing authorities.[21]

The emergence of the new Palestinian leadership and the PLO was both a source and an outcome of the emergence of the Palestinian identity. The PLO helped to reinforce and crystallize this process through various mobilizational mechanisms, and the rise of the PLO to international prominence also sharpened the Palestinian feeling of national pride and identity. On the other hand, the emergence of a strong Palestinian identity was the base from which the PLO drew its resources, according to Rosemary Sayigh.[22]

The Ideological Fragmentation of the Palestinian Elite. The geographical dispersion and the social mobilization of the Palestinians contributed to the ideological fragmentation of the Palestinian political elite, including the PLO leadership. The absence of a well-defined territorial framework and the extraterritoriality of the bulk of the Palestinian leadership have resulted in the absence of agreed upon reference points of political-cum-territorial definitions.[23]

Penetration of the PLO by Arab Regimes. The dispersion of the Palestinians in various Arab countries inevitably involved them in the politics of these countries, and enmeshed them in broader Arab rivalries. The Palestinians became involved in Arab politics either by acquiring citizenship in these countries (Jordan) or through participating in various Arab political movements. This sometimes led to confrontations between them and the host Arab countries,[24] and made the Palestinians highly vulnerable to Arab manipulation. Some Arab regimes used them to bolster legitimacy claims, sometimes to the detriment of the Palestinian cause. Consequently, Palestinian politics often involved a form of "pawn politics."[25]

Social Structure

In addition to the Diaspora and its implications, one can identify certain social-historical factors that have characterized the evolution of Palestinian society and influenced the functioning of the PLO. These relate to historical social cleavages in the Palestinian society, the Palestinian cognitive conceptions of authority, and the Palestinian class structure.

The Palestinian society that evolved under Ottoman rule was characterized by a bifurcation of political power among the Ottoman bureaucracy and the local nobility. Sources of power, instruments of rule, and bases of legitimacy were separate. Moreover, Palestinian society was divided by various social cleavages, most prominently between the urban notables and the rural sheikhs, between various antagonistic segments of the urban notables (e.g., the Hussaini and the Nashashabi families), and between Moslems and Christians.[26] After the 1948 exodus a new cleavage developed between the old notables and the emerging middle-class leadership.

This legacy is reflected in PLO politics in various subtle ways. The evolution of the PLO before and after 1969 reflects the cleavage between the old notables and the leaders of the new middle class. During its first five years, the PLO was dominated by Palestinian notables who almost alienated broad middle-class sectors from the newborn organization. Consequently, when the new leadership took over in 1969 it eliminated the notables from key policy-making organs of the PLO. The formation of various commando organizations can be likened to the politics of the old family cleavages. For example, it has been argued that some resistance organizations are extensions of the old family networks or reflections of some religious-political traditions.[27]

These divisions are further reinforced by the tendency of the Palestinians to personify authority. Palestinians tend to identify authority with the personalities of their leaders, which helps to produce a spectrum of clique-like coalitions around certain leaders and fosters organizational fragmentation.[28] Some resistance organizations have evolved mainly around certain key personalities. This tendency limited the cohesiveness of the PLO.

However, the structural evolution of Palestinian society over the last thirty years has influenced Palestinian politics in a different way. After the 1948 exodus, Palestinian society developed a broad middle class and a relatively broader proletariat of workers. These two classes constitute the social power base of the PLO. Most of the PLO's financial and human resources, as well as its leadership, are essentially drawn from these two classes.

Economic and Military Capabilities

As a transnational revolutionary movement lacking a territorial base of its own, the PLO is mostly dependent upon external economic support. PLO financial resources are drawn in large measure from three sources. The first source is the "liberation tax" levied on Palestinian workers by some Arab governments. These governments usually deduct 5% of salaries paid to Palestinian employees and channel the total taxes collected to the PLO. Cash outlays by Arab governments constitute the second source. According to a resolution passed by the second Arab summit in 1964, Arab governments are committed to pay certain annual financial contributions to the PLO. The actual amount and breakdown of these contributions varies from year to year. For example, the Arab summit held in Rabat in 1974 granted the PLO a subsidy of $50 million, mostly paid by the Arab oil-producing countries. The Arab summit held in Baghdad in 1978, in the wake of the signing of the Camp David agreements, allotted the PLO $400 million annually for the ensuing ten years.[29] Most Arab governments have not honored their commitments to the PLO either because of financial hardships or to show their displeasure with the PLO's policies. Between 1964 and 1971, Sudan, Morocco, and Yemen failed to pay their shares. Iraq and Tunisia paid only for one year and the rest of the Arab governments paid only for two years. According to Shukairy, during this period Arab governments owed the PLO 19 million Egyptian pounds (about $44 million) in arrears.[30] This pattern has not drastically improved since 1971. Contributions from friendly individuals and governments are the third source of support. For example, Dubai imposed taxes on hotel bills, cables, and air tickets for the benefit of the PLO. Kuwait deducts 1% of the salaries of Kuwaiti teachers for the PLO. The Jordanian Chamber of Commerce also pays financial contributions to the PLO. These are drawn from levies on merchants based on the amount of their registered capital, and from a fixed fee paid for every business transaction.[31]

The reliance of the PLO on Arab financial support limits its political options. It created a dilemma for PLO leaders who attempted to strike a balance between the necessities of compliance, especially in relation to major contributors, and the quest of autonomy, prestige among the Palestinian population, and progress toward its goals. The PLO also attempted to create an income-generating mechanism of its own through an industrial infrastructure known as Samid (literally, the "steadfast"). Samid was originally established in Jordan in 1971 as a rehabilitation center for the children of martyrs, and it evolved into an economic system for self-sufficiency for the PLO. It consists of thirty-three industries and employs some 5,000 mostly female Palestinian workers.

The total financial revenues of the PLO are secret, but have been estimated at approximately $500 million annually.[32] This is perhaps an inflated figure. The financial report submitted to the Palestine National Council in June 1970 listed the total expenses of the PLO during the fiscal year 1969-1970 at $3.9 million, 68% of which was allocated to the armed forces.

Militarily, the PLO has a broad base of human resources for recruitment, almost half a million. The PLO has established across-the-board conscription for all Palestinian men between the ages of eighteen and thirty. As a result, the PLO is able to maintain three military forces: a regular force known as the Palestine Liberation Army (PLA), guerrilla forces, and a people's militia.

The PLA consists of three basic formations: (1) the Ain Jalut Brigade of about 1,000 men, stationed in Egypt until the late 1970s; (2) the Qadissiya Brigade of almost 1,500 men, deployed in Iraq until 1971; and (3) the Hittin Brigade of almost 1,500 men, stationed in Syria and Lebanon. Most of these forces are now deployed in Syria and Lebanon. The PLA is mainly an infantry army equipped with Soviet-made infantry weapons such as assault rifles, machine guns, light and heavy mortars, light and medium field artillery, recoilless rifles, armored cars, and some T-34 tanks.[33] The army is controlled by a Palestinian chief of staff, whose headquarters are situated in Damascus. He is directly accountable to the PLO Executive Committee, on which he sits as a permanent member.

The PLA is to a large extent controlled by the Arab governments in whose territories it operates. Arab governments, including the staunchest allies of the PLO, have traditionally insisted on controlling the PLA units stationed on their territories. This applied in particular to Egypt in the 1960s and Syria in the 1970s. Consequently, the PLA actually became a separate body from the PLO, sometimes serving the interests of the sponsoring Arab regimes rather than those of the PLO. Syria used the Hittin Brigade against the PLO commando forces during the Lebanese civil war in 1976, and in the course of the war, PLO commando forces took the chief of staff of the PLA as a prisoner of war.

In addition to the PLA, each PLO member organization maintains its own guerrilla forces. These forces are organized as relatively self-sustained cells and equipped with light arms. Some groups, such as Fateh, possessed heavy weapons such as armored cars, 106-mm field guns, and antiaircraft guns. Most of this equipment was lost in the PLO-Israel war in 1982. It is difficult to give an accurate estimate of the exact manpower strength of the PLO, especially after the 1982 war. Prewar estimates for Fateh, the largest group, varied between 8,000 and 12,000 men with another 15,000 in the militia, which could be mobilized within forty-eight hours. Add to this an additional few thousands for each of the handful of resistance organizations.[34] These forces are under the direct control of their sponsoring organizations, with the PLO performing a coordinating function.

Finally, the PLO maintains an auxiliary people's militia. The PLO militia operate as a rear guard to the resistance forces. They are also trained to master urban guerrilla tactics including first aid, morale raising, and supply operations.[35]

PLO military forces are strategically controlled by the military departments of the PLO through the General Command of the Forces of the Revolution (GCFR). The Executive Committee of the PLO appoints the commander general of the GCFR and his chief of staff. The commander general, in turn, appoints the Supreme Military Council (SMC) under his chairmanship. The SMC consists of the top military leaders of the resistance organizations. The GCFR formulates the military plans of the

PLO, coordinates the military activities of all PLO forces, drafts the budget, and administers the PLO court martial.[36] The military department also supervises the "War College of the Palestine Revolution," which trains officers to serve in the PLO forces.

The PLO forces are plagued by certain structural weaknesses that limit their effectiveness. Most of these forces operate from outside Palestine. They have not been able to build a network of cells in the occupied territories or to mobilize the Palestinians living in these territories. This has made them highly vulnerable to Israeli incursion and to Arab manipulation. Israel has exploited this vulnerability by attacking military and civilian targets of the PLO in Arab host countries, putting a strain on PLO relations with these countries that finally forced Arafat in July 1981 to halt all military operations against Israel. The extraterritoriality of the PLO put it on a collision course with most Arab host countries (notably Jordan and Lebanon) and forced it to resort to commando actions rather than guerrilla warfare.[37]

In the course of the PLO-Israeli war of 1982, the second major PLO-Israeli direct confrontation since the Karama battle of March 1968, the PLO forces suffered tremendous casualties. The PLO lost its heavy equipment and a sizable portion of its military forces.[38] The rest of the forces have been dispersed over seven Arab countries, especially Tunisia, where PLO headquarters is presently situated. The PLO, in turn, inflicted heavy casualties on the Israeli forces: losses were 3,500 killed and 20,000 wounded.[39] Further, the PLO chief has confidently asserted that the PLO-Israeli war has not eliminated the PLO military capability. During the three months following the PLO exodus from Beirut (September–November 1982), the PLO launched 360 military operations against Israeli targets, killing or wounding an estimated 340 Israelis.[40]

Political Structure

Unlike the Palestinian nationalist movement of the 1930s and 1940s, the PLO created an elaborate set of political institutions. Together, these institutions form an integrated political regime that, by virtue of its composition, influences the PLO's foreign policy. The PLO political structure consists of the following basic institutions:

The Palestinian National Council. The PNC is the highest policy-making institution of the PLO. It formulates basic policies, issues instructions and guidelines to the Executive Committee and nominates its members, and has the power to create or abolish any PLO institution. Membership in the PNC is around 180 strong. Members are nominated by a committee of the preceding council, which ensures the representation of various Palestinian groups including resistance groups, trade unions, professional organizations, and independents. In 1983, eight resistance organizations were represented in the PNC: the Palestinian National Liberation Movement (Fateh), the Popular Front for the Liberation of Palestine (PFLP), the Democratic Front for the Liberation of Palestine (DFLP), Al-Sa'iqa, the Arab Liberation Front (ALF), the Popular Front General Command (GC), the Palestine Liberation Front (PLF), and the Palestine Popular Struggle Front (PPSF). Ten Palestinian unions and syndicates, e.g., the General Union of Writers and Journalists and the General Union of Palestinian Workers, were also represented. The PNC has a three-year term; it meets every year or meets in extra-ordinary sessions upon the request of the Executive Committee or 25% of its members. The PNC also has a chairman, who is directly elected by the membership at the beginning of each term.

The Executive Committee. The Executive Committee (EXCOM) is the highest executive body in the PLO. It has full operational authority over all the institutions of the PLO within the policy set up by the PNC. According to the PLO's basic statute, the EXCOM represents the Palestinian people, supervises all the formations of the PLO, issues instructions and takes decisions regulating PLO actions within the policy, implements the fiscal policy of the PLO, and prepares the budget. The committee consists of 12 members elected by the PNC from among its members. In electing members of the EXCOM, the PNC ensures the representation of major resistance groups. Committee members, in turn, elect the chairman of EXCOM. The committee is in permanent session and its members work on a full-time basis. Each EXCOM member has his own portfolio (e.g., foreign affairs, education and culture).

The Central Council. The Central Council (CC) is an intermediary advisory institution between the PNC and the EXCOM. It consists of sixty members, representing various resistance organizations, who meet every three months under the chairmanship of the head of the PNC to review the activities of the EXCOM and plan for future activities.[41]

The PLO Departments. In addition to these three institutions, the PLO maintains nine functional departments that resemble the ministries of state governments. The activities of these departments are supervised by the EXCOM. Each department has its own head except the military department, which is directly headed by the chairman of the EXCOM. Whereas the PNC, the EXCOM, and the CC are staffed so as to ensure the representation of various Palestinian groups, these departments are organized on a professional basis.

Chief among these are the political and military departments and the Palestine National Fund. The political department represents the PLO at international conferences, supervises its offices abroad, and undertakes various diplomatic activities on its behalf. The military department's basic function is to coordinate the activities of the PLO military forces in collaboration with the GCFR. The chairman of the EXCOM is ex officio head of this department. Finally, the Palestine National Fund (PNF) resembles a finance ministry. It supervises all the financial activities of the PLO, handling all financial donations and supervising spending and investing within the framework of the budget approved by the PNC. The PNF administers Samid and supervises the

Institute for Social Affairs and Welfare and its affiliate institutions—the Palestinian Society for the Blind, Social Care for the Wounded, and Social Care for Martyrs' Families, among others. The PNF director is elected by the PNC from among its members and is also ex officio a member of the EXCOM.

Other departments include the education department, which administors the educational affairs of Palestinians living in Arab countries; the health department, which supervises the Palestine Red Crescent Society; the Department of Popular Organizations, which acts as coordinator between the PLO and Palestinian professional associations, syndicates, and input groups; the information and national guidance department, which conducts all information activities of the PLO; the Department of National Relations, which represents the PLO in Arab governments, especially regarding the status of the Palestinians; and the Department of the Occupied Homeland's Affairs, which deals with the Palestinians under Israeli control.

Generally, a political structure can influence the direction of foreign policy in a number of ways. It can provide policy-makers with social and political resources, and it can also act as a constraint on the policy-making process. The resources provided by a political structure depend upon the scope of societal activities under its control, the degree of political institutionalization, and the level of public support.[42] Judging from the scope and domain of the PLO political structure, one may argue that it provides the PLO with ample resources.

The extent and intensity of the PLO's political and social activities deserve further attention. The scope of the PLO political structure may be illustrated by several examples:

1. The PLO has been able to exercise what amounts to sovereign powers over the Palestinians in war situations. The PLO represented the Palestinians in war situations with Jordan and Lebanon and during various incursions into Israel.
2. The PLO exercises extradition powers over the Palestinian people. On many occasions Arab governments have turned over to the PLO Palestinians charged with criminal activities. They were tried and sentenced by the PLO judicial system.
3. The PLO exercises taxation powers over the Palestinians through Arab governments.
4. The PLO exercises judicial powers. It established a revolutionary court, a revolutionary penal code, a revolutionary code of criminal procedures, and a revolutionary rehabilitation code. These codes apply to all sections of the Palestinian people.[43]
5. The PLO sponsors various social, economic, and educational activities, which provide the Palestinians with basic services.
6. The PLO plays a crucial political role in inter-Palestinian conflict resolution, especially among various resistance organizations. For

example, when the conflict between the PFLP and DFLP escalated in 1969 to the point of armed clashes, the PLO Executive Committee intervened to mediate between the two organizations.

The PLO has established both a cohesive set of structural arrangements to regulate its many activities and a well-defined set of decision-making rules, which operate within the context of an elaborate bureaucracy.[44] It is the consensus of the foreign policy literature that all of these dimensions and resources increase an actor's capacity to act in the arena of foreign policy. On the other hand, the political structure can limit the capacity of an actor to conduct foreign policy. The constraining role of the political structure depends upon the degree of coherence and unity both within the regime itself and between the regime and other institutions, the nature and extent of its accountability, and the degree to which the regime represents the wider society.[45] An examination of the PLO political structure reveals that these three variables have tremendously limited the PLO's capacity to make and implement a well-defined foreign policy.

By its nature as an umbrella organization, the PLO comprises a number of resistance organizations. These organizations entered the PLO as groups retaining their ideological and organizational identity. Consequently, PLO institutions are structured to reflect proportional representation of each organization in addition to the few independent members. This has turned PLO politics into coalition politics. Furthermore, these organizations are not a homogeneous set. They differ in their conception of Israeli-Arab conflict (moderates vs. rejectionists), their ideological orientation (Islamic nationalists, Arab nationalists, and Marxist-Leninists), and in the strength of their linkage with Arab regimes (universalists vs. subservients).

An examination of the ideologies of some of the leading organizations may be in order. Fateh adopts an instrumental definition of the conflict that guarantees the mobilization of all resources regardless of ideologies. It perceives the Arab-Israeli conflict as essentially a Palestinian-Israeli conflict, with Arabs and national liberation movements on one side and Zionists and imperialists on the other. The PFLP and DFLP reject Fateh's nationalist approach and advocate a class analysis of the conflict. According to these two organizations, the social dimension of the conflict cannot be ignored because the establishment of Israel was a result of an alliance between various Arab and Jewish bourgeois classes. Consequently, the PFLP and the DFLP include Arab reactionaries among the prime adversaries of the Palestinian revolution, and emphasize the revolution's proletarian nature.

The PLO resistance organizations also differ in the nature and scope of their connections with Arab governments. Some of them are highly institutionalized; others maintain a universalist orientation. The institutionalized or subservient organizations are organically linked with specific Arab regimes; they reflect the ideology and implement the strategy of their patron regime. Prominent among these institutionalized organizations are Al-Sa'iqa (affiliated with the Syrian Ba'th party), and the ALF (affiliated with the Iraqi Ba'th party). The universalists, such as Fateh and the PFLP, reject control by or affiliation with any Arab government. They fear that affiliation with any Arab government will reduce their freedom of action.[46] The representation of these conflicting organizations in the PLO political structure (the PNC, the CC, and the EXCOM) tends to hamper its ability to formulate policies. This has sometimes resulted in inaction. For example, in the fourteenth session of the PNC, Fateh and other resistance organizations became polarized over the issue of their representation in the new EXCOM, with the result that the old EXCOM was retained. The constraining impact of these competing organizations has been further exacerbated by the inability of the PLO to make dissent disadvantageous for these organizations. Resistance organizations that disagreed with the PLO foreign policy did not encounter substantial costs for departing from the umbrella structure. Arab governments also tend to protect and support client dissenting groups.[47] However, the negative consequences of this factionalism have been considerably reduced as a result of the increasing role of Fateh in the PLO. Fateh's dominance has reduced the impact of dissent in the PLO and increased the PLO's capacity to adopt a more flexible foreign policy.

FOREIGN POLICY ORIENTATION

Evidence of the PLO's foreign policy orientation can be found in the PLO Patriotic Charter issued in 1968, the resolutions and programs of the sixteen sessions of the PNC, and the statements by the successive chairmen of the EXCOM: Shukairy, Hammouda, and Arafat. Although these sources differ in the depth of commitment expressed, they articulate a well-integrated foreign policy belief system whose elements can be outlined as follows:

The Global System

The PLO leadership views international politics at the global level as fundamentally anarchic and conflict-ridden. It views the global system as characterized by wars, arms races, and imperialist conspiracies. Structurally, the system is perceived as a loose bipolar system, consisting of two basic contending global powers with a group of Third World actors endeavoring to reduce the threat of a global war. The basic stances of the two superpowers are viewed as intrinsically irreconcilable.[48]

The global system is also viewed as highly unstable. The basic interactions of the system are undergoing a process of fundamental transformation. The crux of this process is the collapse of the old world order of imperialism, colonialism, and racism, and the emergence of a new order whose basic features have not yet been specified.[49]

Within the present global system, the PLO perceives Western imperialism led by the United States and Great Britain as the major adversary of all national liberation movements, including the PLO.

> World imperialism under the leadership of the United States of America is the foremost adversary of all peoples. It is also responsible for various forms of aggression against the liberty and independence of peoples and the usurpation of their resources. This has been clearly manifested in the creation and support to the Zionist entity in our Palestine.[50]

The Soviet Union, the People's Republic of China, and other socialist countries are viewed as major supporters whose collaboration is always appreciated.[51] In an interview with the *New Times* of Moscow, Arafat said "The USSR and its communist party have always supported the just struggle of the Palestine people."[52] Furthermore, because of its geographic location, the PLO considers itself a part of the Third World in general and of the national liberation and nonalignment movements in particular.[53] In this respect, the PLO strives to unify the forces of global revolution and at the same time benefit from the lessons and advice of other liberation movements.[54] The PLO considers itself to be part of the militant group within the nonalignment movement. For the PLO, nonalignment does not mean equidistance towards the global powers, because one of them (the United States) is a mortal adversary. It means active support of national liberation movements against global imperialism, racism, and Zionism.[55] As a result of this global identity, the PLO views itself as playing a particular global role: that of a global anti-imperialist agent and a liberator-supporter of all national liberation movements in Africa, Asia, and Latin America.[56]

The Regional System

The foreign policy domain of the PLO is essentially the Middle East region. The basic issues, interactions, and conflicts of the PLO's foreign policy are located in this region. In fact, the PLO's global orientation is mostly shaped by its view of the basic issues of the regional system. The PLO views the Middle East regional system as containing elements of harmony and conflict. There is a harmony of interests among the Arab peoples; the conflict is between the Arabs and Israel.

The PLO leadership believes that the Arab peoples enjoy a fundamental harmony of interests by virtue of their common language, culture, and history. Conflict in inter-Arab politics is viewed as an aberration. Accordingly, Arab unity is seen as an inevitable historical process. The liberation of Palestine and Arab unity are viewed as complementary and mutually supportive values. The Palestinian charter states that "Each one paves the way for the realization of the other. Arab unity leads to the liberation of Palestine and the liberation of Palestine leads to Arab unity. Working for both goes hand in hand."[57] The organic link between the Palestinians and the rest of the Arabs places the Palestinian cause at the heart of the Arab integrative process and puts special responsibilities upon all Arabs to liberate Palestine.[58] Further, the PLO considers Arab territories surrounding Israel as hinterlands for resistance action. Any attempt to restrict Palestinian resistance in any Arab country is tantamount to betrayal of the goals of the Arab nation.[59]

However, such complementarity does not mean the subservience of the Palestinian struggle to Arab regimes, or the minimization of the Palestinian dimension in the Arab-Israeli conflict. The PLO rejects all forms of "official" Arab intervention in its own affairs. Meanwhile, it does not interfere in the domestic affairs of Arab regimes "except when" these affairs affect the Palestinian cause.[60]

The PLO views the Middle East system as essentially a revolutionary Arab regional system, characterized by sociopolitical conflicts between the forces of Arab national liberation and the forces of imperialism and social exploitation. The PLO maintains that underlying the Arab regional system is a pan-Arab liberation movement that is going through the state of national democratic revolution. According to the PLO, the basic tasks of this revolution are: (1) the realization of full political and economic independence; (2) the destruction of all forms of imperialism and its local subordinate forces; (3) the liberation of Palestine; (4) the liberation of the Arab masses from all forms of exploitation practiced by foreign and local counterrevolutionary forces; and (5) the mobilization of Arab resources in order to achieve pan-Arab socioeconomic development and Arab integration.[61] The PLO clearly identifies with the Arab revolution against Arab "reactionary" forces. Arab revolutionaries are considered the strategic allies of the PLO, and Arab reactionaries are perceived as adversaries even if they provide the Palestinian struggle with limited support in order to protect themselves.[62]

However, the main conflict defining the basic system of interactions in the region is still the Arab-Israeli conflict. The PLO views this conflict as containing core and peripheral actors. The core actors are the PLO, Western imperialism, and Israel. The PLO is supported by an outer circle of Arab and global national liberation movements and regimes.

The national liberationist self-image has led the PLO to de-emphasize the role of social ideology in its program. The PLO adopts an instrumental self-image that guarantees the mobilization of all resources regardless of ideology. Social contradictions among various Palestinian classes are considered secondary to the basic national contradiction with Israel and Zionism. Liberation requires the unity of all forces regardless of ideology.[63] Arafat succinctly stated this conception as follows: "Is this the proper time to stipulate a social content (of the revolution)? We are still in the stage of national liberation. How could I then deprive some classes of the Palestinian people from taking part in the nationalist struggle?"[64]

Image of the Opponent

The PLO perceives Israel as a political adversary whose basic goal is the annihilation of the Palestinian people. Israel is also viewed as a Zionist state that espouses expansionist aspirations in the Arab territories and racist views toward the Arabs.[65] It is not interested in any compromise with the Palestinians; as Arafat states: "Israel insists on and wants only one thing, the non-existence of the Palestinian revolution."[66] The PLO further believes that Israel is pursuing a maximalist policy in its dealings with the Arabs. A resolution of the Palestine National Council stated: "The Zionist invasion of Palestine was and still is a prelude for the occupation of other parts of the Arab land and converting it into a Zionist colony which serves imperialist interests."[67] The PLO also likens Israel to the apartheid regime of South Africa. By virtue of its Zionist ideology, Israel views Arabs as inferior subjects. The Israeli-Zionist racist image of the Arabs, the PLO maintains, is clearly exhibited in the structure of the Israeli state and its laws, which discriminate against the Palestinians. "Settler colonialism in Southern Africa and Zionist settler colonialism in Palestine are not only phenomena that resemble each other from a distance. They are also strategically and organically linked,"[68] Arafat stated. The PLO interprets Israeli expansionist and racist policies as emanating from the Zionist character of the state. Expansionism and racism are intrinsic to the Zionist ideology. Consequently, as long as Israel remains a Zionist state there is no hope of changing its present goals.

The PLO's dispositional attribution of Israel's goals is further reinforced by a perception of Israel as an imperialist agent. Israel is viewed by the PLO as a part of a system designed and coordinated by imperialism. Israel plays a crucial role in safeguarding imperialist interests, dividing the Arab land, and destabilizing Arab regimes.[69]

Article 22 of the PLO Patriotic Charter summarizes these perceptions of Israel as follows:

> Zionism is a political movement organically related to world imperialism and hostile to all movements of liberation and progress in the world. It is a racist and fanatical movement in its formation; aggressive, expansionist and colonialist in its aims; Fascist and Nazi in its means. Israel is the tool of the Zionist movement and a human and geographical base for world imperialism. It is a center and a jumping-off point for imperialism in the heart of the Arab homeland, to strike at the hopes of the Arab nation for liberation, unity and progress. Israel is a constant threat to peace in the Middle East and the entire world.[70]

One of the major areas of change in the PLO's image of Israel is its view of the homogeneity of the Israeli society and elite. Initially, the PLO saw Israel as a monolithic actor. Policy differences among various segments of the Israeli society or political elite were considered to be negligible and not likely to bring about any radical change in the character of the Israeli society.[71] By the early 1980s, however, the PLO began to view Israel as composed of various political groups espousing different policies toward the Arabs. Although the Israeli political establishment remains fundamentally united on major policies, there are new democratic and progressive forces in Israel, such as the Peace Now Movement, the Shelli party, and the Rakah party, which oppose Israeli aggression. Arafat believes the PLO ought to accommodate these forces as the basis for Palestinian-Israeli coexistence.

Goal Selection and Goal Definition

The PLO believes that it should select optimal goals for political action. Settling for the most feasible goals or compromising on maximalist goals, the PLO argues, means losing the battle before it begins. The task of goal selection ought to be approached within this historical paradigm of politics, regardless of the short-term prospects of success or failure. Once the optimal goal has been defined it should not be modified or abandoned, and any tactical goal must represent a step toward the realization of that optimal goal.

The PLO's approach to goal selection is based on its conception of the Arab-Israeli conflict. Arafat argues that history is an inevitable and circular process. History repeats itself, and contemporary and future events are basically replays of past scenarios. Consequently, one can predict the outcome of present policies by analyzing past trends, and one can also choose political goals according to the nature of previous historical patterns.

An analysis of these patterns, Arafat maintains, reveals that the PLO's goal of liberating Palestine will be achieved eventually. The history of the Crusades points to this inevitable outcome. "One who reads history will realize that the logic and inevitability of history support this."[72] If this is the basic pattern of Arab history, then it is only logical to subscribe to the optimal goal of liberating the entire territory of Palestine. This goal may not seem to be feasible today, yet in the long run it will be achieved, Arafat asserts. "Our generation is the generation of suffering, the generation of pain and hardships; it is the next generation that will win, that will reap the harvest of this harsh and wearisome struggle. We have never claimed that we should liberate our territory in a year or two or three. We believe in the necessity of a long-term people's war of liberation."[73]

The PLO's approach to goal selection is reflected in its goal definition. For the PLO, Palestine is the territory of mandatory Palestine. This territory is an indivisible unit and belongs to the Palestinian people.[74] The PLO's basic objective is to establish a democratic state in the territory of mandatory Palestine. This objective was first articulated by Fateh in 1968 and later adopted by the PLO in the sixth session of the PNC in September 1969, which resolved that, "The Palestinian struggle aims at terminating the Zionist entity in Palestine, the return of the Palestinian people to their homeland and the establishment of the democratic Palestinian state on the entire Palestinian territory without any form of racial discrimination or religious fanaticism."[75]

The democratic state is to replace the present political structures in the territory of mandatory Palestine. As a result the PLO initially rejected the establishment of a Palestinian state on a part of the territory of Palestine.[76] In this sense, the notion of the democratic state represents a reaffirmation of the view of the old PLO leadership, which called for the eradication of Israel. As Ahmed Al-Shukairy phrased it: "We believe that the existence of Israel is fundamentally null and must be eradicated as the imperialist existence has been eradicated from many Afro-Asian and Latin-American countries. Israel has no place amidst us. These who want Israel must carry it on their shoulders and plant it in their own territories."[77]

However, the notion of a democratic state does represent a shift from the PLO policy as stated in the 1968 charter. Whereas the charter would permit only Jews who lived in Palestine before 1948 to live in the future Palestinian state, the democratic state would incorporate all Jews who presently live in Israel, provided that they renounce Zionism. This was made clear in a 1970 document, which stated that "All Jews, Moslems and Christians living in Palestine or forcibly exiled from it will have the right to Palestinian citizenship. . . . Equally, this means that all Jewish Palestinians—at present Israelis—have the same right provided, of course, they reject Zionist racist chauvinism and fully accept to live as Palestinians in new Palestine."[78]

According to the PLO, the future democratic state will embrace secularism, democracy, and social justice. The state will assure the adherents of all religions an equal civic status. Popular participation, protection of basic liberties, and political accountability will also be ensured. Socially, the future state, dedicated to a high degree of social justice, will attempt to end all forms of social exploitation.

The PLO-Jordanian confrontation in 1970 and the ensuing expulsion of resistance groups from Jordan forced the PLO to rethink its options and to assess the tactical feasibility of the democratic state proposal. By early 1972, the PLO Research Center initiated studies on the feasibility of a Palestinian state in the West Bank and Gaza.[79] The international legitimacy bestowed upon the PLO after the 1973 October War encouraged it to shift its emphasis from the democratic state goal to the goal of a Palestinian state in the West Bank and Gaza, especially when the former was subjected to severe criticism in Israel and the West. Consequently, the PNC resolved in its Transitional Political Program, issued in June 1974, to accept a separate Palestinian state in a part of Palestine: "The PLO is fighting by every means, primarily by armed struggle, to liberate the Palestinian land and to establish a national independent and fighting authority in every part of the Palestinian soil which can be liberated."[80]

This shift was reinforced by the outbreak of the Lebanese civil war in 1976. The war helped to discredit the notion of a secular state and underlined the urgency for the Palestinians to obtain some sort of a sovereign state. In January 1978, Arafat emphasized that he would be content with a West Bank–Gaza state and would welcome protection from United Nations forces.[81] He reiterated this objective in May 1978, maintaining that the "only possible solution" is for a Palestinian state and Israel to coexist under the joint guarantee of the superpowers.[82]

The PLO quest for a Palestinian state is explicitly for a state alongside Israel in the West Bank and Gaza. However, the PLO is prepared to establish this state on any part of the Palestinian land that can be liberated. Regarding the relations between the new Palestinian state and Jordan, the PLO proposes a confederal connection between the two countries on the basis of sovereignty[83] and the enactment of international guarantees.

The PLO does not, however, consider the Palestinian state as a final solution to the Arab-Israeli conflict, nor does it imply the abandonment of the democratic state objective. The Transitional Political Program of June 1974 stipulates that the Palestinian state is a step toward the democratic state.[84]

Although the PLO's emphasis on the linkage between ultimate and tactical goals is consistent with its approach to goal selection, it seems that this emphasis is a bargaining strategy rather than a reflection of actual goal definition. The PLO has given various signals that this is the case. Arafat argues that the PLO has not put all its cards on the bargaining table because Israel has not done so. Consequently, beyond the strategy of the democratic state, Arafat adds, the PLO prefers to be the last actor to define its final stand. It prefers to listen to offers and comment upon them in order to keep all its bargaining chips.[85] Further, the PLO has privately given assurances that once a Palestinian state has been established, it will not press for further aggrandizement of this state. Former U.S. congressman Paul Findlay received the assurance from Arafat that in return for an independent Palestinian state in the West Bank and Gaza, the PLO was prepared to renounce all violent means to enlarge the territory of that state, and the new state would accord de facto recognition of Israel.[86] Also, in December 1982, Arafat announced that he was prepared to recognize Israel provided it first recognized the rights of the Palestinians. He also hinted that the PLO might change its Patriotic Charter if the Likud coalition and the Labor group also amend their political platforms, which deny the rights of the Palestinians.[87]

Foreign Policy Strategies

The PLO's conception of the Arab-Israeli conflict as a historical process necessarily entails a long-term strategy of goal implementation. Foreign policy goals will not be decided by a single action, but by a series of strategies that will inevitably culminate in the realization of goals.

The PLO follows two interrelated strategies: the popular war of liberation and mass political mobilization. A war of liberation launched by a revolutionary vanguard creates the right atmosphere for mobilization of the masses, which in turn provides the war of liberation with new momentum. In theory, the strategy goes as follows: A long series of small attacks on virtually all Israeli targets is to be launched. During these attacks, the resistance movement will avoid direct military engagements with the adversary in order to neutralize the latter's technological superiority. By persisting in this process regardless of short-term setbacks, the resistance movement will finally achieve its ultimate goal. For the PLO, the popular war of liberation has many advantages. It prevents Israel from enjoying the fruits of a peaceful occupation, continues the spirit of resistance, wears Israel down, and keeps the problem on the agenda of the world community.[88]

A companion strategy to the popular war of liberation is the mobilization of the Palestinian masses. The PLO considers "the Palestinians both inside or outside the occupied lands as the instrument of the revolution."[89] These masses ought to be activated and involved in the various functions of the Palestinian revolution. The mobilization of the masses is a sine qua non for the success of the popular war of liberation.

According to the PLO, military force plays a crucial role in implementing the strategy of the popular war of liberation and in cementing the mobilization and unity of the masses. This has been a consistent line in the PLO's definition of strategy. However, one may distinguish between three phases in the PLO's conception of the role of military force in goal attainment. During the Shukairy phase, military force was perceived as the only instrument to liberate Palestine. This line of thinking continued to characterize the PLO's conception of military force after the resistance organizations came to power in the PLO. Military force was perceived as a *foco* strategy, as advocated by Ché Guevara.

By the early 1970s, the PLO's view of military force became more complex. Although the PLO continued to value it as the major instrument, it argued that military force ought to be supplemented by other forms of political struggle. International negotiations and diplomatic contacts would help the PLO to reap the fruits of armed struggle, the PLO asserted.[90] Arafat articulated this view after the PLO departure from Beirut as follows: "The struggle is a political and military one. Armed struggle is one form of political struggle which has a loud voice. The Palestinians have the right to struggle by all military, political, diplomatic and information means."[91]

THE DECISION-MAKING PROCESS

In analyzing the foreign policy decision-making process in the PLO, one must differentiate between the formulation of general foreign policy objectives and the making of foreign policy decisions. This is because the structures involved in the two areas are not the same. Whereas the PNC is the supreme foreign policy–making unit in the PLO, the Executive Committee is entrusted with the task of making specific foreign policy decisions. Following the Hermann model, the structural characteristics of the two units may be compared in terms of their size, power distribution, and the role of members.[92]

The PNC (which has about 180 members) is a general assembly that represents various Palestinian groups. It elects the EXCOM, which is a small group of 12 members who take care of the day-to-day decision-making tasks. However, the two units converge as far as the power distribution and the role of members are concerned. Power is more or less evenly distributed in the two units. There is no authoritative leader who can commit either of the units to decisions against the majority opposition of the members. The chairman of the EXCOM does not enjoy the autocratic powers traditionally exercised by most Third World leaders.

This balance of power is a change from the Shukairy years. Shukairy used to nominate members of the EXCOM himself, and as a result he enjoyed tremendous power in deciding PLO policy. For example, the PLO-Tunisian conflict in 1966 was completely handled by Shukairy himself without any input from other members of the EXCOM, Shukairy recalls in his memoirs.[93] After Shukairy was oustered in 1968, the PNC limited the powers of the committee chairman and subjected him to continuous scrutiny by the EXCOM and the PNC. However, since the fifteenth session of the PNC in 1981, Fateh has increasingly played a major role in the decision-making process by virtue of its ever-increasing majority in the PNC and the EXCOM. Finally, the majority of the members of the PNC and the EXCOM are representatives of resistance groups. As a result, they are constrained in their deliberations by the policies advocated by their parent organizations. Using Hermann's terminology, the PNC and the EXCOM may be labeled as a delegate assembly and a delegate group respectively.

Foreign policy–making in the PNC is a collegial process. Policies are formed by all members of the council through a process of public debate and majority voting. As a result, the foreign policy–making process is essentially a process of ideological conflict. Delegates advocate policies that reflect the ideology of their parent organizations. Because of the constitutional equal power distribution and the public debate and majority voting system, representatives enter into political skirmishes trying to prove to other delegates the righteousness of their advocated policy or to convert undecided independents to their side. As a result, ideological alignments dominate the deliberation process, and ideological compromise becomes the basic foreign policy–making mechanism. Bilal Al-Hassan, a member of the PNC, outlines the deliberation process in the PNC as follows:

> The members of the National Council have become accustomed, at every session, to witness dialogue and conflict about a number of questions or

about a single central question that polarizes attention in the debate. They have also become accustomed to finding themselves aligned with or opposed to a certain view, with the Council automatically dividing up into two conflicting trends, so that argument is heated, impetuous and stormy, and quiet does not return to the hall until the democratic process acts as umpire in any disagreement and settles it in its own way.[94]

The PNC's response to the Brezhnev Middle East initiative in 1981 was typical of its policy-making process. The PNC's fifteenth session witnessed a heated debate over the initiative with members polarized into three alignments: those who rejected the initiative because it referred to the right of Israel to exist, those who unreservedly accepted the initiative because it emphasized the PLO's role in the final settlement, and those who advocated reserved support of the initiative. The final outcome was a compromise through which the PNC welcomed the Brezhnev initiative, emphasizing those points which affirmed the role of the PLO and the rights of the Palestinians.[95]

The primary decision-making process in the EXCOM is one of collegial incremental bargaining. It is collegial because all members take part in deliberating the issue before any decision is taken. For example, the decision to leave Beirut in 1982 was made by all the members of the EXCOM.[96] The process is incremental because the EXCOM is accountable to the CC and the PNC and because of the need of some participants to confer with parent organizations. The EXCOM cannot take major decisions without at least checking with the CC. It must also justify its decisions to the PNC. Members of the EXCOM, including its chairman, must adapt their views to the needs of other members if a decision is to be taken.

The chairman of the EXCOM plays a coalescent role in the decision-making process. He manages the proceedings of the deliberation process, reviews all important considerations and expedient alternatives, attempts to narrow the gaps between various delegates, and channels the deliberation process toward the options he perceives as consistent with the policy set by the PNC.

FOREIGN POLICY BEHAVIOR

During its two decades of existence, the PLO has developed stable patterns of dyadic, regional, and global behavior. These patterns are influenced by Palestinian national attributes and the PLO's political structure, and also by other systemic, relational, and situational variables in the global and regional systems. The patterns are directly determined by the PLO's orientations toward its external environment.

In order to describe the basic patterns of the PLO's foreign policy behavior, we have followed the international events approach,[97] making use of the data set of the Conflict and Peace Data Bank (COPDAB). The bank is an extensive, computer-based, longitudinal collection of daily international and domestic events between 1948 and 1978 of almost 135 international actors. An event is defined in the COPDAB data set as an official, newsworthy communication. It must be articulated or undertaken by an official representative of the government involved and reported in the press. An event involves (1) an actor, (2) a target, (3) a time period, (4) an activity, and (5) an issue. Each event record contains variables describing the actions, reactions, and interactions of the actors listed in it, in terms of the activity (the verbal or physical act that an actor initiated), the scale value of the event (the degree of cooperation or conflict), and the issue involved.

We compiled all the events in which the PLO was an actor between 1964 and 1978, which gave us the 102,727 events listed in Table 8.2. The events are tabulated according to the dyad of actors (e.g., PLO behavior toward the United States and U.S. behavior toward the PLO). The behavior of each actor in a dyad is divided into two types of behaviors—cooperation and conflict—and each type is broken down by period: 1964–1967, 1968–1973, and 1974–1978. Finally the behavior is aggregated by type of interaction and by period. The data set forth in Table 8.2 reveal certain basic patterns in the PLO's foreign policy behavior:

First, the total amount of foreign policy activities generated by the PLO has been increasing over time. If we divide the total number of events initiated by the PLO in each period by the number of years included, we find that the average annual foreign policy activity has increased from 720 incidents in the first period to 4,307 and 4,698 in the second and third periods. This reflects the PLO's increased capacity to act in the international system due to the growing availability of resources and skills necessary for the conduct of foreign policy behavior.

Second, the initiation of contact is divided equally between the PLO and other actors. Almost 51% of foreign interactions are initiated by the PLO; 49% are initiated by external actors. This is a consistent pattern that cuts across the two types of behavior and the three time periods. It reflects world awareness of the importance of the PLO in Middle East politics.

Third, most PLO foreign policy actions (almost 75%) involve conflict. This is a function of the liberationist role and change-oriented goals of the PLO. We have seen that the PLO perceives its global and regional role as that of an anti-imperialist liberator. Its behavior, therefore, challenges the global and regional status quo and creates a conflict relationship with most political regimes. This explains why almost 54% of the PLO's negative interactions involve countries that defend the status quo in the Middle East, namely Israel and the United States; whereas only 0.2% of its conflicts involve countries that reject the status quo, namely the USSR and the People's Republic of China.

However, the prominence of conflict in the interactions of the PLO has changed over time. Whereas conflict characterized 87% and 90% of the total interactions during periods 1 and 2 respectively, the percentage

TABLE 8.2
International Interactions of the PLO, 1964-1978

Dyad[a]	Cooperation			Conflict			Total by Type of Interaction		Total by Period			Total Interactions
	1964-67	68-73	74-78	64-67	68-73	74-78	Co-op	Conflict	64-67	68-73	74-78	
PLO-West[b]	12	125	136	72	1,543	674	273	2,289	84	1,668	810	2,562
West-PLO	6	163	218	50	1,054	215	387	1,319	56	1,217	433	1,706
PLO-U.S.	--	7	25	5	43	57	32	105	5	50	82	137
U.S.-PLO	--	4	25	1	48	30	29	79	1	52	55	108
PLO-UK	12	37	18	56	132	144	67	332	68	169	162	399
UK-PLO	6	30	22	50	76	--	58	126	56	106	22	184
PLO-France	--	12	42	--	94	222	54	316	--	106	264	370
France-PLO	--	6	88	--	157	85	94	242	--	163	173	336
PLO-East[c]	62	242	588	--	180	--	892	180	62	422	588	1,072
East-PLO	140	208	230	--	272	73	578	345	140	480	303	923
PLO-USSR	--	112	372	--	60	--	484	60	--	172	372	544
USSR-PLO	--	107	--	--	32	--	107	32	--	139	--	139
PLO-PRC	62	94	30	--	--	--	186	--	62	94	30	186
PRC-PLO	124	30	16	--	--	--	170	--	124	30	16	170
PLO-Third World	--	26	3,001	--	422	218	3,027	640	--	488	3,219	3,667
Third World-PLO	70	152	2,931	--	385	226	3,153	611	70	537	3,157	3,764
PLO-Israel	6	58	108	1,922	10,941	8,273	172	21,136	1,928	10,999	8,381	21,308
Israel-PLO	65	175	285	1,875	11,107	6,974	525	19,956	1,940	11,282	7,259	20,481
PLO-Arabs	289	2,143	6,269	519	10,160	4,223	8,701	14,902	808	12,303	10,492	23,603
Arabs-PLO	500	3,415	6,275	284	9,463	3,704	10,190	13,451	784	12,878	9,979	23,641
PLO-Jordan	61	561	417	503	6,938	403	1,039	7,844	564	7,499	820	8,883
Jordan-PLO	96	733	471	243	5,524	356	1,300	6,123	339	6,257	827	7,423
PLO-Lebanon	--	534	851	--	2,295	1,474	1,385	3,769	--	2,829	2,325	5,154
Lebanon-PLO	16	432	674	6	2,387	1,559	1,122	3,952	22	2,819	2,233	5,074
PLO-Syria	65	170	1,078	--	152	1,205	1,313	1,357	65	322	2,283	2,670
Syria-PLO	154	363	1,028	--	224	1,073	1,545	1,297	154	587	2,101	2,842
PLO-Egypt	56	198	732	--	132	710	986	842	56	330	1,442	1,828
Egypt-PLO	132	346	842	--	117	243	1,320	360	132	463	1,085	1,680

PLo-Saudi Arabia	--	86	419	16	204	6	505	226	16	290	425	731
Saudi Arabia-PLO	22	243	370	6	200	--	635	206	28	443	370	841
PLO-Iraq	67	102	227	--	110	239	396	349	67	212	466	745
Iraq-PLO	50	305	229	29	47	224	584	300	79	352	453	884
PLO-Libya	--	78	563	--	99	6	641	105	--	177	569	746
Libya-PLO	--	443	480	--	185	90	923	275	--	628	570	1,198
PLO-Algeria	20	76	308	--	6	--	404	6	20	82	308	410
Algeria-PLO	10	149	275	--	6	--	434	6	10	155	275	440
PLO-World[e]	369	2,594	10,102	2,513	23,246	13,388	13,065	39,147	2,882	25,840	23,490	52,212
World-PLO	781	4,113	9,939	2,209	22,281	11,192	14,833	35,682	2,990	26,394	21,131	50,515

Source: Data are taken, with thanks, from Edward Azar's COPDAB, formerly at the University of North Carolina, Chapel Hill, and now at the University of Maryland. An event is a statement in a public source about who does or says what to whom when and about what issues. Edward E. Azar and Thomas J. Sloan, *Dimensions of Interaction*, International Studies Association Occasional Paper No. 8.

aOrder of listing indicates which party initiated event. PLO-U.S. interactions are those initiated by the PLO.

bAll Western countries including the United States, Great Britain, and France.

cAll Communist countries including the USSR and the PRC.

dTotal interactions with the West, the East, and the Third World, Israel, and Arab Countries.

declined to 57% during the latest period. This decline corresponds to the shift of the PLO toward accepting a limited Palestinian state in the West Bank and Gaza Strip, and to the PLO's emergence to assert its international legitimacy. Obviously, the more the PLO becomes integrated into the international system, the more it shifts toward cooperation rather than conflict.

Fourth, the PLO seems to be locked in a complex process of reciprocal interactions. When it initiates a great deal of conflict, it inspires other actors to do the same. Almost 71% of actions initiated toward the PLO by other international actors are conflictive. Israel and the United States account for 56% of the total conflict actions initiated toward the PLO.

This pattern of reciprocity holds for both positive and negative interactions. Changes in behavior by the PLO were accompanied by similar changes in the behavior of other international actors toward the PLO. As the PLO annual average for conflict changed from 628 to 3,874 to 2,678 in the three successive periods, international actions against the PLO went from 552 to 3,714 to 2,238. As the annual average cooperative behavior by the PLO increased from 92 to 432 to 2,020, international cooperative actions toward the PLO increased correspondingly, 195 to 686 to 1,988.

Finally, the basic domain of PLO foreign policy is the Middle East region. Almost 87% of the total foreign policy interactions of the PLO occur in this region, especially with Arab countries (46%) and Israel (41%). Israel and the PLO have the most active relationship (41%), followed by PLO-Jordanian relations (16%). At the global level, PLO international interactions are basically with the Third World (7%), the West (4%), and the Communist East (2%).

Having identified some basic patterns in the PLO's foreign policy behavior, we will illustrate them by looking at specific international actors. At the global level, we will focus upon PLO policy toward the United States, the USSR, and the PRC; at the regional level, we will review PLO policy toward Israel, Jordan, Egypt, Lebanon, and Syria.

The PLO and the United States

Although the United States does not occupy a prominent place in the PLO's interactions with the West, PLO-U.S. interactions have markedly increased since 1964, with almost 75% of interactions characterized by conflict. This holds equally for PLO behavior toward the United States (77%) and U.S. behavior toward the PLO (72%). Relations between the PLO and the United States have become increasingly more complex and differentiated over the years. This is reflected in the relative decline of conflictive interactions and a modest increase in cooperative contacts. For the PLO it went from 86% conflict between 1968 and 1973 to 70% conflict from 1974 to 1978. Comparable percentages for the United States were 92% and 55%.

The United States attempted to discourage the establishment of the PLO in 1964. It sent secret aides-mémoires to moderate Arab regimes warning against the establishment of the new organization and promising a settlement through the UN.[98] This was partly a response to Shukairy's anti-American posturing when he was Syria's representative to the UN. The PLO-U.S. pattern of conflict continued after 1967. The PLO rejected the 1970 Rogers Plan. It charged that the plan conceded part of Palestine to Israel, recognized Israel's legitimacy, and consolidated imperialist influence in the Middle East.[99] The PLO also accused the United States of orchestrating the Jordanian attack on the PLO in September 1970.

With the signing on September 1, 1975, of an Egyptian-Israeli interim agreement mediated by Kissinger, the United States made a commitment to Israel that it would neither recognize the PLO nor negotiate with it as long as the PLO refused to recognize Israel's right to exist and refused to accept Security Council resolutions 242 and 338. The commitment has since been reaffirmed many times by the Ford, Carter, and Reagan administrations. The PLO rejected Resolution 242 outright because it dealt with the Palestinian question as a refugee issue only. It demanded an amendment to the resolution that would add a reference to Palestinian national rights; a demand that the United States opposed. Furthermore, the PLO welcomed, with some reservations, the Soviet-U.S. statement of October 1977, which referred to the rights of the Palestinians. However, under Israeli and Egyptian pressure the United States shelved the statement a few days later.[100]

Despite its outright denunciation of the Camp David agreements and the Egyptian-Israeli treaty in 1979, and despite its refusal to join the autonomy talks, the PLO began to make some approaches to Washington. In July 1979, Arafat declared that he was prepared to send a PLO delegation to Washington to begin a dialogue with the United States for a new framework for peace.[101] The United States insisted on the PLO's unilateral recognition of Israel as a precondition for such a dialogue.

The PLO-U.S. impasse deepened with the Israeli invasion of Lebanon in June 1982. The PLO charged that the United States had played a major role in the Israeli operation. "The USA took part with Israel in the Lebanese war. It gave Israel military, political, financial, and diplomatic support. The USA made a record out of using its veto power to block any Security Council action,"[102] said Arafat. The PLO also charged that the United States had broken promises given to the PLO to protect Palestinian refugees in Lebanon after the PLO's departure from Beirut. The PLO, Arafat asserted, had protected U.S. civilians and diplomats during the Lebanese civil war, but Washington did not honor its promise.[103] The PLO adopted a middle-of-the-road approach toward the Reagan Plan of September 1982. Various prominent PLO leaders declared that the plan contained some positive points but fell short of the minimum demand of the PLO for a West Bank and Gaza state.[104]

The PLO and the Soviet Union

PLO-Soviet interactions—unlike PLO-U.S. interactions—are predominately positive (87%). About 80% of them are initiated by the PLO. When the PLO was established in 1964, Shukairy took the initiative in contacting the USSR and requesting arms supplies. The Soviets politely rebuffed him, pleading for more time to assess the situation.[105] As a result, Shukairy turned to the People's Republic of China, which was quite willing to replace the Soviets. The Arab defeat in 1967, the change in the PLO leadership, and the PLO's adoption of a new Arab-Israeli strategy created new opportunities for a closer relationship with the Soviet Union. The PLO-Soviet rapprochement was slowed down because of sharp criticism by the PLO of the Soviet endorsement of the Security Council Resolution 242.

The turning point in the relationship came in 1968, following Arafat's secret visit to Moscow as part of an Egyptian delegation.[106] The visit marked the beginning of Soviet recognition of the Palestinian resistance movements. This was clearly articulated by Kosygin in December 1969 when he affirmed Soviet support of the Palestinian struggle.[107] In February 1970, Arafat visited Moscow in his capacity as chairman of the PLO Executive Committee. Although the Soviets expressed their support of the PLO, they remained noncommittal regarding Arafat's request for military aid. It was not until July 1972 that the Soviets agreed to provide the PLO with arms, which began arriving in September 1972. The Soviets began to view the PLO as a genuine national liberation movement that truly represents the Palestinian people. However, they took issue with the PLO's emphasis upon armed struggle as the basic means for goal attainment. They criticized the PLO for not recognizing the possibility of a political resolution of the conflict with Israel.

The PLO-Soviet rapprochement deepened after the October War of 1973. Four basic issues dominated relations during this period: PLO and Soviet participation in the Arab-Israeli negotiations, recognition of the PLO, the Lebanese civil war, and the Israeli invasion of Lebanon. The PLO demanded Soviet participation in the Arab-Israeli negotiations as a safeguard against a U.S.-imposed settlement. The Soviet Union insisted in turn on the PLO's active role in the negotiations. In July–August 1974, Arafat visited Moscow. During this visit the Soviet Union endorsed the Arab summit's decision to recognize the PLO as the sole legitimate representative of the Palestinian people and agreed to open a PLO office in Moscow. The Soviet Union further supported the PLO stand during the Lebanese civil war in 1976. It openly denounced the Syrian intervention in Lebanon, risking the loss of its valuable Syrian connection.[108] Soviet support of the PLO increased in the wake of President Sadat's visit to Israel. Both the PLO and the Soviet Union condemned the Camp David agreements and the Egyptian-Israeli treaty of 1979.

Because of several factors that go beyond the PLO-Soviet relationship, the Soviet Union adopted a cautious approach toward the PLO-Israeli war in Lebanon in 1982. The Soviet Union restricted its response to verbal condemnations of Israel and the United States and the shipment of limited quantities of arms to the PLO, which were seized by Syria.[109] This muted response led to the disenchantment of some PLO leaders with the Soviet Union. Hawatema, the leader of the DFLP, criticized the Soviet policy as ineffective. Salah Khalaf, one of the prominent leaders of Fateh, accused the Soviet Union of collusion in the Israeli invasions.[110] However, Arafat moved quickly to patch up the disagreements. In January 1983, Arafat conferred in Moscow with Yuri Andropov. After the talks, he announced that Andropov supported the PLO plan for a confederal link between Jordan and the Palestinian state.[111]

The PLO and the People's Republic of China

The People's Republic of China is the only international actor whose interactions with the PLO have been cooperative ever since 1965.[112] It was the first non-Arab state to establish ties with the PLO and remains the only great power that has consistently supported it. In March 1965, a PLO delegation headed by Shukairy was warmly received in Peking. A PLO office was opened in Peking and de facto diplomatic recognition was accorded. China provided the PLO with arms and ammunition and some PLO cadres were trained in the PRC. PLO-PRC relations seemed to have cooled in the wake of the Great Cultural Revolution and the removal of Shukairy from the leadership of the PLO, but the new PLO leadership moved to recement its Chinese connection. In March 1970, Arafat paid a visit to Peking during which he secured the continuous flow of arms to the PLO. On the eve of the September 1970 PLO-Jordanian war, the PLO was heavily influenced by Chinese thought and tactics on the utility of military force and guerrilla warfare.[113]

After the 1970 war, PLO-PRC relations continued at a different level. China concentrated upon behind-the-scenes pressuring of various PLO groups to unite. PLO-PRC communications continued but the Chinese restricted their PLO connection to the level of verbal support. A 1977 visit by Arafat to Peking did not result in any noticeable change in this stand. This was essentially because of the growing connection between the PLO and the Soviet Union, the PRC's major adversary.

President Sadat's peace initiatives in 1977 threatened the PLO-PRC relationship. China had an interest in strengthening Sadat's anti-Soviet role, which ran counter to the PLO's anti-Sadat policy. In October–November 1978, a PLO delegation visited Peking with an aim of persuading Chinese leaders to oppose Sadat's Middle Eastern policy. The Chinese were ready to express support for the PLO and to condemn Israel, but refused to criticize Egypt.[114] Since then, PLO-PRC interactions have been kept at this low-key but cooperative level.

The PLO and Israel

The PLO and Israel are engaged in a relationship of pure conflict, and there has been no change in this pattern since the two actors began interacting in 1964. The two actors initiate about the same amount of negative interactions toward each other. This pattern of interaction is a reflection of the issues at stake in the conflict and of the two actors' views of each other. The PLO and Israel both claim an exclusive historical right to the same territory. Neither envisages the possibility of a long-range mutual accommodation, and each denies the legitimacy of the other.

During the first five years of its existence, the PLO's reaction toward Israel was mainly restricted to verbal condemnations and military preparations for the future. After 1969, the PLO emerged as a coordinator of resistance operations against Israel and as a sponsor of the organized Palestinian resistance in the West Bank and Gaza. The 1969–1979 period witnessed the greatest volume of PLO-sponsored guerrilla operations against Israel. Israel responded by attacking various PLO targets.

After the expulsion of the PLO forces from Jordan, guerrilla operations declined considerably, but by 1973 operations began to escalate again from new Lebanese sanctuaries. The Lebanese civil war and Israeli reprisals forced the PLO in April 1982 to offer to sign a nonaggression pact. Israel refused.[115] Shortly after the PLO offer, Israel initiated a large-scale invasion of Lebanon (in June 1982) in order to destroy the PLO's infrastructure. The ensuing three months of fighting between the PLO and Israeli forces resulted in the eviction of most of the PLO guerrilla forces from Lebanon.

After the PLO-Israel confrontation in 1982, the PLO concentrated on three areas of interaction with Israel: rapprochement with the Israeli peace groups, rejection of unilateral recognition, and escalation of military operations. For the first time, PLO leaders openly met with leaders of various peace groups in Israel, as a sign of the possibility of Palestinian-Israeli coexistence.[116] However, the PLO insisted on mutual Israeli-Palestinian recognition rather than the unilateral recognition envisaged by the United States. Arafat justified this policy on three grounds: (1) unilateral recognition would result in increased Israeli intransigence; (2) recognition is a major bargaining card for the PLO, and it ought not be abandoned without a guaranteed gain; and (3) the political platform of the Likud coalition negates the independent existence of the Palestinians and it ought to be amended along with the PLO position.[117] Finally, the PLO began to regroup its forces and to stage guerrilla operations against Israel. The PLO leadership claims that between September and December of 1982 it staged 361 military operations against Israeli positions in southern Lebanon.[118] Meanwhile, the Israeli government has repeatedly asserted that it rejects any compromise with the PLO even if the latter recognizes its existence.

Relations with the Arab Countries

The PLO interacts most frequently with Arab countries. One would normally expect this interaction to be mostly cooperative, but this is not the case. Almost 60% of PLO-Arab interactions are conflictive. During the last period considered (1974–1978), however, a new pattern of cooperative behavior did emerge and the percentage of conflict behavior dropped. As a general rule, the PLO initiates more negative interactions with the Arab world than the latter initiates toward the PLO. This holds equally true for the three periods of interaction.

By virtue of its character as a nonstate actor, the PLO is vulnerable to the manipulations of Arab regimes. The PLO's efforts to create a "Palestinian Hanoi" in Jordan in the 1960s and in Lebanon in the 1970s, and the subsequent damage inflicted upon these countries by the Israelis, caused constant tension between the PLO and the governments of these countries. The existence of a majority of the Palestinians under the control of various Arab regimes also caused a PLO-Arab conflict over the loyalty of these Palestinians. The PLO's attempt to ensure its autonomy and establish a direct relationship with the Palestinians inevitably engulfed it in conflict with most Arab regimes.[119] Differences of opinion between the PLO and the Arab governments over the appropriate solution to the Arab-Israeli conflict exacerbated this underlying tension. Finally, the difference in decision-making style between the PLO and other Arab countries complicated their conflicts. Arab regimes viewed the PLO's more democratic decision-making style as a potentially destabilizing force in their own countries.[120]

PLO-Arab interactions are also cooperative, however. The Arab countries recognize the PLO as the sole legitimate representative of the Palestinian people. The emergence of the PLO to international prominance after 1973 was basically an outcome of a collective Arab effort. Furthermore, the PLO has played the role of interlocutor in inter-Arab disputes such as the Algerian-Moroccan dispute in 1976 and the Egyptian-Libyan war in 1977.

In order to review the interplay of all these factors in the making of the PLO's foreign policy toward Arab countries, we will briefly outline PLO foreign policy behavior toward major interacting countries: Jordan, Lebanon, Egypt, and Syria.

The PLO and Jordan. By virtue of the geographic and demographic connections between Jordan and the Palestinians, Jordan has the most active relationship with the PLO of any Arab country. PLO-Jordanian interactions represent almost 35% of total PLO-Arab interactions, and almost 85% of these interactions involve conflict.

The conflict between the PLO and Jordan in the mid-1960s was in essence a fight for the loyalty of the Palestinians living in Jordan and a struggle over territorial control of the West Bank. King Hussein did not permit the PLO to solicit support among the Palestinians until the PLO assured him it did not aspire to control the West Bank. The PLO also demanded the militarization of the Palestinians in Jordan under its partial supervision, a demand which the king rejected.

After the 1967 defeat, resistance organizations began to operate from Jordanian bases. The Egyptian-Jordanian post-1967 rapprochement helped them to consolidate their military presence in Jordan. After the Karama battle in March 1968 and the ensuing upsurge in the popularity of the resistance organization, King Hussein opted for a closer cooperation with the organizations. However, clashes escalated between the Jordanian army and the resistance organizations because of the latter's undisciplined behavior. The spark that lit the civil war in September 1970 was provided by the PFLP when it hijacked civilian airplanes and blew them up on Jordanian territory. The defeat of the PLO was completed by the end of 1971, when the Jordanian army eliminated PLO strongholds in northwest Jordan.[121]

PLO-Jordanian relations began to improve again after the 1973 war, and after Hussein agreed at the Arab summit of October 1974 to recognize the PLO as the sole legitimate representative of the Palestinian people. In April 1978, a PLO-Jordanian joint National Consultative Council was established. The thaw of enmity between the PLO and Jordan was accelerated by their common opposition to the Camp David agreements. In December 1978, Arafat visited Jordan. A "working charter" was signed to coordinate future relationships. The two parties also formed the "PLO-Jordan Joint Coordinating Committee for the Support of Steadfastness" as the mechanism for joint action supporting the Palestinians of the West Bank and Gaza.[122]

For the PLO, the harvest of the 1978–1980 rapprochement with Jordan was dismal. The PLO wanted a political dialogue that would lead to the return of its former military bases in Jordan, but Jordan restricted the dialogue to economic issues pertaining to the support of the Palestinians under Israeli occupation. The report of the EXCOM to the fifteenth session of the PNC in 1981 was rather pessimistic in its assessment of the record of the new PLO-Jordanian dialogue.

The PLO rapprochement with Jordan gained a new momentum after the PLO's departure from Beirut in 1982. The PLO entered into extensive negotiations with King Hussein through which the two sides agreed to establish a confederal connection between Jordan and the suggested Palestinian state. However, the PLO refused to authorize King Hussein to negotiate on its behalf with the United States or Israel.[123]

The PLO and Lebanon. Relations between the PLO and Lebanon resemble PLO-Jordanian relations in their intensity and in the issues at stake. The PLO became active in Lebanon as early as May 1968. Lebanon offered the PLO a center of communications and accessibility to northern Israel. As Israeli strikes against guerrilla bases became more frequent and as their electrified barrier along the Jordan river went up, PLO forces moved increasingly into Lebanon. As PLO activities in Lebanon increased, Lebanese politicians became apprehensive. They feared Israeli retaliatory measures against Lebanese targets and the disruptive impact of Palestinian militancy on the delicate Lebanese communal balance. This led to military clashes between PLO forces and the Lebanese army in April and October 1969. Through Egyptian mediation, the PLO and Lebanon signed the November 1969 Cairo agreement, which set certain guidelines for their future relations. It recognized the right of the Palestinians to work, reside, circulate, and participate in the armed struggle within the framework of Lebanese sovereignty and security.

The Cairo agreement pacified PLO-Lebanese relations temporarily. Later, army units and right-wing militia members, especially Phalangists, began to clash with resistance members more often. Matters worsened as PLO forces moved into Lebanon after their defeat in Jordan. Israeli retaliatory measures forced Lebanese policy-makers to demand the evacuation of the PLO units from southern Lebanon, and the PLO leadership agreed.[124] The situation in southern Lebanon returned to normal until the Israelis reactivated their military operations against the PLO in early 1973. This led to a new round of fighting between the PLO forces and the Lebanese army.

The involvement of the PLO in the Lebanese civil war and incessant Israeli incursions against PLO targets finally forced the PLO in 1979 to halt all military operations against Israel from Lebanese territories. Further, as the Lebanese felt the brunt of the Israel all-out invasion in June 1982, virtually all Lebanese factions, including the pro-PLO leftists, asked the PLO to evacuate Beirut in order to save Lebanon from total destruction. In September 1982, the bulk of the PLO leadership left Beirut.

The PLO and Syria. The dilemma of Arab regimes in dealing with the PLO is nowhere more pronounced than in Syria. Although the Syrians are among the most outspoken supporters of the Palestinian cause, they have always kept the PLO presence in Syria under firm control and have helped to weaken the authority of the PLO by creating their own organization, Al-Sa'iqa.

Initially, the Ba'thist regime of Amin Al-Hafez was not enthusiastic about the creation of the PLO in 1964. It was already involved with Fateh, which was launching military operations against Israel. The Syrian regime considered the PLO to be a reactionary organization and a facade for Nasser. Consequently, it rejected the integration of Fateh forces with the PLO units and insisted upon Ba'thist control of the PLO units in Syria.

It was not until the chairmanship of Arafat that the PLO began to make a breakthrough with Syria. This new connection was further cemented during the PLO struggle against the Jordanian regime in 1969–1970. During the September 1970 clashes, Syria pushed some PLA units to intervene in Jordan on the side of the PLO.

In November 1970, Hafiz Al-Asad took over as president of Syria. The Asad regime imposed new restrictions on the PLO. When the PLO criticized the Asad-Sadat agreement of September 1973, Syria closed down the PLO's radio station in Damascus. Badly in need of Syrian support, the PLO had very limited options indeed. In March 1975, the PLO agreed to set up a joint political-military command at the suggestion of President Asad, but by early 1976, relations had deteriorated sharply. The catalyst was the Lebanese civil war. When the PLO rejected Syria's conceptions of a Lebanese settlement, the Syrian army intervened in Lebanon in June 1976 to prevent the victory of the alliance between the PLO and the Lebanese leftist forces and to reassert its primacy over the PLO.

The Sadat peace efforts in 1977–1978 brought the PLO closer to Syria once again. The enemies who had bitterly fought each other in Lebanon both became members in the Steadfastness Front. Syria's dismal performance during the Israeli invasion of Lebanon in 1982 revived the underlying sources of tension between the PLO and Syria, and this was reflected in the PLO's decision to move its headquarters to Tunis from Damascus. As the PLO began to adopt a more conciliatory tone and to break away from Syrian guardianship, the Syrians began to criticize the PLO leadership and to challenge Arafat's right to speak on behalf of the PLO. In June 1983, relations came to the breaking point. Arafat accused Syria of supporting the mutiny within Fateh's military ranks and Asad reacted by expelling Arafat from Damascus.

The PLO and Egypt. The PLO's interactions with Egypt are significantly different from its relations with other Arab actors. Because of the absence of a substantial Palestinian community in Egypt or a territorial base for anti-Israeli operations, the issues in PLO-Egyptian relations have been basically restricted to different approaches toward the resolution of the Arab-Israeli conflict. In formulating its Palestinian policy, Egypt has been able to perform without significant PLO pressure.

Only 34% of PLO-Egyptian interactions involve conflict. The PLO tends to initiate more negative behavior toward Egypt than does Egypt toward the PLO. During the three periods under consideration, 46% of the PLO's total behavior was conflictive; the corresponding percentage for Egypt was 21%. A brief review of the evolution of PLO interactions with Egypt will clarify this pattern.

Nasser played a major role in the establishment of the PLO. As a result, the PLO was widely perceived, especially by Syria and Saudi Arabia, as a tool of Nasser's policy. However, PLO-Egyptian relations were not as smooth as might have been expected. Nasser insisted on full Egyptian control of PLA units stationed in Egypt and refused any PLO participation in their military affairs. He also became displeased with PLO leadership when Shukairy agreed with the Chinese to ship light arms to Alexandria without Nasser's prior permission. Moreover, Egypt did not pay its contributions to the PLO and charged the PLO heavily for the various services it used.[125]

After June 1967, Egypt helped in training and arming PLA units, building the PLO intelligence network, and strengthening its broadcasting facilities.[126] However, relations deteriorated after Nasser's acceptance of the Rogers Plan in 1970. The PLO severely criticized the Egyptian move and Nasser, in turn, closed down the PLO radio facilities in Cairo.

Under Sadat, PLO-Egyptian relations were more conflictive than cooperative. Sadat implied that PLO leadership was involved in the student demonstrations against his regime in 1972. However, Sadat managed to calm his tense relations with the PLO after severing his relations with Jordan in protest over the United Arab Kingdom proposal. As a goodwill gesture to the PLO, the assassins of Wasfi Al-Tall, former prime minister of Jordan, were never brought to trial. The PLO politely turned down Sadat's suggestion to establish a Palestinian government in exile.

After October 1973, the PLO severely criticized the Sinai I and Sinai II Egyptian-Israeli interim agreements. The two sides managed to patch up their relations when Sadat sided with the PLO in its conflict with Syria during the Lebanese civil war. Arafat played a role in the mediation efforts between Egypt and Libya in July 1977. The uneasy alliance between Sadat and the PLO finally broke down when Sadat, in a parliamentary meeting at which Arafat was present, announced his decision to visit Israel in November 1977. From then on Sadat became the archenemy of the PLO. Relations deteriorated further when Sadat accused the PLO of being involved in the assassination of Yusuf Al-Siba'i, the editor-in-chief of *Al-Ahram*, in Cyprus in February 1978. In July 1979, an unknown Palestinian organization called the "Eagles of the Revolution" attacked the Egyptian embassy in Turkey.

After the PLO's departure from Beirut, a new pattern of PLO-Egyptian rapprochement emerged. The catalyst for this rapprochement was President Mubarak's condemnation of the Israeli invasion and his decision to withdraw the Egyptian ambassador in Israel. Arafat responded by cabling Mubarak to hail his decision. After his departure, Arafat appealed to Mubarak to shoulder Egypt's historical responsibility toward the Palestinians. No Arab country, he said, had been able to fill the gap created after Egypt opted out of the Arab system.[127] Relations deteriorated very briefly after the announcement of the resolutions of the sixteenth session of the PNC, which seemed to snub the Egyptian government by hailing the opposition as representing the true patriotic Egyptian sentiments. Mubarak viewed the resolution as an unacceptable interference in Egypt's domestic affairs.

CONCLUSION

The analysis of the foreign policy of the PLO illustrates the dilemmas that revolutionary nonstate actors confront when they formulate foreign policy. Lacking a secure power potential or a territorial base, such actors face a real dilemma: to guarantee external support even at the expense of their goal pursuit or to sacrifice the former for the latter. In the case of the PLO, this is further complicated by the dispersion of its population, which is controlled by often conflicting regimes. This engulfs the PLO in the domestic affairs of these regimes and in the various conflicts between them. The difference in legal definitions and perceptions of appropriate strategies between a revolutionary organization that challenges the status quo and established political regimes also adds to the perplexity of the foreign policy–making process. Once established regimes envisage an opportunity for the attainment of their limited goals, they are tempted to crack down upon the maximalist actor. All of this leads to a decentralized foreign policy process, mostly uncontrolled by a sufficient degree of executive authority. It also leads to a foreign policy behavior characterized by incessant conflicts with the state actors who strive to control the behavior of the PLO.[128]

NOTES

1. Raymond Hopkins and Richard Mansbach, *Structure and Process in International Politics* (New York: Harper & Row, 1973), p. 4; Howard Lentner, *Foreign Policy Analysis* (Columbus, Ohio: Charles Merril, 1974), pp. 17–19; and Oran Young, "Actors in World Politics," in James Rosenau, V. Davis, and M. East (eds.), *The Analysis of International Politics* (New York: Free Press, 1972), pp. 125–144.

2. For recent works analyzing the foreign policies of various nonstate actors see Judy Bertelson (ed.), *Non-State Nations in International Politics: Comparative System Analyses* (New York: Praeger Publishers, 1977); Stanley Thames, "The Multi-national Corporation as a Foreign Policy Maker," Paper presented at the seventeenth meeting of the International Studies Association, Toronto, 1976; Samuel Huntington, "Transnational Organizations in World Politics," *World Politics* 15, 3 (1973), pp. 333–368; and Nassif Hitti, "The League of Arab States: Toward an Independent Foreign Policy," *Arab Affairs* (Tunis), December 1981, pp. 76–86 (in Arabic).

3. Ernest Haas, *Beyond the Nation-State, Functionalism and International Organization* (Stanford, Calif.: Stanford University Press, 1964), pp. 469–475; Judy Bartelson, *The Palestinian Arabs: A Non-State Nation System Analysis* (Beverly Hills, Calif.: Sage, 1976), pp. 11–12; and Ronald Macintyre, "The Palestine Liberation Organization: Tactics, Strategies and Options Towards the Geneva Peace Conference," *Journal of Palestine Studies* 4, 4 (1976), pp. 76–79.

4. Rashid Hamid, "What Is the PLO?" *Journal of Palestine Studies* 3, 4 (1975), p. 4.

5. *Compendium of Palestine Documents* (Cairo: State Information Service, 1970), Part 2, p. 1273.

6. Ahmed Al-Shukairy, *From the Summit to the Defeat with the Arab Kings and Presidents* (Beirut: Dal Al-Awada, 1971), pp. 60–62 (in Arabic).

7. Abdel-Moniem Al-Sa'adoun, "The Palestine Liberation Organization," Diploma diss., Institute of Arab Studies and Research, Cairo, 1976, pp. 180–211 (in Arabic).

8. Al-Shukairy, *op. cit.*, p. 112.

9. George Kossaifi, "Demographic Characteristics of the Arab Palestinian People," in Khalil Nakhleh and Elia Zureik (eds.), *The Sociology of the Palestinians*

(London: Croom Helm, 1980), p. 25; and Edward Hagopian and Antoine Zahlan, "Palestine's Arab Population: The Demography of the Palestinians," *Journal of Palestine Studies* 3, 4 (1974), p. 61.

10. Gamil Hilal, "Class Transformation in the West Bank and Gaza," *Journal of Palestine Studies* 6, 2 (1977), pp. 172–173; and Pamela Ann Smith, "Aspects of Class Structure in the Palestinian Society, 1948–1967," in Uri Davis, A. Mack, and N. Yuval-Davis (eds.), *Israel and the Palestinians* (London: Ithaca Press, 1975), pp. 98–112.

11. Sammy Mar'i, "Higher Education Among Palestinians with Special Reference to the West Bank," in Gabriel Ben-Dor (ed.), *The Palestinians and the Middle East Conflict* (Ramat Gan, Israel: Turtledove, 1978), pp. 181–182; and Nabil Shaath, "High Level Palestinian Manpower," *Journal of Palestine Studies* 1 (1972), pp. 80–97.

12. Mar'i, *op. cit.*, p. 441.

13. Philip Davies, "The Educated West Bank Palestinians," *Journal of Palestine Studies* 8, 3 (1979), p. 65.

14. Muhsin Yusuf, "The Potential Impact of Palestinian Education on a Palestinian State," *Journal of Palestine Studies* 8, 4 (1979), pp 70–93; and Michael Hudson, "The Palestinian Resistance Movement Since 1967," in Willard A. Beling (ed.), *The Middle East: Quest for an American Policy* (Albany: State University of New York, 1973), p. 109.

15. Bassam Sirhan, "Palestinian Refugee Camp Life in Lebanon," *Journal of Palestine Studies* 4, 2 (1975), p. 107.

16. Rosemary Sayigh, *Palestinians: From Peasants to Revolutionaries* (London: Zed Press, 1979), p. 125.

17. Rosemary Sayigh, "Sources of Palestinian Nationalism: A Study of a Palestinian Camp in Lebanon," *Journal of Palestine Studies* 6, 4 (1977), pp. 22–23.

18. Abdel-Meguid Amer, *The Patriotic Identity of the Palestinian People: A Field Study of a Camp*, M.A. diss., University of Cairo, 1982, pp. 93–94, 117–118, 129, 136 (in Arabic).

19. *Ibid.*, p. 167.

20. Karl Deutsch, *Nationalism and Social Communication, An Inquiry into the Foundations of Nationality* (Cambridge, Mass.: MIT Press, 1962).

21. Hamid Ansari, "Palestinian National Identity: Challenges and Continuity," Working Paper No. 32, Comparative Interdisciplinary Studies section of the International Studies Association, 1975, pp. 3–8.

22. Rosemary Sayigh, "The Palestinian Identity Among Camp Residents," *Journal of Palestine Studies* 5, 3 (1977), pp. 11–12.

23. John Amos II, *Palestinian Resistance: Organization of a National Movement* (New York: Pergamon Press, 1980), p. 150.

24. Ibrahim Abu-Lughod, "The Palestinians Today," in Hatem Hussaini and F. El-Boghdady (eds.), *The Palestinians* (Washington, D.C.: Arab Information Center, 1976), p. 30.

25. Fawaz Turki, *The Disinherited, Journal of Palestinian Exile* (New York: Monthly Review Press, 1974), pp. 37–38.

26. Donna Robinson Divine, "The Dialectics of Palestinian Politics," in Joel Migdal (ed.), *Palestinian Society and Politics* (Princeton, N.J.: Princeton University Press, 1980), pp. 212–229.

27. *Ibid.*

28. William Quandt, Fuad Jabber, and Ann Lesch, *The Politics of Palestinian Nationalism* (Berkeley: University of California Press, 1973), pp. 80–82.

29. Amos, *op. cit.*, pp. 163–164.

30. Al-Shukairy, *op. cit.*, pp. 192–194.

31. Amos, *op. cit.*, p. 161.

32. *Ibid.*, pp. 158–159.

33. Sara Bar-Haim, "The Palestine Liberation Army, Stooge or Actor," in Gabriel Ben-Dor, *op. cit.*, pp. 181–182.

34. *Ibid.*, pp. 58, 61, 71, 205.

35. *Ibid.*, pp. 167–168.

36. Resolutions of the thirteenth session of the Palestine National Council, held in March 1977, *Journal of Palestine Studies* 5, 3 (1977), pp. 194–195.

37. Y. Harkabi, "The Weakness of the Fedayeen," in Y. Harkabi, *Palestinians and Israel* (New Brunswick, N.J.: Transaction Books, 1975), pp. 102–114.

38. From an interview with Salah Khalaf, member of the Palestine National Council, *Al-Mussawar* (Cairo) 3025 (October 1, 1982).

39. From a lecture delivered by Ahmed Sidky Al-Dajani, member of the Palestine National Council, at the Centre for Political and Strategic Studies. *Al-Ahram* (Cairo), November 21, 1982.

40. From an interview with Arafat in *Al-Hawadess* (London), January 7, 1983, and in *Al-Siyassa* (Kuwait), January 8, 1983. See also Arafat's interview with Saad Ibrahim, "With Yasser Arafat," *Al-Ahram Al-Iktisadi* (Cairo), January 17, 1983, p. 34. Inverview with Abu Al-Zaim, head of PLO military intelligence, in *Al-Ahram Al-Iktisadi*, October 25, 1982, pp. 24–26.

41. Al-Sa'adoun, *op. cit.*, pp. 127–130.

42. Barbara Salmore and S. Salmore, "Political Regimes and Foreign Policy," in Maurice East, S. Salmore, and C. Hermann (eds.), *Why Nations Act: Theoretical Perspectives for Comparative Foreign Policy Studies* (Beverly Hills, Calif.: Sage, 1978), p. 111.

43. Anis Kassim, "The Palestine Liberation Organization's Claim to Status: A Juridical Analysis Under International Law," *Journal of Palestine Studies* 10, 4 (1981), pp. 142–153.

44. Amos, *op. cit.*, p. 176.

45. Salmore and Salmore, *op. cit.*, pp. 111–113.

46. For a full review of the programs of all Palestinian guerrilla organizations, see Ghazi Khorsheid, *A Handbook of the Palestinian Resistance Movement* (Beirut: PLO Research Center, 1971) (in Arabic). For further analyses of these programs see Muhammad Muslih, "Moderates and Rejectionists Within the Palestine Liberation Organization," *Middle East Journal* 30, 2 (1976), pp. 127–140; Paul Jureidini and W. Hazen, *The Palestinian Movement in Politics* (Lexington, Mass.: D. C. Heath and Co., 1976), pp. 19–40; Fouad Moughrabi, "The Palestine Resistance Movement, Evolution of a Strategy," Paper presented at the seventeenth annual convention of the International Studies Association, Toronto, 1976; and Fawaz Hamed Al-Sharkawy, "Palestinian National Liberation Movement, Fateh," M.A. diss., University of Cairo, 1974.

47. Bruce Stanley, "Fragmentation and National Liberation Movements: The PLO," *Orbis* 22, 4 (1979), pp. 1053–1054.

48. Yasser Arafat's speech in the United Nations on November 13, 1974. Text printed in *Journal of Palestine Studies* 4, 2 (1975), pp. 181–192.

49. Arafat's interview with *Al-Muharrer* (Beirut), April 27, 1972.

50. Arafat's interview with *Al-Hawadess* (Beirut), August 2, 1974.

51. Resolutions of the second session of the PNC in *ibid.*, p. 75, and of the third session of the PNC in Rashid Hamid (ed.), *Resolutions of the Palestine National Council, 1964–1974* (Beirut: PLO Research Center, 1975), p. 94.

52. Arafat's interview with the *New Times* (Moscow), November 1973. In *Palestinian Arab Documents for 1973* (Beirut: Institute for Palestine Studies, 1976), p. 497.

53. Arafat's speech at the OAU meeting in Kampala on July 29, 1975. Text in *Journal of Palestine Studies* 5, 1 and 2 (1975 and Winter 1976), p. 258.

54. Resolutions of the fourth session of the PNC, in Hamid, *Resolutions*, p. 111.

55. Arafat's speech at the Fourth Summit of the Nonaligned Movement, held in Algeria in 1973. Text of the speech is in George Nasrallah (ed.), *The Palestinian and Arab Documents for 1973* (Beirut: Institute for Palestine Studies, 1976), pp. 279–280. Resolutions of the fifteenth session of the PNC are in the *Journal of Palestine Studies* 10, 4 (1981), p. 187.

56. Resolutions of the fifteenth session, *ibid.*

57. Article 13 of the Palestinian Patriotic Charter, in Hamid, *Resolutions*, p. 123.

58. Article 15 of the Palestinian Patriotic Charter, in *ibid.*, p. 123.

59. Resolutions of the seventh session of the PNC, in *ibid.*, p. 166.

60. Resolutions of the sixth session of the PNC, in *ibid.*, p. 152.

61. The political program of the tenth session of the PNC held in April 1972, in *ibid.*, p. 218.

62. *Ibid.*

63. Article 9 of the Palestinian Patriotic Charger, in *ibid.*

64. Arafat interview with Talal Salman, "With Fateh and the Fedayeen" (Beirut: Dar Al-Awda, 1969), p. 10.

65. Resolutions of the tenth session of the PNC, in Hamid, *Resolutions*, p. 199.

66. Arafat's interview with *Al-Hawadess*, August 2, 1974.

67. Resolutions of the fifth session of the PNC, in Hamid, *Resolutions*, p. 137.

68. Speech by Arafat at the OAU meeting in Kampala, July 29, 1975, *op. cit.*, p. 259.

69. Resolutions of the fourth session of the PNC, in Hamid, *Resolutions*, p. 111.

70. In *ibid.*, p. 124.

71. Resolutions of the seventh session of the PNC, in *ibid.*, p. 166.

72. Arafat's interview with *Filastine Al-Thawra* on January 1, 1973, in *Journal of Palestine Studies* 2, 3 (1973), p. 168.

73. *Ibid.*, p. 167.

74. Articles 1 and 2 of the Palestinian Patriotic Charter, in Hamid, *Resolutions*, p. 122.

75. *Ibid.*, p. 151.

76. Resolutions of the fifth session of the PNC, in *ibid.*, p. 138.

77. Ahmed Al-Shukairy, *Decisive Situations in the Palestine Issue* (Cairo: PLO Office, n.d.), p. 79 (in Arabic).

78. "Towards a Democratic State in Palestine," Paper submitted to the Second World Conference on Palestine, held in Amman in September 1970. Reprinted by the Arab Information Centre, Ottawa, Canada, n.d., pp. 15–16.

79. Ann Lesch, "Palestinian Politics and the Future of Arab-Israeli Relations," in Robert Freedman (ed.), *World Politics and the Arab-Israeli Conflict* (New York: Pergamon Press, 1979), p. 225.

80. In Hamid, *Resolutions*, p. 247.

81. Quoted in Lesch, *op. cit.*, p. 230.

82. Arafat's interview with the *New York Times*, May 4, 1978.

83. The official spokesman of the PLO, as quoted in *Al-Akhbar* (Cairo), October 13, 1982.

84. Resolutions of the twelvth session of the PNC, in Hamid, *Resolutions*, p. 247.

85. Arafat's interview with *Rose Al-Youssef* (Cairo), October 21, 1974, and with *Al-Akhbar*, November 28, 1973.

86. *Journal of Palestine Studies* 8, 2 (Winter 1979), p. 173.

87. Arafat's interview with *Al-Mussawar*, December 31, 1982.

88. Resolutions of the fourth session of the PNC, in *ibid.*, p. 103.

89. Resolutions of the fourth session of the PNC, in Hamid, *Resolutions*, p. 105.

90. Resolutions of the thirteenth session of the PNC, in *Journal of Palestine Studies* 5, 3 (1977), p. 188.

91. Arafat's interview with *Al-Hawadess*, January 7, 1983.

92. Charles Hermann, "Decision Structure and Process Influences on Foreign Policy," in East, Salmore, and Hermann, *op. cit.*, pp. 77–78.

93. Al-Shukairy, *Summit to Defeat*, p. 211.

94. *Journal of Palestine Studies* 11, 1 (1981), p. 172.

95. *Ibid.*, p. 177.

96. Arafat's interview with *Al-Majallah* (London), October 9, 1982, pp. 2, 5.

97. For a review of the international events approach, see Charles W. Kegley, Jr., et al. (eds.), *International Events and the Comparative Analysis of Foreign Policy* (Columbia: University of South Carolina Press, 1975).

98. Al-Shukairy, *Summit to Defeat*, pp. 93, 118, 122.

99. Resolutions of the sixth session of the PNC, in Hamid, *Resolutions*, p. 169.

100. Raymond Cohen, "Israel and the Soviet-American Statement of October 1977: The Limits of Patron-Client Influence," *Orbis* 22, 3 (1978), pp. 613–634.

101. Arafat's interview with *Al-Safir*, July 23, 1979.

102. Arafat's interview with *Al-Majallah*, September 17, 1982.

103. Arafat's interview with *Al-Siyassa* (Kuwait), January 8, 1983, and with Saad Ibrahim, "With Yasser Arafat."

104. Arafat's statement in *Al-Akhbar*, October 14, 1982; statement of Khalil Al-Wazir in *Al-Ahram*, October 16, 1982; statement of Nabil Shaath in *Al-Akhbar*, October 13, 1982.

105. Al-Shukairy, *Summit to Defeat*, pp. 216–217.

106. It is important to note that Arafat visited Moscow in his capacity as leader of Fateh.

107. Galia Golan, *The Soviet Union and the Palestine Liberation Organization* (New York: Praeger Publishers, 1981), p. 11.

108. *Ibid.*, p. 11–28, 123–125, 232–233.

109. As revealed by Arafat in his interview with Saad Ibrahim, "With Yasser Arafat."

110. Mohamed Selim, "The Soviet Union and the Palestinian-Israeli War," *Al-Siyassa Al-Dawliya* (Cairo) 18 (1982), p. 152.

111. *Al-Ahram*, January 14, 1983.

112. For a full review of the PLO-PRC relations, see the following: Yitzhak Shichor, *The Middle East in China's Foreign Policy: 1949-1977* (Cambridge: Cambridge University Press, 1979), pp. 114–119, 140–144, 155–159; Hashim Behbahani, *China's Foreign Policy in the Arab World, 1955-1975* (London: Routledge and Kegan Paul, 1981), pp. 20–133; Yitzhak Shichor, "The Palestinians and China's Foreign Policy," in Chun-tu Hsueh (ed.), *Dimensions of China's Foreign Relations* (New York: Praeger Publishers, 1977), pp. 156–190; Mohamed Selim, "The People's Republic of China and the Palestine Question," *Al-Siyassa Al-Dawliya* 7, 25 (July 1971), pp. 58–83; John Cooley, "China and the Palestinians," *Journal of Palestine Studies* 1, 2 (1972), pp. 19–34; and Moshe Maoz, "Soviet and Chinese Influence on the Palestinian Guerrilla Movement," in Alvin Rubinstein (ed.), *Soviet and Chinese Influence in the Third World* (New York: Praeger Publishers, 1975), pp. 109–130.

113. Lillian Craig Harris, "China's Relations with the PLO," *Journal of Palestine Studies* 7 (1977), pp. 142–145.

114. Aryeh Yodfat and Y. Arnon-Ohanna, *PLO Strategy and Politics* (London: Croom Helm, 1981), p. 80.

115. Statement of the Israeli minister of tourism, *Al-Ahram*, January 15, 1983.

116. *Al-Ahram*, January 22, 1983.

117. Arafat's interview with *Al-Mussawar* (Cairo), December 31, 1982.

118. Arafat's interview with *Rose Al-Youssef*, January 3, 1983.

119. For a review of the linkages between the PLO and the Arab system, see Gabriel Ben-Dor, "Nationalism Without Sovereignty and Nationalism with Multiple Sovereignties: The Palestinians and Inter-Arab Relations," in Ben-Dor, *op. cit.*, pp. 143–172; and Walid Kazziha, *Palestine in the Arab Dilemma* (London: Croom Helm, 1979).

120. Alan Taylor, *The Arab Balance of Power* (Syracuse, N.Y.: Syracuse University Press, 1982), pp. 57–58.

121. P. J. Vatikiotis, *Conflict in the Middle East* (London: George Allen and Unwin, 1971), pp. 168–179; Mahmood Hussain, *The Palestine Liberation Organization* (Delhi: University Publishers, 1975), pp. 55–64; and Riad El-Rayyes and Dunia Nahas, *Guerrillas for Palestine* (London: Croom Helm, 1976), pp. 89–91.

122. Yodfat and Arnon-Ohanna, *op. cit.*, pp. 12–14.

123. Arafat's interview with *Al-Mussawar*, December 31, 1982.

124. Vatikiotis, *op. cit.*, pp. 180–181; and Jureidini and Hazen, *The Palestinian Movement*," pp. 67–70.

125. Al-Shukairy, *Summit to Defeat*, pp. 152, 277.

126. Amin Hewaidi, *Abdel-Nasser's Wars* (Cairo: Dar Al-Mawkef Al-Arabi, 1982).

127. Arafat's interview with *Al-Mussawar*, December 13, 1982; with *Al-Hawadess*, January 7, 1983; and with *Rose Al-Youssef*, January 3, 1983.

128. Editors' note: The summer 1983 mutiny within Fateh ranks could have serious implications for the PLO, the Arab system, and the conduct of the Arab-Israeli conflict. During its twenty years of existence, the PLO has managed to cope with internal factionalism, manipulation and interference by Arab states, and Israeli attacks. How will it cope with the effects of the Lebanon war: the dispersal of its fighting forces to seven Arab countries, the loss of a military base contiguous with Israel, and the ensuing frustration within its ranks?

Depending on the outcome of the mutiny, a number of possibilities exist. If Syria succeeds in its "power grab" and dominates the PLO, other Palestinian groups and Arab governments may encourage an alternative spokesman for the Palestinians. Syria is likely to use its added influence to negotiate a settlement in Lebanon and the Golan Heights. Or perhaps the PLO will follow a more militant line, halting the search for a peaceful solution to the conflict. In either case, Arafat will be the loser, and the PLO is likely to emerge as a weaker and less autonomous actor.

9

Defending the Faith: The Foreign Policy of Saudi Arabia

Bahgat Korany

1. INTRODUCTION: HEART OF ISLAM AND OIL GIANT

Saudi Arabia is of unparalleled importance to the 800 million Moslems of the world. Never colonized by a Western power, it is the core of both Islam and the Arab race, and the keeper of their purity. The migration that began from this Arab-Islamic state spread Islam as far as China, Russia, and Yugoslavia. Two of Islam's holy places, Mecca and Medina, are in Saudi Arabia, and it is toward these that practicing Moslems all over the world turn five times a day to pray. Islam is not the only determinant of Saudi policy, whether domestic or foreign, but it is paramount.

Saudi Arabia, two-thirds the size of India, is a barren land. Occupying roughly three-quarters of the Arabian Peninsula (about two million square km), Saudi Arabia would have continued—at the economic level—as a sandbox were it not for one commodity: oil. The country has a quarter of the world's supply, is the third largest producer and the largest exporter of oil, and has accumulated six times more overseas assets than the United States.[1]

Yet before the early 1970s, no books and only a handful of articles had been published on this country's foreign policy. Other aspects of Saudi Arabia were only slightly better analyzed. After a survey of 120 books and 5,500 articles in 11 U.S. scholarly journals, Braibanti and Farsy emphasize "the scholarly aridity comparable to Al-Rub Al-Khali, that vast empty quarter of the Arabian Desert rarely traversed by man."[2]

Scarcity of information also characterized newspapers and other nonscholarly sources. Malcolm Peck puts it succinctly:

Base 503597 1-78

In 1968, the *New York Times Index* revealed twice as much reporting on Albania as on Saudi Arabia, five or six times as much on Malaysia in 1969 and four times as much on Burma in 1970. *Time* had only one story relating to Saudi Arabia in 1969, reporting the death of King Saud and commenting on his physical ailments and the size of his harem. No mention was made of Faisal's visit to Washington in 1971. *US News and World Report* did not mention Saudi Arabia in 1969 or 1971 . . . [For] the duration of the 90th and 91st Congresses, 1969–72, the index to the Congressional Record reveals that no reference was made to Saudi Arabia."[3]

The quality of resources was equally poor. The information provided was frequently careless, shallow, erroneous, or stereotyped. For instance, in covering the fourth nonaligned summit in Algeria (September 1973), the *New York Times* mentioned that Saudi Arabia did not attend, although the country's delegation was headed by King Faisal in person. A month later the oil embargo and price rises followed. The quantity of reporting on Saudi Arabia increased greatly, but its quality did not improve.

To earlier shortcomings was added a new distorting factor—a compound of fear and hostility in face of the threat which the oil weapon and visions of endlessly accumulating petro-dollars conjured up. While a *Washington Post* editorial of April 1973 dismissed the first Saudi warning linking oil and politics, it suggested that the "more important oil becomes, the less important the Arab-Israeli dispute." An editorial of 2 January 1974, in the same newspaper, noted the threat of a reduction in Saudi oil production and attacked the "feudal government and its aging monarch" over the King's position on terms of a settlement.[4]

Formidable handicaps thus exist to the analysis of the country's foreign policy decision-making. But available data on social structure, the economy, development plans, and oil policy are increasing, data that can be used to reveal the workings of the political system. In few countries is the relationship between foreign policy and the pattern of state formation and state structure so close.

The second section of this chapter discusses how elements of the domestic environment (geography, population, social structure, and the basis of political authority) affect foreign policy. The third section concentrates on foreign policy orientation, discusses Saudi Arabia's "Islamic theory of international relations," and examines whether the different components of Saudi Arabia's world view are consistent. The fourth section concentrates on decision-making and the role of different social groups. The fifth section uses several indicators to measure the tilt of Saudi international behavior toward the West, and examines how political-strategic interests determine its policy in the Arab system, in its own backyard (the Gulf region), and on the issue of oil within OPEC. The last section touches on the policy-maker's dilemma in the face of vertiginous social change and the limits of attempting to carry out a regional and world role through one-dimensional financial power. It emphasizes the importance of planning and managing foreign policy. Saudi foreign policy is the result of an interplay between Islam's legitimizing function, geostrategic determinants, oil power, and the use of "riyal politik"[5] as a privileged instrument of diplomacy.

2. THE DOMESTIC ENVIRONMENT

Geography and Population

The dominant historiographical trend accounting for the rise of the Saudi state is highly personalized and romanticized. An alternative thesis could emphasize the role of "objective" or ecological factors such as geography. These factors provide the parameters, the context, which limit the range of individual decisions.

The land of Saudi Arabia is barren, and its climatic conditions are harsh. Because of the aridity and relatively cloudless skies, the extremes of temperature range from 50°C in the summer to severe frosts and even weeks of snow in winter. Near the coast (the Gulf and the Red Sea), high atmospheric humidity makes living conditions extremely unpleasant. Several sociopolitical consequences follow from these geographical "givens."

First, in an age of colonial scramble, geographical hardships acted as a protective shield. To the south of Najd (the headquarters of the Al-Saud family) lies what is commonly known in Saudi Arabia as *Al-Ramla* or *El-Rimal*, literally "the Sands," commonly known in the West as Al-Rub-Al-Khali or the Empty Quarter. The first European to enter it was Bertram Thomas in 1930, and information about this region was gathered only after oil was discovered. Rainfall is rare at best, and sometimes stops altogether for as long as ten years, which explains why even local tribes only skirted its fringes. Ibn Saud realized this protective dimension of his country's geography when he said: "My kingdom will survive only as far as it remains a country of difficult access, where the foreigner will have no other aim with his task fulfilled, but to get out."[6]

The little agriculture that exists (about 0.2% of Saudi Arabia is under cultivation) is maintained only at subsistence level. As late as 1978, agriculture contributed only 2.4% of the non-oil gross domestic product, though it employed 30% of the population.[7] As a result, population settlement was rare, in the 1920s and 1930s, as people were literally on the run in search of rainfall and wells. This determined the pattern of state formation and the bases of political legitimacy.

Al-Badya, the bedouins or nomads, still made up 25% of the population in the 1970s.[8] Their society—least tarnished by foreign penetration or population settlement—is highly segmented. The nomadic social organization determines this population's skills and political culture (i.e., the basic values and beliefs governing political organization and practice), and makes accurate estimates of their number difficult.

TABLE 9.1
Saudi and Foreign Work Force in Saudi Arabia in 1980, by Occupational Group

Occupational Group	Saudi Workers		Foreign Workers	
	Number (thousands)	% Increase 1975-1980	Number (thousands)	% Increase 1975-1980
Managers and officials	8.7	1.3	12.4	6.1
Professionals	52.9	4.5	23.5	7.8
Technicians	33.4	8.4	81.3	49.9
Clerical workers	99.6	32.1	121.8	90.4
Sales workers	97.2	14.9	112.6	65.6
Service workers	134.5	29.3	145.2	98.1
Operatives	57.1	17.1	51.4	26.3
Skilled workers	93.5	23.4	101.9	54.8
Semiskilled workers	265.0	95.0	162.5	99.7

Source: Adapted from Ragaei El-Mallakh, *Saudi Arabia: Rush for Development* (London: Croom Helm, 1982), p. 116. El-Mallakh's figures are based on the estimates of the Saudi Ministry of Planning, as included in its publication *Second Development Plan 1395-1400/1975-1980* (Riyadh, 1976), p. 217 (1395-1400 refers to A.H., or *anno Hegirae*).

Estimates of Saudi Arabia's total population also vary.[9] On January 1, 1956, the estimate was 6,036,400. A census was held in 1962-1963, but the results were officially repudiated. In preparation for the Second Development Plan (1975–1980), a census was conducted in 1974, but the results were unclear. First reports put the census total at 4.3 million, but later, a figure of 7,012,642 was announced. In 1975, Saudi officials were still quoting the figure of 5 to 6 million. The UN estimates that total Saudi population rose from 7,251,000 in 1975 to 8,960,000 in 1980.

Whatever their number, no ambiguity exists about the level of skills of the general population. According to World Bank statistics, adult literacy did not exceed 16% in 1977.[10] This lack of basic skills has been a major handicap in the country's rush to development following the huge oil revenues of the 1970s. The First Development Plan (1970–1975) and the Second (1975–1980) spent as much as 31.1% and 25.2% respectively on human resource development.[11] However, the Saudi government still depended on foreign manpower to carry out the country's development projects. As late as 1980, foreign manpower—especially at the high managerial level—still outnumbered Saudis[12] (see Table 9.1). Saudi Arabia is thus dependent on the outside world not only for revenue but also for manpower, and with the influx of foreigners come foreign values and social practices. One dilemma of the Saudi policy-maker is how to maintain the development drive while keeping the society "untarnished."

The ruling elite's political culture is still the "untarnished" heritage of geography. The bedouin population is significant beyond mere numbers; its sociopolitical import is considerable. Helms reports that over

80% of the population of the Najd—the northeastern region of the Arabian Peninsula—presently identify themselves with some tribal group.[13] "Moreover, the present ruling elite . . . the Al-Saud, descends from one of the major Bedouin tribal confederations of Najd, the Anazah, a kinship affinity of which they are conscious and proud. The moral fabric, the social order, and the value system of Saudi society today cannot be fully comprehended without an understanding of its Bedouin component."[14]

Social Structure, Political Authority, and the Legitimizing Role of Islam

Two elements underline Saudi Arabia's social organization and political authority: the tribal system based on kinship and *asabiya* (sense of tribal solidarity) and Islam (of the strict Hanbali type). Whereas tribal organization constituted a formidable barrier to the constitution of a centralized state, Islam was the raison d'être of the impressive army, Al-Ikhwan (literally Moslem Brethren), who fought until central political authority was achieved in the late 1920s.

The inspiration for both Al-Ikhwan and the present Saudi state was a 1745 alliance between Sheikh Mohamed Abdel-Wahab (a strict Islamic revivalist who preached *Tawhid*, the unity of God, and aimed to purify Islam from innovation) and the Al-Saud (rulers of Dar'iyah in Najd in the center of Arabia). This first Saudi state came to an end in 1818, when Egyptian troops (in the name of the Ottoman caliph) and the Al-Rashid, forced the Al-Wahab–Al-Saud dynasty to take refuge in Kuwait. In 1901, Abdel-Aziz Al-Saud, with a handful of tribesmen, left their refuge to recapture Riyadh in 1902 and thus revive a kingdom based on the Al-Wahab–Al-Saud alliance. This was the second Saudi state. It took Abdel-Aziz thirty years and the help of Al-Ikhwan to establish his political control and declare the unified kingdom of Saudi Arabia in 1932.[15]

Saudi Arabia is modeled on the original Islamic state of the seventh century. It has no legal political parties. Its constitution is the Qur'an and its source of laws and regulations is the *Shari'a* or Islamic law. In March 1980, Crown Prince Fahd appointed a small committee of ministers, religious leaders, and judges. Under the chairmanship of his brother and minister of the interior, Prince Nayef, the committee drew up a basic system of government and prepared a formula for the establishment of a consultative council. Saudi government is based on Islamic principles, a direct result of the pattern of Saudi state formation and the role of Al-Ikhwan in this process.

The Ikhwan were bedouin warriors who left their nomadic life to settle down and lead a life consonant with Islamic teachings and practice.[16] Between the year of their establishment in 1913 and their demise in 1929 after their conflict with Abdel-Aziz Al-Saud, the Ikhwan were able to win for Abdel-Aziz every battle they fought.[17] The Ikhwan replaced tribal segmentation, eternal shifting balances, and *razzias* (tribal raids) with Islam as a unifying element, and thus transformed tribesmen from undisciplined warriors into an army. They achieved this task without losing the fervor and dedication typical of earlier intertribal wars. The political control scheme used to weaken the tribal bands was the establishment from 1912 to 1913 of *hijras*,[18] cooperative, agriculturally oriented colonies that recognized the Al-Saud as the holder of the lawful Islamic leadership, or imamate.[19] These *hijras*, which numbered between 200[20] and 222,[21] gave Abdel-Aziz in 1926 a formidable Ikhwan army of 150,000.[22]

Colonel Dickson, a British agent in Bahrain, described Abdel-Aziz's control scheme in 1920:

[Abdel-Aziz] would send for the Shaikh and tell him in blunt terms that his tribe had no religion and they were all "Juhl" [ignorant, like in pre-Islamic days]. He next ordered the Shaikh to attend the local school of ulama [religious scholars], which was attached to the great mosque in Riyadh, and there undergo a course of instruction in religion. At the same time half a dozen ulama, attended by some genuinely fanatical Akhwan . . . were sent off to the tribe itself. These held daily classes teaching the people all about Islam in its original simplicity. . . . When the Shaikh of the tribe was supposed to have received sufficient religious instruction, he was invited to build a house in Riyadh and remain in attendance on the Imam.[23]

In a rare letter dated January 17, 1928, Abdel-Aziz Al-Saud revealed to Dickson his acute awareness of the problems of political centralization in a segmented tribal society and the importance of Islam in coping with these problems. "The Government . . . has been established in this wide desert . . . by the virtue of the social teachings of religion . . . [which] made all the desert tribes within the lands under our control."[24]

3. FOREIGN POLICY ORIENTATION: THE PRIMACY OF ISLAM

The analyst is indeed struck by the prevalence of Islamic symbols in social values, political culture, state apparatus, and leadership declarations. Does domestic Islamism extend to the international scene through Saudi foreign policy? If so, to what degree, and in what form?

This question touches on one of the basic debates in foreign policy analysis: the importance of ideology or religion versus national political interest in determining a country's foreign policy. The most notable example of this debate is the controversy over Soviet foreign policy: is it primarily determined by the teachings of Marx and Engels, or by the perennial characteristics and objectives of the presocialist Russian state?

Even though the Qur'an contains no explicit theory of international relations, there is an Islamic view of the international system. This view developed with the establishment of the first Islamic state and its transformation into an empire. The basis of this Islamic world view was the dichotomy between *Dar Al-Islam* and *Dar Al-Harb* (territory of Islam versus territory of war). By propagating Islam through *jihad* (holy war), Moslems were to increase their *umma* (Islamic community) at the expense of *Dar Al-Harb*, the non-Moslem territory.

The fragmentation of the Islamic empire and the realities of international politics led to the decline of this classical Islamic view of the world. Even in the heart of the Arab world, many countries replaced the concept of *umma*, with its emphasis on religious identification, with the secular concept of "people," with its emphasis on citizenship. The latter was the basis of the Arab nationalist ideology of both Nasserism and Ba'thism. The Saudis reacted to this trend by emphasizing its foreignness to the Arab-Islamic tradition and by promoting even more ardently a pan-Islamic view of the world. In the heat of the confrontation between Nasserist pan-Arabism and Saudi pan-Islam in 1963, King Faisal expressed the inherent opposition between these two world views: "We do not need to import foreign traditions. We have a history and a glorious past. We led the Arabs and the World. With what did we lead them—the word of God and the Shariah [Islamic law] of His Prophet."[25]

Saudi ulamas joined in. They published articles to stress the foreign character and divisive function of secular Arab nationalism. One of those ulamas was Sheikh Abdel-Aziz Ibn Al-Baz, who in his *Critique of Arab Nationalism Based on Islam and Reality*, wrote:

> If advocates of Arab nationalism desire to raise the banner of Islam and rally the Arabs behind it, they would have advised the Arabs and urged them to follow Islamic principles and implement them. . . . Arab nationalism . . . was introduced by Christian Westerns to fight Islam. . . . Many Arabs, opponents of Islam, adopted this call and were followed by ignorants . . . [Thus Arab nationalism] is an assault against Islam and its followers. A number of reasons can be given: the call to Arab nationalism differentiates between Moslems; it separates the non-Arab Moslem from his Arab brother; it divides the Arabs among themselves, because not all of them accept it; any idea that creates divisions in the ranks of Moslems is rejected, because Islam calls for unity, solidarity and cooperation to help the poor and enforce the word of God.[26]

Does this then mean that the kingdom's policy-makers give priority to the Moslem world[27] rather than the Arab region?[28] For many Saudis, no such distinction is feasible, since Arabs are part of the *umma*. Geography and history play a part in determining this world view, for Arabia was both the cradle of Islam and of the Arabs, and thus the two are hardly separable or even distinguishable. Consequently we can redraw the basics of the Saudi world view as shown in Figure 9.1.

As for the non-Moslem world, it is seen as a potential threat to the essence of *umma* and its norms. The West, however, is preferred to the

FIGURE 9.1
The Structure and Components of the Saudi World View

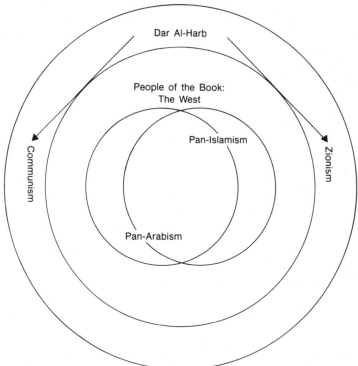

Source: Adapted from David Long, "King Faisal's World View," in Willard Beling (ed.), *King Faisal and the Modernization of Saudi Arabia* (Boulder, Colo.: Westview Press, 1980), p. 176.

East, more out of necessity than moral choice. Close cooperation with the West and not the East is justified on the grounds that the East's Communist, revolutionary doctrine, its materialist theory of history, and its atheism are more morally abhorrent and dangerous to the kingdom's policy-makers.

How does Zionism, the West's stepchild and its ally, fit into the Saudi world view? The three main sources of tension according to the Saudi world view are Zionism, radical Islamic regimes such as Qaddafi's Libya and Khomeini's Iran, and the Soviet bloc. The Saudi policy-makers have faced each in such a way as to emphasize harmony and consistency in their world view.

Zionism. Israel has been the privileged ally of the West, especially of the United States. It is with the United States that Saudi Arabia maintains the highest level of cooperation, and hence Saudi Arabia and

Israel end up being *objectively* in the same camp. Saudi policy-makers have reacted to this dilemma by emphasizing Zionism's early association with socialist ideology and the Communist political backing it received in the initial stages of Israel's creation. Moreover, to show that they are not soft on Israel, Saudis emphasize the pan-Islamic dimension of the Arab-Israeli conflict. The 1967 occupation of Jerusalem—the third holiest city in Islam—helped them to promote this pan-Islamic dimension and thus put Saudi Arabia at the forefront of the anti-Israel coalition. In 1969, following the fire in Al-Aqsa Mosque, Saudi efforts succeeded in convening the First Pan-Islamic Conference, in Rabat, Morocco. Moreover, King Faisal had talked repeatedly of his desire to pray at Al-Aqsa Mosque. After his assassination in 1975, his successors continued the attempt to mobilize all Moslems and Arabs behind this demand and thus behind Saudi policy. Saudi leaders have also seized the opportunity of the annual pilgrimage to Mecca to emphasize, as King Khaled did during the 1977 pilgrimage ceremonies, "the regaining of the third holiest mosque in Jerusalem, and noble Jerusalem itself, and for clearing them of all the impurities."[29] To emphasize this pan-Islamic context of the conflict with Israel, the Saudi foreign minister stated in May 1977 his opposition to Israel's attempt to transform the "Jerusalem problem from a religious to a political one."[30] Several statements by Saudi officials refer to jihad as the only means of confronting Israel, but these statements make clear that jihad does not mean outright war, but rather the mobilization of all resources for a concentrated effort in the political, diplomatic, economic, and military fields.[31]

It is in this context that Saudis tend to defend their close relations with the West, Israel's prime backers. Not only is the West the privileged source of sophisticated technology and necessary arms, it can also be pressured to reduce its support for Israel or at least moderate its policies. In this respect, they emphasize to their Western partners—especially the United States—Zionism's destabilizing effects in the region. They argue, for instance, that the 1947–1948 defeat of traditional Arab regimes encouraged the rise of a radical Arab order and brought Soviet influence into the region—both unwelcome risks to stability. As late as 1981, Sheikh Zaki Yamani, the Saudi oil minister, used this argument with Western journalists. "When the United States, due to internal political pressures, refrains from performing its duty in bringing peace to the area, it thereby serves the Russian interests, to the detriment of its own interests and perhaps those of Israel itself."[32]

Islamic Radical Regimes. Conflicts with the radical Islamic regimes are the most serious for Saudi Arabia since they strike at the very basis of the Saudi state and its legitimacy. Consequently each side has tended to put up a die-hard defense of its concept of Islam, even though the conflicts have had other sources. During the 1970s and early 1980s, the Saudi kingdom faced serious challenges from two activist and radical Islamic regimes almost on its doorstep; Qaddafi's Libya (1969–) and Khomeini's Iran (1979–).

Although both Libya and Saudi Arabia claim Islam as the basis of their regimes, the gap between the Saudis' conservative version of Islam and Libya's radical one has kept the two countries' world views far apart. They tend to disagree strongly on everything from military relations with their respective patrons to oil policy. For instance, in October 1980 the Saudi government invited the United States to send four AWACS planes to use Saudi airfields as a base for observing the evolution of the Iran-Iraq war to detect any potential threats to oil lines or to the kingdom itself. This was the occasion for a diatribe by Qaddafi against Saudi leaders. On October 19, 1980, he urged Moslem pilgrims not to make the traditional trip to Mecca that year because Saudi Arabia and its Moslem holy places were "under U.S. occupation," and he urged jihad to liberate them.[33] King Khaled replied in person to Qaddafi, "It is regretful to see you join Israel, the enemy of Islam and the Moslems, in opposing our request [for the AWACS's visit]. You have proved that you have become a spearhead against Islam and its sanctities."[34] Three days later the Saudi foreign ministry announced the country's decision to break off diplomatic relations with Libya because Qaddafi "was disparaging Islam and sowing discord among the Moslem people."[35] Though Islam seemed to be at the center of the controversy, Libya's siding with Iran was the immediate cause of this Saudi-Libyan name calling.

Seventeen months later, there was another verbal flare-up between the two governments. The immediate cause was their divergent oil policies. Radio Tripoli quoted Qaddafi as saying that Saudi "overproduction" was deliberate "in order to serve the imperialist interests of the U.S. and to undercut oil producers." Typically, the controversy spilled over to the two countries' policy orientations. At the beginning of March 1982, Qaddafi called for a revolt in the Saudi kingdom and said that "the Saudi oil income of more than $100 billion a year is shared by 5,000 princes of the royal family."[36] The Saudi mass media counterattacked. The Saudi daily *Al-Madina* stated that Qaddafi "has afflicted the Arabs like the plague."[37] *Al-Nadwah* accused him of using Libyan oil income to serve the cause of world Communism "by helping international terrorists" instead of helping his own people.[38] *Al-Jazirah*, in an editorial quoted by Radio Riyadh, continued the same theme. Colonel Qaddafi, it said, "is a perfect example of a communist agent." It charged that he had been financing "terrorist movements" in the world, and that he "murdered" Imam Musa Al-Sadr, the spiritual head of Lebanon's Shi'ite Moslems.[39] On March 11, Saudi Arabia called for Libya's expulsion from the Arab League and from the Organization of African Unity. A week later, the Saudi-based Council of High Ulamas described Colonel Qaddafi as a heretic and "a devout servant of evil," who had publicly ridiculed the teachings of Islam, urged pilgrims not to go to Mecca, and dedicated himself to spreading anarchy and dissension.[40]

On December 31, 1982, however, diplomatic relations were resumed. A joint statement issued simultaneously in Riyadh and Tripoli on

December 30, 1982, emphasized the need to insure unity of Arab ranks to face the common enemy, an allusion to Israel and its invasion of Lebanon. This resumption of relations, however, did not change the divergence in the two countries' world views.

Khomeini's Iran, though not Arab, is the major power in the Gulf, Saudi Arabia's strategic underbelly. Before Khomeini's rise to power, Saudi relations with Iran followed contradictory lines. On the one hand, there was competition and mutual fear, as shown by the arms flowing to the two countries. On the other hand, they had a common interest in preventing the political upheavals of radical ideologies (from Iraq or South Yemen) from upsetting either their traditional domestic political structure, or the balance within the peninsula and the Gulf region. This mutual interest led to routine relations conducted on a friendly basis and an unwritten agreement during King Faisal's reign (1964–1975) regarding "areas of influence." The Saudis were apparently allowed a relatively free hand within the peninsula, while Iran was allowed preponderance in the Gulf waters.[41]

When serious resistance developed against the shah's regime in 1978–1979, the official Saudi reaction was that the events were an "internal Iranian affair."[42] Nevertheless, official Saudi statements tilted in favor of the shah's regime "based on legitimacy." Several Saudi commentators denounced the alliance between "religious extremists in favor of the subversive ideologies" and the "Communist Tudeh party" that undermined the rule of the "legitimate authority." As for Khomeini, they condemned him and his "clique" for advocating "these wrong subversive ideologies" and criticized Khomeini's "involvement" with and "trust" of the Communists.[43] Once the shah's demise and Khomeini's rise were accomplished, the serious threat to the kingdom became more concrete and immediate.

First, repeated calls to overthrow the Saudi regime made by Tehran were combined with propaganda campaigns among Shi'ites in Hasa and pilgrims in Mecca. Secondly, Iran's radical posture was viewed by the Saudis as considerably increasing uncertainty about the security of the Gulf in general, and that of the Straits of Hormuz in particular. Thirdly, there were Iranian threats against some of the Gulf principalities, considered to be the Saudi "soft underbelly," and above all, there was a revival of the Iranian claim for ownership over Bahrain on historical and religious grounds.[44]

Yet when the war broke out between Iran and Iraq in September 1980, Riyadh had difficulty choosing between two radicals. Instead, it maintained adherence to the principle of Islamic solidarity. In an interview in New York on October 5, 1980, Saudi foreign minister Saud Al-Faisal affirmed his government's neutral stand. Al-Faisal insisted that "the conflict between two brother Muslim countries . . . has to be brought speedily to termination. It is not a conflict [in which] we want to support one side against the other in order to gain advantage. . . . It is a fratricidal war."[45]

However, by December 1981, Saudi policy-makers emphasized the threat from Khomeini's regime to the Gulf countries and to the legitimacy of these regimes. Relations between the two countries started to deteriorate. On December 1, 1981, the Saudi newspaper *Okaz* countered Khomeini's attack on Fahd's eight-point Middle East peace plan (issued on August 8, 1981). The editorial accused the ayatollah of cooperating with Israel in draining Iraq's energy away from the conflict with Israel.[46] In the same month, and after an attempted coup in Bahrain (allegedly backed by Iran), the Saudi minister of the interior, Prince Nayef, signed a security accord with Bahrain. Nayef accused Iran of training, arming, and financing terrorists with the aim of undermining stability throughout the Gulf.[47] He declared that "the Iranians, who said after their revolution that they did not want to be the policemen of the Gulf, have become the terrorists of the Gulf."[48] Consequently, Saudi Arabia "placed its entire potential in the service of Bahrain's security."[49] As for the Iran-Iraq war, it was no longer considered a fratricidal war. Nayef believed that Iraq's war against Iran was "not in defense of its lands and sovereignty alone, but also of the whole Arab nation" and that "Saudi Arabia stands with Iraq in the same position . . . in facing the dangers confronting the Arabs."[50] Consequently, on December 26, 1981, Saudi Arabia and Iraq signed an agreement ending a border dispute nearly sixty years old amid signs of growing cooperation between the two countries against Iran.[51]

Disturbances by Iranian pilgrims against the Saudi regime and Khomeini's repeated declarations that monarchy is incompatible with the Qur'an's basic tenets show the degree of divergence between the two countries in the politics of Islam. This is the main reason Saudi Arabia and the other Gulf regimes are bailing Iraq out, enabling it to continue the war.

The Soviet Bloc and Saudi Nonalignment

One of the basic components of Saudi foreign policy orientation is nonalignment. Saudi Arabia is a founder-member of the nonaligned movement, and has participated in five out of the seven summit conferences (1961–1983), yet Saudi Arabia has no diplomatic relations with the Soviet bloc; all its relations are with the West. The Soviet Union was, however, one of the very first countries to recognize Abdel-Aziz Al-Saud's new authority and to establish diplomatic relations in the 1930s. Moreover, the Soviet bloc has been in the forefront in supporting the Arab cause, whether against the old colonial empires or against Israel since 1954. Did not these countries (with the exception of Rumania) break off diplomatic relations with Israel following its initiation of the 1967 Six-Day War?

This absence of Saudi-Soviet relations is not due to a lack of Soviet overtures. On January 30, 1979, Igor Bilayev, one of the leading Soviet specialists on the Arab world, stated in an article in *Literaturnaya Bazeta* that Saudi Arabia and the USSR "had never fought each other" and had never had "any insoluble conflict." Instead of continuing the earlier Soviet practice of labeling the kingdom "reactionary," "feudalist," the "Kingdom of Darkness," the article portrayed the country in sympathetic terms and stressed common positions, such as the rejection of the Camp David Accords.[52] Although he adopted a conciliatory tone in the context of U.S. support of Camp David and its "inaction" in the face of Khomeini's threatening regime, Prince Fahd continued to talk about "ideological differences" with the Soviet Union and stated that "the question of diplomatic relations is . . . premature."[53]

The Saudis fear the Soviet military threat,[54] the revolutionary ethos of its doctrine, and the radicalism of its regional allies, but they couch their distrust in terms of inherent opposition between spiritual Islam and atheist, materialist Communism. When Soviet troops entered Afghanistan in late 1979, the Saudis capitalized on this action to defend their position. The Saudis emphasized the strategic-political dangers of the Soviet move as well as the threat against Moslem peoples as a whole. Oil Minister Yamani warned that the main motive "of the Soviets was the oil fields and the Soviets' future oil needs."[55] In the same spirit, Foreign Minister Saud Al-Faisal suggested that the Soviet presence so close to the Straits of Hormuz was merely "a step in the direction of the sources of oil in the Gulf."[56]

In addition, most Saudi statements carried strong Islamic overtones, claiming that "the hour of confrontation between Islam and Communism had begun violently," and that "the atheist threat" had to be checked.[57] Consequently, the Saudi newspaper *Al-Bilad* called on January 1, 1980, for a meeting of heads of state to lay down a common strategy on "the Soviet threat . . . [which] is pointed directly at the Islamic faith."[58] The Saudi government played a leading role in convening the Islamic conference in Islamabad (Pakistan) in late January. In his speech to the conference, Saud Al-Faisal described the Soviet action as a "flagrant challenge to the Islamic world, a gross disregard for Moslems and Islam."[59] The conference ended by supporting the Saudi position. It condemned "Soviet military aggression against the Afghan people," called for the "immediate and unconditional withdrawal of all Soviet troops," and urged the Soviets to "refrain from acts of oppression and tyranny against the Afghan people and their struggling sons." The conference suspended Afghanistan's membership in the Organization of the Islamic Conference, discouraged recognition of, and recommended severing diplomatic relations with, "the illegal regime in Afghanistan," affirming "solidarity with the Afghan people in their just struggle to safeguard their faith, national independence and territorial integrity." Stating its "complete solidarity with the Islamic countries neighbouring

Afghanistan," the conference called for the collection of "contributions from member states, organizations, and individuals" in support of the rebels, and for "nonparticipation in Olympic Games being held in Moscow in July 1980."[60]

In cases like these,[61] Saudi policy-makers attempt to reconcile the kingdom's immediate strategic interests and its inherent Islamic beliefs. Consistency among the different components of the Saudi world view is important to reinforce the regime's legitimacy. This brings us to the Kingdom's pattern of foreign policy decision-making.

4. THE ROLE OF GROUPS IN DECISION-MAKING

Given the paucity of financial resources in the majority of Third World countries, many leaders would be happy to trade places with Saudi Arabia's policy-makers. The country's reserves rose from under $4 billion in 1973 to over $30 billion in 1977, surpassed only by those of West Germany for that year. Its foreign assets were around $100 billion and its oil revenue was $102 billion in 1981.[62] However, because of the structure of political authority, and because of the regional and global contexts they must work with, Saudi policy-makers face hard choices.

For instance, in September 1978, President Sadat continued his go-it-alone diplomacy and signed the Camp David agreements with Israel under the U.S. umbrella. Radical Arab states—with whom Saudi Arabia has little in common politically—championed an anti-Sadat coalition and held the Baghdad conference to ostracize Egypt. Saudi Arabia went along with this, but the choice was not an easy one. On the one hand, the Saudi regime could not support Sadat and the United States lest it be labeled reactionary and a renegade to the Arab cause and Islam. Moreover, Syria and the PLO might react to any Saudi alignment with U.S.-Egyptian-Israeli positions by seeking increased Soviet involvement in the region. On the other hand, Saudi Arabia did not wish to overthrow Sadat, sharing as it did the basics of his strategic outlook, his anti-Soviet stance, and his emphasis on U.S. partnership. In the face of such hard choices, Saudi policy-makers usually drag their feet while working to avoid polarization and a clear-cut alignment.

These dilemmas reflect the contradictions in the Saudi polity itself. As Quandt put it succinctly, Saudi Arabia

is a monarchy, but the King is only one among several key personalities who participate in most important decisions. It is a family enterprise, but the family itself is not united and commoners are anxious to gain power. It is an Islamic state, but secular influences are everywhere present. It is an authoritarian government, but access to rulers is comparatively easy and citizens' demands for individual redress of grievances are often met. It is a society avidly seeking the comforts of the modern world, but traditional elements such as tribes remain influential. It is a country in which unbelievable wealth coexists alongside pockets of subsistence-level poverty.[63]

Thus the locus of foreign policy decision-making is not limited to the foreign ministry, with its prestigious, Princeton-educated young minister and its 500 diplomats.[64] Even at the technical level, jurisdiction does not seem to be clear. Rather, the decision-making process has the following four characteristics:

First, there is an organic link between domestic and foreign policies because of the historical legacy of the state. As a result, foreign policy decision-making is not limited to the ministers of defence, oil, or the head of intelligence, but includes other members of the elite (the royal family or religious establishment) whose primary concern might be domestic. Second, although the power of the Al-Saud family is paramount, other groups do participate and wield differing degrees of influence depending on the issue area. For instance, in the field of relations with foreign Islamic groups, the role of the ulama is substantial.

The third characteristic of Saudi decision-making is that much bargaining occurs before an important decision is announced. In some cases, there can be an "ambiguous" decision or a "nondecision" because of the necessities of compromise or the need to avoid serious dissension. The tendency is to defer and delay issues, especially when they are unduly divisive or difficult to cope with. Quandt gives an example:

> Many foreigners have been concerned about the vulnerability of Saudi oil-fields to sabotage or attack. When asked, most Saudis will avoid the issue. In private they may acknowledge that they are worried, but since no easy solution can be found, a public stance of denial is adopted. This has the virtue, perhaps, of not advertising one's vulnerability . . . but it may also have the effect of preventing serious discussion of the issue altogether.[65]

This points up the fourth characteristic of the slow and improvised process of Saudi decision-making. The Saudi leadership often feels "lost" in crisis situations (e.g., the 1979 Mecca incident, the Iran-Iraq war). Unable to cope, the leadership usually turns to outside powers to settle the problem. French expertise in "counterterrorist" activities was sought during the Mecca incident, and U.S. AWACS planes were invited in at the beginning of the Iran-Iraq war. In brief, Sadat's style of "electric shock diplomacy" is inconceivable in Saudi decision-making. Despite the consistency of the different elements of the Saudi world view, Saudi Arabia's foreign policy behavior is plagued with delays and a failure to follow through.

These four characteristics are influenced by the increasing complexity of Saudi Arabia's regional and global environment, and by the growing demand on the country to perform an active role. More importantly, these characteristics reflect the multiplicity of groups participating in the decision-making process.

The Royal Family and the Foreign Ministry

The country's name—Saudi Arabia—indicates to whom belongs, in theory and practice, the final power to decide. No one seems to know the exact number of the royal family's male members, let alone its female ones. Estimates range from 3,000 to 5,000, a figure equivalent to the number of dedicated members in an effective political party in most Third World countries. This is why an analysis of Saudi decision-making cannot be based on the role of one man or his psychological traits. To understand Saudi decision-making, one must understand Al-Saud family politics: the structure of relations between brothers from different mothers, between senior and junior princes, and between traditional and Western-educated family members; and the techniques of consensus-building that ensure the family's survival.

This structure of family politics is the direct result of the formation of the Saudi state. Very few leadership patterns in the Arab world mirror the state of their society as well as that of the Al-Saud of the Najd region. As mentioned earlier, to achieve primacy Abdel-Aziz Al-Saud formed an alliance with Sheikh Abdel-Wahab and used religion to offset tribal affiliation and social segmentation. To consolidate Al-Saud's overall and hereditary control, Abdel-Aziz formed strong alliances through marriage with the Sudairi, Ibn Jelawi, and Shammar tribes. Estimates put the number of Abdel-Aziz's legal wives at 15, producing 37 to 45 sons, 150 grandsons, and 500 great-grandsons.[66] If his 10 brothers produced the same number of progeny, the majority of the country's settled inhabitants could easily be Al-Saud family members.

Though intertribal marriage guaranteed allegiance, it also created disunity and tension among royal family members with different maternal/tribal affiliations.[67] Competition and tension increased when seniority was not followed as the basis of accession to the throne. For instance, Abdel-Aziz's fourth son, Mohamed, gave up his claim to the throne in favor of the fifth son, Khaled (1975–1982). Tension within the family is also created when a strong individual or clan attempts to accumulate maximum power and hence threaten the share of the others. The death of Khaled (a Jelawi) could have created fears and opened the succession issue within the family. With the accession of Fahd (the head of the strong "Sudairi Seven") to the throne, and the presence of his two full brothers at the head of crucial ministries (Sultan for defense, and Nayef for the interior), the balance of power among the different clans was threatened. Thus, it was mandatory that Abdallah become the crown prince. Though he has no full brothers to assist him in the contest for power, his mother belongs to the strong Shammar tribe of the North, a tribe which has traditionally been hostile to the authority of Al-Saud. In addition, Abdallah has been the head of the dedicated National Guard since 1962.

Whether a member of the royal family will belong to the inner circle of decision-makers depends on several factors: age, clan affiliation, and the balance of power within the family.[68] In 1958, when Saud was endangering the family's rule by his mismanagement of the country's resources and his inability to cope with the Nasserist tide, the senior princes limited his powers and finally forced him to abdicate in favor of his half-brother, Faisal.

Very few leaders have had such long and direct association with foreign policy as Faisal.[69] In 1919, at the age of thirteen, he was appointed by his father to head the Saudi delegation to the Paris peace conference, after which he met King George in London. In 1930, four years after the establishment of the foreign ministry structure, Faisal was put in charge of it. From the age of twenty-four until his death in 1975 at the age of sixty-nine (with the exception of the December 1960–March 1962 period of conflict with Saud), Faisal was almost supreme in foreign policy.[70] He was the king's representative in Hejaz from 1925 until his father's death in 1953. Hejaz held a very distinct international status because of the annual arrival there of the Moslem world's dignitaries to perform the pilgrimage to Mecca. Faisal's repeated involvement in world politics, as well as the autonomous budget he handled, reinforced his position within the royal family. He brought the country's international relations under his own jurisdiction. Even when he became the official head of state, Faisal retained the post of foreign minister and appointed only a deputy foreign minister and some advisors.

Since the establishment of the Saudi kingdom, the foreign ministry has evolved very slowly. When first established in 1926, it was called the Directorate of Foreign Affairs, and consisted of four departments (legal, political, administrative, and consular). The royal decree stipulated that Abdel-Aziz would be responsible for the first two departments and Faisal for the others. When the directorate became a ministry and Faisal minister, he was assisted by a director-general and fifteen civil servants. The 1930 decree stipulated, though, that the king was still in charge, and it limited the authority of the minister. In 1954, a year after Abdel-Aziz's death, the ministry was reorganized, following Western models, and Faisal was put completely in charge. This coincided with Faisal's official nomination as president of the council of ministers, after becoming its de facto head a few months earlier.[71]

The work of the ministry increased in scope and complexity. At the *bureaucratic level*, it grew from a few departments into a complicated structure with a permanent undersecretary and deputy and assistant deputy ministers to head the six major departments and desks: diplomatic missions abroad, Western affairs, Afro-Asian, Islamic, petroleum, and Arab affairs. Additional functional, or technical, desks were established to deal with commercial, financial, and cultural affairs.[72] Supporting these departments are the offices of protocol, consular affairs, administration, cables and wireless, and public relations and press.[73] The technical nondiplomatic support staff for this bureaucratic structure numbered about 500 civil servants in 1982.[74] A diplomatic institute on the model of institutions such as Vienna's Diplomatic Academy or Cairo's Diplomatic Institute was established in the late 1970s to give young diplomats the proper training.[75]

At the *diplomatic representations* level, the ministry's work expanded to keep pace with Saudi Arabia's increasing international status. In 1937, the kingdom had but three delegations (in Cairo, London, and Baghdad) and two consulates. In mid-1983, the ministry organized a general consultation and evaluation meeting for its seventy ambassadors.[76]

Given the increasing complexity of the kingdom's international relations, even Faisal had to delegate authority. In April 1968 a royal decree instituted the post of minister of state for foreign affairs and entrusted it to Omar Al-Saqqaf. The position was filled by Mohamed Masood after Saqqaf's death, and passed to Faisal's son Saud in March 1975 after Faisal's assassination.

The product of "inherited" and "achieved" social status, Saud Al-Faisal is typical of the new generation of young royal technocrats. Born in 1941 to Faisal's most favored wife (Iffat Bint Ahmed Al-Thunayyan), he was tutored by his father and by Kamal Adham, King Faisal's Turkish-born brother-in-law and his intelligence chief. But Saud is also the prototype of the bright, ambitious, college-educated second generation of Saudi princes. A graduate in economics from Princeton, he is particularly skillful in addressing the U.S. public, and has done well in international conferences. Saud attended the 1980 Islamic conference in Pakistan, which condemned the Soviet intervention in Afghanistan.[77] In January 1983, he was the first Saudi foreign minister to visit Beijing (Saudi Arabia has diplomatic relations only with Taiwan) as a member of the Arab summit's delegation on the Palestinian question. Saud emphasizes the centrality of the Palestinian issue in the Arab-Israeli conflict, and believes in linking oil politics to this conflict.

As foreign minister, Saud Al-Faisal has worked with two kings: Khaled and Fahd. Khaled was very different from his predecessor, King Faisal. Frequently described as a "man of the desert," he was interested in the society's traditional groups and in practicing the time-honored sport of falconry. Khaled's poor health forced him to delegate authority, and consequently the number of participants in decision-making increased. Press reports talked about the Khaled-Fahd "duarchy"[78] as a decision-making system. Other influential princes were also increasingly involved in the decision-making process. Sultan, the defence minister; Nayef, the interior minister; and Abdallah, head of the National Guard, negotiated agreements of international cooperation or arms deals. Abdallah intensified his Arab contacts, and in 1980 he capitalized upon his close relations with Syria's president Asad and the president's brother and intelligence chief, Rifa'at Al-Asad, to successfully mediate the rising tension between Syria and Jordan. Even nonmembers of the royal family, like Faisal's protégé Zaki Yamani, accrued influence. Yamani, in conjunction with Fahd, had great freedom in oil affairs. This attenuation, after Faisal's death in 1975, of the one-man primacy in foreign affairs did not change the structural characteristics of decision-making. Senior princes still had their word, and secrecy in visits, payments, and agreements was still the order of the day.[79]

In terms of foreign policy decision-making, King Fahd is bound to follow the Faisal pattern more closely than Khaled. Before Khaled's death, Fahd was already the kingdom's strong man, described by an informed scholar as being "the single most important figure in shaping Saudi foreign policy."[80] Some consider him more pro-American and less anti-Egyptian than many of the other influential senior princes, such as Crown Prince Abdallah. Abdallah, a harsh critic of U.S. foreign policy on the Palestinian question, told a *Time*-sponsored delegation of businessmen and editors visiting Saudi Arabia in 1981 that the most dangerous threat to the Middle East was not the USSR, as the Reagan administration had argued, but the United States. He explained: "I say this because of your total alliance with Israel, which makes the mass of our people take it for granted that Americans are anti-Arab, and makes it convenient for the Arab people to look to the Soviet Union as a friend, since they feel they have been abandoned by the Americans."[81]

This difference in view between the two top men of the kingdom helps to balance the different factions of the royal family's power system. Abdallah's influence, together with that of Saud Al-Faisal, prevents a monopoly of the Sudairi Seven over decision-making and keeps foreign policy from being Fahd's show alone.

The Religious Establishment: The Ulama

Due to its historical legacy, Saudi Arabia considers itself the guardian of Islam and Islamic values throughout the world. Islam is more than a religion; it is a way of life in the kingdom. As a result, the ulama's influence is all-pervasive. They participate directly in decision-making, but more importantly, they shape the social values and the frame of reference of those who judge issues, determine political priorities, decree legal practices, and interpret behavioral results. The views of the ulama are at the basis of the social fabric and the regime's legitimacy. Are they not called "Ahl al-hal wa al-akd," the final arbiters and definitive decision-makers?

The ulama's direct influence in decision-making follows three channels: (1) direct and privileged access to the highest locus of decision-making; (2) monopoly over some ministries and areas of policy, and (3) popular mobilization.

Through Wahabism, the religious establishment was a partner in both the establishment and management of the Saudi state. The Al-Shaikh family of Abdel-Wahab enjoyed continuous prestige and intermarried with the Al-Saud family. King Faisal's mother was from the Al-Shaikh family. Even prominent ulama who were not members of the Al-Shaikh family enjoyed influence, for Abdel-Aziz permitted them direct access to the Majlis, the council that directed the state's affairs. In addition, the ulama had a regular weekly meeting with the king on Thursday afternoons, during which views were exchanged and policy coordinated.[82] Subsequent kings followed the tradition of the Thursday meeting.[83]

Traditionally, the religious establishment has monopolized the Ministries of Education, Justice, Pilgrimage Affairs, and *Awqaf* (religious endowments); the Departments of Missionary Activities, Religious Research, and *Ifta* (verdicts); and the Committee for Commanding the Good and Forbidding the Evil.[84] The influence and activities of these institutions far exceed that of their secular counterparts. If the ulama have not managed to monopolize the Saudi government, they have at least created a parallel one.

Through the regular Friday sermon, usually well attended, the ulama have a public forum to question or support not only religious issues, but also social values and political and economic practices. As a result, their views on Arab and Moslem affairs are very influential. Historically, the ulama have arbitrated intra-elite conflicts. In 1929, Abdel-Aziz had to separate from his formidable army of Al-Ikhwan, but first he needed to secure his continuing legitimacy with the ulama, through a *fatwa* (a religious verdict) that he had not deviated from the right Islamic path. Abdel-Aziz was also willing to delay the introduction of Western mechanical equipment—wireless communications, telegraph, and automobiles—until the ulama were persuaded to give their sanction. In 1950, when the ulama objected to the king's plans to celebrate a golden jubilee marking the fiftieth anniversary (in lunar years) of the capture of Riyadh from the Al-Rashid, the project was duly abandoned.[85] In 1958, when conflict raged within the royal family, the ulama's pressure was crucial in allowing Faisal to take Saud's place. When Faisal himself was assassinated in 1975, the designation of Khaled as his successor had to be approved by the ulama. Last but not least, when the Al-Saud dynasty faced its most serious challenge during the 1979 Mecca incident, even military necessities were subordinated to the ulama's verdict: the counterattack to dislodge the rebels had to await the ulama's green light.

The Military

The Al-Saud family has ambiguous feelings about the armed forces. On the one hand, increased covetousness and threats from the outside are factors pushing the government to strengthen the armed forces. On the other hand, Third World and Arab experience shows that the armed forces are usually serious contenders for political power: Syria had three coups d'état in 1949; the military took power in Egypt in 1952, in neighboring North Yemen in 1962, in Algeria in 1965, and in Libya and the Sudan in 1969. Even in countries where the military are not *formally* in power, a few violent attempts have occurred (e.g., Morocco in 1970–1971). Is it coincidence that in 1934, after the brief war with Yemen, and Saudi Arabia's acquisition of Najran, the army was disbanded entirely?[86]

The 1962–1967 Yemen war greatly revived interest in the army. As a result, in the mid-1960s a huge program of military modernization was begun. The 1967 Arab defeat at the hands of Israel made the Saudi government realize that for both domestic and regional political reasons, it was dangerous not to have at least token military participation in the Arab-Israeli conflict. The 1968 British announcement of its intention to withdraw from the Gulf then stripped the region of its permanent foreign military protection.

With the oil boom of the 1970s, the military modernization program progressed rapidly, at least in terms of hardware. The military sector, like the civil sector, suffers from a chronic manpower shortage, especially of skilled personnel. From 1979 to 1981, despite huge investments in training, incentives, and the building of facilities,[87] the armed forces only rose from 36,000 to 47,000 men. Because of the manpower shortage, there has been a conscious effort to create a capital-intensive military force. Defense expenditures rose from $387 million in 1969 to $24.4 billion in 1981, and was to be $28 billion, or 25% of GNP, in 1982.[88] Defense has been the largest expense in the three development plans. At least 105 arms purchase agreements were made between 1970 and 1982.

To counterbalance any potential danger from the military to the present structure of decision-making in the kingdom, the royal family adopted three "insurance policies."

The first is the presence of members of the royal family within the army, not only at the top but also at lower levels of command. Sultan, King Fahd's full brother, has been minister of defense since 1962. Fahd Ibn Abdallah is head of air force operations, Turki Al-Faisal heads intelligence, and Bandar Ben Sultan (recently appointed ambassador to the United States) has been a practicing and influential pilot.

Second, the training of military personnel has been entrusted to "safe" hands. In the 1950s, Saudi Arabia was in conflict with Britain over the Buraimi Oasis on the frontiers with Kuwait, and so sent Saudi military cadets to Egypt's military training schools. But in the late 1950s, long before the 1962 Yemen revolution, the royal family stopped this practice to eliminate any risk of socialization in Nasserist ideology. This left the United States, which now enjoys a virtual monopoly in the training of Saudi army personnel. Between 1973 and 1977, no less than 4,300[89] upcoming officers of the army, navy, and air force were sent for varying periods of training in the United States. Additional cadets were sent to the U.S. base in Bahrain. Moreover, the armed forces are supervised by the U.S. government or its companies at the structural level. The U.S.-Saudi Joint Commission on Security and Cooperation was established in the 1970s. Bendix Corporation is very involved in the army, Lockheed in the air force,[90] and Northrop in the development of military personnel. In addition, there are about 40,000 U.S. military men and women in different parts of Saudi Arabia.[91]

As a final protection, the government maintains other autonomous military institutions. Prominent among these are the National Guard, the Royal Guard, and to a lesser extent, the Coast Guard and Frontier Force, but most important is the National Guard. Estimates of its strength vary from 20,000 to 35,000 men.[92] The National Guard developed out of the White Army (composed of swordsmen), which in turn was a later version of the old Ikhwan army of the 1920s. The National Guard is composed of loyal tribesmen, who receive the same incentives (land and cash) as the personnel of the regular army. Since 1962 they have been under the direct command of Crown Prince Abdallah, Fahd's half-brother. In 1975, serious efforts were made to modernize the National Guard and provide it with armored cars and other mechanized weaponry. In 1975, a $77 million contract was awarded to the U.S. Vinnell Corporation to train the guard and modernize its methods.[93] At present, the guard is becoming computerized. It was the National Guard's responsibility to flush out the attackers who took the Ka'aba Mosque in Mecca in November 1979.[94]

As a further protective measure against excessive military pressure on the decision-making process, two Pakistani brigades have been stationed in Saudi Arabia as part of the close cooperation policy between the two countries.[95]

The Technocrats

Technocrats are the representatives par excellence of what M. Halpern[96] dubbed "the new middle class." The influence of this class does not depend on family origin, tribal convictions, religious support, or other traditional qualifications. The influence and upward mobility of technocrats depend, above all, on education, training, expertise, skill, and talent. These qualifications have been in demand since the establishment of the kingdom's first Council of Ministers in 1953 and the subsequent establishment of technical ministries. Abdallah Tariki was oil minister until 1965,[97] followed by Zaki Yamani. The influence of this class was increasingly felt with the rush to development that followed the 1970s oil boom.

Technocrats complete most of their studies and training outside the kingdom, in secular, mainly Western, universities. Egyptian universities used to receive many Saudi students, but to avoid contamination by Nasserist ideology they were increasingly sent during the 1960s to U.S. universities. In 1971-1972, Saudi students were the twenty-seventh largest group of foreign students in U.S. universities. Five years later, they were the twelfth largest. By 1977, about 30,000 Saudis had finished their studies in the United States.[98] According to the Saudi newspaper *Al-Jazirah*, by 1980 there were more than 11,000 Saudi[99] students studying at U.S. universities. Of the 64 ministers and deputy ministers in the Saudi government in 1979, 19 had Ph.D.s, mostly from U.S. universities.[100]

Though they are not a homogeneous group and lack the institutional base of the ulama or the military, Saudi technocrats "nonetheless represent a serious group with an impact on economic and financial decisions," if not yet on "high politics" across the board.[101] Their political hopes were raised during the 1958–1960 period of fighting within the royal family between King Saud and his brother Faisal. To regain his influence, Saud used the technocrats' support and established a cabinet where they made up the majority. However, this was a short-lived tactical move on Saud's part.

However, their participation in government has continued and accelerated. In 1965, the Saudi Council of Ministers was composed of fourteen ministers: five princes, three representatives of the Al-Shaikh family, and six technocrats (in the fields of oil, agriculture, communications, information, health, and labor). After the shuffle in 1975, the number of cabinet members rose to twenty-five. The representatives of the Al-Shaikh family remained at three; the number of princes rose to eight; and that of technocrats to fourteen. After Khaled's death and Fahd's accession to power in June 1982, the number of cabinet members was increased to twenty-seven, and the two new members were technocrats. On foreign policy issues members of this group are generally nationalistic, insisting on an "even-handed" U.S. foreign policy in the Arab-Israeli conflict. Cooperation will grow between them and young royal family members such as Saud Al-Faisal, the foreign minister. Moreover, their resistance to waste and undisciplined consumerism could appeal to some members of the religious establishment. Even without an independent institutional base, the impact of Saudi technocrats will be increasingly felt in the different sectors of decision-making.

The Commercial Class

Even though it is generally accepted that Saudi Arabia is a bedouin state par excellence, some specialists attach great importance to the role of commercial interests at the basis of the state.[102] Put succinctly, this thesis holds that commercial interests provided revenue to the Al-Saud and linked the whole area to the world economic system, thus making the major powers of the period concerned for the survival of the Al-Saud.

The present context, however, is quite different, for the rise of the oil economy has led to less dependence by the Al-Saud on the financial support of the commercial class. This does not mean that the partnership between the ruling family and the commercial class has ended, but the partnership has changed form. Despite the fact that large traditional families continue to dominate commerce in the kingdom, their composition, orientation, and relationship with the ruling family has changed. The influx of oil revenues has led to the rise of a new class of businessmen, a second generation of naturalized Saudis like billionaires Adnan Khashoggi and Ghaith Pharaon.[103] This second generation capitalizes on its international business connections and partnership with Najdi aristocrats or members of the royal family. With so many government contracts going around, and with the government policy of prohibiting wholly foreign firms and banks from engaging in business, a bonanza of joint ventures has linked the royal family and the commercial class.[104] The commercial class thus has effective supporters at the highest echelons of the decision-making process, and as long as the commercial class is receiving windfall profits from the oil wealth, it is supportive of both the system and its foreign policy.

Both Yassini[105] and Shaw and Long[106] confirm this transformation of the commercial class and its relationship of mutual benefit with the ruling dynasty. The Rajhis of Riyadh and Jeddah have their money exchange offices throughout the kingdom. The Ali Rizaz family of Jeddah, who founded an import-export company in 1862, now has holdings that include engineering and construction firms, heavy equipment importing, and a petroleum exploration company. Another case is that of Mohamed Ben Laden, formerly a mason at Aramco, "who through construction contracts for the royal family and the government, became the biggest contractor in the country."[107]

Whether it affects decision-making directly or by proxy, this commercial class is in favor of the present economic policy, the free market mechanism, and the consolidation of the private sector. It supports resistance to any "socialist" contagion and continuation of relations with Western and "moderate" countries, even at the expense of a militant nationalist line. This brings us to the analysis of the country's foreign policy behavior.

5. FOREIGN POLICY BEHAVIOR

Although the Saudi kingdom's foreign policy orientation may suffer from internal inconsistencies, no such discrepancy exists between this orientation and its translation into specific behavior. At the global level, almost all Saudi interactions are with the West, especially the United States. At the regional level, the majority of the country's relations are with Arab-Moslem countries, with a preference for those considered "moderate." The watershed of the 1973 oil embargo did not change this pattern; it only helped the country to pursue it more effectively. In short, Saudi international behavior emphasizes the primacy of Islam, pursues a close strategic alliance with the dominant Western power, and promotes "moderate" or pro-Western regimes in the Arab-Islamic world.

The Global Pattern

These trends are inferred from data on four indicators of Saudi international behavior: bilateral intergovernmental visits, diplomatic representation, trade patterns, and arms purchases.

Visits. The available data[108] indicate the number and direction of visits.[109] For the period from January 1970 to June 1982, the total number of visits exchanged was 257: 38 by Saudi representatives and 219 by foreign dignitaries visiting the kingdom. The fact that the country receives more visits than it pays indicates its rising international status and influence, especially since 1973. In 1970, Saudi Arabia received slightly over twice as many visits as it paid to other countries; by 1979 the ratio was almost ten to one.

The distribution of visits is equally significant. Of the total of 257 visits, 72 were with the West (30 sent and 42 received) and 174 with the Arab-Moslem countries (6 sent and 168 received). The large imbalance between visits to and from the Arab-Moslem countries can be explained by two factors: (1) many foreign dignitaries came for pilgrimage as well as for bilateral visits; and (2) with its oil revenues, Saudi Arabia initiated a generous aid program, and many leaders of these developing countries came to try to profit from this "riyal politik."

Diplomats. Regular diplomatic representation[110] for the period 1970–1982 confirms two trends of Saudi foreign policy: (1) rising international status (total value of representation has doubled from 181 points in 1978 to 380 in 1982) and (2) the tilt of Saudi foreign policy toward Western countries and "moderate" regimes. While diplomatic interaction more than doubled with Western and moderate Arab countries (from 82 to 170 points), relations declined with the radicals (from 25 to 18 points), and are still nonexistent with COMECON countries, as Table 9.2 indicates.

Trade. The skew in Saudi relations is confirmed by the third and fourth indicators. Trade patterns for the 1972–1980 period show that Saudi Arabia is becoming increasingly integrated in the Western economic system at the expense of exchanges with other parts of the world (see Tables 9.3 and 9.4).

Armaments. The data for arms purchases are very eloquent. For the period from 1970 to 1982, the kingdom concluded no less than 105 arms agreements, 104 with the West and 1 with Pakistan. The latter, concluded in 1974, was for the "peanut sum" of $145 million. Sixty-one agreements were signed with the United States, and one source[111] indicates that in the eight-year period from 1973 to 1980 Saudi purchases of U.S. arms and equipment totaled $34 billion (compared to $1.2 billion for 1950–1972). The $34 billion estimate does not, of course, include the value of such handsome agreements as the $9 billion AWACS deal in October 1981.

TABLE 9.2
Regular Diplomatic Representation in Saudi Arabia, 1970-1982

Year	OECD (the West)	COMECON	Arab Countries[a] Conservative	Radical	Others	Non-Arab Moslem Countries[b]	Non-Arab and Non-Moslem[c]	Total
1970	56	--	26	25	10	41	23	181
1971	56	--	35	25	10	43	35	204
1972	58	--	35	25	10	43	36	207
1973	58	--	45	25	10	47	38	223
1974	80	--	43	25	10	56	64	278
1975	91	--	45	25	10	56	67	294
1976	91	--	49	26	10	61	67	304
1977	95	--	55	28	10	67	86	341
1978	95	--	54	30	10	67	85	341
1979	96	--	59	25	5	64	102	351
1980	97	--	57	18	5	70	97	344
1981	100	--	70	13	5	62	116	366
1982	100	--	70	18	5	67	120	380
TOTAL	1,073	--	643	308	110	744	936	3,814

Source: The Middle East and North Africa, 1970-1971 to 1982-1983 (London: Europa Publications).

aArab countries classified as radical are Algeria, Iraq (which became conservative in 1980), Libya, Somalia (which became conservative in 1979), South Yemen, and Syria. Those classified as conservative are Bahrain, Djibouti, Jordan, Kuwait, Lebanon, Mauritania, Morocco, North Yemen, Oman, Qatar, Saudi Arabia, Tunisia, and the United Arab Emirates. Egypt and Sudan, which changed from radical to conservative in the early 1970s, make up the "others" category.

bThis category includes Afghanistan, Bangladesh, Indonesia, Iran, Pakistan, Turkey, and also such countries as Chad, whose population in 1982 was 50% Moslem and 5% Christian, with the rest described as "animist."

cAmong others, countries in this category include Argentina, Brazil, Burundi, Ghana, India, Mexico, South Korea, Sri Lanka, Taiwan, Uruguay, and Venezuela.

TABLE 9.3
Volume of Saudi Exports by Region, 1970-1978 (in millions SRls)[a]

Year	Western Hemisphere	Europe	Middle East	Asia	Africa	Oceania	Others	Total
1970	591	4,820	609	3,339	474	309	765	10,907
1971	1,707	8,386	806	4,414	759	254	977	17,303
1972	2,523	12,580	839	5,532	425	214	650	22,763
1973	4,678	17,466	1,266	8,219	586	245	848	33,308
1974	17,155	65,141	4,135	31,973	1,157	1,129	5,533	126,223
1975	14,810	45,420	3,574	31,135	1,154	1,480	6,839	104,412
1976	21,275	55,598	4,209	41,074	1,246	1,682	10,170	135,254
1977	28,291	60,538	5,756	47,162	926	2,154	8,383	153,210
1978	29,636	51,538	4,900	46,947	853	1,746	2,622	138,242

Sources: SAMA, *Statistical Summary:* 1973-1974, pp. 60-61; 1975-1976, pp. 84-85; 1978, pp. 60-61; SAMA, *Annual Report,* 1979, pp. 152-153. As adapted from Ragaei El-Mallakh, *Saudi Arabia: Rush to Development* (London: Croom Helm, 1982), p. 347. Because of the unreliability of data on Saudi Arabia, the figures should be taken as representing tendencies and not precise numbers.

[a]In September 1981, one U.S. dollar equaled 3.64 Saudi riyals.

TABLE 9.4
Volume of Saudi Imports by Region, 1968-1978 (in millions SRls)[a]

Year	United States	Europe	Middle East	Asia	Africa	Oceania	Others	Total
1968	571	807	554	463	145	31	8	2,579
1969	622	1,281	629	625	152	62	5	3,376
1970	569	1,150	636	611	127	95	10	3,198
1971	615	1,295	810	712	152	66	17	3,667
1972	917	1,438	1,009	1,025	216	86	17	4,708
1973	1,407	2,079	1,625	1,641	225	183	36	7,196
1974	1,735	2,696	2,836	2,487	272	89	34	10,149
1975	2,538	4,669	3,647	3,152	321	104	392	14,823
1976	5,739	10,844	7,296	5,673	366	128	536	30,582
1977	9,621	19,424	7,243	10,468	451	310	3,868	51,385
1978	14,434	31,323	2,739	17,612	710	537	1,341	68,696

Sources: SAMA, *Statistical Summary:* 1973-1974, pp. 60-61; 1975-1976, pp. 84-85; 1978, pp. 60-61; 1979, pp. 62-63; SAMA, *Annual Report,* 1979, pp. 152-153. As adapted from Ragaei El-Mallakh, *Saudi Arabia: Rush to Development* (London: Croom Helm, 1982), p. 352. Because of the unreliability of data on Saudi Arabia, the figures should be taken as representing tendencies and not precise numbers.

[a]In September 1981, one U.S. dollar equaled 3.64 Saudi riyals.

Regional Diplomacy

This focus on the West, and especially the United States,[112] at the global level is matched by Saudi opposition to "radical" regimes at the regional level. Saudi Arabia countered the radical wave of Ba'thist-Nasserist Arab nationalism by insisting on pan-Islamism. In May 1962, an international Islamic conference in Mecca, sponsored by Saudi Arabia, declared that "those who disavow Islam and distort its call under the guise of nationalism are actually the most bitter enemies of the Arabs whose glories are inseparable from the glories of Islam."[113] The conference established the World Moslem League, with headquarters in Mecca. Its objective is to counter "all alien ideologies and habits inconsistent with Islam, and to coordinate the effort of Islamic organizations around the world."[114] In 1965, King Faisal toured Moslem countries such as Jordan, Malaysia, and Pakistan to regroup them in a pan-Islamic coalition to counter the radical nationalist trend. The Egyptian-Syrian humiliating defeat in the 1967 war with Israel facilitated the rise of the Saudi trend. In 1969, the first pan-Islamic summit was held in Rabat, Morocco.

Following Nasser's death on September 28, 1970, Saudi Arabia intensified its efforts to deradicalize Egypt and to get rid of the 20,000 Soviet advisors invited in by Nasser. In November 1970, King Faisal sent Adham, his personal advisor and intelligence chief, to meet Sadat discreetly. His mission was to persuade Sadat to get rid of the Soviets so that relations might improve with the United States,[115] whose help might then be enlisted in solving the Arab-Israeli conflict. When Sadat expressed his readiness to work along these lines, Adham passed the word to Washington. The Saudi role of go-between for Egypt and the United States was just one aspect of the increasing coordination between Saudi Arabia and Egypt.

Faisal was the only person trusted by Sadat and Asad with the exact time of the Egyptian-Syrian attack against Israeli troops on October 6, 1973. During the war Saudi Arabia, overcoming earlier hesitation to use the oil weapon against the United States,[116] was crucial in the oil embargo decision. After the war, the Riyadh-Cairo axis (based on a trade-off between Egyptian muscle and Saudi money) aimed to discourage any revolutionary ideology or "practices subversive of the status quo."[117] The axis acquired military teeth through the official formation of the Arab military armaments organization (AMIO), which combined Gulf money and Egyptian production capabilities.[118] Even when Sadat accelerated his go-it-alone diplomacy and signed the second disengagement agreement with Israel in 1975, Saudi Arabia still managed to bring Syria and Egypt together in Riyadh for reconciliation, thus avoiding polarization in the Arab world. Only when Sadat pushed rapprochement to the point of recognizing Israel did Saudi Arabia find association with this policy too risky.

It was also in the name of "moderation" that Saudi Arabia was active in chasing Soviet advisors from Somalia and financing Somali arms purchases from the West in the late 1970s. In both cases, Saudi Arabia managed to make its stand effective and thwart much of the resistance against it thanks to its oil power, as manifested in its impressive commercial balance (see Table 9.5). Saudi diplomacy of the 1970s was predominantly characterized by the rise of "riyal politik," illustrated by Tables 9.6 and 9.7.

Of course, an Islamic "explanation" can always be found to account for Saudi aid to, and co-optation of, such Arab-Moslem countries as Egypt and Somalia. But what about Kenya, South Korea, or Taiwan? Here we can see that immediate strategic and geopolitical interests are

TABLE 9.5
Saudi Arabia's Commercial Balance, 1970-1980 (in millions of US$)

Year	United States	Japan	Italy	West Germany	United Kingdom	France
1970	-104,623	-389,959	-230,607	-18,833	-136,912	-138,763
1971	-5,363	-502,836	-356,837	-64,720	-267,863	-138,763
1972	-51,191	-667,838	-568,675	-106,820	-362,098	-355,401
1973	-61,288	-1,004,522	-853,071	-176,332	-597,024	-794,757
1974	-761,168	-5,216,320	-3,597,097	-1,388,312	-3,172,851	-4,055,000
1975	-481,990	-5,176,813	-2,080,290	-751,210	-1,477,362	-3,116,250
1976	-210,566	-6,619,113	-2,011,736	-494,624	-1,398,199	-4,182,555
1977	-1,422,057	-6,550,854	-2,277,709	-35,857	-954,625	-3,681,991
1978	-2,153,561	-5,063,049	-1,298,183	-1,090,019	-78,304	-3,564,396
1979	-6,106,518	-7,127,720	-3,355,346	-892,906	-372,062	-4,196,013
1980	-10,848,435	-13,616,668	-4,499,907	-577,655	-1,889,120	-8,446,805

Source: U.N. *Yearbook of Trade Statistics,* 1970-1980 (New York: United Nations, 1973-1981).

TABLE 9.6
Saudi Aid to Arab League Countries, 1974-1980

Country/Year	Loans and Grants (millions U.S.$)	Purpose
Algeria		
1980	15.0	Aid to earthquake victims
Egypt		
1974	100.0	Rebuilding of Suez Canal towns damaged during October 1973 war
	300.0	Rebuilding of Suez Canal areas
1975	7.7	Construction of Islamic university in Assuit
1976	800.0	To assist Egyptian economy
Jordan		
1976	215.0	Finance five-year plan
1980	10.0	Flood and heavy snow-damage repair
Lebanon	38.1	First installment of $114.3-million annual contribution to five-year, $2-billion Arab aid program agreed upon at the November 1979 Tunis summit
1980		
Yemen Arab Republic (North Yemen)		
1975	82.0	Budget support
	30.0	Electricity projects
	146.0	Road construction
	15.0	Grain mills and silos
	13.7	Drilling of artesian wells
	4.3	Flood aid
1977	101.6	Budget support
1978	101.6	Budget support
1979	101.6	Budget support
	4.8	Compensation for higher prices paid for imports of Saudi oil
Oman		
1975	100.0	Development projects
Somalia		
1975	11.5	Famine and drought assistance
1979	20.0	Grant
1980	10.0	Budget support
People's Democratic Republic of Yemen (South Yemen)		
1976	100.0	Development assistance
Sudan		
1974	200.0	Development assistance
1978	2.9	Flood relief

(continued)

TABLE 9.6 (cont.)

Country/Year	Loans and Grants (millions U.S.$)	Purpose
1980	11.0	Exploration for minerals (zinc, silver, copper, gold, and chromium)
Syria		
1975	200.0	For weapon purchases
	219.9	For various development projects
1977	50.0	Economic assistance
Tunisia		
1979	7.0	Expenses of Arab Summit conference
	7.0	Expenses of Arab Summit conference
	13.0	Economic development purposes
Djibouti		
1973	10.0	Economic assistance

Source: Middle East Economic Survey, 1970-1980, as cited in Ragaei El-Mallakh, *Saudi Arabia: Rush to Development* (London: Croom Helm, 1982), p. 379.

the real motives behind Saudi international behavior. This was clearly illustrated by the recent constitution of the 1981 Gulf Cooperation Council, and Saudi policy during the 1982–1983 world oil glut.

The Gulf region is Saudi Arabia's soft underbelly, and present relations among Gulf countries have their historical origins in tribal and dynastic relations. When the Al-Rashid defeated the Al-Saud in the nineteenth century, the Al-Saud found refuge at Al-Sabah, in what is now Kuwait, and it was from Kuwait that Abdel-Aziz departed to regain Al-Saud power in 1902. However, the impetus for inter-state institutionalization in the 1970s and 1980s was the rise of petropower. As the secretary-general of the Gulf council, Abdallah Bishara, reminds us, the proposal officially came in May 1976 from A. G. Al-Sabah, the amir of Kuwait.[119] The project at the time included both Iraq and Iran, whose ministers attended a preliminary meeting in Muscat (Oman) in 1977. With Iran's revolution and the Iran-Iraq war, the idea of a Gulf council changed. By excluding the two warring countries—Iran and Iraq—the new council proposal gave Saudi Arabia the chance to be the sole regional power present in the projected institution. Consequently, Saudi Arabia overcame its hesitation about collective security pacts and on February 4, 1981, convened the foreign ministers of the five small Gulf states (Bahrain, Kuwait, Oman, Qatar, and the United Arab Emirates) to meet in Riyadh. The meeting established the Gulf council machinery, with headquarters in Riyadh. During the eighteen months that followed the First Gulf Council Summit (Abu Dhabi, May 25, 1981), no less than thirty-four meetings of ministers and specialized committees were held.[120] The council works to integrate the members' economic, defense, and foreign policies in the interest of the "stability of the Gulf region," as the

TABLE 9.7
Saudi Aid to Non-Arab, Non-OPEC Institutions, 1975-1980

Institution/Year	Contribution (millions U.S.$)	Disposition of Aid
Asian Development Bank		
1975	50.0	Loan from SAMA
International Monetary Fund		
1975	1,200.0	Oil facility special drawing rights
1977	1,700.0	Oil facility
Islamic Conference Organization (ICO)/Islamic Solidarity Fund (ISF)		
1975	14.99	Islamic News Agency; ISF; Islamic Philanthropic Society (Makased, Beirut); construction of Islamic mosques, schools, and centers in Australia
1977	28.0	ISF for development projects in Islamic countries; Islamic News Agency; Jerusalem Fund
1978	38.7	ISF; Jerusalem Fund; Islamic universities of Uganda and Niger; Islamic News Agency; Islamic Waqfs Fund (a religious endowment)
1979	54.8	ICO; $30 million addition to ISF's capital for scientific research and Islamic universities, natural disaster relief, mosques, schools, and hospitals; Jerusalem Fund; Islamic missions; celebration of the Hegira fifteenth century (New Year's celebration)
UNESCO		
1975	5.6	Grants to finance educational projects; interest-free loans for educational programs
United Nations Relief and Works Agency		
1975	0.6	
1976	1.2	
1977	1.2	
1978	10.2	Regular annual $1.2-million payment plus two special contributions
1979	3.5	Regular contribution plus $2.3-million special contribution
1980	5.0	Regular contribution plus $3.8-million special contribution
United Nations World Food Programme		
1976	50.0	
1980	55.0	For the fourth consecutive year, Saudi Arabia was the larges donor to the World Food Programme
World Bank		
1980	401.6	SAMA purchase of 28.6% of a 700-million DM bond issue arranged by German banks

Source: Middle East Economic Survey, 1975-1980, as cited in Ragaei El-Mallakh, *Saudi Arabia: Rush to Development* (London: Croom Helm, 1982), p. 388.

communiqué of the first summit affirmed. But the establishment and functioning of this council goes beyond the regional objectives of Saudi diplomacy.[121] The council's aims—as a professor[122] at the United Arab Emirates University took pains to emphasize—have to be situated within the global strategic context and Saudi oil policy. Saudi behavior during the 1982–1983 glut in the world oil market is a good illustration of this policy.

Faced with the crisis of a world oil glut and lower prices in the 1980s, OPEC's thirteen members were in danger of undercutting each other on the world market. Increasing oil supplies (from the North Sea, Alaska, and Mexico) led to the decline of OPEC's world share from 68% in 1976 to only 46% at the end of 1982, and a decline in its financial resources from a peak of $109 billion in 1980 to a deficit of $18 billion two years later.[123] An OPEC meeting in late January 1983 ended in disagreement, and some observers started talking about the end of OPEC.

It was in this context that Saudi Arabia convened the oil ministers of the Gulf council in Riyadh (February 20–23, 1983). Together, these countries hold the major share of both oil production and petrodollars; consequently, they can adjust more easily to fluctuations in the world oil market. Did not Saudi oil minister Yamani affirm in autumn 1975 that to ruin the other countries of OPEC, all that his country need do was to produce oil to its full capacity?[124] In conjunction with the other members of the Gulf council, Saudi Arabia was certainly in a good position to shape OPEC's decision on production and price levels.

Confident of the crucial influence of its own coalition, Saudi Arabia conducted its diplomacy in a typical velvet-fist style. The Riyadh Gulf council meeting of oil ministers agreed on a lower price, but Riyadh would not declare this price on the world market before a "last chance" OPEC meeting to agree on a common price and level of production. The suggestion was then made to reconvene an OPEC meeting. A month or so before the OPEC meeting, Dr. Oteiba, the oil minister of the United Arab Emirates (and also the president of OPEC at that time), declared that his country had decided to increase its production by 45% to meet a swelling budget deficit.[125] The message was clear: the Gulf states are ready to flood the market. In this context, OPEC members had to choose between accepting a version of the decision of the Saudi-led coalition, or provoking a price war on the world market with the probability of being beaten and blamed for OPEC's demise. Consequently, when OPEC members met in London in March 1983 an agreement was reached: reduce production to 17.25 million bpd, and reduce the official price from $34 to $29 per barrel. In this way, Saudi Arabia managed to restore a measure of "stability" to the world oil market.

CONCLUSION: THE MIXED BLESSING OF OIL POWER

It is easy to conclude that from an economic point of view, the 1970s have seen the rise of Saudi Arabia from the status of sandbox to regional and international power. Saudi Arabia is a large aid donor and Saudi oil power forms the base for a new coalition in the global system—the African-Arab-European dialogue. It lent the International Monetary Fund $11 billion in 1981-1982, and thus holds the sixth largest voting share, after the United States, Britain, Germany, France, and Japan.[126] Even with the 1982–1983 world oil glut, which cut the kingdom's 1981 oil earnings by two-thirds,[127] Saudi Arabia still receives $13 billion from its overseas investments, the equivalent of the GDP of seven developing countries combined (Central African Republic, Chad, Haiti, Mali, Sierra Leone, Somalia, and Togo), or more than thirteen times the GDP of neighboring South Yemen. The kingdom may thus successfully continue to base its diplomacy on both Islamic influence and "riyal politik," keep its self-image as guardian of the Islamic spirit, and bolster "moderate" systems of government.

Our conclusion, however, would not be complete without considering the limits of Saudi foreign policy. These limits are not unrelated to Saudi Arabia's biggest asset: oil power. Saudi Arabia is asked to play a regional and world role, but does not possess the basic capabilities (industrial base, developed transnational organizations, military force, or skilled manpower) to maintain this role. Saudi power is not only one-dimensional (financial); it is also wholly dependent on the whims of the outside market. Saudi minister of finance Abu Al-Khail put it nicely: "We don't have surplus, we have temporary liquidity."[128]

The result is, as both the *Washington Post*[129] and N. Ayubi[130] expressed it, the vulnerability of the rich: the Saudi's perception of exposure to danger and susceptibility to accident, change, and the uncontrollable forces loose in the world. Saudi Arabia faces the problem of developing a solid base from which to manage its foreign policy in an increasingly complex environment. The problem is aggravated for the Saudi policy-maker *because* his country is no longer a "sandbox" that can be ignored by the world system. The rate of social change with which the Saudis must cope is too fast.

At the beginning of his political career thirty years ago, Nasser described in a metaphorical way the effects of social change on his own Egypt.

Our modern awakening . . . began with a crisis. In my opinion our case very much resembled that of . . . a man who spent a long time in a closed room. The heat in that closed room became so intense that the man was in anguish. Suddenly a violent storm blew, smashing all windows and doors, and strong currents of cold air began to lash the body of the . . . man who was still perspiring. The . . . man needed a breath of air. Instead, a raging hurricane assailed him, and fever began to devour his feeble body.[131]

Egypt's "opening up," however, started almost 200 years ago, whereas Saudi Arabia has passed from the camel to the computer age within a decade. The magnitude of this change can be seen through the sums allocated to the three development plans. The first plan (1970–1975), described by Minister of Planning Hisham Nazer as an experiment in social transformation, cost a relatively modest 56,223 million riyals ($12 billion). The amount for the second plan (1975–1980) rose to 498,230 million ($142 billion), and the budget for the third (1980–1985) was 782,000 million riyals ($235 billion)—nine and fourteen times the cost of the first plan respectively. The huge petrochemical and industrial complexes in Yanbu and Jubail indicate the degree of transformation, and the developing road and transport system indicates how fast the country is "opening up." Until 1964, the only surfaced roads, besides those in the oil network, were in the Jeddah-Medina-Mecca area. By May 1981, there were 21,470 km of asphalted roads, with 9,400 km built under the second plan and another 6,600 km to be built under the third. Saudia, the government-operated airline, carried 9.5 million passengers in 1980. To cope with increasing traffic, the new Jiddah airport, completed in 1983 at a cost of $5 billion, is the largest in the world.[132]

In the face of these massive changes, how can the kingdom—the result of an alliance between ulama and umara (princes) and modelled on a seventh-century Islamic state—cope? The gap between the kingdom's official puritanical posture and daily reality is causing social tensions, as reflected in the growing divorce rate and the decrease in mosque attendance, particularly by youngsters and schoolchildren. Sheikh Abdel-Aziz Ibn Al-Baz, the highest authority in the religious establishment, considers Western-style economic development a threat to Islamic values and the serene, tranquil Moslem way of life. Al-Baz believes Saudi Arabia should take advantage of Western technology while repelling "dangerous ideas," i.e., Western culture.[133] The fact that computer print-outs begin with the Quranic expression "in the name of god" may reflect Al-Baz's view of "take the best and eschew the rest," but the problems of the Saudi policy-maker in coping with change and managing national and international political behavior are too serious to be solved in such a simplistic way. Two cases, one domestic and one regional, illustrate the policy-maker's present dilemma.

The 1979 seizure of the Grand Mosque in Mecca by religious zealots was to protest the kingdom's deviation from the "true Islamic path." Until then, the kingdom had faced only external attacks on its legitimacy, from Qaddafi's Libya or Khomeini's Iran. The January 1980 decapitation of the sixty-three "fanatics"—according to due process of law—put an end to this particular incident, but the problem itself remains.

The regional case concerns Fahd's eight-point plan (autumn 1981) for the settlement of the Arab-Israeli conflict. The usual pattern of Saudi behavior in inter-Arab affairs was to avoid clear-cut public identification with any country or camp, and to work toward mediation and consensus-building. In this way, the kingdom maintained its bridges with all Arab regimes, and its active mediatorial role identified it with Arab solidarity.

Crown Prince Abdallah mediated the 1980 conflict between Syria and Jordan, and King Fahd personally mediated the Western Sahara conflict between "radical" Algeria and "moderate" Morocco. King Hassan of Morocco was invited to Saudi Arabia in February 1980; a month later President Benjedid came; and in May Fahd himself visited the two countries.

In the fall of 1981, the kingdom departed from its discreet diplomacy of consensus-building and submitted the Fahd plan to the eleventh Arab summit (Morocco, November 1981). The plan divided the conference. Overall opposition included the "Steadfastness Front" (Libya, Syria, South Yemen, and the PLO); Iraq, North Yemen, Mauritania, and Lebanon abstained; and Jordan, Kuwait, and the United Arab Emirates gave only "shy support, asking for changes in wording." Only eight countries supported the plan: Bahrain, Djibouti, Morocco, Oman, Qatar, Somalia, Sudan, and Tunisia.[134]

The problem, however, was not with the plan itself, but rather with planning and timing. Saudi policy-makers failed to make a systematic study of the context of the conference, its timing, and the objectives and the influence of supporters and critics, and failed to tailor Saudi Arabia's capabilities to its objectives. Only in this way could policy-makers have evaluated the chances of success or failure for the move, and hence decide whether and at what time to submit the proposal. The "science" of planning and managing foreign policy was lacking.

This lack is significant because it reflects the problems of both the Saudi state and its foreign policy, which are essentially problems of adaptation to a new context at the levels of both social development and foreign policy. The Saudi state and Saudi policy-makers need time to reflect on these changes, grasp their pace and direction, and adjust. It is through this process of adaptation that oil power could be transformed from cash to capabilities, and these capabilities could be used to plan and manage foreign policy that would make Saudi Arabia less vulnerable.

NOTES

1. Standard yearbooks as well as good journalistic accounts emphasize these aspects. See, for instance, *The Middle East and North Africa, 1982-1983* (London: Europa Publications, 1982), pp. 677–705. David Holden and Richard Johns, *The House of Saud* (London: Pan Books, 1982); Robert Lacey, *The Kingdom* (New York: Avon Books, 1982).

2. Malcolm C. Peck, "The Saudi-American Relationship and King Faisal," in Willard A. Beling (ed.), *King Faisal and the Modernisation of Saudi Arabia* (Boulder, Colo.: Westview Press, 1980), pp. 235–236.

3. *Ibid.*, pp. 238–239.

4. *Ibid.*

5. Concerning the Saudi currency—the riyal—see Lacey, *op. cit.*, pp. 445–457.

6. Holden and Johns, *op. cit.*, p. 385. Helms confirms: "the absence of a peasant class bound to the land and incorporated into the urban structure . . .

meant that the Ottomans and later the British found the prospect of establishing their control in Najd very daunting." Christine M. Helms, *The Cohesion of Saudi Arabia* (Baltimore, Md.: Johns Hopkins University Press, 1981), p. 58.

7. *Middle East and North Africa,* 1982-1983. In his in-depth analysis of the Saudi economy, El-Mallakh estimated the agricultural share of the GDP as 5.8% for the same period. Ragaei El-Mallakh, *Saudi Arabia: Rush to Development* (London: Croom Helm, 1982), p. 85.

8. Saad E. Ibrahim and Donald P. Cole, "Saudi Arabian Bedouin," *Cairo Papers in Social Science* 1, 5 (1978), p. 3.

9. *Middle East and North Africa,* 1982-1983, pp. 677–705.

10. The World Bank, *World Development Report 1982* (London and New York: Oxford University Press, 1982), p. 110.

11. El-Mallakh, *op. cit.,* p. 169.

12. *Ibid.,* p. 116.

13. Helms, *op. cit.,* p. 60.

14. Ibrahim and Cole, *op. cit.,* p. 3.

15. Abdel-Aziz, known as Ibn Saud, governed for more than fifty years (1902–1953). He was followed by his sons Saud (1953–1964), Faisal (1964–1975), Khaled (1975–1982), and Fahd (1982–).

16. John S. Habib, *Ibn Saud's Warriors of Islam* (Leiden, Netherlands: E. J. Brill, 1978), p. 19.

17. Ayman Al-Yassini, "Saudi Arabia: The Kingdom of Islam," in Carlo Caldarola (ed.), *Religions and Societies: Asia and the Middle East* (The Hague, Netherlands: Mouton, forthcoming), p. 6. I am grateful to Dr. Al-Yassini for making available to me, before publication, both this excellent paper and another one on Islam and Saudi foreign policy.

18. Literally, *hijra* means immigration, and was first used to label the prophet Mohamed's move from Mecca to Medina to establish the first Islamic state. The word is thus pregnant with important religious and emotional associations.

19. Helms, *op. cit.,* p. 130.

20. Al-Yassini, *op. cit.,* p. 6.

21. "Although this number may not be definitive . . . [this] writer has been able to identify 222." Habib, *op. cit.,* p. 58.

22. Helms, *op. cit.,* p. 138.

23. Habib, *op. cit.,* p. 30.

24. Helms, *op. cit.,* p. 78.

25. David E. Long, "King Faisal's World View," in Beling, *op. cit.,* pp. 177–178. On April 20, 1963, at the height of the Arab cold war and the conflict in Yemen, King Faisal reiterated: "We stretch out our hands . . . [and] open our breasts to our Arab brethren. . . . We are prepared to reach the goal set before us, which is complete Arab unity, but we cannot forget in any situation that this country has . . . her geographical location and the presence of the holy places . . . [which] distinguish her from other Arab countries. . . . We support Islam above all things; and we look upon Islam as our solid foundation." Ayman Al-Yassini, "Islam and Foreign Policy in Saudi Arabia," Center for Developing Area Studies Paper, McGill University, Montreal, 1983, p. 12.

26. Al-Yassini, "Islam and Foreign Policy," pp. 10–11.

27. Long, *op. cit.,* p. 176.

28. William Quandt, who appears to follow the Saudi position, emphasizes the Arab world and the Palestinians over the Islamic world. See his lucid book, *Saudi Arabia in the 1980s* (Washington, D.C.: Brookings Institution 1981).

29. Haim Shaked and Tamar Yegnes, "Saudi Arabia," in Colin Legum, Haim Shaked, and Daniel Dishon (eds.), *Middle East Contemporary Survey*, 1976-1977 (London: Holmes and Meier, 1978), pp. 565–585. (Hereafter referred to as *Middle East Survey*.)

30. *Ibid.*

31. Jacob Goldberg, "The Saudi Arabian Kingdom," in Legum, Shaked, and Dishon, *Middle East Survey*, 1979-1980, pp. 681–721.

32. *New York Times*, April 24, 1981, pp. A1 and A7.

33. *New York Times*, October 25, 1980.

34. *Ibid.*

35. *Keesings Contemporary Archives*, August 7, 1981, p. 31011.

36. *New York Times*, March 7, 1982.

37. *Ibid.*

38. *Ibid.*

39. *Ibid.*

40. *Keesings Contemporary Archives*, September 3, 1982, p. 31682.

41. Shaked and Yegnes, *op. cit.*, p. 574.

42. Jacob Goldberg, "The Saudi Arabian Kingdom," in Legum, Shaked, and Dishon, *Middle East Survey*, 1978-1979, pp. 736–769.

43. *Ibid.*

44. Goldberg, in *Middle East Survey*, 1979-1980.

45. Ami Ayalon, "The Iran-Iraq War," in *Middle East Survey*, 1979-1980, p. 23.

46. *Keesings Contemporary Archives*, June 4, 1982, p. 31523.

47. *New York Times*, December 21, 1981.

48. *Keesings Contemporary Archives*, June 4, 1982, p. 31523.

49. *New York Times*, December 21, 1981.

50. *Keesings Contemporary Archives*, June 4, 1982, p. 31523.

51. *New York Times*, December 28, 1981.

52. Quandt, *op. cit.*, p. 145. On the death of King Khaled in June 1982, Brezhnev sent a message of "profound condolences" to King Fahd, the Soviet press agency Tass reported. *New York Times*, June 15, 1982.

53. Goldberg, *op. cit.*, p. 755.

54. For the views of Prince Bandar Ben Sultan, expressed to me during a meeting at Harvard University on September 19, 1979, see Bahgat Korany, "Petro-puissance et système mondial: Le cas l'Arabie Saoudite," *Etudes Internationales* 10, 4 (1979), pp. 797–819.

55. Goldberg, in *Middle East Survey*, 1979-1980.

56. *Ibid.*

57. *Ibid.*

58. *Ibid.*

59. *Ibid.*

60. See the *New York Times*, January 30, 1980, p. A13, for the complete text.

61. For other cases, see Quandt, *op. cit.*, p. 44.

62. *Middle East and North Africa*, 1982-1983.

63. Quandt, *op. cit.*, p. 76.

64. Talk with Mr. Ziyad Al-Shawaf, Saudi Arabia's ambassador to Canada, Ottawa, July 5, 1983.

65. Quandt, *op. cit.*, p. 109.

66. Ghassan Salama, *The Foreign Policy of Saudi Arabia Since 1945* (Beirut: Institute of Arab Development, 1980), p. 47 (in Arabic). This Arabic edition is

based on Dr. Salama's well-researched Ph.D. dissertation, University of Paris, Sorbonne. For more data on the royal family see also *Time*, June 28, 1982.

67. Helen Lackner, *A House Built on Sand* (London: Ithaca Press, 1978), pp. 57–58.

68. Some foreigners have also participated in decision-making. Dr. Rashad Pharaon, Abdel-Aziz's Syrian physician, also became his personal advisor; and Turkish-born Kamal Adham was both King Faisal's brother-in-law and the kingdom's intelligence chief. Lacey, *op. cit.*, pp. 169, 358–359, 393, 447–448; Holden and Johns, *op. cit.*, pp. 102, 139, 179, 364–365.

69. This information is from Salama, *op. cit.*, pp. 47–84.

70. The one exception was relations with the Gulf principalities, which Abdel-Aziz handled himself because of his relations with the different tribal chiefs.

71. Charles Harrington, "The Saudi Arabian Council of Ministers," *Middle East Journal* 12, 1 (1958), pp. 1–20.

72. Conversation with Ambassador Al-Shawaf, *op. cit.*

73. Richard Nyrop et al., *Area Handbook for Saudi Arabia*, 3d ed. (Washington, D.C.: American University, 1977), pp. 216–217.

74. Conversation with Ambassador Al-Shawaf, *op. cit.*

75. *Ibid.*

76. *Ibid.*

77. Quandt, *op. cit.*, p. 84.

78. *Time*, June 28, 1982.

79. Salama, *op. cit.*, pp. 47–83.

80. Quandt, *op. cit.*, pp. 81–82.

81. *Time*, June 28, 1982, p. 23.

82. Tim Niblock, "Social Structure and the Development of the Saudi Arabian Political System," in Niblock (ed.), *State, Society and Economy in Saudi Arabia* (New York: St. Martin's Press, 1982), p. 92.

83. Al-Yassini, "Saudi Arabia," *op. cit.*, p. 15.

84. *Ibid.*

85. Niblock, *op. cit.*, p. 92.

86. John A. Shaw and David E. Long, *Saudi Arabian Modernization* (Washington D.C.: Center for Strategic and International Studies, 1982), pp. 67–74.

87. *The Military Balance* (London: International Institute of Strategic Studies), data on Saudi Arabia in the different volumes from 1970-1971 to 1982-1983.

88. "Facts and Figures on Defense: Saudi Arabia," *Military Technology* 5, 28 (1981), pp. 69–73.

89. Data calculated from the information provided by Salama, *op. cit.*, pp. 319–328. Salama draws upon Congress reports on U.S. arms policies in the Gulf and the Red Sea Area.

90. Jean-Louis Soulié and Lucien Champenois, *Le royaume d'Arabie Saoudite à l'épreuve des temps modernes* (Paris: Albin Michel, 1978), pp. 201–202.

91. *Middle East Intelligence Survey* 7, 17 (December 1-15, 1979), p. 129; "Facts and Figures on Defense," *op. cit.*

92. "Facts and Figures on Defense," *op. cit.*

93. Nyrop et al., *op. cit.*, p. 323.

94. *Middle East Intelligence Survey* 7, 17 (December 1-15, 1979) p. 129.

95. "Facts and Figures on Defense," *op. cit.*

96. Manfred Halpern, *The Politics of Social Change in the Middle East and North Africa* (Princeton, N.J.: Princeton University Press, 1963), Chapter 4.

97. For a detailed analysis of this group as represented by Tariki, see Stephen Duguid, "A Biographical Approach to the Study of Social Change in the Middle East: Abdallah Tariki as a New Man," *International Journal of Middle East Studies* 1 (1970), pp. 195–220.

98. Peck, *op. cit.*, p. 240.

99. Al-Yassini, "Saudi Arabia," *op. cit.*, p. 20.

100. Niblock, *op. cit.*, p. 101.

101. Quandt, *op. cit.*, p. 87.

102. Niblock, *op. cit.*, p. 76–77.

103. Holden and Johns, *op. cit.*, pp. 244–245, 359–366; Lacey, *op. cit.*, pp. 464–470, 507.

104. David B. Ottaway, "Sudden Drop in Oil Wealth May Give Saudis Severe Jolt," *Montreal Gazette*, June 11, 1983.

105. Al-Yassini, "Saudi Arabia," *op. cit.*, p. 23.

106. Shaw and Long, *op. cit.*, pp. 78–81.

107. Al-Yassini, "Saudi Arabia," *op. cit.*, p. 23.

108. Data, on the whole, are of modest quality and hard to come by, but they do show certain trends. The data for the visits are calculated from the chronology in the *Middle East Journal*, 1970–1982; data for diplomatic representation are from the volumes of *The Middle East and North Africa* for 1970–1982. Data for trade patterns are from the *U.N. Yearbook of International Trade Statistics*, although El-Mallakh's *Saudi Arabia* is much easier to use and just as good on trade. For arms agreements and purchase, the main sources used were *The Military Balance*, 1970–1982, and *SIPRI Yearbook*, 1974–1981 (New York: Crane, Russak & Co. for SIPRI). The SIPRI data are not as recent as those of *The Military Balance*, but they are more detailed.

109. For a more detailed scale using *both* frequency *and* rank of visits, see Bahgat Korany, "Dependence financière et comportement international," *Revue Française de Science Politique* 28, 6 (1978), pp. 1067–1093.

110. The measurement of Saudi Arabia's rising diplomatic status is based on calculating both the level and directness of regular diplomatic representation. The tool used is a 5-point scale, with a resident ambassador counting 5 points; a nonresident ambassador, 4 points; a resident chargé d'affaires, 3 points; a nonresident chargé d'affaires, 2 points; and unidentified diplomatic representatives, 1 point.

111. Shirin Tahir-Kheli and William O. Staudenmaier, "The Saudi-Pakistani Military Relationship," *Orbis* 26, 1 (1982), pp. 155–171.

112. Using different data and technique, Edward Azar confirms the patterns of behavior emphasized here. See his "Saudi Arabia's International Behavior: A Quantitative Analysis," Paper presented at the Symposium on "State, Economy and Power in Saudi Arabia," Centre for Arab Gulf Studies, University of Exeter, England, July 4–7, 1980. I am grateful to Dr. Mustafa Elwi (of Cairo University) and to Dr. Azar for making this paper available to me. For another approach that emphasizes the same trends, see the insightful chapter by Fred Halliday, "A Curious and Close Liaison: Saudi Arabia's Relations with the U.S.," in Niblock, *op. cit.*, pp. 125–147.

113. Al-Yassini, "Islam and Foreign Policy," p. 13.

114. *Ibid.*

115. This information is confirmed by diverse sources, for instance: Holden and Johns, *op. cit.*, p. 392; Lacey, *op. cit.*, p. 393, Mohamed Heikal, *The Road*

to Ramadan (New York: Ballantine Books, 1976), p. 118; David Hirst and Irene Beeson, *Sadat* (London: Faber and Faber, 1981), p. 97.

116. King Faisal said as late as August 1972: "The use of the oil weapon against the USA should be ruled out," *Middle East Journal* 26, 3 (1972).

117. Paul Jabber, "Oil, Arms, and Regional Diplomacy," in Malcolm H. Kerr and El Sayed Yassin (eds.), *Rich and Poor States in the Middle East: Egypt and the New Arab Order* (Boulder, Colo.: Westview Press, 1982), pp. 415–447.

118. *Ibid.*

119. Abdallah Bishara, "The Gulf Cooperation Council," Paper submitted to the Symposium on "The Domestic and International Framework of Cooperation in the Arab Gulf Region," sponsored by Kuwait University and the Economic Society of Kuwait, Kuwait, April 18–20, 1982 (in Arabic).

120. *Middle East Magazine* (London), December 1982, p. 8.

121. Interview with A. Bishara in *Middle East Magazine*, September 1981.

122. Abdullah El-Nefissi, "The Gulf Cooperation Council: The Politico-Strategic Framework," Paper submitted to the Symposium on "The Domestic and International Framework of Cooperation," *op. cit.* (in Arabic).

123. *Time*, February 7, 1983, pp. 34–38.

124. Saudi Arabia produced 40% of OPEC's world production in 1981. *Middle East and North Africa*, 1982-1983, pp. 677–705.

125. *Time*, February 7, 1983.

126. Quandt, *op. cit.*, p. 149.

127. Ottaway, *op. cit.*

128. *Middle East Economic Digest* 22 (July–September 1978), p. 3.

129. Meg Greenfield in the *Washington Post*, May 26, 1980, p. A15, as quoted by Azar, *op. cit.*

130. Nazih N. Ayubi, "Vulnerability of the Rich," Paper presented to the Gulf Project Symposium, Center for Strategic and International Studies, Georgetown University, Washington, D.C., June 1982.

131. Gamal Abdel Nasser, *The Philosophy of the Revolution* (Cairo: Department of Information, 1954), pp. 42–43.

132. *Middle East and North Africa*, 1982-1983, pp. 677–705.

133. Goldberg, *Middle East Survey*, 1980-1981, pp. 730–731.

134. *Middle East Magazine*, January 1982, pp. 13–16.

10

Revisionist Dreams, Realist Strategies: The Foreign Policy of Syria

Raymond A. Hinnebusch

INTRODUCTION: HISTORICAL BACKGROUND

Syria's foreign policy orientation has been rooted, ultimately, in the frustration of Syrian nationalist aspirations by Western imperialism. In the wake of the 1917 Arab revolt, Syrians expected the creation of an independent Arab state in historic Syria (Bilad Al-Sham); instead, betraying their promises to the Arabs, the Western powers subjugated this land and dismembered it into four ministates: Syria, Jordan, Lebanon, and Palestine. They also collaborated in the colonization and establishment of the state of Israel in Palestine.[1] In time, Syria gained political independence, but its separation from Lebanon, Palestine, and Jordan proved irreversible, and in Israel Syria encountered a formidable enemy entrenched on its borders. These developments produced a powerful brew of anti-imperialist, anti-Zionist, pan-Arab (or pan-Syrian) sentiment that has imparted an enduring revisionist and irredentist thrust to Syrian foreign policy. This revisionism reached a climax under the radical wing of the Ba'th party (1963–1970), which tried to make Damascus the bastion of a pan-Arab revolution. Through support for a war of liberation in Palestine and attacks on Western interests and clients in the region, this regime sought to mobilize the resources of the whole Arab world against the regional status quo. This challenge brought on the 1967 defeat and the Israeli occupation of new Arab lands, including the Syrian Golan Heights. This defeat, which generated intense new security fears in Syria and gave new roots to revisionism, only further locked Syria into the conflict with Israel and its backers.

A foreign policy is, however, shaped by capabilities as well as frustrations, fears, and desires. The truncated Syrian state provides a slim resource base for a revisionist foreign policy. The country is no match for the United States, the guarantor of the regional status quo,

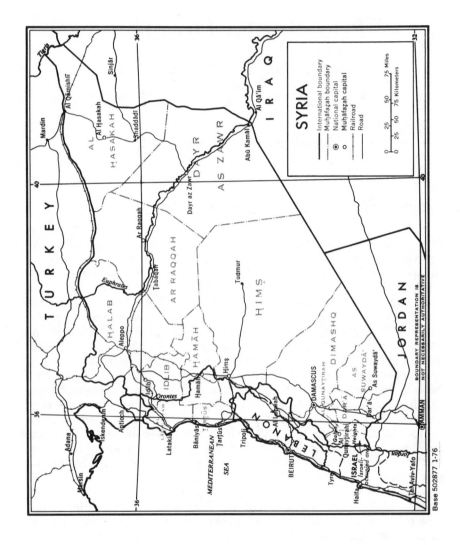

SYRIA

International boundary
Muḥāfaẓah boundary
⊛ National capital
○ Muḥāfaẓah capital
Railroad
Road

0 25 50 75 Miles
0 25 50 75 Kilometers

Base 502877 1-76

and is at a lower level of development and military prowess than its main adversary, Israel. Its inter-state environment is dominated by threats and constraints. To be sure, Syria has sought with some success to broaden its resources through alliances with other states. Superpower rivalry allowed Syria to win arms and some protection from the USSR. The Soviet alliance diluted but did not decisively check the freedom of action of Syria's opponents, and it never provided Syria with the means to seriously challenge the status quo. Syria also drew to an extent on the economic and military power of other Arab states, but the fragmentation of the Arab world and its dependence on the West largely frustrated Syrian efforts to mobilize Arab power behind its foreign policy goals. Syria faced a large and enduring gap between goals and capabilities.

The 1967 defeat brought home the high costs of messianic revisionism in these conditions, and provoked the rise to power of Hafiz Al-Asad, a leader who was prepared to chart a more realistic foreign policy strategy. Asad radically scaled down Syria's foreign policy objectives, focusing on the recovery of Arab lands taken in 1967. The defense of Syria from further attack and the preservation of the regime were given higher priority than under his incautious predecessors. Toward these ends, Asad developed new diplomatic and military means. In a new spirit of diplomatic flexibility, he accepted the principle of a political settlement of the Arab-Israeli conflict in return for Israeli evacuation of the conquered territories, and sought to mobilize the international support needed to force a settlement acceptable to the Arabs. He also greatly expanded Syrian military capabilities as a defense against attack, to gain diplomatic leverage from a credible threat of war in the absence of a political settlement, and ultimately with the aim of recovering the lost lands by force if diplomacy failed. He worked to develop alliances with the USSR and other Arab states, needed to sustain Syrian capabilities. However, the gap between goals and means persisted, because the attainment of even Syria's scaled-down objectives proved illusive, and because Syria had not wholly forgotten earlier ambitions and grievances and continued, at heart, to reject the legitimacy of the status quo. Syrian foreign policy continued to be shaped by the conflict between residual but deep-seated revisionist dreams and an ascendant realist strategy dictated by the limits of Syrian power and the constraints of the environment.

THE DOMESTIC ENVIRONMENT

Society, Political Structure, and Economic Capability

Syria is poorly endowed with the attributes of inter-state power. A small country, it lacks the territory and strategic depth of a major power. Its long borders, unprotected by natural boundaries, are difficult to defend; the Golan Heights, Syria's one natural defense against Israel, were captured in 1967. Syria has also been vulnerable to Israeli movements to outflank its forces through neighboring Lebanon or Jordan.[2] Syria's relatively small population (6.3 million in 1970) provides a limited manpower base and no great obstacle to invaders. The population is at a medium level of social development as measured by such indicators as literacy (about 60%); most Syrians are either peasants or a step removed from the village or rural town. Hence Syria's modern skills and organizational capabilities, though growing, remain inferior to those of its main enemies. Syria is a fragmented society, divided by a multitude of sectarian, ideological, ethnic, and class cleavages that despite an overarching national consciousness and common language, have dissipated much of its political energies in internal conflict. Not only have these divisions frustrated national mobilization, but the willingness of local dissidents to ally themselves with rival Arab powers (Jordan, Saudi Arabia, and especially Iraq) has frequently weakened the regime and its policies.

Syria's economic base is too slim to support its foreign policy commitments. Although it has enjoyed a good rate of growth, the Syrian economy remains transitional. Mainly agrarian, it has only a modest industrial sector. Under the radical Ba'th, Syria embarked on a socialist course that sought to curb economic ties to the West, seen as obstacles to integrated national development and constraints on a nationalist foreign policy. A new state-dominated economy emerged, aimed at self-sufficiency but supported by the Soviet bloc. The regime's simultaneous commitment to an ambitious development program, populist welfare, and an activist foreign policy put severe strains on its resources; defense expenditures alone consumed 15–20% of the GDP and around a third of public expenditures by the 1970s.[3] Under Asad, Syria was forced to rebuild ties to the Western market and the Gulf in a search for new resources. Unabated growth in military, investment, and consumption expenditures ·made Syria increasingly dependent on external economic support, chiefly from the Arab oil countries (Libya, Saudi Arabia, etc.) and the Soviet bloc.[4] This support was crucial in sustaining Syria's foreign policy stance, but Syria's dependence was also a constraint on policy, diluted only by its distribution among several ideologically disparate sources. Dependence on Saudi Arabia, in particular, had a powerful moderating effect on Syrian policy.

Syria's political structure has been shaped in many ways by the external environment. The product of a nationalist movement and based on the military, Syria's political system has developed into a huge authoritarian "national security state" that harnesses society to the exigencies of foreign policy. The concentration of power permits the making and implementation of foreign policy decisions relatively free of institutionalized constraints; government control of the economy readily permits the commitment of the country's resources toward realizing foreign policy goals. A huge professionalized military establishment has emerged, increasingly disciplined after years of unreliability. The political apparatus—the single party, its "mass organizations," and the mass media—though unable to overcome sharp societal cleavages or submerge persistent opposition, has nevertheless mobilized indispensable support for the regime. In times of tension or war with Israel, the population has tended to close ranks around the regime, but the latter's fragile legitimacy prevents the total national mobilization to which leaders have occasionally aspired. Moreover, the appreciable growth of opposition at the end of the 1970s threatened to undermine the foreign policy as well as the domestic position of the regime.

Military Capabilities

Syria's military capabilities have continuously expanded, especially under Asad. At independence, Syria had only a tiny, rudimentary army; by the late 1960s, this had grown to a 75,000-man force equipped with 450 tanks and 140 combat aircraft,[5] and by the late 1970s, to a 230,000-man military machine with over 2,500 tanks and about 500 combat aircraft.[6] This is an enormous defense establishment for a state the size of Syria. Syrian capabilities are not, however, equal to those of its opponents, chiefly Israel. Under Asad, Syria seemed to become more of a match for Israel than heretofore. The military received more and better weapons than ever before.[7] The quality of the officer corps, damaged by the political purges and infighting of the 1950s and 1960s, was restored by growing professionalization under the tutelage of a large Soviet training mission. The fighting spirit of the Syrian army was, at least in the 1973 war, probably equal to that of the Israeli army. Nevertheless, Syria has remained inferior to Israel in organizational and command capabilities.[8] Syrian weaponry has tended to remain a step behind Israel's in quality, and the technical, maintenance, and logistic capacity of the Syrian army has lagged a step behind the supply of increasingly sophisticated weaponry. The air force has remained a weak link in the Syrian military structure; its aircraft are inferior and its pilots less experienced than Israel's. Thus, the air force has proved unable either to mount effective offensive strikes against Israel or even to defend Syrian air space. A growing antiaircraft missile defense system has only partly compensated for this weakness.[9]

Although there is always a possibility that in a future war an Israeli blitzkrieg might (as in 1967) swiftly defeat the Syrian armed forces, Syria's performance in the 1973 war is probably more representative of its true capabilities. In that war, the army's lack of experience in offensive warfare was manifested in its unsophisticated "steamroller" tactics and its failure to seize certain strategic points on the Golan.[10] Big gaps in Syria's air defense umbrella allowed Israel to carry out damaging strikes against nonmilitary targets. However, the Syrian army never collapsed, as it did in 1967; and in defense, well dug-in Syrian forces proved extremely stubborn, making Israeli advances slow and costly.

The U.S. supply to Israel of massive amounts of very sophisticated weaponry after Sinai II threatened to shift the military balance sharply against Syria. The subsequent detachment of Egypt from the Arab war coalition (and the deterioration of the Egyptian armed forces) further enhanced Israel's position vis-à-vis Syria. An effective alliance with Iraq and Jordan could probably have made up in part for the defection of Egypt, but this proved beyond the capacity of Syrian policy. Syria tried instead to achieve military parity with Israel, and sought help from the Soviet Union to restore the former weapons balance. However, Syria remains at a serious quantitative and qualitative disadvantage in facing Israel alone,[11] and in the 1982 Lebanese war, the continuing vulnerability of Syrian defenses led to a major defeat. Currently, Syria lacks a credible offensive capability against Israel, but defensively, Israel might still find it a tough nut to crack.

Political-Diplomatic Capabilities

Under Asad, Syria developed its political-diplomatic capabilities to a higher pitch of sophistication. Asad's Arab diplomacy aimed at constructing an effective all-Arab coalition against Israel that could combine a credible war option with the threat of the oil weapon. Asad was thus quick to set aside his predecessors' ideological quarrels with other Arab rulers in favor of a diplomacy of inter-Arab consultation and coordination. This included bilateral relations with all Arab states regardless of ideology, and participation in the regular Arab summit meetings through which Syria tried to commit the resources of the Arab world to a common Arab stand against Israel.

At the international level, Syria's main aim is to secure international support for Israeli withdrawal from Arab lands and for Palestinian rights. A realist, Asad has never believed that diplomacy could substitute for the threat or use of military force, but he has been more astute than his predecessors in the use of diplomacy to manipulate global forces and rivalries. In the post-1973 period, in particular, Syrian leaders calculated that a diplomatic exploitation of the apparent shift in power and wealth to the Arabs might win back territory that war alone had failed to recover. They also believed that a flexible diplomacy would be useful in gaining international support against Israel and in preventing the isolation of Syria, which hitherto had allowed Israel to attack with relative political impunity. Syria abandoned the uncompromising stance that had previously isolated it, in favor of a policy combining flexibility with adherence to principle. Syria's position has since been to accept a political settlement with Israel on the condition of total Israeli withdrawal from the lands taken in 1967. In spite of U.S. support for Israel, Asad also reestablished diplomatic relations with the United States in order to take advantage of divergences in U.S. and Israeli interests.

Asad's diplomacy has some real achievements to its credit. It has played a vital role in keeping the Palestinian issue on the world agenda.

Asad significantly increased Syria's world diplomatic stature and forced the great powers to recognize Syria as a key to peace and war in the Middle East. Asad developed connections with both the East and the West, and with the radical and conservative Arab capitals, in order to increase Syria's options and resources and to overcome its isolation.[12] He was able to acquire a sliver of the lost Golan Heights through a tough and astute policy of "talking while fighting" in the disengagement negotiations. Syrian diplomatic links to the United States, direct or via Saudi Arabia, narrowed Israel's freedom of military action against Syria.

There have also been failures. Syria built the coalition with Egypt needed to launch the October War but could not prevent Egypt from subsequently breaking ranks, and thus lost much of the bargaining leverage created by the war. Saudi Arabia was persuaded to support Syria diplomatically and financially but not to a point where it would risk its U.S. connection for the Arab cause. Syria's failure after Camp David to strike an alliance with Iraq and to maintain the existing alliance with Jordan has left the eastern front more vulnerable than ever. Finally, Syria's heavy-handed policy toward the Palestinians during the Lebanese conflict permitted Israel and the Maronites to outmaneuver and undermine Syrian policy in Lebanon.

FOREIGN POLICY ORIENTATION

The Syrian Role Conception

Syria has traditionally thought of itself as, above all, the "beating heart of Arabism." Historically, Syrian national identity focused on the idea of a larger Arab nation embracing all Arabic speakers, rather than on the contemporary Syrian state, which has been regarded as an artificial creation of imperialism.[13] Ba'thist doctrine, reflecting the dominant Syrian view, regarded the regional state system—the division of the Arab world and of historic Syria into a multitude of ministates, and the establishment in their heart of a Western bridgehead, Israel—as a mutilation of the Arab nation. Overcoming this "mutilation" was the "eternal mission" of the Ba'th. Syria was seen not as a national unit, but as a base for this national mission. Hence, Syria has been the strongest and most consistent center of pan-Arab sentiment, and a main source of projects for Arab union.[14]

Yet nowhere is the gap between ideal and performance more marked than in Syria's pan-Arab role. Traditionally, two rival centers of Arab power, Iraq and Egypt, and more recently a third, Saudi Arabia, have served as more well-endowed resource bases for pan-Arab leadership. Rather than leading the Arab world, Syria has often found itself at the mercy of pressures and decisions emanating from these other centers. Moreover, Syrian regimes have always been impelled by a narrower raison d'état designed to protect and advance their own Syrian base, and this has frequently conflicted with the pan-Arab ideal. Since the establishment of the United Arab Republic in 1958, no Syrian political elite has been prepared to sacrifice its power on the altar of pan-Arabism. In 1963, the ostensibly pan-Arabist Ba'th government helped scuttle plans for union with Egypt and Iraq in the fear it would mean the surrender of power to Nasser; in the late 1970s plans to merge Syria and Iraq in the face of a common Israeli threat foundered for similar reasons.

After thirty-five years of statehood, disappointments with several unity experiments, three wars, and the loss of Syrian territory in pursuit of Arabist designs, Syrian preoccupation with pan-Arabism seems to have significantly receded. Indeed, the main thrust of Syrian foreign policy in the 1970s was entirely conventional: to recover Arab lands through a classical strategy of military threat, alliances, balance-of-power politics, and acceptance of a peace amounting to a reluctant accommodation with the regional state system. Raison d'état seemed to have triumphed over pan-Arab messianism.

Nevertheless, Syrians still do not perceive the regional environment as a classical state system of distinctive national entities; the Arab states are still thought to make up a nation with an overriding national interest that ought to govern their foreign policies. Identification with the current Syrian state has yet to take the form of an exclusive Syrian nationalism. Rather Syria's special identity is Arab: Syrians consider themselves the most Arab of the Arabs, the "conscience of the Arabs," and the main champions of the Arab cause. On this basis, Syrian leaders regard themselves as better able than other Arab leaders to interpret the higher overall Arab national interest. Even when following policies apparently motivated by a Syrian raison d'état, Syrians have justified themselves with the argument that "what's good for Syria is good for the Arab nation." Syria's immediate military-security needs vis-á-vis Israel—given its status as the most "steadfast" of the Arab front-line states—are considered to be indistinguishable from the higher Arab national interest. In the Syrian view, Syria is entitled to draw by right on the wealth of the Arab oil states, to demand the ouster of Egypt from the Arab community, and even to discipline the pursuit of Palestinian "particularism" by the PLO. In the Ba'thist world view, Syria's special role remains that of the "vanguard" of a larger Arab nation.[15]

Not surprisingly, Syrian attitudes toward and relations with other Arab states have been profoundly ambivalent: a mixture of alliance and rivalry. The feeling of common nationhood, a common enemy, and a recognition of the benefits of cooperation have often brought Syria together with the other Arabs. But Syria's policies, whether they follow its own special interpretation of the higher national interest or lesser reasons of state, have often met with opposition from other Arab states. Hence Syria has often seen these states as threats, rivals, and obstacles to its policies. In the 1960s, Syria saw itself as a base for the export of revolutionary nationalism against other Arab kings and presidents. Traditional Arab regimes were included in the same category as Israel and viewed as agents of Western imperialism. Syrian insistence on its superior nationalist virtue—justified or not—isolated Syria from both the conservative states and more moderate nationalist states like Egypt. Under Asad, a residual radicalism has largely been eclipsed by a new conception of Syria as leader of a concert of all Arab states, regardless of ideology, aimed at recovering Arab rights from Israel. Yet even this more cooperative stance has not prevented intense rivalry between Syria and other major Arab powers, such as Egypt, Iraq, and Saudi Arabia, who have contested the Syrian view of a proper foreign policy.

Perceptions of the Global System

Syria's perceptions of, and role in, the global system turn chiefly on its relations with the United States, the USSR, and Western Europe. The Syrian view of the global arena and the rival great powers has been shaped by Arab nationalist reaction against the historical victim-ization of the Arab nation by Western imperialism. Syria has traditionally thought of itself as a member of the anti-imperialist Third World camp.[16] Aligned with neither East nor West, Syria has not, however, remained equidistant between these two poles. Syria's attitude toward the East and West has been determined by their positions on the issues of importance to Arab nationalism, in particular the Palestine cause. By this standard, the record of the Eastern bloc is far superior to that of the West; hence friendship with the socialist states and hostility to (chiefly U.S.) "imperialism" have been traditional features of Syrian foreign policy under the Ba'th.

The United States. Syria and the United States have a history of mutual animosity. President Nixon's reference to Syrian leaders as "crazies" was not untypical of the view from Washington. Syria, for its part, had ample reason to dislike the United States. U.S. efforts to harness Syria to anti-Soviet alliances in the 1950s, several CIA intrigues against nationalist governments in Damascus, interventions with Britain against Arab nationalist forces in neighboring Lebanon and Jordan, and efforts, in the name of the Eisenhower Doctrine, to "quarantine" Syrian radicalism: all were part of the formative experiences of the current political elite.[17] Even more important has been the role of the United States in establishing and sustaining Israel. Syrians have not forgotten that in 1967, UN ambassador Arthur Goldberg, as Security Council president, deliberately delayed a meeting of the council until Israel could—in violation of an earlier UN cease-fire—complete its conquest of the Golan.[18] They know that the United States was prepared to directly intervene against them during the Jordanian-Palestinian war of 1970. They know, too, that it was massive U.S. arms shipments that enabled Israel to reverse Syrian advances and keep the Israeli hold on the Golan in 1973. Hence Syrians have traditionally thought of the

United States as the head of the "world imperialist camp." U.S. ties with Israel have been seen as organic, not accidental. Israel was seen not only as a U.S. client but as a surrogate acting in U.S. interests; for Israel, the United States represents a vital lifeline and strategic depth without which it could not survive.

Under Asad, this traditional view has altered. The rise of Arab military and economic power at the time of the 1973 war and the consequent U.S. need to placate the Arab world was understood by Syrian decision-makers as introducing a potential divergence between U.S. and Israeli interests and providing new Arab leverage over the United States. The United States might, it was thought, be brought to consider Arab interests in order to protect its own, and to pressure Israel to withdraw from the lands taken in 1967. After 1973, Syria thus accepted Kissinger's mediation efforts and reestablished long inactive diplomatic connections with Washington. To a lesser extent, cooperation with the United States was a concession to Saudi Arabia, Syria's paymaster. Unlike Sadat, however, Asad expected that the United States would bring pressure to bear on Israel only if, in the absence of a peace settlement, its own interests were under threat of renewed war and an interruption of access to oil.

Syrian assessment of the extent to which the United States has altered its total commitment to Israel has fluctuated. At times—e.g., after the Kissinger-mediated disengagement on the Golan, and after Carter's 1977 commitment to seek an overall settlement that would provide for Palestinian rights—Syrians were optimistic. More often, this optimism was overshadowed by the suspicion that the U.S. aim was to substitute a partial settlement for a comprehensive one, divide the Arabs, and keep them militarily inferior to Israel. After Sinai II, the accompanying massive arms shipments to Israel, and the U.S. promise not to talk to the PLO; and again after Camp David, Syrian suspicions of U.S. intentions seemed confirmed. Yet at the beginning of the 1980s, Syrian policy-makers still had some hope that the United States might yet be brought to realize the possible costs of its failure to support an Arab-Israeli settlement acceptable to the Arabs.[19]

Western Europe. Western Europe has traditionally been considered by Syrians as part of Western imperialism. France occupied Syria for a quarter of a century, and together with Britain was responsible for the dismemberment of Bilad Al-Sham and the colonization of Palestine. Both powers supplied arms to Israel and stood against Arab nationalism throughout the 1950s. West Germany made large financial payments to Israel. However, as Western Europe withdrew from its imperial role in the Middle East and loosened connections with Israel, relations with Syria improved. Under de Gaulle, Franco-Syrian relations were very good. By the 1970s, European evenhandedness in the Middle East conflict had dissipated much previous Syrian hostility and suspicion. In consequence, Syrian economic ties with Western Europe—in contrast to those with the United States—developed rapidly, overshadowing those forged with the East in the 1960s.[20]

The Soviet Union. The USSR is Syria's major international patron. The basis for good Syrian-Soviet relations was laid in the late 1950s when Moscow extended political protection to Syria from intense Western pressures, broke a Western arms embargo of the country and entered into technical and trade agreements with Syria. In the 1960s, under the leadership of the radical socialist wing of the Ba'th Party, Syria swung sharply toward the East, and forged a dense network of cultural, economic, and interparty relations.[21] The Soviet Union became Syria's main trading partner and source of development credit, aid, and technology. More important, the USSR became Syria's chief backer in the conflict with Israel, the sole supplier of the Syrian army, and Syria's patron in the international arena. The radical Ba'thists fell in 1970, but Syrian-Soviet relations remained close under the subsequent Asad regime. Although there is an anti-Soviet wing inside the regime (reputedly led by Mustafa Tlas) and considerable hostility toward the Soviets among religious and bourgeois elements of the population, most Syrians consider the Soviet Union their only dependable global ally. It is the one country that has consistently been willing to provide Syria with sizable amounts of economic and military aid without unacceptable compromise to Syrian nationalist commitments. Syrians realize that Soviet friendship follows from self-interest, i.e., the desire to keep U.S. influence out, acquire bases, etc., but they believe that their interests coincide with those of Moscow in most issue areas. Barring a Middle East peace settlement, Soviet support is in fact absolutely indispensable to Syria. The Syrian-Soviet relation is, of course, an unequal one, given Syria's dependency and Moscow's preponderance, but the Soviets' desire to maintain influence in the Middle East has made Syria important to Moscow, especially after the loss of their position in Egypt in the early 1970s. Syria thus has some leverage over its huge ally, and has never allowed Moscow to unduly influence its policy; Syria is far from being a Soviet satellite or surrogate.

Syrian-Soviet relations have not been without friction. Syrian leaders objected to Soviet pressures to accept a political settlement with Israel until they decided to pursue such a course themselves. Many Syrian policy initiatives—support of guerrilla warfare against Israel, the 1970 intervention in Jordan, the 1973 war—were taken against Soviet counsels of caution. In the 1960s, Asad objected to the weight thrown by the Soviet embassy in support of his radical rivals, although he did not, after seizing power, allow this to prejudice him against Moscow. The USSR objected strenuously to the Syrian intervention against the left in Lebanon and appears to have slowed down its economic and military aid as a means of exerting pressure on Damascus; but this quarrel, too, proved fleeting, although Damascus made it known that it had expected more understanding from its long-time ally. The post-1973 U.S. intervention in the Arab-Israeli conflict temporarily lessened Syrian dependency on Moscow; but because the United States was unwilling to satisfy Syrian interests, these developments never really threatened Moscow's position in Syria. The most durable source of Syrian discontent with its patron has been the reluctance of the USSR to make commitments to Syria comparable to those made by the United States to Israel. The Soviet Union did nothing to protect Syria from Israel in 1967 and in general has proven unwilling to take major risks on Syria's behalf. Moscow has also been reluctant to supply Syria with advanced weapons comparable to those given to Israel, although the Soviet Union did make huge arms deliveries during the 1973 war, which jeopardized détente with the United States. Since that time the Soviets have at least partially matched U.S. deliveries to Israel. This, combined with Syria's growing feeling of vulnerability and perception of U.S. disinterest in a comprehensive settlement after Camp David, led Asad to alter his traditional policy of formal nonalignment and sign a treaty of friendship and defense with the USSR in 1980.[22] Soviet passivity during the 1982 Israeli invasion of Lebanon and the poor showing of Soviet weapons during this conflict seemed to cast some doubt on the value of this alliance, however.

Perception of the Regional System

Israel. Israel is Syria's main enemy. Syrians perceive Israel as an imperialist-linked colonial-settler state implanted in the heart of historic Syria at the expense of Syria's southern Palestinian cousins. Dividing the eastern from the western Arab world, Israel is a permanent obstacle to Arab unionist aspirations. Syria and Israel have fought three wars and many lesser clashes in which Israel has typically inflicted punishment or humiliation on Syria. Since 1967 Israel has occupied a chunk of Syrian territory, the Golan Heights, which it annexed in 1981.

In the 1960s Syria pursued an active policy of challenging Israel, giving support to Palestinian fedayeen and trying to push the Arab states into preparation for war.[23] In 1967 war broke out, but the Arab forces were defeated. In the 1970s, underlying attitudes toward Israel barely altered. Israel's legitimacy is still not recognized, nor has insistence on Palestinian rights to all of Palestine been abandoned. But the realization that Syria can at present do little to reverse the establishment of the Zionist state has induced a substantial moderation in Syrian policy. In practice, Syria has postponed the "liberation of Palestine" to a remote and indefinite future and is now prepared to end the state of war in return for evacuation of the Arab lands taken in 1967 and creation of a Palestinian state on the West Bank.

In the Syrian view, such a "peace" would come about through a UN accord rather than through a state-to-state peace treaty. The end of belligerency would not entail either diplomatic or trade relations with Israel, which Syria considers to be the right of any sovereign state to pursue or not as it pleases. Demilitarized zones and peacekeeping forces between Syria and Israel are acceptable provided they are on both sides of the border, not merely on the Golan. The end of belligerency would imply no acceptance of Israel's right to Palestine and, indeed, a "political struggle" with Israel would continue over the rights of Palestinians to return to and enjoy equal citizenship inside Israel.[24]

Syria's core demands—total evacuation and Palestinian rights—are probably not negotiable. Syria is unlikely to accept any settlement that would not return all of the Golan. Not only is Syrian public opinion adamant on the recovery of the Golan, but the Ba'th, which was responsible for its loss, could not at the risk of its political survival settle for less. Nor is the regime likely to accept an "autonomy" for West Bank Palestinians that would permit continued Israeli control of the area: the technical distinction in Syrian minds between "Syrian" and "Palestinian" interests is probably not yet sharp enough to legitimize any such cosmetic solution. Indeed, the pre-1973 Syrian rejection of UN Resolution 242 was precisely on the grounds that the resolution ignored Palestinian rights, treating the Palestinian issue as a mere refugee problem. It also left the door open to "minor" border "adjustments," at the expense of Syrian recovery of the Golan. Syria has since accepted the resolution only according to its own interpretation that it provides for Palestinian rights and total Israeli withdrawal to the 1967 borders.

The conditions of a settlement have so far remained purely hypothetical, since Israel has shown no intention of relinquishing further territory, and has legally and demographically attempted to incorporate both the Golan and the West Bank. The United States has not yet felt any strong compulsion to force Israel to exchange territory for peace. Syria at present lacks the military or diplomatic leverage to alter this situation. Syrian policy in the early 1980s concentrated on preventing partial settlements of the Arab-Israeli conflict which ignored Syria's minimal conditions for peace. Ultimately, Syria hopes for a change in the strategic balance through the growth of Arab power and U.S. realization of the dangers to its interests of continuing conflict.

The Palestinians. Syria regards Palestine as a lost part of itself and Palestinians as "southern cousins." There is a sizable and influential Palestinian community in Syria, linked by a multitude of ties to Syrians. Syria has seen itself—perhaps rightly—as the main champion of the Palestinians in the Arab world; Syria played an instrumental role in the formation of the Palestinian resistance movement and has been a major source of its military and political support.[25] Several times it blocked—militarily or politically—efforts by Arab states to repress the resistance movement; alone among the Arab states, Syria came to its aid during "Black September." Syrian rejection of any Middle East peace that does not include Palestinian rights remains critical to Palestinian leverage in any resolution of the Middle East conflict.[26] Defense of the Palestinian cause has been and probably will remain crucial to the legitimacy of any Syrian regime.

In the 1960s, Syria was committed to the "liberation" of all Palestine. Under Asad, this evolved into the lesser demand that Palestinian rights be satisfied in any Middle East peace. Although Syrian spokesmen have often stated that the definition of these "rights" is a matter for the PLO, Asad has made it known that they include not only the establishment of a Palestinian state on the West Bank, but also the right of exiled Palestinians to return to their homes in Israel. The former should probably be taken as a short-range minimum demand, the latter as a long-range maximum demand.

Despite the ostensible Syrian commitment to the Palestinian cause, relations between Damascus and the PLO have nevertheless fallen into the pattern of conflict and cooperation typical of inter-Arab relations. Syria has consistently claimed tutelage over the resistance by virtue of its patronage of the Palestine cause, historic Syrian-Palestinian ties, and Syria's role as the major front-line state in the Arab East. Ba'th leaders have insisted that particular Palestinian interests must not be pursued in conflict with the overall Arab interest the Ba'th claims to represent. This is especially so under Asad, who in contrast to his radical predecessors, has tended to denigrate the resources the PLO, as compared to Syria, can contribute to the common struggle with Israel.

The PLO has tried to minimize its dependence on any one of the Arab states, aware that their raison d'état has often conflicted with Palestinian aims. Palestinian leaders have thus long feared Syria's efforts to impose its will on its smaller partner. Damascus has tried to exert influence inside the PLO through Syrian-controlled Palestinian formations, such as Al-Sa'iqa and Syrian-based Palestine Liberation Army (PLA) units, a presence viewed with misgivings by mainstream Palestinian leaders such as Arafat and even more so by the rejectionists. At times, Syrian leaders have seemed intent on using these clients to capture the leadership of the Palestinian movement. Syria has even used force against the PLO. Both Arafat and George Habaash spent time in Syrian jails. The bloody battles between the Syrian army and the fedayeen in Lebanon, in which many Palestinians have been killed, have caused a growing breach between the two sides. The PLO has tried to preserve its autonomy from Syria chiefly by playing against Damascus the influence of Syria's rivals—Egypt, Iraq, and Saudi Arabia, a practice the Syrian leaders much dislike.

The substantive differences between Syria and the PLO have chiefly turned on goals and strategy in the conflict with Israel. Syria's movement away from commitment to the full liberation of Palestine did not lead to any overt conflict with the mainstream PLO because of a parallel scaling down of objectives by the Palestinians themselves. But it did divide Syria from rejectionist Palestinians and was bound to make even mainstream leaders question the depth of Syria's commitments. Palestinian leaders have also suspected that Syria lacks their commitment to the principle of independent Palestinian statehood on any Palestinian territory recovered from Israel; Syria might accept or even prefer its incorporation into some wider Arab entity, if that advanced Syrian ambitions to bring parts of historic Syria back under its sway. There have also been several typical conflicts over strategy. Syrian restrictions on Palestinian operations from Syrian territory demonstrated the divergence between the Palestinian need for a military front with Israel and the demands of Syrian security. The Palestinians' effort to widen their military base in Lebanon conflicted with Syria's effort to harness them to its political-diplomatic strategy. In short, although Syrian and Palestinian interests overlap, they are not identical.[27]

The Eastern Front States. Iraq, Jordan, and Lebanon are regarded by Syria as parts of the Arab nation and, as such, as natural partners in the Arab eastern front against Israel. Under Asad, earlier efforts to bring them into the struggle through revolution gave way to diplomatic means, but these efforts bore little durable fruit. Cooperation between Syria and its Arab neighbors was repeatedly shattered by new rounds of conflict.

Asad long worked to include Jordan in his strategy against Israel. Jordan's army was a military asset, particularly in preventing Israeli moves to outflank the Golan defenses. Jordan also had to be kept from making a separate peace with Israel. At the beginning of the decade, Jordanian repression of the fedayeen postponed but was not allowed to prevent subsequent development of close relations. In 1973 Jordanian forces fought on the Golan, and in the mid-1970s, the two states were pursuing political and economic "integration." However, at the end of the decade Asad allowed Jordanian tolerance of anti-Ba'th Islamic dissidents to rupture the Syrian-Jordanian alliance, at no little cost to Syrian security and political leverage.

Iraq—militarily powerful, oil rich, and ruled by a wing of the Ba'th party—should have been a natural Syrian ally. The militant wing of Syrian opinion long preferred an Iraqi alliance to the Egyptian and Saudi alliances the regime maintained. Asad did, on and off, try to build a common military front with Iraq, but except for the Iraqi contribution to the 1973 war, intense rivalry has prevented serious collaboration.[28] Leadership conflicts, historical intraparty quarrels, and until recently, Iraqi rejection of a political settlement, were the main forces dividing the two states. The Syrian leadership so feared the hostility of the Iraqis and their ability to foster Syrian dissidence that it tended to consider Iraq more as a threat than as a potential ally. In the wake of Camp David, Arab and Soviet efforts to bring the two states together foundered on these fears and rivalries. When the perceived interests of their regimes diverged from the security interests of their states and of the Arab world in general, both Syrian and Iraqi leaders put regime interests first.

Under the radicals, Syria tried to stimulate revolution in Lebanon and turn it into a base for Palestinian fedayeen. Under Asad, Syria continued to consider a Palestinian presence in southern Lebanon as useful to keep pressure on Israel and intervened a number of times to protect Palestinians against both Israeli and Lebanese attacks. Nevertheless, Asad wanted to maintain Lebanon as a nonmilitarized, Western-protected buffer against Israel. To make it a confrontation state would invite a possible Israeli drive into Lebanon, threatening Syria's soft western flank. Syrian intervention in the Lebanese civil war was motivated chiefly by the desire to maintain a Lebanese buffer against Israel. However, the contradiction between Syria's desire to keep Lebanon as a stable buffer and yet maintain a Palestinian presence in the south became apparent during the civil war; both Israel and the Maronites made sure this double game would not go on.

Egypt. After a long period of revolutionary rivalry,[29] Egypt and Syria struck a close alliance in the early 1970s. Both states shared an incentive for military action against Israel to recover their lost territories and only in alliance was such action possible. Alliance with Egypt also served to satisfy the strong pro-Egyptian trend in Syrian public opinion. This alliance thus became the cornerstone of Asad's foreign policy in the early 1970s. The joint Egyptian-Syrian attack on Israel in 1973 did break the prewar stalemate and opened prospects for a diplomatic settlement that would recover the lost territories. But divergences in Egyptian and Syrian purposes appeared from the outset and ultimately frustrated Syrian aims. During the war, Sadat's cautious strategy allowed Israel to concentrate the bulk of its forces on the Syrian front. Sadat also bid for a cease-fire without Syrian agreement.[30] In the postwar negotiations, he increasingly disregarded the common Arab position in pursuit of agreements with Israel that left Syria out. No combination of Syrian threats and blandishments could, however, deter Sadat from his separate course. Syrian-Egyptian relations deteriorated rapidly after Sinai II.[31] Following Sadat's trip to Jerusalem, Syria broke with Egypt and attempted to mobilize the Arab world against Sadat's effort to lead it along what Syria saw as the road to capitulation. Syria hoped, however, that removal of the Sadat regime might yet bring Egypt back onto the "right" path.

Saudi Arabia and the Gulf States. After three years of conflict in which the Ba'th made no secret of its desire to overthrow the "reactionary" oil states, Syria under Asad set out to forge a strategic alliance with Arab petropower. Asad believed that through a combination of public pressure, appeal to their Arab feelings, and an end to antitraditional radicalism, the oil princes could be brought to serve the Arab cause. In fact, he did secure the financial backing that allowed the reconstruction and almost continual expansion of the Syrian army since 1970. Suspicions and stresses in Syrian-Saudi relations persisted, however. Saudi Arabia did employ the oil weapon in 1973, but this was more to Egypt's benefit than to Syria's. Subsequently the Saudis proved unwilling, in spite of the neglect of Syria's interests in the peace negotiations, to tighten oil pressure on Washington on Syria's behalf. The Saudis were also wary of the growth of Syrian influence in the mid-1970s, notably in Lebanon. They have tried to use Syria's economic dependency to curb its militancy, much to the annoyance of Damascus.[32] Although Syrian decision-makers are aware that the tightening links between the United States and Arab oil power make a strong Saudi stand on the Arab-Israeli issue ever less likely, they have little choice but to maintain their Saudi ties. Not only has Syria become economically dependent on Riyadh and the other oil princedoms, but Saudi Arabia, alone of the Arab states, has real leverage over Washington. Syrian decision-makers seem to hope that ultimately Saudi patience with Washington will exhaust itself and Arab solidarity will prevail.

Syrian-Saudi relations are not, of course, detached from Syria's domestic interests and conflicts. A pro-Saudi group, led by top officers like Mustafa Tlas and supported by Sunni business interests and wider streams of pious Islamic opinion, has held the upper hand. But a radical element remains wary of overtly close relations with, or dependence on, Riyadh, seeing this relationship as a threat to the whole Arab revolution and as a source of corruption and reaction inside Syria.

The Maghreb. In the Syrian view, Algeria and Libya are kindred radical nationalist states whose support for the Arab cause and Syrian policy can usually be counted on. Relations with Libya have been close although checkered. Qaddafi's interference in Syrian politics and his denunciation of the Syrian drive against the PLO in Lebanon marred longer periods of amicable relations in which Libya tried to use its money to bolster the Syrian front against Israel and lure Syria into more militant positions. The high points of Libyan-Syrian relations, in 1971 and again in 1980, were marked by unity arrangements that proved in practice to be chiefly foreign policy alliances. Finally, in contrast to his predecessors, who regarded traditional Morocco and accommodating Tunisia as traitors to the Arab cause, Asad, in pursuit of his all-Arab front, has stayed on good terms with both states. In 1973 Moroccan troops actually fought on the Syrian front.

THE DECISION-MAKING PROCESS

Foreign policy decision-making in Syria is concentrated at the apex of the Ba'th's authoritarian single-party state. The state establishment is dominated by a powerful presidency resting on three institutional pillars: the party, the military, and the ministerial bureaucracy. The leaders of these institutions make up a power elite that the president both leads and consults in the decision-making process.

Although the president is clearly dominant, the decision-making process nevertheless appears to be collegial; other members of the elite are not mere staff readily discarded or ignored. Foreign policy matters are decided by a circle of key leaders of varying scope, dominated by the president and top foreign policy and defense specialists. Top military leaders have been very prominent in this circle because Asad is dependent on military support and because most foreign policy decisions have had immediate military-security implications. During the 1970s the most regular members of the decision-making circle seem to have been Defense Minister Mustafa Tlas, Chief of Staff Hikmet Shihabi, Air Force and Security Chief Naji Jamil, Foreign Minister Abdel-Halim Khaddam, and probably Rifa'at Al-Asad. At times, however, the decision-making circle expanded, embracing the prime minister; the assistant secretary-generals of the two Ba'th party commands; other members of the commands specializing in foreign policy, security, and defense affairs; the heads of the various intelligence agencies; and close presidential advisors. An even wider circle of persons, including the full membership of the party commands, key ministers, and members of the National Progressive Front (a pro-Ba'th coalition of small parties) has sometimes been consulted.

Evidence for this collegial decision-making process is available for two critical decisions: the Golan disengagement and the Lebanese intervention. Kissinger found in the disengagement negotiations that in contrast to Egypt, where only Sadat had to be convinced, in Syria the whole foreign policy inner circle had to be present and collectively persuaded. Dawisha's study of the Lebanese case indicates that when critical and controversial decisions were being taken, the consultation unit tended to broaden; thirty-eight persons were evidently involved in the consultation unit that decided on the intervention.[33] In the consultative process, all actors are not of equal weight. Asad's position was rather more than that of first among equals. The choice of a wider or narrower decision unit was probably largely left to his discretion; in arbitrating between rival factions, he could effectively decide which would prevail; and, if he felt strongly about a course of action, a coalescence of other members of the elite against him was most unlikely. But Asad seems to be a relatively self-effacing consensual leader who carefully weighs the views of his subordinates before taking a stand. Such decision-making by consultation appears to have been critical to Asad's ability to maintain personal support and the stability of his regime. This style may permit more input into the policy-making process than is true in more personalistic authoritarian systems.

Asad's Orientation

Asad has left a perceptible imprint on Syrian foreign policy that contrasts with that of his predecessors. He is a cautious realist whose moves are governed by careful calculation rather than impulse or desire. His harrowing experience in 1967 (when as defense minister he saw his unprepared forces mauled by an Israeli attack brought on by the recklessness of ideologically minded colleagues) no doubt accounts for the new tone he has imparted to Syrian decision-making. He has, in fact, described his policy as "realistic" as opposed to the "theory" of his predecessors. Asad tends to think in the military-strategic terms of a military professional, rather than in ideological-political terms, and his most important decisions have reflected this propensity. Examples are the relative tolerance of King Hussein's repression of the fedayeen in 1970, the decision to bury the hatchet with Saudi Arabia, and the intervention against the Palestinians in Lebanon. All ideological differences must, in his view, be subordinated to the effort to mobilize all Arab resources against Israel. As a negotiator, Asad combines a stubborn defense of principle with flexibility. Believing strongly in the justice of the Arab cause, he will not readily concede major principles, yet is flexible enough to bargain if some advantage can be won from it; he is a shrewd, audacious, and tenacious bargainer who combines the romanticism and sense of honor and wrongs of the bedouin with the cunning and haggling skill of the traditional *suk*. In contrast to Sadat's impulsive tendency to make concessions, Kissinger found that in Damascus, the smallest issue was a matter of stubborn bargaining.[34]

Foreign Policy Interest Groups

Several small groups occasionally exercise influence in the policy process and could thus be called foreign policy "interest groups." This influence may be exerted directly, through representatives included in the policy consultation process, or indirectly, in that decision-makers have felt constrained to take account of their views and expectations. Ba'th party militants, more ideological and inflexible than the relatively pragmatic top leadership, have limited the latter's freedom. In the Golan disengagement negotiations, they seemed to constrain Asad as much as he constrained them. For a time, there was a faction inside the party that wanted Syria to join the rejectionist camp and exchange Egyptian or Saudi alliances for an Iraqi one. A residue of militant socialists also seem to persist inside the party, and their influence is enhanced by the relatively strong current of radical opinion among the intelligentsia as a whole. However, Asad has, through purges and new recruitment over the years, gradually diluted this militancy.[35] The lower and middle ranks of the officer corps—many of whom are party members—are probably also a relatively militant group. The military appear to be "hawkish" toward Israel. The reluctance of the officer corps to accept the cease-fire in the October War of 1973 contributed to the Syrian decision to continue the conflict over Mt. Hermon during the first half of 1974. A strong wave of anti-Egyptian sentiment swept the military after Sinai II, and it is known that elements of the military overtly or covertly resisted Syrian intervention against the Palestinians in Lebanon. On the other hand, certain high-ranking officers, such as Tlas and Jamil, have been often identified with a conservative trend linked to Saudi Arabia and suspicious of the Soviet Union. Other top military men, such as Chief of Staff Shihabi, are thought to be nonpolitical professionals, chiefly concerned with the security, capabilities, and integrity of the armed forces; they are likely to be advocates of greater defense spending and of pressure on the USSR to supply Syria with more advanced weaponry. Under Asad, military discipline has been much more effective than heretofore, and the ever-larger army is increasingly unlikely to be united behind any given policy demand; nevertheless, the Ba'th elite must still take care to satisfy its military constituency, and on issues such as the military budget and peace and war, the voice of the officer corps is uniquely powerful. In comparison to the party militants, the professional foreign policy bureaucracy seems to provide a voice of moderation in regime councils.

Although pressure groups have been described here in institutional terms, the actual units of interest articulation are more likely to be fluid personal factions and opinion groups rooted in, and cutting across, institutional lines. Interest articulation has undoubtedly taken place within the informal units of elite consultation described above. In addition, formal assemblies, notably Ba'th party congresses and the rounds of elections immediately preceding them, appear to have sometimes served as wider arenas within which foreign policy pressure groups have debated regime strategy and occasionally challenged it. Up to now, however, unified, sustained broad opposition to the leadership does not appear to have crystallized inside the regime's institutional base. When they have felt it essential, Asad and his inner circle have not hesitated to override the objections of their followers, or even to repress challenges. They have generally claimed authority to exercise broad discretion in interpreting the party policy ostensibly decided in party congresses. Thus, for example, the formal resolutions of congresses have typically appeared more uncompromising toward Israel than has the actual policy followed by the leadership.

Public Opinion

The broader public plays a role in Syria not dissimilar to what is found in other developing political systems. On the one hand, a "public mood" seems to define certain bounds outside which decision-makers dare not tread without risking their legitimacy. This is not a small matter for a regime that has never enjoyed more than precarious legitimacy, in a country where regime support is very closely linked to positions and performance on nationalist issues, and where deviations from traditional postures readily become weapons used against incumbent elites by their opponents. On several issues, public opinion leaves the elite little freedom of action. Because it was responsible for the loss of the Golan, the Ba'th leadership is under a special burden to recover it without compromise. Syrian opinion also upholds a special obligation to the Palestinians. Moreover, the ruling elite's nationalist credentials are vulnerable to attack in spite of its long record of militancy because many Syrians distrust its Arabism on sectarian grounds.[36] The nationally mobilized segment of the Syrian populace is, owing to the long struggle with Israel, probably quite high in comparison with other states at similar stages of development; this "attentive public" is not easily disregarded in elite calculations.

On the other hand, the government is not without freedom of action in its foreign policy. A half-literate population is vulnerable to manipulation by an elite that enjoys a near monopoly of the mass media and is prepared to forcibly repress overt opposition. On some policy matters, the public is divided or inattentive. The government's ability to win relative public acquiescence in its Lebanese intervention against the Palestinians, a policy that hitherto seemed politically unimaginable, is one indicator of the latitude enjoyed by decision-makers. However, the Islamic uprisings of the late 1970s may have partly been a function of the erosion of regime legitimacy as a result of this venture.

Several major tendencies can be discerned in Syrian public opinion on foreign policy issues. There is a militant rejectionist element on the campuses and among intellectuals that opposes any political settlement accepting Israel and the relative détente with the United States, but it seems to have declined in the 1970s. A pro-Western peace faction, strongest among the commercial bourgeoisie, would like to follow Sadat's course, anticipating greater business prosperity and a reduction of the role of the military in society as a result of a peace settlement. The right wing generally opposes Syria's alliance with the USSR as a threat to its religious ideals and material interests. The dominant trend in public opinion is centrist. It favors nonalignment, but views good relations with the USSR as indispensible. Tired of years of conflict and stalemate and aware of the costs of continuing war, Syrians want a peace settlement, but not at any price: the government position—peace in return for withdrawal from the occupied lands—seems in fact to reflect the mainstream public view fairly accurately.[37]

FOREIGN POLICY BEHAVIOR

The Rise of Hafiz Al-Asad and the Eclipse of Revolutionary Nationalism

The regime and foreign policy of Hafiz Al-Asad emerged as a reaction to the collapse of the Ba'th party's revolutionary-nationalist strategy in the 1967 war. The rise of the Ba'th was itself in many respects an outcome of the nationalist ferment stimulated by the creation of Israel. In 1963, the party came to power with an ambitious program of social revolution and national assertion; a challenge to Israel and its backers was its central national priority. As Ba'th leaders saw it, Israel was the principal obstacle to the realization of all nationalist aims and constituted the last bastion of imperialism in the heart of the Arab nation. Yet while Arab governments talked much, they failed to act. Daily, Israel became stronger; Israeli diversion of the Jordan River would make room for new immigrants, and Israel would soon have nuclear weapons. If the Arabs did not act soon it would be too late. Once radical Ba'thists seized power and were in a position to decide, it was incumbent upon them, as they saw it, to act.

The strategy put forward by the radical Ba'thists was based on the proposition that although Israel might be militarily superior, the Arabs could prevail in a protracted "war of popular liberation" in which the numerically superior Arab masses, the Arab armies, and Arab oil would be totally mobilized in the national struggle. The Ba'th effort to initiate this national mobilization took two main forms: Syria began to train, arm, and support Palestinian fedayeen in a guerrilla campaign against Israel's borders, and the regime also embarked on a revolution in Syria and tried to export it to the rest of the Arab world. Through this revolution, it was thought, the Arab masses could be politically mobilized and the traditional Western-linked Arab regimes, who refused to put Arab resources at the service of the national cause, toppled.[38] This provocative policy helped precipitate the 1967 war in which the Arab armies were defeated and new Arab land was seized by Israel. Yet the Ba'thist radicals were determined to continue their militant course; Syria would continue to back the fedayeen and would stand as a firm obstacle to any attempts at a political settlement in which the Arabs would have to accept Israel at the expense of the Palestine cause.[39] There is little doubt, however, that in spite of this militancy, the precarious legitimacy of the radical Ba'th regime was shattered by the 1967 defeat and the loss of Syrian territory in the war. As a leadership aspiring to total national mobilization, it had been fatally compromised.

Although Hafiz Al-Asad had been a part of the leadership that pursued this course, he soon came to doubt its efficacy. As defense minister, he was especially sensitive to the immediate military risks and costs of provoking new Israeli attacks on a Syrian army unprepared to repulse them. Thus in 1968, Asad emerged as the leader of a faction inside the Ba'th regime calling for a change of course. Asad argued that Syria was incapable of sustaining a costly, interminable, and in his view, ineffective guerrilla war with Israel. Rather, Syria should focus its efforts on the more realistic goal of recovering, through limited conventional war, the territories lost in the 1967 war. Although he did not say so, Asad seemed to believe that since the Ba'th had lost the Golan, it had a special responsibility to get it back. Asad's strategy called for (1) priority for the buildup of the regular Syrian army and the subordination of all guerrilla activities to conventional military strategy; (2) a close alliance with Egypt, a necessary partner in any war against Israel, as well as with other eastern front Arab states; (3) détente with the traditional Arab oil states who alone possessed the resources to finance an Arab military buildup; and (4) an end to the pursuit of revolution inside and outside Syria because it divided Arabs and diverted them from the struggle with their main opponent, Israel. Against this, the radicals argued that concentration on recovering the occupied territories as a goal separate from the liberation of all Palestine meant, ultimately, an acceptance of the existence of Israel. They also asserted that without revolution in the Arab world, all Arab resources could never be mobilized for the struggle.

Two years of conflict inside the regime between the "radical" and "realist" factions came to a head in late 1970 when the two sides split over the proper Syrian response to King Hussein's onslaught on the Palestinian fedayeen. The radicals, in order to save the fedayeen and if possible overthrow the monarchy, ordered the intervention of Syrian and PLA units on the Palestinian side. Asad, however, deterred by Israeli and U.S. threats, refused orders to commit air support.[40] As a result, the Syrian-PLA force was repulsed with losses, although not before it provided some relief to the hard-pressed fedayeen. Enraged at the insubordination of the defense minister, the party leadership tried to dismiss Asad. He responded with a coup d'état, deposing his radical rivals and bringing his own faction to power. This conflict was symptomatic of the underlying differences between the two factions. The radicals, in pursuit of their messianic vision of revolutionary nationalism, were prepared to take high risks in the apparent belief that to do nothing for the cause was worse than to suffer defeat. Asad, ever conscious of the actual balance of power and unwilling to commit his forces against another Arab state, had a much more cautious and conventional conception of political-military strategy. His 1970 victory marked a decisive turning point in Syrian foreign policy: an end to revolutionary activism and the beginning of a policy of realpolitik. Most Syrians seemed to welcome removal of the leaders most identified with the reckless policies that had produced the 1967 disaster.[41]

Toward the October War (1971–1973)

Asad lost no time in putting his stamp on Syrian foreign policy. At the Eleventh National Congress of the Ba'th Party in 1971, a major scaling down of the objectives of Syrian policy was officially ratified. The object "for the advancement of which all resources and manpower should be mobilized" would now be "the liberation of the occupied territories." "The liberation of Palestine" was replaced in Syrian discourse by the more ambiguous—and, in practice, far less comprehensive—demand for "Palestinian rights." From this key shift in goals flowed a whole series of alterations in strategy and tactics.

Since Asad believed that recovery of at least some of the lost territories was possible through regular military action against Israel, his first priority was to prepare for such an engagement. This required a major buildup in the Syrian armed forces, a greatly increased supply of arms, and the money to pay for them. It also required military allies.

To acquire arms, Asad maintained the close alliance forged with the Soviet Union in the 1960s. As Syria fell in with the Soviet view that the Arabs should ultimately seek a political settlement with Israel, relations actually grew closer. When Sadat expelled Soviet advisors from Egypt, Asad did not follow suit, and fearful that Soviet-Egyptian conflict would jeopardize the Arabs' ability to make war, tried to mediate the quarrel. By 1972, Soviet arms, although still inferior to those received by Israel, began to flow into Syria in quantities that would make a military challenge to Israel possible. This increase in Soviet liberality was mainly due to a desire to reward Syrian loyalty and demonstrate to Sadat what his hostile act would cost him; in part it was also recompense for the use of certain Syrian facilities by Soviet forces, and an acknowledgment that Moscow could not long keep its Arab friends if it refused to help break the humiliating and intolerable stalemate that allowed Israel to keep Arab lands.

Acquiring the money to finance the military buildup and finding partners to help fight Israel required a new Arab policy, and Asad immediately undertook to forge one. First he built new alliances with the Arab oil states, thereby replacing the radical idea of pan-Arab revolution as the operative concept of Syria's Arab policy with that of all-Arab solidarity. Before long the oil Arabs were indeed making large contributions to Syria's military budget. Second, Asad struck a strategic alliance with Egypt, the most militarily powerful of the Arab states, and indispensable to any successful war with Israel.

Asad's effort to create an effective eastern front was, however, less successful. Relations with the Iraqis, in spite of Asad's desire for military cooperation, remained poor. Personal and political rivalries divided the two regimes, and Asad's Egyptian alliance signified to Iraq tacit Syrian complicity in Egypt's acceptance of UN Resolution 242. Iraq's significant military contribution to the 1973 war was less effective than it might have been had it been prearranged.

Efforts to build an alliance with Jordan bore even less fruit and, indeed, proved politically costly. Despite Hussein's continuing repression of the Palestinians, Asad regarded him as within the pale because Jordan was needed as part of the eastern front and because Asad saw little possibility of, or profit in, removing the monarchy. Instead of denouncing Hussein, Asad tried to mediate the conflict with the fedayeen; Arab guns, he argued, should be turned against Israel, not against each other. These conciliatory policies brought on Asad's first major foreign policy crisis. As the intention of the Jordanians to fully liquidate the resistance became clearer, Asad's mediation looked increasingly ineffectual, especially in comparison with the risks taken by his predecessors on behalf of the Palestinian resistance. When Syria prevented the fedayeen from continuing the war with Hussein across the Syrian border and even held up a shipment of Algerian arms to them, Asad appeared to be an accomplice in Hussein's plans. The Syrian regime finally resorted to border closings and skirmishes to pressure the Jordanians into restraint, but the latter accomplished their objectives: the PLO presence in Jordan was liquidated. Asad's policy followed chiefly from a calculation that the Jordanian army was a more important asset in war than the commandos, precisely the opposite of his radical predecessors' convictions. This new Syrian attitude was a major factor in Hussein's calculation that he could liquidate the resistance without paying a big cost. For Syria, the ultimate result of détente with Hussein was ambiguous. Jordan did help cover Syria's southern flank in the October War, but it did not make a major contribution to the fighting.

Guerrilla tactics and the fedayeen did, however, continue to have a place in Asad's strategy. Syria remained a main patron of, and base for, the fedayeen. The Ba'th-controlled Al-Sa'iqa organization, purged of radicals, was developed as a tool of Syrian policy. Syria continued to permit or even sponsor guerrilla operations from Syrian bases, which occasionally escalated into clashes between Syrian and Israeli regulars or precipitated Israeli air raids. When in the spring of 1973 the Lebanese government sought to follow King Hussein's example toward the Palestinians, Syria permitted PLA units to move to the assistance of their compatriots. Apparently, Asad found it politically important to demonstrate continuing commitment to the Palestinian cause. Commando operations were also a way of demonstrating that Syria would not accept the post-1967 status quo and of contesting Israel's tightening hold over the Golan. But the guerrillas were now regarded chiefly as auxiliary forces to be subordinated to Syria's overall strategy, rather than as the cutting edge of liberation.

Finally, there were alterations in Syria's diplomatic strategy under Asad. Officially, Syria continued to reject UN 242 because it failed to clearly specify that Israel must fully evacuate the conquered territories and because it did not acknowledge Palestinian political rights. Anyway, there was little to gain by overt acceptance of the resolution in the absence of any Israeli inclination to return the territories or international pressure to force it to. Moreover, Asad had to contend with elements inside his own regime who remained opposed to accommodation with Israel. Syria did not overtly object to Egypt's unilateral pursuit of a diplomatic settlement in 1971–1972 or Egyptian courtship of the United States, perhaps because this never showed any signs of likely success. Syria, in any case, had little confidence in the efficacy of such measures in the absence of a demonstrated Arab capacity to challenge Israel militarily. But diplomatic efforts could, at least, satisfy world opinion that the Arabs had exhausted all peaceful options before resorting to war. Syrian decision-makers could have had no illusions, however, that in the aftermath of such a war they could avoid being drawn, if only under international auspices, into negotiations for a general settlement in which they might have to formally accept Israel. No less than the Egyptians, Syria went to war in 1973 precisely to shift the balance of power sufficiently to force a settlement incorporating the minimum Arab demands.[42]

From the October War to Camp David (1974–1978)

Syria failed to recover the Golan in the October War and even ceded some additional ground before accepting a cease-fire,[43] but the war did shift the balance of power in favor of the Arabs. Syria's postwar objective was to translate the leverage won in the war into a comprehensive Middle East settlement under international auspices. For the first time, Syria formally accepted UN 242 and 338, reinterpreting them to mean an end to the state of war in return for the Israeli evacuation of all Arab lands and the creation of a Palestinian state on the West Bank. Syria believed the key to this outcome was Arab solidarity: continued use of the threat of renewed war and an oil boycott to get a U.S.-Soviet imposed Israeli rollback.

Obstacles to the success of this strategy soon became apparent. The United States was unwilling to impose a general settlement on Israel and tended instead to seek a partial settlement. Egypt showed a growing readiness to fall in with the U.S. effort and seek a separate deal with Israel. The Saudis proved reluctant to use the oil weapon for the Arab cause, and as their wealth and prestige mounted, they were increasingly invulnerable to nationalist pressures to do so. Damascus had hoped for a quick overall settlement, but once Sadat accepted a partial disengagement and persuaded Saudi Arabia to lift the oil boycott, this prospect—and much of Syria's bargaining leverage—quickly evaporated. King Faisal had, however, induced Kissinger to "do something for Syria" similar to the Israeli pullback on the Egyptian front. Syria's immediate attention was thus diverted to an effort to maximize its gains in the Kissinger-mediated disengagement negotiations.

The Syrian leadership appears to have been seriously divided over how to respond to Kissinger's initiative and to his overall concept of "step-by-step" diplomacy. A hard-line group (whose initial spokesman was Foreign Minister Khaddam) argued against partial agreements. Since the power balance—both military and economic—was shifting toward the Arabs, this group believed Syria could hold out for a comprehensive settlement on its own terms. It also feared that a peace obtained under U.S. patronage would spell a virtual end to the Arab revolution. Khaddam also rejected the concept of direct negotiations with the Israelis.[44] A second group (whose spokesman was Prime Minister Ayubi) favored disengagement and the exploration of the step-by-step approach in order to get something to show for the war. It argued that the outcome of the 1973 war was as favorable as Syria could hope for, and hence that Syrian bargaining leverage was at a maximum. Moreover, Syria's wartime allies could not ultimately be depended upon to help force a general settlement. Egypt would look to its own interests; Iraq was untrustworthy; and the USSR had shown that it would take few risks for Syria in the face of U.S. power. Nor would the United States permit a substantial shift in the balance of power against Israel.

In the end, Asad agreed to negotiate and pulled his hard-line colleagues along after him. That "shuttle diplomacy" did not require face-to-face negotiations with the Israelis made the decision easier; so too, did U.S. assurances that disengagement was only a prelude to subsequent and greater Israeli withdrawals. Asad's aim was to force the Israelis back as far as possible on the Golan, without permitting disengagement to become a substitute for an overall settlement. To strengthen his hand in the negotiations and in dealing with his own militants, Asad conducted a war of attrition on the Golan and Mount Hermon, forcing the Israelis to maintain a costly mobilization. He bargained tenaciously with every card at his disposal, including the Israeli prisoners of war. Kissinger, in order to show the Arabs that reliance on the United States paid, pressured Israel to make concessions comparable to those made to Egypt.[45] In the end, in fact, Asad had to settle for a partial disengagement similar to the Egyptian one, recovering only the sliver of land lost in 1973 and a small part of that lost in 1967, in return for a UN observer force between the Syrian and Israeli lines. Only at the last minute and evidently with great reluctance did he agree to this. To make the disengagement more acceptable to Syrian opinion, Asad insisted that it was only a first step linked to an ultimately complete Israeli withdrawal. He was also careful to acquire the stamp of approval from other Arab states. The rollback of the Israeli army, uncomfortably close to Damascus, was a security gain; and the recovery of even a small piece of lost territory was a political gain vital to the regime's internal position. Syria had not had to negotiate face-to-face with Israel—thus tacitly recognizing it—as had Egypt. But the agreement was purchased at the cost of reducing military pressure on Israel: the UN presence would make a future surprise attack to recover the bulk of the Golan more difficult, and another potential front for the Palestinian fedayeen was, in practice if not in principle, forfeited. Syria refused to formally promise an end to fedayeen operations from the Golan, but in actual fact they ceased. The agreement facilitated the U.S. effort to defuse the wartime crisis as a substitute for solving the Arab-Israeli dispute.

Syria's disengagement committed it to the negotiation process, shifting the internal balance against the hard-liners. But Syria was very wary of the U.S. policy of arranging agreements between Israel and the separate Arab states, an approach that weakened the Arab's hand and was likely to penalize those parties to whom the Israelis were least willing to make concessions—Syria and the PLO. Gradually, Syrian policy hardened against step-by-step diplomacy. Instead, Syria aimed to steer the negotiations toward an international conference in which a united Arab delegation would face the Israelis and settle for nothing less than a total Israeli withdrawal to the 1967 lines. At such a conference the USSR could balance U.S. influence; the PLO could be represented, hence its national demands could be legitimized and satisfied; and a second damaging unilateral deal on the Egyptian front could thus be prevented.

At the Rabat summit in 1974 Syria worked to contain Sadat's go-it-alone propensity through the pressure of an all-Arab consensus. Syria also supported recognition of the PLO as the only party empowered to speak for the Palestinians. As Kissinger's intention to seek another Israeli-Egyptian deal became clear, Syria and the PLO formed a "joint political command," declaring that Palestinian and Syrian demands could not be separated and that they would make peace together or not at all. Asad visited Jordan to solidify Jordanian opposition to any separate deals. However, these efforts did little to check movement toward a second separate agreement on the Egyptian front. Kissinger seems to have misled Asad into muting his opposition to a second Sinai disengagement by hinting at a similar substantial Israeli pullback on the Golan. Sinai II, however, destroyed Syria's bargaining hand by largely removing Egypt from the military confrontation. Both the Israelis and the Americans apparently believed Syria to have lost virtually all its leverage,[46] and since Damascus was, in any case, insisting on linkage between the Golan and West Bank, the idea of a second Syrian disengagement was quickly shelved. Subsequently, Israel refused to make any more territorial concessions to Syria or on the West Bank. Kissinger relieved the pressure on the Israelis to do so by promising not to demand further concessions, rearming them to the teeth, and ruling out the PLO as a party to the conflict. The Israeli arms buildup, combined with the virtual neutralization of Israel's southern front, greatly increased the threat to Syria's security. Syrian leaders condemned the agreement on the grounds that it allowed Israel to concentrate its forces on Syria and freeze the lines in the north and east. To Syria, it seemed that the United States was more interested in dividing and weakening the Arabs than settling the Middle East conflict.

In the post–Sinai II period, however, Syria had little choice but to pursue a diplomatic settlement: without Egypt another war was impossible. Feeling vulnerable and alone in facing Israel, Asad set out to build an alliance in the Arab East embracing Lebanon, the PLO, and Jordan. This bloc would help contain any Israeli efforts to outflank Syria militarily through Lebanon or Jordan and help deflect U.S. efforts to lure Amman into a separate agreement with Israel. As leader of such a bloc, Syria's interests could not be lightly disregarded. Syria would be better able to resist pressures to join either Egypt or the rejectionists, and would be positioned to pose as champion of the Palestinian cause. Jordan and the PLO proved amenable and this effort had a brief success.[47] It enabled Syria to mobilize Arab opinion against Egypt and to signal to Washington the futility of a peace process that ignored Syrian interest.[48] The subsequent apparent establishment of Syrian hegemony in Lebanon also strengthened Syria's hand. In 1977 President Carter acknowledged the Palestinian issue as the heart of the Middle East conflict and proposed an all-party peace conference aimed at an overall settlement. To Damascus, it seemed that a comprehensive settlement might still be in reach if Arab solidarity and the new U.S. approach stood the test of time. Both, however, were defeated by Israel's refusal to talk with the PLO or consider more than cosmetic changes in the status quo. Carter, under intense Zionist pressure, had second thoughts about imposing a peace on Israel. Sadat embarked on his trip to Jerusalem, convinced that Israel would never agree to an overall settlement, but might, to break Arab solidarity and relieve U.S. pressure, concede the Sinai. This brought Syrian-Egyptian relations to a total break. Asad refused Sadat's pleas to join him in negotiations, having lost all confidence that the Egyptian leader could be held to a common negotiating position. Sadat had dissipated Arab bargaining power by showing himself ready for peace at any cost and overtly recognizing Israel and the Israeli annexation of Jerusalem beforehand. For Asad, to associate himself with this course would only legitimate a spurious undertaking and antagonize Ba'thist militants, who demanded that Syria stand firm.[49] Syria joined the Steadfastness Front opposed to the Egyptian course, but was powerless to stop Sadat. As Egypt and Israel made peace, ostensibly defusing the Middle East conflict, U.S. pressures on Israel for a wider peace disappeared, and with them any incentive for Israel to deal with Syria and the Palestinians. Thus Syria's interests were again ignored in the Middle East "peace process."

The Syrian Intervention in Lebanon

The stage was set for Syrian intervention in Lebanon by the breakdown of order in Lebanon and by Syria's ambition to build a Syrian-led block in the Arab East after Sinai II. The prospect of a partition of Lebanon and Israeli intervention posed a grave security threat to Syria; but the conflict also presented an opportunity for Syria to insert itself as arbiter and draw Lebanon under its political-strategic wing. In the early stages of the conflict Syria supported the Palestinian and Lebanese leftist forces with arms and aid against rightist Maronite attacks. In early 1976 Syria first overtly intervened to halt a rightist drive of partition and conquest. This enabled Damascus to put forth a Syrian peace plan. It provided for a moderate redistribution of power in favor of the Moslems and a disengagement of the Palestinians from Lebanese affairs in exchange for Maronite tolerance of their presence. By this time, however, the Lebanese left and radical Palestinians had gone on the offensive in the name of a secular radical state that would serve as a base for struggle with Israel. They were soon joined by Fateh in a drive that put the Maronites in jeopardy. The Syrian peace plan had failed. A growing rift opened between Syria and its traditional allies. Syrian diplomatic and military pressures were now turned on the left, and Damascus entered a tacit alliance with the Maronites. The Palestinians and the leftists resisted, to the point of attacking Syrian forces. As the conflict escalated, Syrian military intervention increased, aimed with tacit approval from Washington and Israel at the forcible pacification of the Palestinian-leftist forces.

The motives behind this radical departure from traditional Syrian policy were complex. Syria held that a leftist military victory could not succeed except at grave cost. It would embitter the Maronites against the Arab world, drive them into the arms of Israel, and escalate partition, further balkanizing the Arab world. Syrian leaders feared sectarian strife might even spill across the border, threatening the multisectarian base on which their own power rested. The Syrians also feared a radical state in Lebanon sponsoring guerrilla warfare against Israel would only give the Israelis an excuse to evade pressures for a peace settlement, destroy the fedayeen presence in southern Lebanon, and realize their historical ambition to seize this area. Israeli intervention, whether in response to Maronite distress or against radical forces, would drag Syria into a war on terms favorable to Israel, in which the Israelis could threaten Syria's soft Western flank. This military security threat was unquestionably the dominant ingredient in Syrian policy. Instead of a radicalized Lebanon, Damascus far preferred a situation in which Syria could play the role of balancer between two rival communities and hence exercise hegemony in Lebanon. Dominance in Lebanon would put Syria in a stronger position to resist rival Arab forces—those pressuring for accomodation with Israel and also the Iraqi-backed rejectionists aiming to upset the prospects for a political settlement. The PLO could be more readily harnessed to Syrian objectives; there was no question of "delivering" the Palestinians into a peace settlement against their will, but Syria did not relish the idea of a Palestinian resistance impervious in its Lebanese bastion to Syrian influence or aligned with rival Arab states. Neither did Syria want the PLO bogged down in governing Lebanon; this would divert the Palestinians from the struggle with Israel and weaken pressures on Israel to give up the West Bank. Syria no doubt felt special rights and responsibilities in "fraternal" Lebanon, reinforced by pan-Arabist contempt for the imperialist-created boundaries between the two countries. But Ba'thist dreams of incorporating Lebanon into Syria were hardly operative: they would have dictated smashing, not protecting the Maronite militias. Finally, certain personal emotions influenced Syrian leaders. The Alawites among them, long subject themselves to Sunni Moslem hostility, may have sympathized with the Christians; Asad's personal ties with former Lebanese president Sulayman Frangieh also disposed him to Christian views. As Palestinian and leftist leaders defied Syria, personal animosity for them grew in Damascus; Syrian leaders were outraged that their junior allies were so ungrateful as to defy them and even attack the Syrian army that had made so many sacrifices for the Palestinian cause. Once Syria's prestige was put on the line by armed resistance to its forces in Lebanon and by Iraqi and Egyptian support for this defiance, Syrian determination to chastise the Palestinian and leftist forces solidified. Only after inflicting a military defeat on them did Asad accept Arab mediation to end the conflict.

The outcome appeared to be a Syrian victory. The Palestinians, the leftists, and the Arab world accepted Syria's "peacekeeping" role in Lebanon and Syria's army settled down in force to guard the soft spot on the Syrian western flank. The regime set out to impose a Pax Syriana, to reverse the movement toward partition and to reconstruct a Lebanese state amenable to Syrian control. But Asad's plans soon encountered growing resistance from the Maronites, who opposed Syria's effort to penetrate Christian areas and were bent on de facto partition. Syria wanted to keep a Palestinian guerrilla option in the south as a political bargaining chip; the Maronites, however, began to carve out a southern enclave in cooperation with Israel meant to seal the border. Syria then threw its support to Palestinian and leftist forces fighting in the south. Yet in May 1978, when Israel invaded, Syria stood by and allowed the consolidation of this disputed zone. Subsequent Syrian military drives to punish the Maronites for their alliance with Israel marked the collapse of Syrian-Maronite relations. Syria pushed the militias back but, deterred by Israel, could not bring them to heel. Two small Maronite enclaves overtly aligned themselves with Israel, presenting stubborn obstacles to the reconstruction of a united Lebanon and a threat to Syrian security. In 1979 and 1980 Syria supported Palestinian efforts to reestablish a southern presence and tried halfheartedly to challenge regular Israeli incursions into the area. In 1981 Syria pushed back a Maronite drive to extend their control into Syrian-held areas. When the Israeli air force intervened on the Maronites' behalf, Syria moved antiaircraft missiles into eastern Lebanon. Israel threatened to destroy them if they were not removed, but Syria stood firm, the United States restrained Israel, and the crisis petered out. Israel's 1982 invasion of Lebanon marked a vast new escalation of the conflict. Syrian forces engaged the Israelis but suffered serious losses and retreated from strategic sections of Lebanese terrain. Syria left the PLO to its fate and left Israel occupying large parts of Lebanon.

Syria's intervention in Lebanon brought about everything it was meant to prevent and thus proved to be an unmitigated disaster. To be sure, Syria had fortified its Western flank, but involvement in Lebanon had also dissipated its forces. Weakening the Palestinian and leftist forces opened the door to the Israeli-Maronite combination and the expansion of Israeli power into Lebanon. The potential for Israel to outflank Syria's Golan defenses increased. Conflict with the Palestinians also weakened the political front against capitulation to Israel: it gravely damaged Syrian-Palestinian solidarity and made it easier for Sadat and perhaps others to settle separately with Israel at Syria's expense. This disaster resulted from Syria's pursuit of too narrow a raison d'état, which blinded it to the interests of its natural allies and led Syria to use force against them to the benefit of historical opponents. Asad allowed his fear of Israel to draw him into a conflict with his own allies that weakened him and strengthened Israel.[50]

The Post-Camp David Era (1978–1983)

Syrian policy after Camp David was aimed at containing the threat of an Israel strengthened and emboldened by the withdrawal of Egypt from the conflict, preventing the legitimation of the Camp David process in the Arab world, and claiming the support to which Syria was entitled as the only remaining front-line Arab state. Initially, Camp David drew the Arab states together to Syria's benefit. Jordan's rejection of Camp David helped prevent its legitimation and Syria's isolation. Syria's demands for Arab money to achieve military parity with Israel after Egypt's defection were received sympathetically. Syria and Iraq seemed on the verge of burying the hatchet. A brief Syrian-Iraqi concert provided the political weight to force an Arab break with Egypt and the potential to reconstruct the eastern military front.[51] But before long, Arab ranks were again in disarray and Syria was threatened with isolation. The Iraqi alliance was stillborn: Asad would not give up on a political settlement and remained wary of a large Iraqi military presence on Syrian soil. Mutual mistrust put an end to the rapprochement. The Jordan-Syria alliance born of Sinai II also collapsed, largely over Jordan's tolerance of anti-Ba'th dissidents on its soil. The Iran-Iraq war further split the Arab world to the benefit of Israel and Sadat; by committing a major Arab power to an enervating conflict far from the Israeli front, it sharply reduced Syria's military options. Yet Syria supported Iran. This and its growing Soviet ties strained Syrian relations with the conservative Arab oil states whose aid supported Syria's military position. Except for ties with the Steadfastness Front (including Libya, Algeria, South Yemen, and for a while, the PLO), most of the links Asad had long worked to forge with the Arab world were either badly frayed or broken by the 1980s. The Steadfastness Front could not substitute for a diplomatically united Arab world or a militarily effective eastern front.

As Syria found itself at odds with much of the Arab world, troubled by internal dissidence and after Camp David, convinced that nothing good could be expected from the United States, it moved closer to the Soviet Union. A weakened and isolated Syria needed Soviet protection and arms. Hence, in 1980 Syria signed a treaty of friendship with the USSR on the grounds that the Egyptian alliance with the United States had to be balanced. Soviet arms deliveries did partly restore the military balance with Israel and the enhanced Soviet commitment to Syria's defense probably had some deterrent effect on Syria's enemies.[52] On the other hand, relations with Washington deteriorated rapidly. The Reagan administration, which viewed Syria as a Soviet surrogate, had little interest in accommodating Syrian demands. The neglect of Syrian interests by the Reagan Plan and the green light given to the 1982 Israeli invasion of Lebanon far overshadowed U.S. restraint of Israel during the "missile crisis."

Thus, Syria's position significantly deteriorated after Camp David. Israel's annexation of the Golan showed that Israel considered both the international political balance and the local military balance sufficiently unfavorable to Syria to rule out, a priori, any negotiated settlement. Syria could only stand by in impotent frustration. Then, Israel's victory in Lebanon dealt Syria a major military setback and also, by demonstrating the impotence of Arab power, strengthened "capitulationist" forces in the Arab world. Even the PLO began to explore diplomatic initiatives that left Syria out. Before long Syria was backing a revolt by Palestinian radicals against PLO moderates led by Arafat; this policy further damaged Syrian-Palestinian solidarity and dissipated forces that could have been confronting the common enemy. The U.S.-sponsored agreement on Israeli withdrawal from Lebanon, backed by a growing U.S. military presence in that country, seemed to show that the United States sought a Maronite-dominated Lebanon at peace with and open to Israeli influence. The threat of political isolation and military danger to Syria was perhaps graver than that arising from the Camp David agreements. Another Arab state would be drawn into a separate partial peace with Israel and Syria's western flank exposed to Israeli military and political penetration. To counter this threat, Syria engaged in a risky challenge to U.S. policy. Syria encouraged subversion against the Maronite government in Lebanon, and by refusing to withdraw from the country, tried to scuttle its accord with Israel. By the end of 1983, Syria was involved in a dangerous military confrontation with the United States itself. The Syrians' view was that if they could not impose a Middle East peace compatible with their vital interests, they could at least prevent one that ignored them. Ultimately, the political-military balance was bound to shift more to Syria's favor.

CONCLUSION:
THE RECORD OF SYRIAN FOREIGN POLICY UNDER ASAD

When Hafiz Al-Asad came to power he inherited the reins of a state committed to revolutionary Arab nationalism, an intense revisionism shaped by a quarter of a century's struggle with imperialism and Zionism in which Syrian national ambitions had largely been frustrated. The gap between the goals of foreign policy—the virtual overthrow of the regional state system—and Syrian capabilities was wide. Syria's resource base was too slim and external constraints too powerful to sustain this messianic policy. The attempt to continue this policy regardless of limitations invited the stunning defeat of 1967, which in effect shattered the dreams of Arab nationalism.

Asad attempted to close the gap between goals and capabilities. Policy objectives were greatly scaled down: revolutionary nationalism gradually gave way to realpolitik and a practical acceptance of the Middle East state system. The revision of Syrian policy can be seen in the limited objectives of the 1973 war, the détente with traditional Arab states, and Syrian acceptance of UN 242. Narrower, more immediate interests began to shape policy more closely. Where they diverged, the interests of the Syrian state largely took precedence over pan-Arab visions. This was clear in the repeated subordination of the Palestine cause to Syrian strategy and security, and particularly in the Lebanese intervention. In the same spirit of realism, Asad also set out to expand Syria's capabilities. The replacement of a divisive pan-Arab radicalism with a policy of pan-Arab solidarity helped, at least for a while, to unite Arab energies for national and Syrian goals. A pragmatic diplomacy mobilized both Arab money and Soviet arms in an extraordinary expansion of Syrian military power. A greater willingness to play the game of international realpolitik seemed to pay dividends in the first disengagement. Syria was acknowledged by the middle 1970s as part, with Egypt and Saudi Arabia, of the "Arab Triangle," that is, as one of the three most consequential Arab states.[53]

Yet by the 1980s, it was clear that the gap had not been effectively bridged. On the one hand, Syria had failed to attain even its scaled-down objective: Israeli withdrawal from the occupied lands. This was due to constraints largely outside Syria's control, notably the U.S.-Israeli ability to continuously up the military ante and to detach Egypt from the Arab camp, and the unwillingness of Saudi Arabia to use the oil weapon again. But failures of its own policy also weakened Syria's hand. Paradoxically, some of these failures were due to the same realist raison d'état that had seemed to strengthen Syrian capabilities. The disaster in Lebanon showed that pursuit of too narrow a state interest could be self-defeating. Also, on occasions where Arab and Syrian interests diverged from the survival imperatives of the regime, Syrian leaders were prepared to put the latter first at great cost to the former: one example of this was the post–Camp David collapse of the eastern front with Jordan and Iraq.

On the other hand, Syria was not fully reconciled to the regional status quo. Syria probably remains the most committed of the Arab states to the aspirations of Arabism, the least prepared to fall back on a separate statehood apart from the Arab nation or to abandon the Arabs' minimal demands in the conflict with Israel. This persistent pan-Arabism flows in part from the fact that Syria's parochial state interests coincide more than those of other Arab states with wider Arab national goals, and without pan-Arab solidarity these interests cannot be attained. Syria's dilemma is that its interests and dreams cannot be satisfied within the status quo system, but challenges to this system can be made only at great risk of further disasters. Syria appears likely, thus, to remain frustrated and dissatisfied, a major source of revisionism in the regional state system.

NOTES

1. A. L. Tibawi, *A Modern History of Syria* (London: Macmillan, 1969), Chapters 8–11; and Zeine N. Zeine, *The Struggle for Arab Independence* (Beirut: Khayats, 1960), provide the most authoritative accounts of these developments.

2. In the 1973 war, for example, Israeli aircraft tried to outflank Syrian antiaircraft defenses by way of Lebanon.

3. These calculations are based on figures from official budgets in the Central Bureau of Statistics publication *Statistical Abstract*, issued annually in Damascus by the Syrian government.

4. Syrian economic growth from 1970 to 1975 was 8.2% (GDP at constant 1963 factor cost), but by 1976 imports were double exports. The deficit in the trade balance was covered in great part by grants from Arab oil states.

5. Richard Nyrop et al., *Area Handbook for Syria* (Washington, D.C.: Government Printing Office, 1971), pp. 287–296.

6. These estimates are based on reports from several sources. Estimates by the London Institute of Strategic Studies are reported in *Middle East*, March 1978. Israeli estimates appear periodically in the *Middle East Intelligence Survey*. See also the yearly analyses in Colin Legum, Haim Shaked, and Daniel Dishon (eds.), *Middle East Contemporary Survey* (London: Holmes and Meier, 1976-1977 to 1979-1980); Roger Pajek, "The Soviet-Syrian Military Aid Relationship," in Anne Sinai and Allen Pollack (eds.), *The Syrian Arab Republic* (New York: American Academic Association for Peace in the Middle East, 1976); and Yehoshua Raviv, "Arab-Israeli Military Balance," *Jerusalem Quarterly* 18 (Winter 1981), pp. 122–144.

7. Syria has recently acquired an armory of increasingly sophisticated weapons greatly superior to what it had in 1973. Generally, Syria has aimed at acquiring weapons with an operational profile equivalent to those in Israel's arsenal. Raviv, *op. cit.*; *Middle East Intelligence Survey*, January 1981.

8. Dawisha contends that the Syrian soldier has exhibited considerable bravery, especially in the October War and in the struggle for Mt. Hermon, and that the officer corps demonstrated a much higher level of commitment in these two encounters than they had previously. See A. I. Dawisha, *Syria and the Lebanese Crisis* (New York: St. Martin's Press, 1980), pp. 40–41. McLaurin, Mughisuddin, and Wagner argue that the Syrian military remains overcentralized and poorly led at the senior level, but that the junior officers and enlisted ranks have been vastly improved and have shown themselves to be good fighters. Large numbers of Syrian troops, they note, have been exposed to advanced military equipment by the Soviet military mission. See R. D. McLaurin, Mohammed Mughisuddin, and Abraham Wagner, *Foreign Policy Making in the Middle East* (New York: Praeger Publishers, 1977), pp. 236–237. By the late 1970s, there were a reported 5,000 Soviet advisors assigned to the Syrian army, a big increase over the previous decade.

9. McLaurin, Mughisuddin, and Wagner (*op. cit.*) note that the Israelis have superior aircraft with respect to delivery capability and range, and have also had a larger number of qualified pilots. See also the *Area Handbook* assessment and the analysis of the relative quality of weaponry in Michael Vlahos and Geoffrey Kemp, "The Arab-Israeli Military Balance," in Legum, Shaked, and Dishon, *op. cit.*, 1976-1977, pp. 74–81.

10. Most notably, the Syrian army, in its initial offensive into the Golan, failed to capture a strategic bridge that allowed Israel to retain a foothold on the plateau. Without this bridge, an Israeli counteroffensive would have been much more difficult and costly. See P. R. Chari, "Military Lessons of the Arab-Israeli War of 1973," *Institute for Defense Studies and Analysis Journal* (New Delhi, April–June 1976); and Riad Ashkar, "The Syrian and Egyptian Campaigns," *Journal of Palestine Studies* 14, 2 (1974), pp. 15–33.

11. If Egypt were still in the Arab war coalition, the Arabs would together have a 3 : 1 advantage, similar to that of 1973; however, without Egypt the ratio drops to 1 : 1.5 or 1 : 1.8. The removal of Iraq owing to its war with Iran further enervates the Arab war option. Acting alone, Syria is at a disadvantage in the ratio of forces vis-à-vis Israel. However, the ratio between Syrian and Israeli forces stationed permanently on the Golan is in Syria's favor, so that a surprise attack might be able to seize much of the Heights before Israel's main forces were mobilized; once they were mobilized Syria could not do without Iraqi or Egyptian help. Defensively, Syria has a better chance of holding its own on the Golan. Raviv, *op. cit.,* p. 137.

12. By the beginning of the 1980s, however, Syria appeared more isolated than at any time since Asad took power; only time will tell whether this situation will continue.

13. Even the minority of Syrians who have identified with a "Syrian" nation have not taken that to mean the current state, but historic Syria, Bilad Al-Sham, which embraces Lebanon, Jordan, and Palestine as well as modern Syria. Some have even considered Iraq to be part of the Syrian nation.

14. For good analyses of Syrian political identity, see Moshe Maoz, "Attempts at Creating a Political Community in Modern Syria," *Middle East Journal* 36, 4 (1972), pp. 389–404; Michael H. Van Dusen, "Syria: Downfall of a Traditional Elite," in Frank Tachau (ed.), *Political Elites and Political Development in the Middle East* (Cambridge, Mass.: Schenkman Publishing Co., 1975), pp. 117–120; and Leonard Binder, "The Tragedy of Syria," *World Politics* 19 (1967), pp. 521–549.

15. Thus, Ba'thi parlance refers to Syria as Al-Qutr (the region) rather than as the nation: this contrasts with current Egyptian usage of the word *Watan* (nation), which refers unambiguously to Egypt.

16. A typical statement of Syria's view of itself as part of the Third World is found in the "Speech by President Hafiz al-Asad at the 4th Conference of the Heads of State of Non-Aligned Countries," Algiers, September 1973, Syrian Arab News Agency release, Damascus.

17. For the definitive analysis of these events, see Patrick Seale, *The Struggle for Syria* (London: Oxford University Press, 1965).

18. See the speech by Noureddin Atasi to the UN General Assembly, June 20, 1967.

19. On more recent U.S.-Syrian relations, see Edward Sheehan, *The Arabs, Israel, and Kissinger: A Secret History of American Diplomacy in the Middle East* (New York: Reader's Digest Press, 1976).

20. For example, the Syrian *Statistical Abstract* for 1976, pp. 401–403, shows the rapid growth of trade with Western Europe, the leveling off of trade with Eastern Europe, and the modest amount of trade with the Americas, only one-third of which was with the United States.

21. A. I. Dawisha, "The Impact of External Actors on Syria's Intervention in Lebanon," *Journal of South Asian and Middle Eastern Studies* 2, 1 (1978), pp. 23–25, discusses some of these ties. See also Jaan Pennar, "The Soviet Road to Damascus," *Mizan* 9 (1967), pp. 23–29; and I. Valentin, "The Syrian Ba'th Party," *International Affairs* (Moscow), October 1969.

22. On more recent Syrian-Soviet relations, see Galia Golan, "Syria and the Soviet Union Since the Yom Kippur War," *Orbis* 21, 4 (1978), pp. 777–802.

23. For good analyses of Syrian policies and attitudes toward Israel in the mid-1960s, see Maxime Rodinson, *Israel and the Arabs* (Harmondsworth, Eng.:

Penguin, 1968), especially pp. 167–171; Abraham Ben-Tsur, *The Syrian Ba'th Party and Israel* (Givat Haviva, Israel: Center for Arab and Afro-Asian Studies, 1968); Tabitha Petran, *Syria* (London: Ernest Benn, 1972), pp. 187–200. My analysis also relies on the reports of various Ba'th party congresses, especially the Eighth National Congress, 1965, and the Ninth Emergency Congress, 1967, published by the Ba'th party in Damascus.

24. Syria's acceptance of UN Resolutions 242 and 338, interpreted as requiring total Israeli withdrawal from the lands taken in 1967 and guaranteeing that the Palestinians have national rights and are not treated merely as refugees, represents a formal Syrian commitment to end the state of war with Israel. Several statements by Asad have explicitly expressed Syria's desire for a negotiated political settlement of the conflict. However, a residual ambiguity in the Syrian position must be noted. The Twelfth National Congress of July 1975, which spelled out Syria's strategy in the negotiations process, declared that Syria will stand against "turning the Palestinian cause into a case of removing the consequences of the aggression of 1967," and speaks of the recovery of the West Bank as a "step . . . toward liberating all the Palestinian lands."

Thus, although the negotiations process would end in a termination of the state of war, the regime seeks to reconcile this with Ba'th principles and nationalist opinion by representing it as a mere first step in a continuing struggle over Palestine. Some Syrian leaders seem to envision the end result of this "struggle" to be "levantization" of Israel. Through a gradual historical process Israel would lose its ties to the West and its exclusively Jewish character, Arabs in Israel would acquire equal citizenship, and a binational Middle Eastern state would emerge. Recent Syrian attitudes toward Israel are reflected in the Ba'th National Leadership's "Declaration de la direction nationale du Parti Baas Arabe Socialiste au 5eme anniversaire de l'agression," Damascus, June 1972; the interviews given by Asad in *Time*, May 18, 1974; *Newsweek*, June 10, 1974; *Time*, December 8, 1975; and Joseph Kraft, "Letters from Damascus," *New Yorker*, June 17, 1974. An Israeli view that seems to exaggerate Syrian militancy but is otherwise useful is Moshe Maoz, "Syria Under Hafiz al-Asad: New Domestic and Foreign Policies," Jerusalem Papers on Peace Problems, Leonard Davis Institute for International Relations, Jerusalem, 1975, especially pp. 12–18. Syria's official strategy in the negotiations process is represented in the Ba'th party publication, "Statement of the National Leadership on the Activities of the 12th National Congress of the Arab Socialist Ba'th Party," Damascus, 1975.

25. On Palestinian-Syrian relations, see Rodinson, *op. cit.*, pp. 161–171; Fuad Jabber's analysis in William Quandt, Fuad Jabber, and Ann Lesch, *The Politics of Palestinian Nationalism* (Berkeley: University of California Press, 1973), especially pp. 157–175, 188–194, 201–204.

26. Asad has detailed the Syrian perception of its role as supporter of the Palestinian cause. "In the course of one day at Arqoub, thirteen of our planes were destroyed while defending the Resistance. . . . Again in the course of one day . . . 500 of our soldiers fell in action against the enemy who had bombed a commando base somewhere in Syria. . . . Why have we declined after the Sinai agreement to enter into negotiations in order to restore part of the Golan? Had our approach been strictly based on Syria's interests alone, we would have entered into negotiations in order to restore a part of our territory. . . . Our sacrifices here in Syria are as clear as the sun; we have sacrificed our own sons, our economy, our land, everything for the sake of the Palestine cause." "Speech Delivered by the Secretary-General of the Ba'th Arab Socialist Party, Comrade

Hafiz al-Asad, Before a General Plenum of Local Government Councils," published by the Ba'th party, Damascus, July 20, 1976.

27. On conflicts between Syrian and Palestinian policies and Syrian attitudes regarding their "rights" of tutelage over the Resistance, see Jabber, *op. cit.*, p. 194; Itamar Rabinovitch, "Syria," in Legum, Shaked, and Dishon, *op. cit.*, p. 616; and Edward Said, *The Question of Palestine* (New York: Vintage Books, 1979), p. 201.

28. In fact, both the Syrian and Iraqi regimes have tried to overthrow each other. Syria also used its control over the flow of the Euphrates River—on which Iraq is dependent—to pressure Iraq, while the Iraqis have cut the flow of oil through Syrian pipelines, costing Damascus substantial transit revenues.

29. For the best account of Egyptian-Syrian "revolutionary" rivalry, see Malcolm Kerr, *The Arab Cold War*, 3d ed. (New York: Oxford University Press, 1971).

30. See Muhamed Heikal, *The Road to Ramadan* (New York: Ballantine Books, 1976), for an insider's account of the disagreements between the two leaderships during the war.

31. For an account of Egyptian-Syrian disputes over postwar negotiating strategy, see William R. Brown, *The Last Crusade: A Negotiator's Middle East Handbook* (Chicago: Nelson-Hall, 1980), pp. 37–53.

32. Syrian leaders have on occasion made public their dissatisfaction with Saudi Arabia and its junior Gulf partners. A common complaint has been that Syrians bore the brunt of fighting in the 1973 war, but the Arab oil states reaped the benefits (of increased oil prices).

33. See Sheehan, *op. cit.*, for an analysis of Syrian decision-making in the disengagement negotiations; see A. I. Dawisha, "Syria's Intervention in Lebanon, 1975–76," *Jerusalem Journal of International Relations* 3, 2–3 (1978), pp. 245–276, on decision-making during the Lebanese crisis.

34. See Sheehan, *op. cit.* For an analysis of Asad's personality, see also Moshe Maoz, "Hafiz al-Asad: A Political Profile," *Jerusalem Quarterly* 8 (1978), pp. 23–24.

35. Nevertheless, the results of a 1974 survey of newly recruited party youth showed very militant attitudes. Of the respondents, 83.1% did not believe that Syria should restrict fedayeen activity from bases in Syria, whatever the cost, and 86.1% thought Syria should economically boycott Western nations that support Israel. See Raymond A. Hinnebusch, "Political Recruitment and Socialization in Syria: The Case of the Revolutionary Youth Federation," *International Journal of Middle East Studies* 11 (1980), pp. 143–174.

36. Syria's political elite is particularly vulnerable to a loss of legitimacy on nationalist grounds because of the high proportion of Alawites in it. This is because the minorities are perceived by many members of the Sunni majority community as former collaborators with the French or, by virtue of their heterodoxy, as less Islamic, thus less Arab, than Sunnis. Thus the current Ba'th leadership must, to prove its nationalist commitment, be more militant and less flexible on national issues than a Sunni Muslim–dominated leadership (like the Egyptian) might be.

37. This is an impressionistic assessment based on the writer's residence in Syria in 1973–1974 and in the summers of 1977 and 1979.

38. For documents setting out the Ba'th strategy, see Ba'th Party, "Statement of the National Command About the Achievements of the 9th National Congress," Damascus, October 1966; Agence Arabe Syrienne d'Information, "Discours

prononcé par le Docteur Noureddine Atassi, chef de l'état," Damascus, 1967. The analysis by Petran, *op. cit.*, pp. 194–200, is the best scholarly treatment of the subject.

39. See National Leadership, Ba'th Party, "Statement on the Results of the 9th Emergency Congress," Damascus, 1967. For the best analysis, see Petran, *op. cit.*, pp. 201–204.

40. It is now known that both the United States and Israel were actually preparing to intervene in support of the Jordanian regime.

41. On the intra-Ba'th conflict, see Petran, *op. cit.*, pp. 239–249; and Malcolm Kerr, "Hafiz Asad and the Changing Patterns of Syrian Politics," *International Journal* 28, 4 (1975), pp. 289–706. Internal party documents on the party crisis include: "Al-Taqrir Siyasi Al-Muatamar Qawmi 'Asher Al-Istethnai" [Political report of the Tenth Extraordinary National Congress], Damascus, 1970.

42. The following are reliable accounts of Asad's policies prior to the 1973 war: Aryeh Yodfat, "The End of Syria's Isolation?" *The World Today* 27, 8 (1971), pp. 335–339; Itamar Rabinovitch, "The Limits of Power: Syria Under Hafiz al-Asad," *New Middle East*, March 1973, pp. 36–37; Petran, *op. cit.*, pp. 252–257. Relevant Syrian policy statements include: "Statement of the Regional Command of the Arab Socialist Ba'th Party on the Agenda of the 5th Regional Congress" (1971), "Statement of the National Leadership on the Work and Results of the 11th National Congress of the Ba'th Arab Socialist Party" (1971), and "The Speech Delivered by President Hafiz al-Asad on the 9th Anniversary of the March Revolution" (1972), all published in Damascus by the Ba'th party.

43. The cease-fire was unpopular in Syria. In his speech given on October 29 to the people, Asad claimed that the cease-fire had been imposed by the great powers in consultation with Egypt, but came as a surprise to Syria, and at a time when Syria was prepared for a major counteroffensive against Israel. Asad declared that he had accepted the cease-fire because he was given assurances by Sadat that the Soviet Union had guaranteed Israel would withdraw totally from the territories taken in 1967. He asserted that in his understanding the UN cease-fire solution (338) provided for the rights of the Palestinian people. From "Discours du Président Hafiz al-Asad adressé au peuple le 29 octobre 1973," Syrian Arab News Agency release, Damascus.

44. Khaddam is quoted as having said, "I do not want my son to be told that his father sat down at the same table with Zionists to negotiate peace with them." *New York Times*, January 6, 1974, p. 10.

45. The sources are in agreement on the tenaciousness and audacity of the Syrian bargaining during disengagement talks. On the disengagement negotiations, see Sheehan, *op. cit.*; Matti Golan, *The Secret Conversations of Henry Kissinger* (New York: Quadrangle, 1976), pp. 179–212; and Brown, *op. cit.*, p. 37. On conflicts within the Syrian elite over the negotiations, see McLaurin, Mughisuddim, and Wagner, pp. 243–244.

46. Discussions with a U.S. diplomat, American Embassy, Damascus, 1977. The virtual removal of Egypt from the Arab war coalition destroyed Syria's bargaining leverage because without Egypt, Syria's threats to renew the war if its interests were neglected lacked credibility.

47. It is possible that Syria hoped to promote a PLO-Jordanian reconciliation that would not only permit military coordination between the two parties, but diplomatic coordination as well. On Asad's strategy at this time, see his interview with Patrick Seale in the *Observer* (London), March 6, 1977.

48. See Rabinovitch, "Syria," p. 614.

49. For Asad's view, see his interview in the *Herald Tribune*, January 9, 1978. It is clear from his comments that Asad simply did not believe Sadat's claim that he would insist on Syrian and Palestinian rights.

50. The reader is referred to the following analyses of the Lebanese intervention which were found to be useful: "Why Syria Invaded Lebanon," *MERIP Reports*, 57 (1976); P. Heller, "The Syrian Factor in the Lebanese Civil War," *Journal of South Asian and Middle Eastern Studies* 4, 1 (1980), pp. 56–76; Adeed Dawisha's book-length study, *Syria and the Lebanese Crisis*, Brown, *op. cit.*, pp. 200–203; John Bullock, *Death of a Country: The Civil War in Lebanon* (London: Weidenfeld and Nicholson, 1977); Walid Kazziha, "The Lebanese Civil War and the Palestinian Resistance Movement," Instituto Affairi Internazionali Working Papers, January 1979; Enver Koury, *The Crisis in the Lebanese System: Confessionalism and Chaos* (Washington, D.C.: American Enterprise Institute, 1976); Richard Johns, "Firm Hand at the Helm," *Financial Times*, November 18, 1976; and the Syrian statement in the *New York Times*, November 16, 1976.

51. See "Enter the Eastern Front," *Middle East*, March 1979, for a good analysis of the military implications of a Syrian-Iraqi concert.

52. On the Israeli perception, see Moshe Dayan's analysis in *Yediot Aharanot*, July 17, 1981, translated in the *Journal of Palestine Studies* 11, 1 (1981). On Syrian-Soviet links, see Lawrence L. Whetten, "Soviet-Syrian Moves in the Middle East," *Roundtable* 279 (1980), pp. 258–265; and Karen Dawisha, "Moscow Moves in the Direction of the Gulf," *Journal of International Affairs* 34, 1 (1980/1981), pp. 219–233.

53. Fouad Ajami, "Stress in the Arab Triangle," *Foreign Policy* 29 (1977/1978), pp. 90–108.

11

Foreign Policy Process in the Arab World: A Comparative Perspective

Ali E. Hillal Dessouki
Bahgat Korany

The preceding chapters dealt with the foreign policies of seven Arab actors: six states and the PLO. As stated earlier, the focus of this volume is on the period from 1970 to 1980. Many authors, however, could not analyze the patterns of the 1970s without situating them in their historical context. This context includes constraints imposed by persistent global structures, transformation within the Arab system, Algeria's colonial legacy, the emphasis by Sadat's Egypt on economics as a reaction to Nasser's emphasis on anticolonial politics, Iraq's urge for regional leadership, the reincarnation in Qaddafi's Libya of nationalist politics, dispersion of the Palestinian population, Islam and Saudi state formation, and the Grand Syria dream. But despite differing emphases each chapter's analysis of a country's foreign policy was organized according to the conceptual framework outlined in Chapter 1.

Without coming to an overall agreement, the different chapters do seem to share some conceptual-methodological premises:

First of all, each contributor has combined the advantages of different approaches. In the analysis of the Arab world, there is a dialectic between two major approaches. The *area study* approach has emphasized *specific Arab* behavior with a focus on such determinants as Islam and the structure of the Arabic language, a focus that could lead to the propagation of common stereotypes. The *social science* approach, on the contrary, has emphasized the *general patterns of behavior* in the Arab world, with a focus on quantitative methods and interdisciplinary concepts. This sometimes leads to generalizations divorced from their historical and cultural context. None of the authors has employed one approach to the exclusion of the other. All have been trained in the social sciences, but have also extensive field research in the Arab world, and have lived or are still living there.

The authors have attempted to go beyond present foreign policy and social science conceptualization.[1] In the place of mere static analysis, they have emphasized, for example, the changing bases of conflict and cooperation in the Arab system, the changing patterns of Algerian decision-making, and Egypt's focus on restructuring its foreign policy under Sadat. There has been a systematic attempt to investigate the linkages between social structure and foreign policy.

Despite the scarcity of data, the authors have persisted in researching the process by which foreign policy inputs are converted into outputs, i.e., the decision-making process.[2] Going beyond simplistic psychologistic orthodoxy, they have situated the decision-making process within its social context and traced the part played by the different participants (see especially the chapters on Egypt, Saudi Arabia, and Syria). The emphasis throughout has been on analyzing foreign policy output as both "words" and "action," role conception and role performance, general orientation and specific behavior. We wanted to draw attention in the research on foreign policy to the potential gap between "say" and "do," especially among Third World countries characterized as they are by limited capabilities in relation to their foreign policy objectives. This dimension was often emphasized by authors who sought to explore the problems of combining pragmatic practices with radical ideology, or revisionist dreams with realist strategies.

In reading about the seven actors examined in this book, we understand that the foreign policies of Arab states differ in a number of ways. The actors differ in their perceptions of the global system and of their role within it; they differ in their policies toward major regional issues such as the Arab-Israeli conflict and on ways of achieving a comprehensive peace in the region; they differ in the way they relate to each other; and finally, they differ in their political structures and foreign policy decision-making processes. Generally, theories of foreign policy have explained these differences in terms of: (1) the imperatives of modernization and state building, or the character of the postcolonial state; (2) the need for ruling elites to divert attention away from domestic problems; (3) elite conceptions of national roles; and (4) the impact of external factors and penetration by outside forces. This chapter will briefly underline some of the important patterns that emerge from the case studies presented. We will consider them under three headings: orientation, decision-making process, and foreign policy behavior.

ORIENTATION

In almost all of the case studies, we observe the salience of the regional system. The permeability of political frontiers in the Arab world is explained by recent statehood, the Arab-Israeli conflict, and the impact of transnational ideologies such as Arab nationalism and Islam. This confirms recurrent themes in the literature, that the elite of developing countries perceive the context of their foreign policies as primarily regional and that change of foreign policy behavior is likely to manifest itself at the regional level before it is generalized to the global level. What is more characteristic of the Arab situation is its intricate and almost organic relation with the global system. For the reasons outlined in Chapter 2, the political distance between the global and the regional is insignificant in the Arab world. Because of strategic considerations, Israel, and oil, the global system has paid great attention to regional developments and issues in the Arab world.

Arab perceptions of the global system differ from one actor to another. Sadat's Egypt, following Saudi Arabia, invoked anew the spirit of the cold war era and aligned Egypt with the West. The PLO leadership perceives a bipolar system, views the United States as a bastion of imperialism, and aligns itself with forces of national liberation and anticolonialism. In between, we have Saddam Hussein of Iraq, who sees a welcome transition to a multipolar system. For Hussein, the best policy to be followed by the Arabs is nonalignment and the establishment of close relations with the new emerging centers of global influence— Western Europe and Japan. The case studies underline three propositions.

1. The most salient factor in the analysis of developing countries' foreign policies is their position in a highly stratified international system where unequal exchange seems to entail important attitudinal and behavioral consequences.
2. Elites' perceptions of the structure of the global system, of the norms governing its functioning, and of their position in it have greatly affected their foreign policy orientation of national self-assertion through nonalignment.
3. When the foreign policy elite of a developing country perceives the world as hostile, intense political competition leads the country toward a foreign policy that puts independence first. A less competitive situation will permit a policy that accords priority to the search for aid.

This last proposition is related to the development/security or aid/independence dilemma referred to in Chapter 1. The case of Egypt demonstrates the perception of foreign policy as an activity whose primary concern is the mobilization of resources and foreign aid for development. Syrian foreign policy confirms the thesis that inter-state conflicts in the Third World and military security considerations can be just as important as a focus of foreign policy. This becomes even more true in the context of long-standing conflicts such as the Arab-Israeli confrontation. In the Syrian case, as Raymond A. Hinnebusch argues in Chapter 10, the military-political preoccupations of the conflict with

Israel far overshadow development as a concern of foreign policy-makers. Indeed, developmental considerations sometimes appear peripheral to Syria's main security concerns. This may be explained by the gravity of security threats and Syria's ability to manage the economy thanks to massive economic foreign aid.

THE DECISION-MAKING PROCESS

Much has been written on the role of the leadership variable in the decision-making of developing countries. A dominant trend among North American writers is psychological reductionism, a modern version of the "great man" theory of history, which attributes everything to the leader's idiosyncrasies or to perceptual variables. Consequently, an examination of the psychological traits of different leaders has become a substitute for the analysis of how different foreign policy determinants do in fact influence and shape foreign policy decisions. We are not disputing the relevance of leaders' psychological variables in developing countries' politics, but rather questioning the degree of influence, the level at which they apply, the type of situation, and the method of demonstrating their causal impact. We think that individual psychological variables are better understood as intervening variables, as synthesizers of the myriad factors affecting the foreign policy process. They are like a chemical agent that activates and transforms the different inputs, without negating their influence. The relative importance of the psychological variable also depends on the particular foreign policy output. For instance, in analyzing foreign policy orientation, systemic variables are likely to have greater influence than psychological ones; but the latter would probably rank first when dealing with a foreign policy decision in a crisis situation.[3]

Our work also demonstrates the importance of distinguishing between legal-institutional and social-political constraints. In most developing countries, the legal-institutional structures provide the leader with seemingly unlimited powers, yet social and political realities (such as segmented societies, geographic vulnerabilities, economic dependency, and political instability) impose severe constraints. In this context, we have to emphasize the importance of domestic factors, which seem crucial in almost every case study. Variables such as resources (Egypt), segmented society (Syria and Iraq), or political factionalism (Algeria, the PLO, and Syria) are significant in understanding the foreign policies of these countries. The links between domestic and foreign policies are intricate, and domestic political considerations are crucial in the choice between foreign policy alternatives. This is reinforced by the vulnerability of weak states, the lack of an institutional base, and the pattern of personal legitimacy prevailing in most Arab regimes.

Contrary to the simplistic notion of a domineering leader or "commander of the faithful" with unchecked and unrestricted powers, the case studies of this book present a more sophisticated image of the decision-making process. In most cases, the leader is confronted by a complex situation of sociopolitical and economic constraints, military vulnerabilities, and a number of domestic political demands (on religious, national, or ethnic grounds).

The decision-making process in Arab countries can be approached from three perspectives: presidentialism, oligarchical-collective, and collegial collective. The first emphasizes the presidential center, which includes "the president as a person" and "the presidency as institution" (the presidential palace, advisors, offices, etc.). Egypt comes closest to the presidential or leader-staff type of decision-making, which is characterized by an authoritarian decision-maker who can act alone without consultation with any political institutions other than a small group of subordinate advisors, typically appointed by the leader and lacking an autonomous power base of their own. Usually these advisors have no independent sources of information other than those available to the leader.

The leader-staff pattern is characterized by fragmentation of roles and responsibility on the part of the staff group, reliance on direct negotiation and personal diplomacy with foreign heads of state, the ability to respond quickly to events and to make unconventional and bold decisions. Leaders often repeat their past behavior in similar situations, make important decisions without consulting the foreign minister or even the prime minister, and frequently use presidential emissaries (not necessarily career diplomats) in foreign policy assignments. This type of decision-making provides the opportunity for nonofficials to perform important roles due to their personal relations with the leader.[4]

At the other end of the spectrum is the collegial or delegate assembly type of decision-making, characterized by consultation, bargaining, and search for consensus. This pattern of decision-making—followed by the PLO—may lead to immobility and an inability to innovate or adapt adequately to changing circumstances. Examples of the oligarchical-collective type are provided by Syria and Algeria. This type is characterized by the presence of a strong leader who both leads and consults in the decision-making process.

FOREIGN POLICY BEHAVIOR

The case studies in this book describe a number of behavioral patterns. We observed the dialectic between revolutionary idealism and pragmatism at work in the cases of Algeria, Iraq, and Syria, as well as in the reorientation of Egypt's policy after Nasser. In Sadat's Egypt, the change from the former to the latter was almost complete in both word and deed; in the other cases ruling elites combined revolutionary rhetoric with pragmatic behavior. Ideological considerations were put aside either because of economic hardships, as a result of the death of a charismatic leader and the ensuing political vacuum or legitimacy crisis, or because of the imperatives of a war situation and the need for military assistance. The idealism/pragmatism issue is closely related to the processes of foreign policy adaptation (coping with a changing environment), transformation (response to a radical change in one ingredient of a state's situation), or restructuring of orientation (a fundamental change in basic objectives and general strategy).

Another issue is the aid/independence dilemma referred to in Chapter 1. From our studies, it seems that independence is a core concern for most Arab elites. A favorite theme in their foreign policy orientation is thus to balance off between the two superpowers and the two blocs. The case studies also indicate that influence is a two-way process, and that small states are not just satellites or surrogates. Syrian or Iraqi relations with the Soviet Union have not been without friction, and the leadership of both countries has resisted Soviet pressure to accept a political settlement with Israel they did not want. The case of Egypt is even more instructive; Sadat managed to humiliate the Soviet Union first in 1972 by expelling some 20,000 military advisors, and later in 1980 by dismissing the Soviet ambassador from Cairo.

A third behavioral pattern is the discrepancy between potential and performance. Iraq is a prime example of a country whose power equation has rarely been balanced. In the 1950s and 1960s, it was overshadowed by the leadership of Nasser's Egypt, and constrained both by its political instability and Kurdish insurgency. In 1978, when Iraq was ready to take on an active regional role, the revolution in Iran created a new situation that eventually led to war. Another case of unfulfilled leadership desire is Morocco (population 20 million, per capita income $740 in 1979, 98,000 armed forces and $916 million in military expenditure's in 1980). Due to its peripheral geographic location in the far west of the Arab world and its image of a traditional authoritarian regime, Morocco has not been able to perform a sustained influential role in inter-Arab relations.

In certain Arab countries, we also find a gap between verbal articulation of goals and actual foreign policy behavior. For example, Algeria, a revolutionary country that plays an active role in international councils on behalf of the Group of 77 and for the establishment of a new international economic order, projects a Third World image. Yet in the 1970s, its trade relations with the United States increased, and its long-standing strong economic relations with Western Europe continued. Algeria managed to have close economic relations with capitalist countries and flourishing military relations with the Soviet Union.

Related to incongruence in role conception and performance are sudden changes, zigzagging, and improvisation in foreign policy behavior. In some cases, this is caused by despair at the gap between capabilities and objectives. In others, erratic behavior is due to impatient leadership, incomprehension of the complexity of international politics, and the confusion between national dreams (which are by definition of a long-range nature) and objectives that must be related to operational capabilities.

The Arab world also provides an example of a state with no foreign policy. The Lebanese case is striking; a sovereign state, member of the United Nations and the League of Arab States, finds its territory the battleground of combatting forces, none of which is present with Lebanese consent. Lebanon has become an arena for the foreign policies of other actors, rather than choosing a foreign policy of its own. To the extent that Lebanon has a foreign policy, it is a policy of survival.

Other patterns of foreign policy behavior exist among Arab states not covered in this book.[5] There is the example of South Yemen, a besieged state isolated by geography, poverty, and ideology. The foreign policy of compromise is followed by Jordan, Kuwait, and Sudan. For all, geographic location is crucial. Sudan lives in the shadow of Egypt and its regime survived in the 1970s thanks only to Egyptian help in times of crisis. Sudan has borders with six other countries, a situation that makes her vulnerable to hostile foreign penetration. Jordan exists in the midst of Syria, Iraq, and Israel, and at different times, Syria and Israel have made claims on Jordanian territory. Kuwait feels the brunt of Iraqi and Saudi influence. In fact, its independence in 1960 was challenged from the very beginning by Iraq's irredentist demands. Consequently, the foreign policies of Sudan, Jordan, and Kuwait have been ones of compromise, moderation, and bargaining. In times of Arab cold war, they tend to play the role of mediator between the larger and more influential Arab states. Finally, there are countries such as Mauritania, North Yemen, Somalia, and Djibouti, whose foreign policies are of only limited significance to overall inter-Arab relations. Their peripheral geographic location, poverty, and small population account for their lack of impact on the policies of other Arab states or on the main processes of the Arab system.

WHERE DO WE GO FROM HERE?

To cope with some of the empirical and conceptual gaps in the foreign policy literature (e.g., the analysis of decision-making in the Third World context), there remain at least four promising areas for further research. First, we need more comparative and cumulative studies on the foreign policies of developing countries, either within one region (Africa, Asia, or Latin America) or interregional. Second, we need comparative studies that, instead of analyzing the totality of foreign policy, focus on one of its components, such as particular decisions. For instance, why and how did Libya decide to intervene in Chad, Egypt to sign the peace treaty with Israel, Saudi Arabia to go for the oil embargo, or Iraq to sign the 1975 border agreement with Iran?

At the other end of the spectrum, there needs to be more emphasis on the comparative case study approach: we need in-depth studies of a single country, with conclusions relevant to other countries. In comparative case study analysis, the treatment must be less descriptive and more analytical; the research methodology, initial hypotheses, and general findings must be applicable to, or at least suggestive for, the conduct of other case studies. In this context we need to know more about the different components of foreign policy outputs. For example, if a country restructures its foreign policy, does it begin with orientation or behavior, and how do we assess the impact of one upon the other? As far as foreign policy determinants are concerned, what is the role of information or misinformation (sources, quality, and amount), and what is the effect of public opinion or specific interest groups (e.g., the army) on foreign policy behavior? If Arab and other Third World countries are dependent, how do external factors penetrate their policy-making processes and influence the final output?

Finally, we need more policy-oriented research. Is the conduct of foreign policy an art, or is it also a scientific activity that can be planned and managed? To what degree are the different foreign policy structures (foreign ministries and their embassies, related departments in the ministries of commerce or defense) efficient? To be able to answer these questions, we need rigorous criteria of foreign policy evaluation and a reliable set of indicators to measure the performance of a developing country's foreign policy.

NOTES

1. For a good start in this direction, see for instance Jorge Dominguez, "Consensus and Divergence: The State of the Literature on Inter-American Relations in the 1970s," *Latin American Research Review* 13 (1978), pp. 87–126; E. Ferris and J. Lincoln (eds.), *Latin American Foreign Policies: Global and Regional Dimensions* (Boulder, Colo.: Westview Press, 1981); W. Ofuatey-Kodjoe, "A Theoretical Frame for the Research and Analysis of the Foreign Policies of African Countries," Paper presented to the annual meeting of the International Studies Association, Los Angeles, March 1980.

2. An attempt to address this lack of analysis of Third World foreign policy decisions has been made by the contributors to Bahgat Korany (ed.), *Foreign Policy Decisions in the Third World* (Beverly Hills, Calif.: Sage Publications, 1984), a special issue of the *International Political Science Review* 5.

3. Bahgat Korany, "Absence of Alternatives and Crisis Behavior: Egypt's Decision to Go to War in 1973," Paper submitted to the Eleventh World Congress of the International Political Science Association, Moscow, August 1979.

4. Charles Hermann, "Decision Structure and Process Influences on Foreign Policy," in Maurice East, S. Salmore, and C. Hermann (eds.), *Why Nations Act* (Beverly Hills, Calif.: Sage Publications, 1978), pp. 69–102.

5. Tunisia presents a very special and significant case. A small country (its population of less than 7 million lives in an area not exceeding 164,000 square km) with the oldest political leadership in the Arab world and maverick foreign

policy for the region, Tunisia's regional influence has been increasing, especially since the move of the headquarters of the Arab League from Cairo to Tunis in 1979 and the nomination of a Tunisian as the league's secretary-general. For an analysis of Tunisia's foreign policy and the participation of informal members in its decision-making process, see Bahgat Korany, Jean-Louis Balladier, and Jean-Benoît Gauthier, *Dépendance et politique étrangère: Le cas de la Tunisie*, (Montreal: University of Montreal, Arab Studies, Vol. 6, 1983).

Abbreviations

AID	Agency for International Development (U.S.)
ALF	Arab Liberation Front
ALN	Armée de liberation nationale (Algeria)
AMIO	Arab military armaments organization
ANP	Armée nationale populaire (Algeria)
AWACS	Airborne Warning and Control System
bpd	barrels per day
CC	Central Council (PLO)
CIA	Central Intelligence Agency (U.S.)
CNRA	Conseil national de la révolution algérienne (National Council of the Algerian Revolution)
CNR	Conseil national de la révolution
COPDAB	Conflict and Peace Data Bank
DFLP	Democratic Front for the Liberation of Palestine
EEC	European Economic Community
EXCOM	Executive Committee (PLO)
FLN	Front de liberation nationale (Algeria)
GC	Popular Front General Command
GCFR	General Command of the Forces of the Revolution (PLO)
GDP	gross domestic product
GNP	gross national product
GPRA	Gouvernement provisoire de la république algérienne (Provisional Government of the Republic of Algeria)
IMF	International Monetary Fund
INOC	Iraqi National Oil Company
IPC	Iraq Petroleum Company
LIBOR	London Interbank Offered Rate
LSP	Labor Socialist party (Egypt)
MNC	multinational company
NATO	North Atlantic Treaty Organization
NIEO	New International Economic Order
NPUP	National Progressive Unionist party (Egypt)

OAPEC	Organization of Arab Petroleum-Exporting Countries
OAU	Organization of African Unity
ODEP	open door economic policy
OECD	Organization for Economic Cooperation and Development
OPEC	Organization of Petroleum Exporting Countries
PFLOAG	Popular Front for the Liberation of Oman and the Arabian Gulf
PFLP	Popular Front for the Liberation of Palestine
PLA	Palestine Liberation Army
PLF	Palestine Liberation Front
PLO	Palestine Liberation Organization
PNC	Palestine National Council
PNF	Palestine National Fund
PPSF	Palestine Popular Struggle Front
RCC	Revolutionary Command Council (Iraq; Libya)
SADR	Sahrawi Arab Democratic Republic
SIPRI	Stockholm International Peace Research Institute
SMC	Supreme Military Council (PLO)
SONATRACH	Société nationale de transport et de commercialisation des hydrocarbures (Algeria)
UAE	United Arab Emirates
UAR	United Arab Republic

About the Contributors

Bahgat Korany is director of the Arab studies program and professor in the Department of Political Science at the University of Montreal in Quebec, Canada.

Ali E. Hillal Dessouki is a professor of political science at Cairo University.

Ahmad Yousef Ahmad is an associate professor in the Department of Political Science, also at Cairo University.

Raymond A. Hinnebusch is an associate professor in the Department of Political Science at the College of Saint Catherine in Minnesota.

A. G. Kluge, Fellow in political science at Johns Hopkins University, is a Ph.D. candidate in international relations at the School of Advanced International Studies in Washington, D.C.

Paul C. Noble is an associate professor of political science at McGill University in Montreal.

Mohamed E. Selim is an assistant professor of political science at Cairo University.

I. William Zartman is director of African studies and professor of international politics at the School of Advanced International Studies of Johns Hopkins University in Washington, D.C.

Index